Booth Tarkington

Portrait-sketch of Booth Tarkington in 1914 by Robert Reid. It is a companion piece to the portrait-sketch of Susanah Tarkington, *opposite page 223*, and Mrs. Tarkington's favorite portrait of her husband. It is owned by her and reproduced with her permission.

BOOTH TARKINGTON
Gentleman from Indiana

JAMES WOODRESS

GREENWOOD PRESS, PUBLISHERS
NEW YORK

CONTENTS

ILLUSTRATIONS

Grouped in this order following page 222

Beebe Booth
Mrs. Beebe Booth
Joseph, Booth, and John S. Tarkington
Newton Booth
Hauté Tarkington
Booth Tarkington at the age of three
Booth Tarkington when he went to Phillips Exeter Academy
Booth Tarkington's drawing of Donald Jameson
Tarkington as Cassius in *The Honorable Julius Caesar*
Booth Tarkington, his mother, and nephew
Booth Tarkington and Billie Burke
Seawood
S. J. Woolf's drawing of Booth Tarkington
The Floats on Kennebunk River
Booth Tarkington and his French poodle
Booth Tarkington at the time of publication of *Alice Adams*
Portrait-sketch of Susanah Tarkington

Drawings of himself by Booth Tarkington

Just before sailing to Capri in 1905 *page* 75
From a letter to Dan Calkins written in November, 1889 *page* 96
Letter to father of April 13, 1899 *page* 281

PREFACE

The biographer's chief reward is an intimate acquaintance with a significant and vital personality. Such was Booth Tarkington, who as writer and man exerts an attraction that grows stronger with increasing familiarity. His literary talent is large, well disciplined, authentically American, and worth a secure place in twentieth-century literary history. His genius for friendship draws to him even those who did not know him, and his nimble curiosity affords congeniality with anyone even mildly interested in people or events. He pursued life intensively as long as his health permitted and observed it acutely after he was forced to the sidelines. Totally lacking in guile and pretense, he was a man of integrity, a generous humanist, an inveterate optimist, and an old-fashioned gentleman.

Although Tarkington was immensely popular, his life until now has remained unwritten. He always said he would tell his own story and on that account put off interested biographers; but he carried to completion in 1941 only the first part of his memoirs—the chronicle of his youth and literary apprenticeship —and stopped at the threshold of his life as novelist, playwright, and story writer. He died in 1946 without returning to the work, and the matter of a biography then was left in abeyance while the Indiana Historical Society sponsored the compilation of an excellent bibliography. Mrs. Tarkington thereafter gave her husband's papers to Princeton University. The subsequent cataloguing and classifying of this vast collection has made accessible for the first time the primary source material for his life.

My aim in writing this book has been to meet the dual need for a narrative biography and a critical study. In the first half of this century enthusiastic readers bought more than five million copies of his works (before paperbacks), and for many

Americans over thirty-five Tarkington is an indelible part of their youth. To these persons, I hope that a renewal of acquaintance with Penrod Schofield, Willie Baxter, Alice Adams, and others will recall the days when they too were young, harassed by their elders, and hopelessly in love. For younger readers, I hope to introduce an amiable humorist, a shrewd psychologist, and a skillful storyteller: in short, a writer whose best works ought not to be left unread.

While many of Tarkington's books bring nostalgic promptings to memory, others belong in a serious and significant tradition. When I came to Indianapolis in 1950, I began rereading Tarkington as a means of orienting myself in new surroundings. I soon discovered that he had portrayed urban, middle-class, Midwestern America better than anyone else. His novels, though a generation old, still mirrored the very life I could see about me, and he seemed, therefore, the inheritor and transmitter of the commonplace realism pioneered by Howells in the last century. Because the bulk of Tarkington's work contributes to a more perceptive understanding of the shifting society in which we live, I have tried to put him into the proper historical and cultural frame of reference.

Although many persons have helped make this book possible, I owe the greatest debt to Mrs. Tarkington. She authorized my use of her husband's papers at Princeton, granted me permission to quote from unpublished manuscripts, wrote letters to facilitate my research, and answered all questions patiently. Moreover, she left me free to treat my subject as I thought best so that I am wholly responsible for whatever deficiencies or superfluities this work may have. In addition, I have received important help from other members of her family, particularly Tarkington's nephews, John and Donald Jameson, and their wives, whose reminiscences were illuminating and useful.

I also wish to acknowledge the immense assistance given me by the staff of Princeton University Library, especially by Alexander Wainwright and Alexander Clark of the Rare Book Department. They provided ideal facilities and patient counsel during my considerable stay in Princeton. Furthermore, my book has been greatly enriched because John Jameson, Mrs. Julian Street, Barton Currie, and Ralph Boyd (executor of the Howard Wetherell estate) allowed me to use the Tarkington letters in their possession; and I am under obligation to Carl Brandt of Brandt & Brandt, John Fischer and Miss Dorothy Fiske of Harper and Brothers, Lee Barker of Doubleday and Company for opening their Tarkington files to me. Other large debts I owe to Hugh Kahler and Erwin Panofsky of Princeton, who talked to me about Tarkington, and Mrs. Edgar Rombauer of St. Louis, whose vivid memory of Tarkington and Indianapolis in the Nineties helped bring my picture into sharper focus. Also I wish to thank Colonel Frederic A. Price of Fort Pierce, Florida, for his kindness in permitting me to use a letter he wrote Tarkington and the reply to it.

For reminiscences or help in research, not specifically acknowledged in my notes, I am indebted to Miss Elizabeth Trotter of Philadelphia, Mrs. Laura W. Foster of the Indianapolis Public Schools, Mrs. Eva Leech of the Wright Library of Dayton, Ohio, Miss Evangeline Thurber of the Howard-Tilton Memorial Library of Tulane University, Miss Dolores Cadell of the San Francisco Public Library, and Henry L. Savage, Princeton Archivist. I have further to thank Howard W. Stepp and C. E. Dammon, registrars of Princeton and Purdue respectively; Miss Carolyn E. Jakeman of the Houghton Library of Harvard University, John H. Moriarty, Librarian of Purdue, and Lewis F. Stieg, Librarian of the University of Southern California, for making available to me Tarkington letters in their custody; and my task could not have been completed without the considerable assistance I received from the staffs of the Indianapolis Public Library, the Indiana State Library, the Theater Collection of the New York Public Library, and the libraries of the Pasadena Playhouse and my own institution, Butler University.

For permission to quote from unpublished letters to Tarkington, I am indebted to the following persons: Melville Cane (for Sinclair Lewis), Miss Helen Hayes, J. P. Hennessey (for Alexander Woollcott), Miss Mildred Howells (for William Dean Howells), Mrs. Isabel Lord (for Hamlin Garland), Graeme Lorimer (for George Horace Lorimer), Alfred Lunt, Miss Charlotte Murray (for Harold Murray), Colonel Frederic A. Price, Miss Phyllis Robbins and Mother Elizabeth Keating (for Maude Adams), Kenneth Roberts, Mrs. Julian Street (for Julian Street),

Mrs. Irita Van Doren (for Ellen Glasgow), Leon Wilson (for Harry Leon Wilson).

I wish also to thank W. C. Griffith of the Merchants National Bank and Trust Company of Indianapolis, who as trustee of the Tarkington estate permitted me to quote from unpublished manuscripts. I am further grateful to the *Georgia Review* for permission to reprint from its pages a portion of chapter nine, and to Mrs. S. J. Woolf and the New York *Times* for permission to use the S. J. Woolf drawing of Booth Tarkington. My last acknowledgments are to George Stevens and Ray McCully, Lippincott editors, who gave my manuscript sympathetic and expert reading, and to my wife, whose specific services in this project were without number.

JAMES WOODRESS

Indianapolis
September, 1954

Booth Tarkington

PROLOGUE

HOOSIER GOLDEN AGE

W<small>HEN THE AFTERNOON TRAIN</small> from Bloomington, Illinois, pulled into the Union Station at Indianapolis on the eighteenth of November, 1899, it carried the novelist-critic William Dean Howells, then swinging through the Midwest on a lecture tour. The view from the car windows as the Big Four accommodation entered the city was profoundly impressive to a reflective Midwesterner who had lived most of his adult life in the East. The Hoosier capital was a lively commercial center about to be heavily industrialized, a mushrooming community of nearly one hundred and seventy-five thousand persons. Surrounded by pleasant, undulating plains and magnificent old groves of hard maple and beech trees, it lay at the hub of a state richly endowed with natural resources.

If Howells had been born in Indiana instead of Ohio, he would have seen Indianapolis grow from a country village in the Thirties to a thriving city half a century later. Men of his own generation had watched the muddy streets and wooden houses retreat before acres of asphalt and durable—if ponderous—brick and stone buildings with mansard roofs. Even young men born in the pre-industrial innocence of the Sixties remembered when Indianapolis was a pleasant big town of neighborly people. In the last year of the nineteenth century, however, the oldest citizens, some of whom still talked of Indian fighting, lived with granddaughters whose boldest exploits were charity bazaars and literary teas. This remarkable foreshortening of history must have kindled the imagination of the visiting novelist as his train jolted to a halt in the station.

Howells descended from the platform into the waiting arms

13

of a reception committee that represented the local literati. Books, he already knew, were as important a local product as corn and hogs, and he was pleased to find himself honored for his own vast production of an approved Hoosier commodity. From the station the committee escorted him to the Bates House where, like a visiting potentate, he held court for the rest of the afternoon. Through the hotel parlor and into the privacy of his room flowed the literary constituency of this dean of American letters. A presidential candidate today might command no more homage than Howells received in Indianapolis on the eve of the twentieth century.

Several hours later, Howells barely had dismissed the last of his callers when a carriage arrived to take him to dinner. Although many hostesses coveted the honor, the lucky lady was Mrs. Ovid Butler Jameson, ardent promoter of the arts, who honored her distinguished guest by inviting him to dine with former President Benjamin Harrison and her brother Booth Tarkington, author of a first novel recently published. The dinner was excellent, the conversation lively, and Howells, flattered by this attention, wrote his wife the next morning that from the moment of his arrival he had. been "caught up into the silken arms of the aristocracy."

If Howells read the newspaper reports of his visit, however, he found that his arrival left some disquieting eddies. He had more admirers in Indianapolis than he could accommodate. Even if Mrs. Jameson and the reception committee had not captured him, he could have held audience with only a fraction of his well-wishers during his brief stay. A disgruntled editorial writer, complaining that the guest was not seeing the real city, exploded in an open newspaper letter to Howells: "The 'set' has you in tow . . . and proposes to anchor you to a dais . . . while they do the lionizing act." The criticism was justified: Howells was, in fact, monopolized by the organized devotees of literature—the half dozen literary clubs that sponsored his appearance—and even the so-called public lecture at the Plymouth Church was a closed affair with admission by card only.

Nonetheless, the evening was a glittering success, and even if tickets to the lecture were not generally available, the promoters of the affair managed to turn out twelve hundred of the élite. When Howells appeared on the platform, the auditorium, both floor and gallery, was filled to capacity. Women in rustling silks and satins far outnumbered their reluctant escorts, who quietly wilted in dress suits and starched shirts. A newspaper reporter observed that the hall was jammed with old women, young women, and girls not yet out of school, all of whom took keen delight in the proceedings. Everyone seemed to have read Howells' fiction and applauded the speaker generously. The visitor appeared completely at ease before his listeners: a small, dignified gentleman of sixty-two with white hair and mustache and an air "of great reserve force."

The lecture was on "Novels and Novel-Writing," a topic certainly well suited to an Indiana audience of 1899. Howells knew that any literary gathering in Indianapolis probably would assay higher in published authors than a similar group in any other city except Boston or New York. Besides Tarkington, his listeners that evening could have included James Whitcomb Riley and Kin Hubbard (the creator of Abe Martin), both residents of Indianapolis; Maurice Thompson *(Alice of Old Vincennes)* and General Lew Wallace of Crawfordsville; and Charles Major *(When Knighthood Was in Flower)* of Shelbyville. All of these authors already had gained national prominence and could be assembled on short notice to read from their works for charity or to greet a visiting novelist. Also soon to return home from a brief rustication in Denver was Meredith Nicholson, whose career as a popular novelist presently would begin.

If ample time were allowed to collect the celebrities, George Ade could be counted on to come home from Chicago. His native ties were strong and his trips to Indiana frequent. He might have brought with him John T. McCutcheon, cartoonist and fellow Purdue alumnus, and another Chicago resident who sometimes visited her old Indianapolis neighbors—Mary Hartwell Catherwood. If a Hoosier literary powwow of real importance had been planned, enough Indiana authors might have been summoned home to hold a writers' conference. Edward Eggleston, an author with a critical as well as a popular following, and his brother George then were living in New York, as was Martha Finley of Elsie Dinsmore fame. Annie Johnston, creator of the Little Colonel, could have come from the Pewee Valley near Louisville. Other Indiana authors, living both in the state and out but not yet known, would have included George Barr McCutcheon *(Graustark)*, brother of John and editor of a Lafayette newspaper; David Graham Phillips, a New York newspaper man; William Vaughn Moody, professor of English at the University of Chicago; and Gene Stratton-Porter, housewife from near Fort Wayne.*

Most of the Indiana literary reputations of fifty years ago have proved ephemeral, but an editor beating the brush then could have flushed a covey of writers in nearly every county. Howells no doubt had been prepared for this by Ade, whom, he met in Chicago the month before lecturing in Indianapolis. Ade was fond of telling about the visiting lyceum lecturer who had heard that book-writing was a popular activity in Indiana. The visitor, hoping to ingratiate himself with his Hoosier audience, invited all authors to sit on the platform with him. This was the signal, declared Ade, for the entire audience to rise and start forward. It must have seemed to Howells during his tremendous reception in Indianapolis that the plains and hills of Indiana were somehow peculiarly hospitable to writers.

Howells' pronouncements against the historical romance and his championship of literary realism ought to have given pause to his audience, but his opinions dismayed only a tiny minority of his admirers at the Plymouth Church. Howells was the literary arbiter of 1899, and his ideas, for the most part, went down smoothly. His listeners, however, actually enjoyed reading and writing about Tudor England or mythical kingdoms of Central Europe far more than about contemporary Indiana scenes. Charles Major's best-seller interested Howells not at all; nor would McCutcheon's *Graustark* ever elicit his praise. In the lecture he pointedly commended the realism of Zola and Tolstoy and made his familiar demand for literature that treated life as it really was: "The truth should always be told. It may be indecent, but it cannot be vicious. The imagination can only work with the stub of experience, for experience is life. The difference between realism and romanticism is that the realist takes nature as he finds her; the romanticist colors nature for his own use."

Against the laudatory reports of the *Journal* and *Sentinel,*

* Theodore Dreiser, born at Terre Haute in 1871, is omitted from this list because he was for many years a novelist without honor in his home state.

only the *News* lifted a dissenting voice. When Howells declared that Jane Austen, George Eliot, and Anthony Trollope were more realistic and truthful than Dickens and Thackeray, the *News* representative took sharp exception; and Howells' dictum that Sir Walter Scott continued to be read only by persons in their nonage brought an anguished rejoinder. Tarkington, however, was one listener in the group who neither applauded loudly and went on consuming romance nor took umbrage at the critical judgments of the visiting novelist. On nearly all points, though it took him years to put them into practice, the young man was in full agreement.

Despite Hoosier preference for romance, Indiana had a literary tradition that Howells honored. It had begun before the Civil War with Julia Dumont, whose *Life Sketches from Common Paths,* published in New York in 1856, probably made her the first Indiana author known outside the state. Though her characterizations were wooden and her scenes of Hoosier life artificial, Mrs. Dumont held a minor place in literary history as Edward Eggleston's schoolmarm. What she was unable to do herself, her pupil could accomplish in *The Hoosier Schoolmaster,* which appeared in 1871, the same year that both Howells and Henry James published their first novels. A distinguished contribution to American literature, Eggleston's book became a classic and remains the most vivid picture of Indiana in its unsophisticated adolescence. Indiana literature then flowered in the Eighties with the productions of Wallace and Riley, writers still to be reckoned with in American literature. Howells no doubt regretted that Wallace, who had entertained him in Crawfordsville some years earlier, had chosen to write of Ben Hur instead of his Civil War experiences, but he was well pleased with Riley's verses of Hoosier domesticity.

Howells was particularly anxious to see Riley during his visit to Indianapolis. Although the Hoosier poet was a close friend of Mrs. Jameson, illness had kept him from her dinner party, and Howells, accordingly, paid his respects on the day after the lecture. Driving to the poet's home on Lockerbie Street, he sat for an hour with the man he honored as "the poet of our common life." He had written just seven months before: "I think Mr. Riley a very great artist, with insight as subtle as the best of the new English poets, and sympathy as generous." And he had concluded that Riley's poetry was of such sweetness, sincerity, and purity that "some may not yet prize it aright."

Contemporary critics have dealt severely with Riley's reputation; yet at the time of Howells' visit to Indianapolis he was the star of brightest magnitude in the Hoosier literary constellation. He was much sought after as a public reader, and when he recited "The Old Man and Jim" or "Out to Old Aunt Mary's," the handkerchiefs of his sentimental listeners always fluttered at the weepy passages. Nostalgic collections like *The Old Swimmin'-Hole and 'Leven More Poems,* which reached the best-seller class, had made poetry pay for Riley in reputation and in dollars.

Howells' guide on the day of the lecture was Booth Tarkington, just thirty years old, who had published *The Gentleman from Indiana* only the month before. Howells was pleased to have so deferential a young man to escort him about, but he hardly could have suspected how important he was to be for Tarkington. He could not have guessed that of all writers he was to exert the most profound influence on his companion's career. The attentiveness of his guide might have suggested something of this, but Howells was not egoist enough to realize that Tarkington asked nothing better than to be a disciple.

The two novelists had met once before at the Lantern Club in New York on Thanksgiving Day, 1895. Tarkington then had been living in New York, trying to write, but with no success. When a friend offered to take him to the club, where Howells was to be, he went hopefully planning to ask for literary advice, but the evening ended in a painful experience. Already speechless to find himself in the same room with Howells, Tarkington on that occasion was asked to sing a solo without accompaniment. His fame then rested on an earlier membership in the Princeton Glee Club—not on his writing. Howells may have recalled that the voice Tarkington found was a quavering one at a pitch nature never intended, but four years later when the young man explained apologetically that the sounds had been unintentional and the honor of making them unsought, Howells graciously said he could not remember the embarrassed performance.

Tarkington was not a total stranger to Howells in November, 1899, however, for the visitor told an interviewer that he had read *The Gentleman from Indiana* with pleasure. The new American novel will come from the West, Howells said, and then added generously that Mr. Tarkington was an author of great promise; but his praise seems in retrospect more a gracious gesture than a real conviction. Nevertheless, he was kind to his guide during their rides together, and as they drove to the lecture hall in a slow little cab, Howells gave the young novelist advice that remained vivid thirty-seven years later. Beware the critics, he warned: "You'll find they can still hurt you long after their power to please you is gone!" Tarkington was inevitably to learn the truth of this observation.

The next day as Howells crossed the northern plains of Indiana en route to Detroit, he sorted out his impressions of his Indianapolis sojourn. He was well pleased with the lecture and the flattering reception. People had stuffed him with praise, he wrote his wife from the train. Moreover, he was pleased with the physical appearance of Indianapolis, which he called "a stately and beautifully livable city," and the new, "distinctly noble" Civil War monument in the heart of the capital gave the city "a very European effect." Of the people he had met, Riley and former President Harrison stood out most vividly.

The impression that Tarkington made on him actually had not yet precipitated. Their talks during the brief stay were more important than he knew, for he had been performing unwittingly a sort of laying on of hands. This Howells finally came to realize fifteen years later after reading in *Harper's* the first two installments of *The Turmoil,* Tarkington's first important novel embodying the creed of literary realism that Howells long had preached. In his "Editor's Easy Chair" he wrote: "So fine and strong a talent as Mr. Booth Tarkington's has its sins of romanticism in the past to answer for; but whoever reads his very powerful fiction lately current in these pages must own that he is atoning for far worse transgressions than can be laid to his charge. . . . Here we have a master indeed." Privately Howells wrote twice to congratulate Tarkington, the second time including what amounted to a benediction: "I tremble a little for you. Now you must go on and be of the greatest."

ONE

IMPRIMIS: 1869-1881

In the ninety-third summer of American independence, during the administration of President Grant, the United States devoted its energies to domestic problems. Four years had passed since the end of the paralyzing Civil War, and the country was rebuilding and growing with astonishing vigor. Through the Ohio River Valley flowed the westward migration that spilled out upon the Great Plains. Through the Far West rolled the first transcontinental rail traffic on the Union Pacific's new track. East and West had just been linked on May 10 when the Golden Spike was driven into the roadbed at Ogden, Utah. In the population centers of the Atlantic seaboard, meantime, the postwar expansion of industry and commerce kept pace with the development of the hinterland. While honest men built financial empires in New York, Boston, and Philadelphia, unscrupulous manipulators also were at work. In September the notorious efforts of Jay Gould and Jim Fisk to corner the gold market were to produce the "Black Friday" of infamous memory.

Late in July, however, the swift national growth hardly disturbed the surface calm in Indianapolis near the population center of the country. The city was enjoying showers and temporary relief from a sultry midland summer, and citizens found little in the morning's news, either domestic or foreign, to interest them. The trustees of the state university were meeting, the tailors in New York were on strike, and the American Philological Association was convening at Poughkeepsie. Europe, too, relaxed in a moment of tranquility, and no one suspected that France and Germany would be at war within a year. The great news of the autumn would be the opening of the Suez Canal, an event to fire Whitman's imagination in "A Passage to India" with the vision of a better world in the making. The immediate reports from Europe concerned the Harvard crew, which was practicing on the Thames for a race with Oxford, and the royal honeymoon of a Danish prince and a Swedish princess. Such were the circumstances that accompanied the birth of Booth Tarkington in the capital of Indiana on July 29, 1869.

When the Indianapolis *Journal* announced briefly the next day that John S. Tarkington, Esquire, was the happy father of a thirteen-pound boy, it reported all the facts of the event worth public notice. The day had begun in the Tarkington household only a little before daybreak, and by breakfast time the baby had arrived with a minimum of inconvenience. Leaving the mother and infant in the care of Dr. Tisdale and a nurse, father and only daughter, with pardonable enthusiasm, had rushed to the telegraph office to broadcast the joyful news. Relatives, if not newspaper readers, could appreciate the importance of a first son born nearly twelve years after marriage. The boy would be named for his mother's brother, Newton Booth, who was thus far the most distinguished member of the family.

The Tarkingtons in 1869 were a typical professional-class group—a closely knit, stable, and respected family. They lived at 520 North Meridian Street in what already was the best residential section of the small city. John Tarkington, a lawyer, provided adequately for his wife and eleven-year-old daughter Hauté, owned his own home, and was known and liked throughout the community. Although his income was modest, he possessed a good many well-thumbed books, and his wife had a piano that she played with average ability. About the household there was a casual, unhurried air, a pleasant way of life that belonged to the small American city before it became the industrial metropolis. The Tarkington ménage, moreover, reflected a Southern grace often found in Indianapolis homes of that era.

When his son was born, John Tarkington was thirty-seven years old, already an old resident of Indianapolis. He had graduated from Asbury College (now DePauw) in 1852 and with his commencement oration had won a job as private secretary to Governor Joseph A. Wright. After the Governor's term of office ended, he had stayed on to practice law in the state capital. During the Civil War he had served a term in the state legislature, then joined the Union Army as captain of an Indiana infantry company. At the conclusion of hostilities he had returned to Indianapolis, rebuilt his abandoned law practice, and served a term as judge of the Marion County Civil Circuit Court. Known in later years as "Judge" to his townsmen and "Papa John" to family and close friends, he was a soft-spoken, generous, kindly man. His humanity and gentleness undoubtedly formed his son's most characteristic traits. No father ever was more patient and understanding, and the lifelong relationship between Booth Tarkington and his father was close and affectionate.

John Tarkington's personality, in some respects, was *sui generis,* although his unruffled good nature may have derived from his Southern ancestry. His father, the Reverend Joseph Tarkington, had been a zealous Methodist circuit rider during the backwoods days of Indiana, but the family originally had come over the mountains from North Carolina in 1798 during the great post-Revolutionary War migration. Joseph Tarkington, Booth Tarkington's grandfather, had been born near Nashville, Tennessee, in 1800. The Tarkingtons later had drifted north to the free soil of Indiana along with many other restless Southerners, including Abraham Lincoln's family.

The missionary zeal of Joseph Tarkington was absent from John Tarkington's make-up. Where the Methodist-minister father had belonged to the pioneer generation which cleared the forests and carried the gospel on horseback, the lawyer son consolidated and refined the accomplishments of the trail blazers. Joseph had broken virgin soil with a wooden plow in southern Indiana at the age of seventeen; at the age of twenty he had been converted during a camp meeting near Bloomington. John had gone to college at the pioneer institution that Joseph Tarkington had helped found and there cultivated a taste for literature, the arts, and Oriental mysticism. Although he never lost his father's strict sense of duty and honor, life to John Tarkington was never a relentless struggle with the devil.

Elizabeth Booth Tarkington, his wife, however, was made of sterner stuff. Hers was a New England ancestry that stretched back to Thomas Hooker, founder of Connecticut. Her people had belonged to the second of the two great population streams that mingled in Indiana, and her marriage to John Tarkington was characteristic of the union of New England and the South in the new state. Beebe Booth, her father, had belonged to the hardy race of Yankee shopkeepers. After serving in the War of 1812, he had loaded a stock of merchandise on a pack horse and set off for Indiana via Daniel Boone's Wilderness Road. Elizabeth had been born in Salem, Indiana, where her father owned a store, and was educated in Terre Haute, where the family later moved.

The Booths had faith in themselves and cared little for tradition. Because he believed in education—even for women—Elizabeth Booth's father sent his daughter to the best school in Terre Haute, which happened to be St. Mary-of-the-Woods, a Catholic institution. He did not worry that she would lose her Presbyterian faith, and she did not. Elizabeth Booth in turn sent her daughter to a convent school in spite of the objections that her Methodist-minister father-in-law must have voiced. Her legacy to her son was not in temperament but in intellectual equipment and a cultivated taste. Far better educated than the average matron of Indianapolis, she brought to the provincial lawyer's home a spark of the French civilization that the Sisters of St. Mary's had kindled on the banks of the Wabash.

Elizabeth Tarkington, moreover, was a proud, ambitious woman who provided the dynamo that energized and sometimes overcharged her household. She was not easy to live with, for she demanded the undivided interest of those about her. Being intensely family-conscious, she named both of her children after members of her family, and one imagines that John Tarkington sometimes had his fill of Booth tribal exploits. Yet she gave her husband and children boundless affection that was returned in generous measure.

Newton Booth, who became successively Governor of California and United States Senator, exerted a profound influence on the Tarkington household. Not only was he the great man of the family, but he also was the hero of a Horatio Alger success story. He had made a fortune in the early days of California but never married, and being a generous man and fond of his sister's family, he was a frequent factor in Tarkington finan-

cial and other affairs. It is small wonder that Elizabeth Tarkington took her children to visit Newton Booth in California
in the summer of 1872, the year after he was elected Governor.
On this junket mother, daughter, and small son were gone
nearly a year, during which time they presided grandly over
the executive mansion at Sacramento. Uncle Newton, in his
turn, visited Indianapolis frequently, campaigned for Indiana
Republicans, helped the Tarkingtons build a house in 1876,
and contributed to his namesake's support at Phillips Exeter
Academy. Finally, it was his legacy that tided the nephew over
a long literary apprenticeship after college.

The memory of his visit to California, even though he was
only three at the time, remained with Booth Tarkington all of
his life. Uncle Newton was an admiring, indulgent bachelor
whose official residence was filled with flamboyant miners, merchants, and politicians of the post-gold rush era. Bret Harte's
Poker Flat was not far away; nor was Virginia City, Nevada,
where Mark Twain had spent the Civil War years. The California capital was then the raw little wooden town on the
Sacramento River that Lincoln Steffens recalls in his *Autobiography*. The small boy from Indiana was a much petted and
spoiled youngster in that predominantly male society. He was
glutted with toys, puffed up with flattery.

Uncle Newton, moreover, was fond of children and understood his nephew's deeds and childish fancies. A glimpse of the
relationship between the Governor and his namesake appears
in Tarkington's graceful story *Beasley's Christmas Party* (1909),
in which Newton Booth sits for the portrait of the bachelor-pol-
itician David Beasley, who makes believe with his crippled
ward Hamilton Swift. During the visit to California, as Beasley does in the novelette, Uncle Newton gave a dinner for his
nephew's imaginary playmates, the Hunchberg family from
Constantinople, even putting a plate on the floor for the fancied St. Bernard dog Simpledoria. The Governor remembered
his own childish whimsy when he too had played with an unseen companion, his athletic alter ego Bill Hammersley—a character also incorporated into Tarkington's story.

The visit to California was, all things considered, a triumph
for the nephew—even taking into account his first serious social
error. The Governor on the evening of the indiscretion had

given a dinner party for gentlemen important in the affairs of state. Most of the banqueteers, like the Governor, had gone west to seek their fortunes during the gold rush days. What they lacked in sensitivity, they made up in conviviality. During the evening the Hoosier nephew was presented to the assembly in the dazzling panoply of white dress and blue sash, and after a noisy toast to his health someone offered the child a glass of champagne. Accustomed to accept all tributes to his precocity, young Booth downed the drink unobserved by his uncle at the opposite end of the table. One drink led to another. The delighted guests around him, astonished at his capacity to absorb champagne, kept his glass filled. The result, recalled Tarkington in his memoirs sixty-nine years later, was spectacular and memorable. "In one particular line of accomplishment," he wrote, "I am now probably without a living colleague. I doubt that any other inhabitant of the year 1941 has the right . . . of recording that he got howling drunk in the State of California in 1872."

Several months after Elizabeth Tarkington and her children returned from California, the Panic of 1873 swept away their brick house on Meridian Street and most of their income. When the crash came, John Tarkington once again was rebuilding his law practice, which had dwindled alarmingly while he served his term on the circuit court bench. Suddenly legal fees disappeared, and the Tarkingtons were poor. The panic forced them to New York Street, an unfashionable crosstown thoroughfare, where they lived in a two-family house with another depressed lawyer. Their horses went to pasture in the country, and they no longer were carriage folk. These hard times, however, left no permanent mark on Booth Tarkington, and he might not have remembered them at all if his sister, then fifteen had not reminded him in after years of their trials. His mother's piano survived the financial reverses, and he remembered many boisterous evenings of singing and playing when the three older members of the family grouped themselves about the piano. His most vivid recollection was the lack of a yard and the necessity of playing on the sidewalk or in the dusty, unpaved street.

When Tarkington was six, the nation began to recover from the economic blight, and his father's law practice picked up.

The family then moved back to the avenue, this time North Delaware Street, where they again had a brick house, albeit a rented one, a large shady lawn, and horses in the stable. The little boy's horizon broadened to the confines of the iron fence that enclosed the ample yard. Soon after, Newton Booth's generosity made it possible for Judge Tarkington to build a new house better than the one he had lost in the panic. This followed Uncle Newton's visit to Indiana in the summer of 1876. By then he was Senator Booth, who came to stump the state on behalf of Hayes and Wheeler and the Republican ticket. His nephew excitedly watched the parades, bands, and torchlight processions that accompanied campaigning in that gaudy era of the Gilded Age. Through the smoke of the torches Tarkington remembered his uncle riding calmly in an open carriage on his way to address the multitude. The brilliant political career of Uncle Newton Booth may have provided the motivation for Tarkington's own lifelong interest—and foray once—in politics.

The new house was a tremendous event for the entire family. A year in building, it rose slowly from foundations that seemed cathedral-like at 1100 North Pennsylvania Street, one of the pleasantest avenues of the fashionable North Side. The house was designed by a popular architect, but, remarkably enough, it climbed out of its basement without the gingerbread garnishing popular in the Seventies. It was a tall brick house, austerely Victorian, with high, narrow windows and vertical lines that soon were softened by thick shrubbery and Virginia creeper. Tarkington lived there for forty-six years until in 1923 the smoke, noise, and traffic drove him farther uptown.

Twentieth-century taste antiquated the old homestead, but Tarkington clung to it as long as he could. With its dim interiors and dark woodwork, ancient plumbing and obsolete wiring, the house ultimately became a burden, but it was pregnant with memories—both happy and painful. There were enacted many of the escapades that found a place in the Penrod stories. There he passed his literary apprenticeship and wrote his best novels. There, too, his mother and daughter died, and his first marriage ran on the shoals. The house finally was torn down in 1940 to make way for a parking lot. Even before its ignominious end, however, the front lawn had been invaded by a hamburger stand, and in his last years Tarkington could not bear going to town by way of Pennsylvania Street.

When Tarkington, as an adult, returned to Indiana after periodic absences, the old home seemed a fixed point in a world of change. The furnishings and decorations of his boyhood retained their Victorian flavor undisturbed into the twentieth century. On many occasions, like his fictional playwright Gilbert in *Presenting Lily Mars* (1933), he stood in the front hall profoundly moved by the sight of familiar things. The reception room off the hall remained stiffly formal with its gilded chairs and brown velvet sofa in their accustomed places, and the antique telephone retained its place screwed to the yellow-papered wall behind the wide black-walnut staircase. But the library in later years was the room that conjured up the past most vividly. Within its open double doors across from the parlor rested the old black grand piano near the bay window. Under the room's high ceiling he had spent hours enough to be counted into years. "Here were the same old rows of books on the same old polished brown shelves, and, on the walls above, the same old steel engravings. . . . Upon the same old gayly floral Brussels carpet stood the same old Eastlake sofas and the same comfortable, unpleasantly carved old rosewood chairs in their old places precisely."

Life in Indianapolis was pleasant for the substantial citizens who owned such homes as the Tarkingtons built on the avenue in 1876. Although these houses cost only seven or eight thousand dollars to erect, their owners were judged rich and made up the local gentry. They employed a "girl," usually Irish or German, who lived in the back bedroom and made two dollars a week, and a Negro hired man who was quartered over the stable at the same wages. These homes stood well back from the street in great yards shaded by leftover forest trees and were built with front and back and sometimes side porches. Stables that later became garages lined the unpaved alleys behind the houses. There on pleasant mornings the horses were groomed by Negro coachmen who gossiped along the back fences as they worked superintended by small boys like Booth Tarkington. On the avenue at irregular intervals, meanwhile, passed stunted little street cars pulled by lone mules. Life was so leisurely then that on shopping days a housewife could call to a driver from an upstairs window and while the car waited put on her hat and coat and tell the "girl" what to have for dinner. Horse-drawn carriages, wagons, and pedestrians made up the rest of the traffic along the residential thoroughfares in that smokeless, unsophisticated era.

Fortunately for his biographer, Tarkington's memory clung to many childhood incidents of the Seventies, and the stories that he put into his memoirs provide frequent insights into his adult personality. There is no doubt that the child was father to the man, and the character of young Booth Tarkington stamped itself on the literary productions of the novelist. The man and his works are all of a piece, and the strengths and weaknesses of the one are necessarily the strengths and weaknesses of the other. Specific memories of the ages six, eight, and ten show the direction in which the twig was bending.

When Tarkington was six, he went to visit his Grandmother Booth in Terre Haute. There on a hot afternoon in a dry goods store he divested himself of his self-conceit. His grandmother sent him to buy a needle—one solitary needle: price, one cent. He did not want to run such a trivial errand in an unfamiliar store, but he saw no way to avoid the chore and had to go. Making a one-cent purchase seemed at the age of six a humiliating act, and he protested that he might be held up to ridicule. His grandmother, however, brushing aside his objections, suggested that he say as he bought the needle: "I believe this is the very smallest purchase I ever made in my life." As he walked downtown, he felt that his grandmother's advice would make the ordeal possible.

Inside the store his confidence ebbed. The noon hour had just ended, the heat was withering, and he was the only customer. He walked timidly down the long aisle between two high counters until he came to a clerk languidly fanning himself. When he asked for the needle, the clerk yawned, put down his fan, and rummaged about for the requested object. A moment later, the needle in hand, the boy gave his practiced laugh, then with a sinking feeling said bravely: "I believe this is the very smallest purchase I ever made in my life."

The effect was disastrous. The clerk leaned across the counter, all languor gone. "What did you say?" he asked in a startled voice. The boy already was sorry he had said it but

felt obliged to repeat the remark. He could not, however, duplicate the practiced laugh, and although he wanted nothing so
much as to get out of the store, the clerk had not closed the
incident. "Come listen to this," he called to the other clerks.
"I want you to hear something." They came from all corners
of the store, surrounding him, and when they had gathered, the
clerk told them: "Sold him a needle for a cent . . . I want you
to hear him talk about it." Then turning to the boy, whom he
fixed in a glittering stare, he repeated: "Say it again."

The episode burned itself indelibly into Tarkington's memory. As he walked back to his grandmother's house, millions of
locusts seemed to fill the scorched summer air with unending
proclamations of his shame, hideously letting the world know
that he was a cheap pretender who had been caught showing
off. Also along the homeward route he passed a row of catalpa
trees, and for the rest of his life the sight of catalpa trees and
the sound of locusts brought back Terre Haute at ninety-eight
in the shade and the cure he had undergone of being one special
kind of snob.

On another occasion Tarkington again learned humility
under circumstances ineradicable from his old-age recollections.
At a children's party when he was eight he took part in a kissing game in which all the little girls withdrew to the hall leaving the boys in a circle each with a vacant chair behind him.
After a grown-up hostess monitoring the door had obtained
from one boy at a time the name of the girl nearest his heart,
she would call out: "A lovely letter for little ——." The girl
summoned then appeared coyly, skirted the rear of the boys,
and seated herself behind the lad she thought had sent the
message. If she chose correctly, the boy publicly kissed her. If
she erred, she fled from the room under the hoots and taunts
of the derisive males.

When Tarkington's turn came, he tremulously asked for Hattie. The hostess opened the door and called for the little
maiden who had caused agitations in his juvenile breast. Simultaneously, however, he realized that if Hattie should seat herself behind him, he could not kiss her. He trembled as he
comprehended the crisis that approached. But it never arrived.
Four feet behind him was an open window, and by the time
the little girl had appeared in the doorway, he was falling

through fresh air and late afternoon sunshine, having jumped uncontrollably out of the window. Later, as he sat with his back to a brick wall pondering his predicament, he imagined the party in a turmoil, the game broken up, himself a pariah.

After what seemed hours he had to return to the house. One did not go home from parties without his best hat, and that article was still inside. Furtively he slipped into the kitchen, passed quiveringly through the hall, opened a door, and—was in the party again. Boys and girls in paper caps were whooping and running about. He expected a dozen accusing fingers to point at him, but nothing happened. No chorus of children surrounded him crying: "We've caught Booth Tarkington!" After recovering from his astonishment, he grabbed Page Chapman by the arm as the latter sprinted past. "Page . . . What did Hattie do?"

"When?"

"When I jumped out of the window."

"Did you? . . . Let go me! Sam Miller's after me and I got to run."

The place of that party, once the home of Bushrod Browning—a boyhood friend—still survived in the smoky downtown area of Indianapolis in 1941, and Tarkington never drove past the house in after years without a painful glance at the window he once had jumped from without being missed. He recognized the experience as a valuable lesson in his own cosmic unimportance. He also must have realized that his adult fastidiousness went back at least as far as his demonstrated inability to kiss a little girl in public.

As deeply rooted as Tarkington's modesty and humility, was his amiability. He was unable to get mad at anyone—either as a child or as a man. At the age of ten he practiced the manly art of self-defense on a punching bag in the stable in order to protect himself from his boyhood tormentors, but he might as well have saved his energy. He could not fight even Launce Chapman, a lad of ebullient spirits who pommeled him daily on the way home from school. Launce turned the afternoon exodus from Public School Number Two into a riot, which usually began when he slammed Tarkington into the gutter and sat on his head in full view of the other children. Try as he would, Tarkington could overcome neither Launce nor anyone else.

Most of his friends in conflict could reach a berserk pitch at which they inflicted damage on superior adversaries, but Tarkington's temperament was too equable for such outbursts. "I couldn't get that way," he remembered. "Even when they threw stones at my dog I couldn't fight for him; could only crouch over him, receiving helplessly the missiles upon my own body." Amiability and passivity became perhaps his most dominant traits. They carried him pliantly through bereavement and physical suffering, bound to him friends of vastly different personalities, made him an observer rather than a doer, and stocked his novels with pathos rather than tragedy.

Tarkington compensated for his unathletic body and unaggressive nature by discovering the resources of his father's library. He became a bookish child and associated more and more with his father, mother, and grown sister. While he was still a small boy, his parents read to him nearly every day—his father at night and his mother in the afternoons. One book that he particularly enjoyed with his father was Scott's stories of the history of Scotland in *Tales of a Grandfather*. History also provided the fare for the most memorable hours of his mother's reading, and during the summer he was nine he gladly cut short his play each day to listen to Guizot's *History of France*. For the Midwestern child Guizot's people came alive. From Vercingetorix to Clovis, from Louis XI to Voltaire and Louis XVI, the makers of French history passed vividly through the boy's imagination. The mother successfully transmitted to the son her own fondness for French culture, acquired in student days at St. Mary-of-the-Woods.

When Tarkington traveled through the châteaux country along the Loire twenty-eight years later, scenes from Guizot's history came flooding back at Blois, Cheverny, Amboise, and Loches—especially Loches with its château built by Charles VII and famous dungeons used by Louis XI for political prisoners. He wrote his mother after a day of sightseeing that his memories had returned vividly and with "infinite gratefulness" to the "summer when you and I read Guizot in the back room, with the old desk in the corner; the railed fence around the house; the barn with 'Grey Eagle' in the stall: the Guizot still

showed the imprint of the ... setter pup's teeth. ... You made
history attractive & human to me in that reading."

Tarkington himself began to consume a large number of
books as soon as he learned to read. While still a schoolboy,
he devoured Shakespeare, histories of England and the United
States, and a miscellaneous procession of novels. Dickens and
Scott, of course, provided countless hours of pleasure; so did
Victor Hugo, Wilkie Collins, and Goldsmith. Offsetting this
substantial reading matter were the adventures of Deadwood
Dick and other characters from the prolific output of the
House of Beadle and Adams; but the ten-cent thrillers remained in Tarkington's memory only as titles. This literary
diet was almost infinitely varied and not only included such
moral tales as *John Halifax, Gentleman,* but also the more
memorable exploits of Tom Sawyer, Don Quixote, and Robinson Crusoe. Most of the fare was solid reading matter capable
of building both a taste for excellence and a sound standard of
literary values.

The impulse to write accompanied Tarkington's reading,
and even before starting to school, he dictated tales to his older
sister. She recalled half a century later that when he was only
seven he began a story called the "Unknown Adventure,"
which opened thus: "A fortune having been left me, involving
interests in the gold mines, it behooved me to take a perilous
journey into the Far West." Perhaps his sister's memory embroidered the actuality, but he certainly began scribbling tales
in grammar school. Like the adventures of Harold Ramorez
that Penrod composed in the stable sawdust box, a similar story
written about 1880 has survived in an old copybook. It also
begins precociously: "It was 6 o'clock in the morning on a
rainy damp day about November 10, 18—. The little steamer
City of San Francisco was painfully chugging down the Sacramento toward San Francisco. All was dark about her." These
early stories—the dictated tale, the yarn of the Sacramento
steamer, and Penrod's lurid imaginings—all take place in the
gold-mining regions of the West. Tarkington undoubtedly
wrote under the influence of Uncle Newton Booth's experiences and the heroics of Deadwood Dick.

One would expect a shy, studious child like Tarkington to
be the joy of his schoolteachers, and so he was for three years.

During this time he was a model little boy, loved his teachers, and enjoyed the perquisites of the honor pupil. He sat near the throne and on occasion was allowed to wet the sponges that dangled from the blackboard. In the fourth grade, however, he developed a violent dislike for Miss Fannie Jameson, his teacher, and made no effort to hide his feelings. She reciprocated the hostility and let her annoyance over his peccadillos grow into a small-scale persecution. Within a month the boy lost interest in his studies, slumped to the bottom of his class, and became a rebel against education.

The rewards of being a praised scholar previously had compensated him for ineptness in sports; the loss of his favored status created a serious consequence. He began to itch and twitch, to bat his eyes and wiggle his nose. His head bobbed, and his throat uttered involuntary "glunks" and "glucks." The teacher was exasperated, accused him of deliberately making faces at her, and when the family physician was called in to diagnose the twitchiness, the patient, listening at the door, heard the doctor mention St. Vitus' dance. The boy felt then that he had contracted a disease of real distinction.

The doctor prescribed a villainous-tasting tonic, but the nervousness, of course, continued, and Tarkington went on twisting, scratching, and jerking. He found that he could flutter his nostrils like a rabbit and wiggle his ears so visibly that Miss Jameson could see him the length of the schoolroom. One day his troubles reached a climax. Sitting quietly at his desk, he realized that the neatly braided pigtails in front of him were swaying unaccountably. When the gingham checks behind the braids began to move in circles, he put up his hand.

"May I be excused?"

"You may not."

He protested that he felt sick and Miss Jameson had better excuse him, but she was unmoved. He then proved his illness to be genuine in full view of the teacher and pupils. When the convulsion was over, he walked to the cloakroom, and though he could have reached that sanctuary, he paused and was sick again in the classroom. Not a little pleased with himself, he floundered home and was put to bed.

Tarkington's parents were puzzled by the turn of events. He never told them of his feud with Miss Jameson, not realizing the trouble himself until years later. In his memoirs he recalls: "I didn't myself understand that she was really what was the matter with me or, of course, that I was just a bit of machinery and she was the wrong mechanic to operate it." The elder Tarkingtons concluded that their boy was studying too hard; so they took him out of school for the rest of the semester and sent him to visit his grandmother in Terre Haute. When he returned to school in the autumn, he joined the class behind him and repeated the four-A under a different teacher. His muscular vagaries subsided.

The effect of this experience is not easy to assess. Tarkington carried through life a slight tic that he attributed to Miss Jameson, but more importantly the episode may have influenced his writing. From it perhaps came his perennial interest in children, their moods and attitudes, their dreams and delusions, and his impulse to understand the psychology of youth. As an adult, he was continually absorbed in the activities of his nephews and later their children, and it may be that the Penrod stories owe something to Miss Jameson's assault on his childish sensibilities.

At the beginning of 1881, after his fourth-grade ordeal had ended, Tarkington began making entries in a Christmas diary. This document reveals his thoughts and acts for a one-year period that included his twelfth birthday. The entries show a child of Penrod's age, rather more articulate and reflective than the average twelve year old but normal enough in his interests and aspirations. On May 31, for example, he was wondering what he would be doing one year hence but thought "perhaps the end of the world will come before then." He was not perturbed that a few days earlier the Sunday school authorities had tried unsuccessfully to convert him, and on June 12 he noted succinctly: "Not converted yet." He regarded as more significant, the diary indicates soon after, that "Mr. Riley called & I recited B. Freitche [sic] to him."

The most important event of the year was a summer visit to Marshall, Illinois. His cousin Fenton Booth, later to be Chief Justice of the United States Court of Claims, lived in Marshall, and the two cousins, exact contemporaries, had wonderful times together. On July 28 Tarkington wrote: "Went to Marshall at 3 o'clock," and on the next day he recorded: "I'm 12 years old. First birthday I ever spent away from home." There was too much to do, however, to be homesick. While Fenton had a printing press and was publishing a newspaper, Booth had trained and equipped himself to operate a Punch and Judy show. Most exciting of all, the town's annual "show day" was scheduled for August 8.

Marshall then was a sleepy country village in the heart of the flatlands west of the Wabash River. Although it lay well within the borders of Illinois, it became the setting for Tarkington's first novel, *The Gentleman from Indiana.* In his adult remembrance of things past, Marshall always symbolized the timeless perfection of a boy's heaven. Whittlers in their shirt sleeves on the courthouse steps, farmers' wagons tied to a near-by fence, sunshine filtered through the elms on the village square—these nostalgic impressions pervade a significant portion of Tarkington's fiction. There the people lived happily while the world spun on around them, and the visiting city boy roamed the dusty streets and adjacent fields in barefoot happiness. What Hannibal, Missouri, and Hamilton, Ohio, were for Mark Twain and Howells, Marshall, Illinois, was for Booth Tarkington. Neither Winesburg, Ohio, nor Gopher Prairie, Minnesota, had yet been founded.

During the second week of Tarkington's stay the circus came to town, the occasion known to the village and surrounding farms as "show day." Early that morning the entire length of main street resounded with the rattle of vehicles pouring into town. Farm families from every direction came in their great red and blue wagons drawn by splendid Clydesdales. As the elders rode on the front seats, the bright-eyed and freshly scrubbed children peered over the sides of the wagon beds. Here and there a prosperous farmer's son flashed along in a trim side-bar buggy with his sweetheart by his side. By nine o'clock the square was crowded and the air filled with a thousand cries. The strolling mountebanks jostled the gypsy fortunetellers; the candy peddlers vied with the balloon salesmen. Mingling in the holiday gathering, Booth Tarkington sold palm-leaf fans and Fenton Booth hawked peanuts.

After what seemed an interminable wait, there was a fanfare of trumpets announcing the approach of the circus parade. Down the middle of the street ahead of the procession ran barefoot boys who had been up before daybreak to greet the show. Then came the band with a crash of drums and the blare of brass, followed by the lumbering elephants mounting the spangled performers of the show. In their wake frolicked the clowns, rode the helmeted charioteers, and pranced the horses drawing cages of real tigers. Last of all came the calliope and more carefree boys capering to its mechanical tunes.

In the evening of the "show day" Uncle Lyman Booth took the cousins to the circus. Under the big top the boys completed their day of happy memory. For Tarkington "show day" provided the material for his first successful story, a sketch that won a fifteen-dollar prize from the *Nassau Literary Magazine* at Princeton ten years later. Not only did this story bring in the first money he earned from writing, but it also provided, in a revised and expanded version, the most effective bits of local color in his first novel.

After Tarkington returned to Indianapolis, the autumn began with the death of his dog Fritz and was followed by the death of President Garfield. Both melancholy events, and others, are soberly noted together in the diary at the end of September. "These two last months have been very sad," records the daybook in mournful summary; "Morris & Victor Chapman died in Eau Claire while I was away. . . . Fritz, poor, dear little Fritz has died too. So have Pres. Garfield and Mrs. Holoway. Fritz suffered so much. He died while I was at the grocery."

As Tarkington re-entered school that fall, he was fast growing beyond the age of Penrod. By the next summer he had graduated to long pants and detachable hard collars labeled: "Youth's First Base. Size 13." He found himself then no longer a child but a youth. His collars said so.

TWO

THE EDUCATION OF A WRITER

D URING THE YEAR that Tarkington became a youth, he graduated from writing copybook narratives to constructing plays.
Theatergoing and play-reading were popular diversions for all
members of the family except dour Joseph Tarkington in whose
presence no one dared mention such frivolities. The clerical
grandfather, however, seldom visited Indianapolis to disapprove
of his son's household, and young Booth was encouraged by his
parents and sister to convert the hayloft of the stable into a
theater. With Dan Calkins from next door, Horace Hord, the
Chapman boys, and others he pioneered in the amateur theatricals that Penrod Schofield and Sam Williams later carried
on memorably in the Penrod stories.

For his first attempt at playwriting Tarkington took his inspiration from the newspapers of 1882, the result being a melodrama in fourteen acts entitled "Jesse James." In it he
chronicled with minute fidelity the career of the famous outlaw, whose exploits recently had dazzled the minds of imaginative youngsters. He played the title role himself and assigned
the part of Bob Ford to Page Chapman; but the play was an
artistic failure, for after running along briskly for fourteen stir-
ring acts its melodramatic end took the small fry audience
unawares. When Bob Ford's cap pistol treacherously assassi-
nated the hero, the audience sat dumbly waiting for the show
to continue, and the playwright had to make a curtain speech
to tell the spectators they ought to know enough to go home
when a play ended.

From this theatrical beginning Tarkington went on writing
plays, with unflagging enthusiasm, for nearly fifty years. By

the time he reached high school he had progressed to farce-comedy, and instead of the all-male cast of "Jesse James," his next play contained two feminine roles, though it must be admitted that the masculine parts pretty well monopolized the show. This play was never completed, but the outline and finished portion show it to be a comedy of manners in which the author was to play the role of John Henry Lafayette Beans, a callow country cousin who turns the tables on his superior city relatives. Tarkington's chum Horace Hord was to have the romantic lead. The inspiration for this play probably came from Restoration Comedy, surprising as that seems for Indianapolis in the Eighties. Tarkington later remembered that he was reading Wycherley about this time—albeit with much astonishment—and the innocent intrigues of this unnamed drama dimly suggest the somewhat indecent plot of *The Country Wife*.

It was also during this period of adolescent theatricals that Horace Hord and Tarkington planned to go on the stage. Daily they declaimed Shakespeare to each other in preparation for a partnership that would take them on the road in their own company; and while Tarkington practiced *Richard III,* Horace worked on *Macbeth.* In addition to their favorite plays by Shakespeare, they intended to produce original comedies by Tarkington, and the country cousin play apparently was begun as part of their repertoire. When Tarkington outgrew his plans for an acting career, the idea of this youthful drama remained in the deep well of his subconscious, and years later he used its basic situation for two of his most successful adult plays, *The Man from Home* and *The Country Cousin*.

While Tarkington experimented with playwriting, he also attempted his first poetic flight. His Pegasus, he discovered, soared the first time out of the stable, making a far more spectacular showing than the hayloft melodrama inspired by the James brothers. His first poem was a tour de force that convinced his parents and sister of his genius. To score this triumph, he wrote some melancholy verses of thirteen-year-old *Weltschmerz* and illustrated them himself with sketches of a clown posed tragically on a hilltop and then seated morosely under a tree. Next he bound the pictures and text together into a pamphlet, left them on the library table for his mother and sister to find, and slipped expectantly out of doors.

THE TREES

When the soul knows but sadness
  No hope and no gladness
Then the soul in its sighing
Finds rest in leaves dying
  And shadows of leaves at play.
When the soul knows but sorrow
  And the birth of tomorrow
Will bring but the death of today
  Turns the soul to the trees
  Moving cool in the breeze
Keeping time to the summer's sigh
Finds rest and finds sadness
But no hope and no gladness
  For the Trees answer not
    Passion's cry.

As he lingered about the yard under the library window, he soon heard a pleasant commotion inside the house. Feminine voices were exclaiming delightedly over the masterpiece. Never before had he done anything that produced such an effect on his family. Not only did his parents and sister exult in his talent, but they also sent off copies of the opus to kinfolk far and near. For several days the young poet basked in the rosy glow of his accomplishment, and years later Tarkington the novelist found his material ready made when he wrote the part of *Gentle Julia* (1922) in which young Florence Atwater also composes a precocious first poem.

During Tarkington's fourteenth year the family preoccupation with literature and the theater was temporarily sidetracked in favor of more occult lore. The new interest was spiritualism, which already had generated a great deal of enthusiasm in the East and was spreading its hocus-pocus into the Midwest. The Tarkington household was caught by the fad when sister Hauté discovered psychic powers. For months she entertained and mystified close friends and relatives with table-lifting and spirit-rapping, while her younger brother looked on in fascination.

One evening when Tarkington came into the house at his

nine o'clock curfew hour, he found his father, mother, sister, and James Whitcomb Riley, who was a family friend, seated about a table with hands outstretched on the mahogany top. John Tarkington was slowly reciting the alphabet, and the table was making thumping sounds. Soon there ensued a dialogue between his father and the table:

"Is *G* or *H* the letter you want?"

The table thumped twice.

"Not *G*, then . . . You want *H*. Is that right?"

The table thumped three times. Then Riley laughed and said that he recognized his brother Hum Riley. As the boy watched silently, Riley and the table carried on a conversation purporting to come from the poet's deceased brother.

After stumbling on that séance, Tarkington watched for others on subsequent evenings. Sometimes Riley took part, sometimes visiting members of the family. When Newton Booth visited Indiana, he joined the group and later took back to California a firm belief in spiritualism. Only Grandfather Tarkington never was convinced, for he still believed in the reality of Satan. When he heard of the occult doings, he drove forty miles by buggy from his farm where he lived in retirement to investigate; and after listening to the rappings for an hour, he pronounced them the work of the devil and straightway drove forty miles home again. No one ever mentioned spiritualism to him again; in fact, no one ever argued with the Reverend Joseph Tarkington about anything. On the other hand, Grandmother and Grandfather Booth took great pleasure in the sessions around the library table.

The séances became less and less frequent after the old circuit rider had so emphatically made his pronouncement. Soon the emotional and physical strain began to impair Hauté's health, and after her marriage in 1886 her energies found a different outlet. Tarkington never disbelieved in the reality of his sister's psychic powers and throughout his life was tolerant of other persons' alleged supersensory experience. At mid-career he introduced favorably a book on spiritualism by a former Indianapolis neighbor, May Wright Sewall, suggesting that Mrs. Sewall's reported communications with her dead husband could not be dismissed as mere delusions. He also shared a lifelong interest in spiritualism with Hamlin Garland and agreed with him that psychic phenomena must be accepted as genuine. Finally, in his old age Tarkington urged one of his grand-nephews, who seemed to have inherited Hauté's powers to carry on controlled experiments in table-rapping and levitation.

While spiritualism flourished at home, Tarkington was forming indelible attitudes towards religion at church and Sunday school. His parents were Presbyterians who attended services regularly, and long before he could understand what was going on, he had to sit through interminable sermons. His presence in church was an inescapable obligation of boyhood, a dreary business not unlike a kind of punishment. He grew up, consequently, feeling that church attendance was to be dodged at the first opportunity, and during his adult career, though he was a religious man, he never was a churchgoer. "The boredom of those painful Sundays," he wrote later, "has remained with me all my life." In 1898 he told a friend that he had not been to church ten times, except for weddings, in five years. He had gone once when an aunt gave two stained-glass windows and again when a girl asked him to take her.

Sunday school also left its mark on him. All the boys he knew went, partly because they were made to and partly because they wanted to. They rather enjoyed the Bible lessons and found the weekly experience a refreshing novelty; yet questions began to arise as they grew older, one of which shook profoundly Tarkington's belief in the wisdom and truth of the Bible. When he was fifteen, his class read in the weekly lesson the story of Uzzah, the man who was killed by God for stumbling against the Ark. Tarkington was revolted by the cruelty of God in exacting such incomprehensible vengeance: "It seemed to me a revoltingly cruel thing—*I* wouldn't have done it . . . *no* decent person would! The teacher (kindly but perplexed) declared that the story was true . . . the act good and just." To the boy's mind, however, the story either was not true or God was wicked. For a long while he had been troubled by the biblical accounts of a deity who killed so many people for the sake of a few to whom he was partial. The story of Uzzah convinced him that the whole thing was a fable, since the authorities said each part was as true as every other part, and soon after this he left Sunday school forever, finally being old enough to have his own way about such matters. The passage in II Samuel, nevertheless, was valuable to him, for it made him realize, as he explained later, the necessity of having a religion that could be defended.

The creed that Tarkington later worked out for himself as a young man resembles the liberal theology of Unitarianism. His cosmology, like that of Jefferson, Franklin, and other deists, derived from the Newtonian concepts of the eighteenth century and envisioned a Supreme Intelligence behind the well-oiled clockwork of a harmonious universe. The comet's "royal sweep . . . through caverns of night . . . [in] a precise, defined orbit varying not in its stupendous regularity" convinced him of the existence of God, but not a personal god or a deity available only to Christians. Every religion, he thought, was a different statement of the same truth, definitions of which varied as dialects broke off into languages and men began fighting over semantics. He regarded historical Christianity much as Emerson had described it in his "Divinity School Address": originally a spontaneous worship by primitive man of the wonder and mystery of life but in modern times the well-posted preserve of a highly dogmatic priesthood. Also like Emerson, Tarkington regarded Christ not as God but as the one perfect man whose life exemplified human possibilities.

While Tarkington was wrestling with matters of religion, another problem of adolescence, the awakening consciousness of sex, began to disturb him. He had graduated to long pants and starched collars but remained a bashful boy whose awkwardness in the presence of girls recalls the gaucheries of Willie Baxter in *Seventeen* (1916). Although he had grown up in mixed juvenile company, attended many children's parties, and suffered through dancing school, his attitude towards the other sex had been intolerant, like that of Penrod, whose experiences with girls, in fact, were often his own. Tarkington himself once had written to a little girl, as Penrod did: "Dear Madam Please excuse me from dancing the cotilon with you this afternoon as I have fell off the barn/ Sincerely yours/ Penrod Schofield." He eventually outgrew his shyness, and years later when the lady who had received that note reminded him of it, he was the most popular bachelor in Indianapolis.

At the age of fifteen, however, he was far from poised on the occasion of his first formal call on a girl—an Older Girl of at least sixteen. The instigator of this event was the dashingly handsome Horace Hord, whose aplomb in the presence of girls Tarkington envied. On this expedition Horace took with him both Tarkington and Bush Browning, two painfully shy adolescents. Horace knocked on the door, made the proper inquiries, and introduced his companions, who then sat uncomfortably on the sofa while Horace chattered intimately with the Older Girl. Every once in a while the pair on the couch were asked to corroborate an opinion, upon which they laughed embarrassedly and cleared their throats simultaneously. The muscles of Tarkington's face soon began to hurt from forced smiling; he also felt too warm. The circulation in his legs became sluggish, but he was afraid to change his position. After an interminable period Horace finally ended the agony by announcing that it was time to go:

> Bush and I stood up, coughing, and the Older Girl said she was sorry we had to leave so soon; she hoped we'd come again. Bush and I said we'd certainly like to, and remained where we were, mumbling, making semi-bowing motions, and moving our hanging hands in little arcs, in case she intended to shake them.
> She didn't, but said she was glad we'd like to come again; and we said, yes, indeed, we'd like to; and Horace said, "Well, for heaven's sake, come on; we got to chase our freight!"
> Bush and I, still making little bowing motions, began to move backward toward the door together, saying, "Well, good night, huh, huh!" and then coughing. Every step or so we stopped because she'd say, "Well, good night; I do hope you'll come again!" and we had to respond, "Well, good night, we'd certainly like to!"
> Our progress backward, accompanied by these courteous vocalizings, was impeded. We were too close together; Bush seemed to be both a little behind me and somewhat in front of me. I stepped on him and he stepped on me; our feet became confused; all eight of our limbs seemed to be interlockingly in the way of one another. Bush lost his balance and I mine; there were hopeless clutchings, and then we were both full sprawled upon the carpet, still entangled, and exclaiming scrupulously, "Pardon *me!*"

The Older Girl covered her face with her hands as Bush and Booth struggled to their feet, laughed at themselves, and beat a retreat from the house. As long as they were in earshot, they

continued to laugh boisterously; then the false merriment
ended and the recriminations began.

At the age of sixteen Tarkington was growing fast. He outgrew shoes and suits in a manner that perpetually embarrassed
him and never managed to accumulate enough flesh to cover
his bony frame. His adolescent angularity included prominent
shoulder blades that caused him mental anguish and much self-
consciousness. One summer day when he and a friend were to
play tennis with two girls, he asked his companion for a frank
opinion. Did his shoulder blades stick out too far? The friend
candidly answered yes and advised him to wear two shirts.
Though the day was hot, the game brisk, he played stoically in
both wool and cotton shirts. But as he mopped his brow on
the way home, he felt rewarded when his companion conceded
that the shoulder blades had been nearly obliterated under the
double swathing.

Girls, of course, were vastly important to any high school
boy; yet Tarkington's chief extracurricular activities were literary, theatrical, and artistic. When he was not writing copybook stories or producing hayloft dramas, he spent his free
hours filling notebooks with crayon sketches and pen-and-ink
drawings. His family thought he had real talent, encouraged
his drawing, and later arranged for professional instruction, the
result being that he grew up with the ambition to be an
illustrator. Also because of his interest in art Tarkington's
acquaintance with Indiana's best-known man of letters, Riley,
blossomed into a warm friendship and even artistic collaboration. The poet, who also liked to draw, praised the boy's
sketches and sometimes spent entire evenings drawing with him
and correcting his errors.

The relationship between Tarkington and Riley began when
the boy was eight, and the still-obscure poet was a new staff
member of the Indianapolis *Journal*. Riley came to court sister
Hauté, but he was less an ardent lover than a family friend.
The younger brother benefited handsomely from the many
afternoons and evenings that Riley spent at their house, and
throughout his life the name of the poet always summoned up
pleasant memories. Riley apparently enjoyed the boy's company as much as that of the sister, for he acted stories for him,
turned cartwheels on the lawn, recited poems, and even asked

for advice about verses in the process of composition. One day in 1886, when Riley was preparing a new book, *The Boss Girl*, for publication, he showed Tarkington the cover design he was working on, a picture of an ink-bottle cannon firing a charge that exploded into the words of the title. Tarkington studied the sketch, then added to it a downward-flying imp applying the point of a quill to the touchhole of the cannon. The addition pleased Riley, and the book was published with the imp on the cover, after which, Tarkington remembered, the poet called him his collaborator.

The boy was tremendously proud when his drawing appeared on Riley's book, but this public recognition, stimulating as it was, did not change the delicate balance of his social adjustment. Ever since his fourth-grade feud with Miss Jameson, he had imbibed unwillingly from the springs of formal education, and during his seventeenth year he found himself suddenly unable to drink at all, though his scholastic average for the first two years of high school had been a respectable 83.7. One day while he was on his way to school in the fall of his junior year at Shortridge High School, an insignificant incident touched off a chain reaction of unexpected and widely ramifying developments: he met Bush Browning, who had left school and was driving a horse and wagon in the carefree role of bill collector for his father's business.

Tarkington climbed up on the seat beside Bush to smoke a forbidden cigarette and by the time he had finished, it was too late to go to classes. How could he excuse his tardiness? How could he bear the hostility of his teacher? The answer was obvious: he could do neither of these things. And after he had been absent an entire day, the situation became more and more hopeless. To excuse a day's absence, one had to produce a note from home, and to make his parents a party to his truancy was unthinkable.

On the next day Tarkington set out for school as usual, but he walked about until he again met Bush. The second day of truancy passed, as the first, in a round of riding and bill-collecting; and so went the first week. By the time Sunday came, Tarkington had resolved to end the intolerable situation, but he could not bring himself to discuss the matter with his family. What had begun as a peccadillo had become an enormity, and as the weeks passed, matters became increasingly appalling. While he pondered ways of ending the unbearable predicament, he varied his daily routine, sometimes riding with Bush, sometimes reading in the public library; but each day the dread of exposure became more terrifying, until finally nine weeks after its beginning the agony ended. Tarkington's mother happened to meet his former physics teacher at a reception and innocently asked how her son was doing.

Disclosure of the truth, however, caused no explosion at home. There were tears of sorrow and disappointment, but his parents and sister were kind, sympathetic, and gentle. There was no third degree, no reproach, no suggestion that he again face his former teachers. He would take private lessons in voice and a single high school course in drawing for the rest of the year, then go to Phillips Exeter Academy in the fall. In this situation, as in others, Tarkington's mother and father displayed admirable restraint in handling him. They perhaps had been over-indulgent and over-protective in raising him, but they also had the good sense not to play the martinet when he disappointed them. Patience and understanding ultimately produced the results they hoped for, and sending the boy away from home for his last two years of high school was the most astute move they could have made. Two years at an Eastern school revived his interest in studies, toughened him mentally and emotionally, and removed him from the smothering attentions of his mother and sister.

Tarkington entered a totally new world when he enrolled at Phillips Exeter in the autumn of 1887. The contrast with high school then was even sharper than it would be today, for the preparatory school was small, and the boys were thrown pretty much on their own. Because dormitories were nonexistent, the students lived in boardinghouses scattered about the New Hampshire village, and Tarkington found himself for the first time free from parental supervision. Although there was one other youth from Indianapolis in school, the Midwestern boy landed among strangers in a bewildering new environment. Nearly all of his classmates came from the East, only a handful from the West and South, and to make the transition even more abrupt, he arrived in Exeter nearly a month late. The shock of new people, new places, new ideas, however, jolted him beneficially, as he later realized, for Exeter was the experience that "began to open my eyes to the world."

Surprisingly perhaps, his adjustment to the new life was rapid, and a month after arriving he no longer seemed a callow Midwestern youth. Writing Dan Calkins in November, he reported that a forbidden Sunday-night poker game then was in progress in the boardinghouse. There were six fellows rooming there, he bragged, and they raised more hell than any other six students in town; and he added gratuitously that his German professor was an ass and his landlady a "regular old fraud."

He began immediately, however, to work hard on his studies to make up for his previous lack of application. Uncle Newton Booth was paying part of his expenses and expected results, and his parents were making a sacrifice to send him away to school. Impressing on him the financial drain of his boarding-school bills, his father wrote near the end of the first year that the cost so far had been one hundred dollars a month, whereas his cousin Fenton then was going to DePauw for a quarter of that amount. But the effort seemed worth while when Tarkington's first grades were issued, and his father wrote after Christmas congratulating him on an average of eighty-three, only ten points behind the top mark in the class —and that after entering a month late.

The severity of the New England winter caused the boy his greatest distress during his first year at Exeter. While he spent a lonely Christmas at school, unable to go home for the holidays, heavy snows began piling up outside the deserted boardinghouse, and two and a half months later snow still lay in thick drifts on the New Hampshire countryside. Writing his family in mid-March, he described wearily the bleak landscape still to be seen from his window: an empty expanse of dull white fields stretching away to the tree-lined river. Nothing was visible—no fences, no hitching posts, nothing but snow. He was tired of plowing through "drifts and drifts of clogging heavy snow . . . staggering, flopping, pulling, jerking. . . . Oh to get away to the dry city—to find some dust." No doubt he thought that all New England winters were as severe as his first one, though he realized later that this outburst had been written during the memorable blizzard of Eighty-eight. He had not left Indiana prepared for such weather, and in January, after the mercury touched twenty below zero, his father wrote posthaste that he was sending two suits of the best camel's-hair underwear obtainable in Indianapolis.

The snows of mid-March were slightly more endurable when Tarkington thought of the approaching spring vacation. The president of his class, Arthur Lord, had invited him to spend the Easter holidays in New York. The midland youth had spent Thanksgiving in Boston with an uncle, but the thought of visiting the Lords in New York at Easter was enchanting. His parents consented to the trip, though they had misgivings and warned him against the temptations of the big city. When they admonished him not to go slumming, he replied: "We will go to the theater and Art galleries and all that, but one of the pleasantest things about it will be the home feeling."

The vacation trip was all that he anticipated. More than a generation later, as he wrote a Foreword to John Drew's memoirs, the recollection of that week in New York still was vivid: "What a good and merry town was brown-stone New York then, when one stood at the doors of the Fifth Avenue Hotel to see the pretty girls . . . parading by after the matinee; when the Avenue was given over to proud horses and graceful women." Unforgettable too was the performance he saw of *The Taming of the Shrew,* when Drew played Petruchio to Ada Rehan's Katharina at Augustin Daly's theater. Whether or not he visited the art galleries on that vacation, the record does not say.

Tarkington matured a great deal during his two years away from home. When he summed up his school experiences at the end of the first spring term, he wrote glowingly of his satisfaction with both his friendships and his studies. He had made good grades and good friends. He spoke warmly of Dr. Scott, the principal, and Mrs. Scott, whom all the boys adored. "I have grown to love the school and have tremendous school-feeling," he told his mother as he described the baseball team's victory over Andover. In his studies he had indeed done well, especially in the courses that interested him the most—history and English; and in the autumn of 1888 when he returned for his senior year, he found psychology to be the most fascinating study he ever had encountered. "Dr. Scott," he reported to his father then, "is a marvelous teacher and talker and I wish you could hear him." Tarkington, in short, made good away from home: he applied himself seriously, and the rewards were both temporal and spiritual.

Tarkington fancied himself a gay blade during his senior year, but his notion of deviltry stopped at practical jokes, loud clothes, incessant smoking, and occasional champagne suppers. He was shocked by the sexual license of some of his classmates. Unburdening himself to Dan Calkins on this subject, he complained: "the fellows are handsome, some of them, witty—a few . . . but what a hot-bed of foulness and muck! Portsmouth houses are full of them every night—Boston ones, every holiday." Indiana was not more saintly than the East in 1889, but to Tarkington and his friends in Indianapolis brothels existed only in books. His decency, he added, was wondered at as "something strange and unheard of."

Faith in his own moral code, however, was reinforced by a happy Christmas vacation at home during his senior year. Then for the first time on New Year's Day he was old enough to join the formal holiday callers, those incredibly sophisticated young men who dashed up and down the avenues in silk hats and sleighs from one big open house to another. It was a time when Negro servants in white ties and tails opened polished front doors, violins played against banks of flowers and potted palms, fragrant logs burned in wide fireplaces, beautiful girls graced every house, and over the whole nostalgic scene of mid-winter gaiety gaslight from a hundred jets threw a mellow glow. During the same winter holiday Tarkington also attended a busy round of teas and dances given by his former high school classmates, many of whom he had known from childhood. Some of his friends had entered college; others had finished school and gone to work. Already the couples were getting married or at least talking about matrimony. His crowd was friendly, relaxed, intimate, and within the well-defined bounds of Midwestern mores they enjoyed a large measure of social freedom.

Tarkington's final year at Exeter was protracted through the entire summer by work on the *Pean*, the class yearbook. In the winter he was selected to be one of four editors, but no one found time to perform editorial chores until after graduation, and then two of the four discovered compelling reasons to go home. Tarkington and Edward Cullinan were left to write and illustrate the book alone, a task they struggled with throughout the summer only to have the Boston printer suspend work when funds ran out. As Tarkington labored through the vacation, duty bound to complete the class memorial, his Grandmother Booth was dying in Indianapolis, but he neither would leave his project nor could afford to make a special trip home. His father was understanding, accepted his decision, and let his expenses run on through the summer. Although his mother suggested querulously that he abandon the enterprise, his father advised him to stay as long as need be and wrote at the end of July: "Do what you think is your clear duty by the Pean." When the youth finally returned home at the end of August, his labors had come to naught, but his illustrations were ultimately used in the *Pean* published by the class of 1891.

The summer was gone when Tarkington reached Indianapolis; but his late return did not matter, because he had no immediate plans to enter college. The family exchequer was depleted and needed to be replenished if his mother's dreams of Princeton were to be realized. John Tarkington recently had given up practicing law and had taken a position with S. A. Fletcher & Co., Indianapolis bankers, to insure a steady income during his son's college years. In July, 1889, however, he was still in debt, and his son, therefore, spent the following year at home. He took courses during September and October at a business college and in mid-November began a six-day-a-week program at T. C. Steele's newly opened art school. Having passed his twentieth birthday before returning home, he felt himself a man. "I smoke at home now all the time," he wrote a friend of his larger latitude: "Mother . . . only says 'Booth, how can you?!?!' about three times an hour now—it used to be seventy-eight."

His new freedom also extended to his clothes. When he returned from Exeter, he brought with him all the latest Eastern fads in a wardrobe that not only his family, but neighbors and strangers as well, were quick to ridicule. "Try as hard as I may to suit people," he wrote, "they laugh as I pass. Damn this town. . . . I'm going to emigrate to Africa and wear a coral necklace." Instead of Africa, however, he took his sartorial excesses to Purdue University the following year; but by the time he went to college he had learned to live with the criticism and even to see some humor in his richly caparisoned figure. When he later described a student-faculty reception at Purdue, for a Lafayette, Indiana, newspaper, he ridiculed the affected costume of one student who looked "just like Henry Clay's statue." Then he added archly that Tarkington was dressed the same way. The best portrait of the author as dude occurs in *The Conquest of Canaan* (1905) in the sketch of Gene Bantry, just home from college (*circa* 1890):

> His ulster, sporting a big cape at the shoulders, and a tasselled hood over the cape, was of a rough Scotch cloth, patterned in faint, gray-and-white squares the size of baggage checks, and it was so long that the skirts trailed in the snow. His legs were lost in the accurately creased, voluminous garments . . . [which] . . . permitted a liberal knee action . . . almost without superficial effect. Upon his feet glistened long shoes, shaped, save for the heels, like sharp racing-shells; these were partially protected by tan-colored low gaiters with flat, shiny, brown buttons.

Tarkington switched his plans from Princeton to Purdue during the summer after his winter of private art instruction. While he was vacationing at Lake Maxinkuckee in northern Indiana, he met a captivating girl, Geneve Reynolds, who just happened to live in Lafayette. She was a charming creature who talked delightfully on art and literature and whose father had been a classmate of Newton Booth at Asbury College. By a happy coincidence her home town also was the seat of Purdue, and when Tarkington discovered that Purdue had on its faculty a gifted teacher of art, he abandoned Princeton for apparently logical and compelling reasons. His family, still unable to afford an Eastern school, was surprised at his choice of an agricultural and mechanical college but as usual was indulgent. Lafayette proved to be merely a stop on the road to New Jersey.

"Booth Tarkington, a graduate of Phillips Exeter Academy, is taking special art work under Prof. Knaufft," reported the Lafayette *Sunday Times* on September 21, 1890, in a column of college news. The author of the item was Tarkington himself, who added reporting that year to his studies and his extra-curricular calls on Miss Reynolds. His journalistic experience was perhaps the most useful accomplishment of the period, because he discovered, unfortunately, that Ernest Knaufft, the artist-teacher, was completing his last semester at Purdue and that Geneve Reynolds was discouragingly popular. Nevertheless, for a few months he studied under Knaufft, who simultaneously was teaching the eminent graphic artist Bruce Rogers, and carried on his aesthetic dialogues with Geneve whenever he could. After he transferred to Princeton the next year, he continued his art studies and occasionally corresponded with Geneve.

Tarkington not only worked hard on his art course at Purdue, but he also labored conscientiously over his other studies. Besides the inspired instruction of Professor Knaufft, there were the zoology lectures of Dean Coulter, who "enlightened with brilliant illuminations through the mist that covers the original truth of things." Although his early interest in science had been negligible, Tarkington later concluded that the dean "performed upon me what might easily be called a miracle in the art of educating." His mark in zoology was ninety, and the stimulation of great teaching may have sent him on to botany, in which he did nearly as well. He also continued his preparatory school work in French and German and, of course, took English literature. In all of his courses at Purdue he maintained an eighty-nine average and received his highest marks, ninety-eight and ninety-six, in two elective literature courses.

Absorbing as his college work was, perhaps the most indelible of all his experiences at Purdue were the uproarious week-end visits of George Ade and John T. McCutcheon, both of whom were brothers in Sigma Chi. Although the pair had graduated before Tarkington entered college, they worked on Chicago newspapers and frequently returned to their alma mater. His friendship with Ade and McCutcheon, begun during this year at Purdue, lasted a lifetime, and with Ade, in particular, was renewed periodically in Europe, New York, Chicago, and Indiana. Tarkington was initiated into Sigma Chi on October 12; hence his meeting with Ade and McCutcheon undoubtedly took place soon after his arrival in Lafayette.

Between hilarious week ends at the Sigma Chi house and his

studies Tarkington squeezed in a good many extracurricular activities. Ade, already a successful columnist, perhaps inspired Tarkington's own column in the *Sunday Times,* and McCutcheon, a newspaper cartoonist, may have criticized his drawings for undergraduate publications. His newspaper column was amateurish, but it was always informative, sometimes funny, and gave him a chance to exercise his talent for observation and satire. He continued to draw, as he had at Exeter, and contributed illustrations both to the 1891 yearbook and to the literary magazine. Besides writing and sketching, he went out for dramatics, playing the title role in a production of Sir William Gilbert's Tom Cobb and he joined the Irving Society, before which he spoke on "The Old and the New in Art." His selection as the group's orator, he wrote his family, was "the great honor of the college."

The year at Purdue, however, was marred by financial worries, and the few letters that survive from this period are mainly concerned with money matters. In November he was so broke that he did not have twenty-five cents to go to the football game, and on returning to Lafayette after Christmas he reached the campus with only a dollar to his name. In the spring when he wrote home to thank his mother for sending him "Mr. Milburn's sermon," he needed three dollars for the sophomore picnic, which would be, he said, his first social event since February. He also admonished his mother: "You must give up the idea of Princeton. I must go to work. I have several gray hairs and enough education. If I am ever to be anything, it is time I commenced being." But Princeton it was to be, and when he returned to Indianapolis in June, he was ready for the pivotal experience of his youth—his two years at Princeton.

In July his father dispatched advance notice to a cousin who lived in Princeton: "I write in the interest of our boy, Newton Booth Tarkington, who is destined by his mother to go to the College of N. J. the coming year . . . before devoting himself to journalistic Art, or something of that in-definitive mode of procedure to the poor house." The Tarkingtons, he wrote, planned to give their son a year or two to "study the broadening branches of learning" before going on perhaps to the Art Students League of New York for specialized training. He could not enroll at Princeton for a degree because he did not have the requisite background in classical languages.

His deficiencies, however, were not his fault. Uncle Newton Booth had held that Latin and Greek were useless because they had done him no apparent good in frontier California, and his word was law to his sister. Because John Tarkington never argued with his wife, their son arrived at Princeton with a smattering of science, modern languages, and literature. He frolicked through his Princeton courses as a special student, in contrast to his serious study at Purdue, and felt little regret except on Commencement morning in 1893. The formal education that he absorbed both at Purdue and Princeton was haphazardly planned, but he had a gay time, made many friends, and prepared himself well enough for writing novels.

When Tarkington descended from the station surrey in Nassau Street, a warm September sun flooded the gray-brown stones of the college, and his first sight of the campus was a "vision of the Promised Land." After three quarters at Purdue, then seventeen years old, the graceful eighteenth-century lines of Nassau Hall fairly took his breath away. A college nearly a century and a half old in a town redolent with colonial history enchanted the midland youth.

Tarkington entered the junior class in the autumn of 1891. He was then twenty-one years old, five feet, eleven inches tall, long-boned, and lanky. He had dark brown eyes and hair, a long face, and his father had written, "an ambitiously prominent nose with nostrils to please Napoleon himself." His friends remembered him, in addition, as a sallow-faced, stoop-shouldered young man whose hollow cough marked him as an habitual user of tobacco. "We gave Tark short of a year to live unless he quit cigarettes," wrote one of his contemporaries.

His personality immediately disarmed everyone. He never had outgrown the nervousness of his childhood, but he was gay, sympathetic, affectionate, and utterly lacking in pretense. His classmates accepted him as if he had always been one of them, and by graduation time he was probably the most popular man in the group. The Ivy Club took him in, and the village tradesmen soon were calling him by his first name. His room in University Hall quickly became a clubhouse, operating nearly around the clock, for campus literati, songsters, and thespians.

No one who knew Tarkington during his two years at Princeton ever forgot him. A. P. Dennis, a senior who roomed near by in 1891-1892, first saw him squatting on a sofa, munching doughnuts, drinking beer, and manipulating pencil and paper. "He's sketching," explained Tarkington's roommate, as though showing off a trained animal. Another friend, Jesse Lynch Williams, the playwright, remembered him sitting in a corner devouring toast and writing a poem to the girl he had met most recently at a prom, while elswhere in the room friends ate, drank, played the banjo, and wrestled on the sofa. The quarters were a shambles of cigarette boxes, trophies, signs, photographs, books, and students.

All the reports of Tarkington as an undergraduate emphasize his ability to make friends and to digest anything. He was like a magnet in a box of iron filings. The lively sessions in his room never broke up before one or two in the morning, and "Tark had about as much privacy in his apartment," wrote Dennis, "as Louis XIV at his morning rising." The lethal combinations of food that he consumed are hard to credit, but the witnesses agree that his capacities for food and drink were spectacular. A few months after leaving Princeton, he wrote Dennis that he had changed his night lunch a little, and "if you will follow my plan you'll never have another bad day. Between two and five A.M. every night take unlimited Beer, Bananas, Cheese Sandwiches, Chocolate Creams and Cake, Lemon Ice and a Welsh Rarebit. Don't go to bed too early. This is the secret of my constitution."

Tarkington was seldom known to study, although he passed most of his courses satisfactorily and in some cases brilliantly. Having a quick mind and a photographic memory, he slid through exams so easily that his friends thought he must absorb knowledge through his pores. Yet he remembered many of his teachers and the effects they had on him. Dr. Patton's ethics classes, he recalled, blasted his theories of evolution and convinced him of a real hell until he went to Professor McClure's biology laboratory to study life under a microscope. Allan Marquand was an unforgettable teacher who seemed to live in another realm, the world of art. General Kargé, with whom he read Goethe, he remembered as an Old World gentleman of charm and distinction, and Dean Murray, who "lectured in beautiful English," never had trouble with students cutting his literature courses. Nor did Woodrow Wilson, then professor of political science, whose courses Tarkington perhaps audited: "We crowded his lectures, both kinds of us; the idle apprentice as eagerly as the industrious."

Outside the classroom Tarkington was the most brilliant and industrious student in the undergraduate body, a dynamo of energy and enthusiasm. He had the unique distinction of serving as an editor for three major student publications: the *Nassau Literary Magazine,* the *Tiger* (humor magazine), and the *Bric-a-Brac* (Yearbook). In addition, he was soloist for the Glee Club, and in his senior year Washington's Birthday Orator and president of the Dramatic Association. He wrote and drew voluminously for the publications he edited, and for the drama group, he wrote and acted in the organization's annual presentation.

This production was *The Honorable Julius Caesar,* a burlesque musical comedy that made Princeton history. Full of youthful exuberance and pure "corn," the show played to an enthusiastic student audience in the old commons of University Hall. Although John Mayhew composed the music and Post Wheeler did the lyrics, Tarkington wrote the book, cast the parts, trained the chorus, designed the costumes, and helped build the scenery—all this in addition to singing and acting a leading role. His part was Cassius, described on the program, which he also wrote, as "an old-time villain, wily and tricky, with an unappeasable appetite for crime."

The Dramatic Association during Tarkington's presidency gave hostage to fortune by changing its name to the Triangle Club. Then, to begin auspiciously under its new name the next year, the club successfully remounted *The Honorable Julius Caesar,* thereby inaugurating the tradition of Triangle Club productions. Not until later, however, did the organization tour the country at Christmas time; for in his day, Tarkington afterwards recalled, the club was limited to performances in Princeton and Trenton, because the faculty feared the church people would think that Princeton was getting too theatrical.

The Glee Club was not hampered by such restrictions, and its annual tour was planned enthusiastically by student members and alumni groups alike. Soon after his arrival at Princeton

Tarkington joined the second bass section of the club and immediately became a soloist. When the club visited the Midwest during the Christmas vacation of 1892-1893, Tarkington headlined the concerts in a dozen cities from Pittsburgh to Omaha. In his home town he sang "It's All Over Now," a song of his own composition that stopped the show. His number was the best on the program, reported the Indianapolis *News*, which added that he was twice recalled and then presented, like a prima donna, with flowers. Perhaps the home-town press was biased, but papers in Minneapolis and Kansas City also gave him the highest praise. Mark Sullivan, in his autobiography, recalled attending a Princeton Glee Club concert in West Chester, Pennsylvania, at the age of fourteen and seeing for the first time college men as a group. In their dress suits they seemed demigods, but one man in particular stood out, the bass who sang the solo in "Peter Gray"—Booth Tarkington. That concert, incidentally, was responsible for Sullivan's wanting to go to college.

Although the Glee Club tours were a great success, the singing that Tarkington and his friends did on the steps of Nassau Hall was even more memorable. His "Danny Deever" was a tour de force that he had to repeat every time there was group singing. One night his performance was especially effective, for the inevitable song was requested by late-returning students who had gathered to sing outside the dormitory. As Tarkington sang, an undergraduate audience collected. Just at the end of the song, as the last deep bass notes died away, there came a solemn roll of thunder from the distance. It was an impressive moment.

When he could take time from his singing and acting, Tarkington dashed off contributions for the literary and humor magazines. Most of his undergraduate writing seems to have been turned out like hack work, but there are occasional hints and portents of the future novelist. He wrote quantities of undistinguished verse, stories imitative of Bret Harte and Poe, humorous sketches reminiscent of Twain and Ade, and a trivial talk-of-the-town column. Yet there is apparent in all this a consciousness of style and a developing narrative power. The prize story in the literary magazine, "The Better Man," which drew on his memory of summers spent in Marshall, Illinois, was the

best of the lot because its inspiration came rather from experience than from books. Yet many years were to elapse before
the vogue of the historical novel relaxed its grasp on his
imagination.

An informal literary club known as the Coffee House provided a focal point for undergraduate writers in 1892-1893.
Jesse Williams, then a graduate student, was the oracle of the
group. They admired and discussed all the standard eighteenth-century authors and among the moderns championed
Meredith, Stevenson, Howells, Twain, James, Harte, Barrie,
Hardy, and Kipling. Sometimes they included in their discussions Daudet, Cherbuliez, Balzac, Hugo, and Flaubert, and they
knew Tolstoy and Turgenev but not Dostoevsky and Chekhov.
Zola they had read but regarded as a clumsy writer with gross
tastes and therefore no very great figure in their world of letters.
Whitman and Melville were known to them but not taken so
seriously as Browning and Tennyson. When F. Marion Craw-
ford came to lecture at Princeton, the Coffee Club turned out
en masse and was thoroughly delighted with the literary opinions of that romancer.

Tarkington looked back fondly on his Princeton days, "not
an instant of which I would have changed." He cherished most
his friendships and valued least the old school tie. Scarcely a
year passed in his later life when he did not spend a few days
or weeks at Princeton, but when a nephew matriculated in
1924, he told a friend: "The Ivy prestige is as ridiculous a thing
as comes under my observation." Princeton had given him
wider horizons, a host of memories, and he remained a devoted
alumnus and classmate. Summing up his undergraduate experience many years later, he wrote: "The elms thrived; the
grass before Old North was always crisp and green; and the
gardens at Prospect and through all of Princeton town were
rich with flowers abloom, never a blowsy or dried or faded one
among them. Yet it never rained! It was always sunshine then."

THREE

LITERARY APPRENTICESHIP

ONE AFTERNOON many years after Tarkington had become a successful novelist, he was lying on the beach at Kennebunkport, Maine, with his writing neighbor Hugh Kahler. The two men were accosted by a summer-colony mother who announced that her son wanted to be a writer and she needed help. As Tarkington and Kahler struggled to their feet, they groaned inwardly at the dismal prospect before them: at the very least they would have to read a well-intentioned but impossible manuscript. They politely but unenthusiastically agreed to assist in any way they could, and the lady continued:

"I want you to talk our boy out of it."

"You do?"

"Yes, my husband and I don't want him to be a writer."

"Why not?"

"We want him to *do* something."

Tarkington had encountered a similar attitude in Indianapolis when he returned from college with neither a profession nor a job. He had considered a chance to work on the New York *Tribune* but rejected journalism to become a free-lance writer and illustrator. His neighbors, however, saw him as a young man with no apparent desire to go to work. He settled down comfortably in his father's house, and for five years no one saw any tangible accomplishment. He was a young man without gainful employment, a wastrel who stayed up late, drank, slept most of the day, and often could be seen racing about the city in a red-wheeled runabout behind a lively pair of trotting horses. His parents were embarrassed by their son's unproductive existence, though they waited patiently and indulgently for the eventual harvest.

Indiana, of course, took pride in her authors, but there was a vast difference between wanting to write and succeeding at it. Lew Wallace had combined a military, legal, and diplomatic career with writing, and Riley had made a huge success both as poet and public reader. These authors had won public esteem by the approved manner. Fortunately for Tarkington, Uncle Newton Booth's death in 1892 brought him a small bequest, the income from which met his moderate needs during this apprenticeship, so that he was able to go on writing and collecting rejection slips without becoming a financial drain on his family.

"I was for five years, and more," he recalled in 1900, "one of the rejected—as continuously and successively, I suppose, as any one who ever wrote." During this period he sent off to editors in New York countless manuscripts that came back so fast they seemed to have been intercepted in Philadelphia. The more unsuccessful he was, the longer and harder he worked—sometimes all night. Early one morning after an unusually long session he went for a walk and upon returning met the milkman, who paused to talk:

> "You been up all night?" he asked.
> "Yes," I answered.
> "What you been doin'?" he went on.
> "Working," said I.
> "Workin'!" said he. "What at?"
> "Writing," said I.
> "How long?" said he.
> "Since yesterday noon," said I. "About 16 hours."
> "My God," said he. "You must have lots of time to waste!"

Tarkington may have seemed a lazy and unproductive member of society to his neighbors, but the fact is he learned to write by dint of much practice, and like the nine-tenths of an iceberg that is submerged his first novel represented only a tiny fraction of his apprentice work. From his first childish copybook narratives to the mature novels of his ripest creative period forty years later, his growth as a writer was slow and unspectacular. No serious artist ever worked more diligently than he to master and refine his technique, and no artist ever tried harder to make each creation the best that he was capable of. If craftsmanship sometimes substituted for inspiration, he had no apologies to make.

After leaving Princeton, he spent the summer at Jamestown, Rhode Island, on Narragansett Bay. His mother and sister had gone to Class Day exercises at the college, and after the students dispersed, the three Tarkingtons went on to New England. He felt bereaved for a time at the sudden end of his undergraduate days and often sat whole afternoons on the salty rocks of the bay brooding about the pleasant past and wondering about the future. He managed to sink his regrets in a busy program of summer-resort parties, however, and even began gathering literary material from the people in the summer hotels and cottages. Sometime during the summer he paid a visit to Bar Harbor, Maine, and on the way passed through Exeter, New Hampshire, where the sight of the familiar buildings of his old school choked him up. When he returned to Indianapolis in the autumn, he already may have begun "The Ruse," a full-length play laid in Bar Harbor.

This play, which was finished in time for the Indianapolis Dramatic Club's annual Christmas presentment, starred Tarkington in the role of Dennis Smith, Arkansas lumber dealer who visits a former college classmate at Bar Harbor. The drama was farce-comedy of a type Howells had popularized among amateur theatrical groups, and Tarkington's summer-resort frolic has some of the same gaiety of a Howells creation. "The Ruse" is managed with more hilarity than finesse; but it was a good beginning and was so well received by the Indianapolis audience that it was repeated at a benefit performance in the spring.

The autumn of 1893 was a busy time for Tarkington, because he not only put together a full-length play, but he also began his first novel, *The Gentleman from Indiana*. Although the novel was not finished for five years, forty thousand words were written within a few months after he left college. When his book eventually was published, he recalled that the early chapters of the story had gone smoothly until one day the tale suddenly stopped short. "It wouldn't budge. The hero stuck fast in the middle of a walk he was taking—he wouldn't take another step." The author backed off and tried again without success, then attempted to coax the tale along by drawing illustrations of scenes yet unwritten. When he failed completely to get the story going, he put it away and turned again to play and short-story writing.

One of the difficulties with the early draft of the novel may have been Bar Harbor, a good setting for a farce but hardly the place to start a novel about an Indiana newspaper editor. An early outline of the story opens in a summer resort where the handsome, athletic hero is surrounded by admiring college classmates soon after their graduation. Tarkington also planned to trace the nineteenth-century history of Indiana before getting to his contemporary concoction of politics, journalism, and romance. But when he took the manuscript out of his desk after five years of additional apprenticeship, the fatal charm of the New England summer resort had faded. He finally began the novel where it should have started originally—in Indiana in the Nineties.

Although New York editors seemed engaged in a conspiracy against Tarkington, he was able to obtain local publications for some of his stories and poems. Each year the Indianapolis Flower Mission, a charity, held a fair, and in connection with the fair the ladies in charge published an annual magazine, for which they recruited Hoosier talent. Bruce Rogers designed one of their covers, and Tarkington was a fairly regular contributor, offering stories that he regarded less hopefully than those going the rounds of Eastern editorial offices. Most of these contributions are apprentice work, a story of yachting off Newport, a humorous essay on the origin of golf, a tale of settlement work in the slums, but "Gay Fragments," published in 1894, shows a real hint of Tarkington's best vein.

This piece consists of four snatches of dialogue overheard at a dance. In the first Mr. Tenny and Mr. Brook are discovered sitting out the revels in the men's room, having been dragged to the affair unwillingly by their wives; and in the second, Mr. Tilbury, performing a duty dance with the buxom, bespectacled Miss White, is waltzed along to the accompaniment of a monologue about protozoa and hexapods. In another bit of conversation Tarkington expertly captures Miss Higgins and Mr. Dorking sitting on the sidelines (having danced once an hour ago and long since exhausted all conversation) in a scene

that anticipates the superb wallflower chapter in *Alice Adams*
(1921). The last of the fragments is a tête-à-tête between Miss
Rose Budde, a popular belle who likes to dance all the time,
and a young man who has managed momentarily to get her off
the floor and out of circulation.

If Tarkington had expanded "Gay Fragments" into a novel
of manners about Indianapolis society, his literary apprenticeship might have ended several years before it did. The plan of
The Gentleman from Indiana was more ambitious than he yet
could execute, but the Indianapolis social scene was under his
daily observation, and when he wrote "Gay Fragments," he was
shaping the material that he knew best. In another sketch of
this period, a tale entitled "The Serious Moment," he calls to
life a midland country club scene in an hour of summer revelry.
A portent of the nostalgic evocation that he was later to master
is this snatch of dance music:

> Inside the house an orchestra played. The violins rippled
> gaily together; the harp tinkled above and bubbled below them
> and ran out from the waltz-theme in sparkling rings; the airy
> contralto of the 'cello dived into the warm shallows of the
> dance, lifted above the surface with a burst of plaintive laugh-
> ter, poised, then swam below again, in placid, calm content;
> beneath, boomed the inciting throb of the bass, beating steadily
> in the depths, strong, incessant, immutable—an unanswerable
> admonition to the foot of the laggard.

The same literary impulse that motivated Winston Churchill, S. Weir Mitchell, Charles Major, and others during the
Nineties kept Tarkington producing costume romances for a
decade after he left college. This vogue of the historical novel,
a popular interest that even Mark Twain abetted in *Joan of
Arc*, occupied Tarkington's best creative efforts during his apprenticeship and resulted eventually in two novels, two novelettes, two short stories, and three plays. In addition, even *The
Gentleman from Indiana* and later *The Conquest of Canaan*
are tinctured with the attitudes and preoccupations of the historical romance.

After making a false start on his first novel, Tarkington tried
another play, "The Prodigals," a three-act drama laid in Trenton, New Jersey, in 1790. The plot of the new play was more

elaborately constructed and the dialogue more expertly written than in "The Ruse." Opening on a noisy tavern scene late at night with the hero, Joseph Scovill, a gallant with a tarnished reputation, as the leading merrymaker, the plot makes use of mistaken identity and heroic self-sacrifice in the best tradition of the costume romance. In the final act, just as Scovill is about to be hanged for a crime he did not commit, the real culprit is discovered, and the governor learns that Scovill would have died to protect the honor of his lady. The play ends, of course, with the rehabilitation of the main character and the immediate prospect of matrimony.

The character delineation and plot development of this play follow the romantic stereotypes of a theatrical era long passed. Tarkington's youthful drama, however, is nearly as good as many plays produced with great success in the Eighties and Nineties. Even Bronson Howard's fabulously successful *Shenandoah,* which made Charles Frohman a small fortune, was the same sort of romantic melodrama; and Tarkington himself succeeded later with this genre in *Beaucaire.* When "The Prodigals" was produced by the Indianapolis Dramatic Club with the author in the role of Scovill, optimistic friends saw Broadway possibilities in the script.

Encouraged by the amateur tryout of his play, Tarkington got up his nerve and sent the manuscript to Richard Mansfield. The actor read it with interest, dictated to his secretary some kind things about it, and gently turned it down; but he invited Tarkington to send him another play if he wrote one with a strong character part. He really meant that the chief male role was not inflated enough to let him dominate the stage from opening to closing curtain, and Tarkington admitted readily that the play had been written for Indianapolis amateurs who would have been jealous if any one part had been made too prominent. This slight—though rather routine—encouragement by Mansfield was excitement enough for the time being and may have accounted for Tarkington's insistence later that Mansfield play *Beaucaire.* "I know how little that [praise] would mean to some folks but it gave me a swelled head," he wrote a Princeton literary friend, James Barnes, whom he also asked for advice about sending out his drama again.

The play was soon to take him to New York, but in the meantime he was working on stories and drawings. During his apprenticeship he turned out scores of illustrations, which he offered to various magazines that bought free-lance art work; but in all instances save one they came back. About the time he was beginning "The Prodigals," he sent off to the old *Life* a drawing and some accompanying text captioned "In the Borderland." To his delight the magazine bought them for twenty dollars, his first professional remuneration except for an anonymous joke previously sold to *Life* for two dollars and a half. 'In the Borderland" was a parody of Aubrey Beardsley's art in the *Yellow Book* (the journal of the London literati) and also of Oscar Wilde's prose. This early publication seems remarkably unmirthful today; yet it was a potent stimulus, and Tarkington bombarded Eastern editorial offices with another thirty or forty drawings before his enthusiasm flagged. The acceptance from *Life* stated that thirteen of the twenty dollars were payment for the drawing, the balance for the text; and since the text occupied twice as much space as the illustration, Tarkington concluded hastily that there was far more profit in drawing than in writing; but he never again sold a sketch and no more prose until S. S. McClure bought *The Gentleman from Indiana.*

By autumn, 1895, Tarkington was ready to besiege personally editors and producers in their New York offices. His sister had sent "The Prodigals" to an agent, Elizabeth Marbury, who wrote that he ought to come east to revise the manuscript under her direction. He needed no other prompting and set off for New York to seek his literary fortune, carrying with him a bundle of new, rejected, and partly finished works. Simultaneously James Whitcomb Riley wrote a friend on the *Century Magazine,* asking him to look out for the young man. "In a histrionic way," said Riley, "he has proved himself an embryo Irving. And in dramatics has written his own play; while in art and literary lines he is a youthful Du Maurier, and mark! none of these talents he has yet ripe for marketing." The poet added that the youth wanted merely to see and to know the real producers of literature at their desks, in their studies, and at their clubs; but Riley underestimated Tarkington's purpose in visiting New York, even though he accurately predicted that success would hang fire.

As Tarkington stood on the deck of the ferry boat that carried him from Jersey City to the foot of Cortlandt Street, he hoped fervently that somewhere in the castellated skyline before him there would be a market for his literary wares. All the old thrills of New York from his Exeter and Princeton days returned when he rode up the Ninth Avenue El to the midtown boardinghouse where he would live and write for the next five or six months. He wanted desperately to become part of the glitter and excitement of the metropolis. He wanted to write for the handsome monthly magazines that Howells, Riley, and Mark Twain appeared in and to be identified with the Broadway of the Frohmans, David Belasco, and Richard Mansfield.

New York was an exhilarating place for the young Midwesterner that winter. Although he wrote unsuccessfully and lived on the top floor of a brownstone boardinghouse for fifteen dollars a week, he went frequently to the theater, the opera, and the art galleries. He saw Sarah Bernhardt, who was making an American tour, Joe Jefferson in *The Rivals,* and Maggie Mitchell in *The Cricket*—the same Maggie who had fascinated the young Henry James in Boston in the same role a generation earlier. He sang his embarrassed solo for Howells at the Lantern Club on Thanksgiving and debated with other boarders Crane's new novel, *The Red Badge of Courage,* and Harold Frederic's latest, *The Damnation of Theron Ware.* New York was still largely a city of gaslight, although electricity was beginning to appear, and the bicycle craze was just starting. Hansom cabs still dominated the avenues, and there were as yet no subways. Girls tightly corseted preserved their hourglass figures, and only the most brazen of women appeared in public in bloomers or demanded the vote for their sex.

Soon after taking a room on West Fifty-seventh Street, Tarkington began successive overhaulings of his plays, chiefly "The Prodigals," under the guidance of his agent. His friend Barnes, who already was supporting himself by writing, collaborated on at least one of the revisions of the costume drama; but all of Tarkington's efforts failed, and he remembered later that each time it was worked over, the manuscript of "The Prodigals" seemed to deteriorate. Finally the agent lost interest and tinkering came to a halt. Success appeared possible only twice that

winter, once when Mansfield again read the play with the idea
of producing but not acting in it and again when Edward Soth-
ern showed a brief interest.

After the play project stalled, Tarkington returned to his
top-floor room to write stories. The impulse towards romance
was inveterate, and he went on with the colonial settings that
he had used in "The Prodigals." One of his tales was "Mr.
Brooke's Friends and an Enemy," a story laid in Trenton in
1760 that bears a superficial resemblance to the play. Its title
character, a high-spirited carouser like Scovill, becoming involved in a scuffle with the watch after a late evening at the
tavern, outsmarts his enemies after appropriate complications.
This manuscript, as well as another laid in seventeenth-century
England, had to wait ten years for publication. Then after Tarkington had published three successful novels and a collection
of tales, *Appleton's* and *Everybody's* magazines were glad
enough to get the stories.

During the months spent in New York Tarkington also began a novel of the theater, combining not only his interest in
the drama but also his early enthusiasm for Uncle Newton
Booth's yarns of the Far West. This story, however, was even
less successful than his other undertakings, for it bogged down
in chapter three in California when the hero was about to join
a theatrical company playing Shakespeare in the mining camps.
Yet it is interesting for its narrative technique, being (with a
single exception) utterly different from Tarkington's later
work, and the manuscript survives as tangible evidence of his
complete change between apprenticeship and maturity. He
wrote it in the first-person, a point of view which he later called
about "as lazy as fiction done in the form of letters," instead of
'the upper type" of narration employed by Howells, James,
Meredith, and Hardy.

If Tarkington had not been embarrassed speechless at the
Lantern Club dinner, Howells might have given him the expert criticism that he needed at this stage of his apprenticeship.
But the best literary counsel he could obtain was from Riley,
who was hardly the person to advise a potential writer of realistic fiction. Tarkington's sister again took the initiative and
sent "Mr. Brooke," as the story was later titled, to Riley for
critical evaluation. The poet had no patience with historical

fiction and not knowing the tale was supposed to be flavore
with eighteenth-century archaisms started through the manu
script, peppering it with emendations. On page four he los
interest and read without annotating until he reached the end
Then he exploded in the margin: " 'Out o' window' is not i
life or *fact* or *truth*—*but* in Goldsmith. Watch those dam'
things that give you away! . . . Does anyone on earth talk th
way. Quit *affectation*. You *know* better." As far as this advic
went, it was good, but Riley was a romantic sentimentalist eve
though he used Hoosier dialect with beautiful precision; an
Tarkington was not deterred from pursuing his early intere
in urbane historical fiction by Riley's predilection for bucol
contemporaneousness. He needed a Howells or a James to sho
him the superior merits and *raison d'être* of realism.

When spring came in 1896, Tarkington returned to India
apolis to the routine he had followed before his unsuccessf
New York sojourn. In the three years since he left Princet
he had earned an average of seven dollars and fifty cents a ye
from his chosen vocation, but he went doggedly on writin
drawing, and imitating historical romancers. In the next tv
years he turned out two more plays and a long story—all la
in the eighteenth century: one in Revolutionary France, one
Revolutionary America, and one in Bath, England, in tl
days of Beau Nash. By then his family was perplexed over l
failure and the neighbors indignant that the Tarkingtons co
tinued to indulge their idle son. Perhaps it was at this tin
that he had a talk with Lew Wallace on the subject of his fa
ure to get published. The old man was not very helpful, T:
kington remembered, and suggested that his parents could w
have worse things to explain than a son who apparently d
nothing. "Every community," he said "has a few loafers and
accustomed to see them hanging around the saloons or po
rooms . . . Our people look down on them, of course, but u
derstand them."

If a young man had to be an unsuccessful writer, Indiana
lis in June was a pleasant place to suffer from editor
indifference. An observer on the top of the yet unfinished w
memorial at the center of the city seemed to be on a tow
rising from an island of stone surrounded by verdure. The
were only glimpses of roofs and chimneys immediately visi

among the thick leaves of shade trees, while to the north the ample brick houses of the best residential section marched towards the city limits along green-vaulted avenues. Beyond the northern fringes of town, about Sixteenth Street, lay open country; then still farther off among great sycamores wandered the lazy, silken thread of Fall Creek. In the evenings along the pleasant residential streets the normal sounds audible from verandas were murmurings of voices from other verandas, the plod-plod of horses drawing family groups out for cool drives, or occasionally in the distance soprano voices singing sentimental songs to piano accompaniments. Tarkington made the best of his situation, and when he was not writing, he drove out in his red-wheeled runabout, attended dances at the Country Club, listened to literary discussions at the Contemporary Club, mingled convivially at the University Club, and acted in plays with the Dramatic Club.

His newest play, the French Revolutionary drama, provided a one-act comedy for the Dramatic Club the following November. This was "Mlle. de Marmantel," published later as *Beauty and the Jacobin* (1912), in which Tarkington played the part of Valsin, an agent of Robespierre. After his New York discouragements he apparently despaired of writing plays that Broadway would produce and turned to one-act dramas especially created for his friends. "Mlle. de Marmantel," a lively comedy duel between the agent and a lovely émigrée, was a distinct improvement on his earlier plays, and when he later revised the ending for book publication, the play began a successful career on the amateur stage. He also wrote another one-acter about this time, "The Kisses of Marjorie," a slight drama of the American Revolution placed in Philadelphia during the British occupation.

While Tarkington was writing one-act plays, his college classmate Robert Sloss launched in Greenwich Village a "little" magazine called *John-a-Dreams*. The publication appeared only seven times between August, 1896, and May, 1897, but during its short life Tarkington, the unpaid staff artist, contributed prose, poetry, and drawings—"The Kisses of Marjorie," for instance, first appearing there. One significant item, "A Letter of Regrets," drew its inspiration from the coffee house society of Addison and Steele. A four-page illustrated poem, it depicts a convivial lover who has forsaken his drinking companions to attend his fiancée, and the verses are set appropriately in an eighteenth-century type face. Tarkington's interest in the early eighteenth century was soon to bear more important fruit and to be instrumental in ending his apprenticeship.

Before that happy event, however, his contributions to *John-a-Dreams* brought him a remarkable fan letter from Louisiana. Addressed to Cecil Woodford (Tarkington's pseudonym) in a feminine hand, the epistle piqued the curiosity of Sloss and his editorial assistants, who forwarded the envelope, unopened but irreverently inscribed, in a valentine and demanded a copy of the contents. By sheer coincidence the correspondent was Helen Pitkin, a newspaper woman and New Orleans belle whom Tarkington once had known. He had met her when he was fifteen during a visit to New Orleans with Uncle Newton Booth and his cousin Fenton, and there he had fallen in love for the first time with the golden-haired Helen. This unexpected recrossing of long-diverged paths led to an extensive correspondence, a whirlwind romance, and, in time, a brief engagement.

Most of Tarkington's contributions to *John-a-Dreams* are unimportant, though they illustrate a poetic preoccupation that began at the age of thirteen and lasted till he was thirty. Throughout the Nineties he composed poems, and only after his first novel was published did he Forswear verse. Then he abandoned poetry completely, except when his fictional characters occasionally were moved to lyric expression. Before 1899, however, about two dozen of his poems appeared in print, many in Princeton publications, a handful in the Indianapolis *Journal,* and three in Sloss' magazine. Even then he was able to look at his own poetry objectively and to evaluate his metrical output in this previously unpublished verse:

> When a fellow's not a poet
> It is better he should know it
>   And be still.
> Peg may spread his wings and fly it
> I should be too wise to try it.—
>   But I will.

Although Tarkington was unable to sell his drawings, art was his springboard to literature. There is a close correlation between his efforts to be an artist and his literary creative process, for the two forms of expression interlocked and reinforced each other during his early career and remained closely allied in his subsequent life. He often let his sketches fertilize his imagination, and after drawing pictures with dramatic value, he plotted tales to accompany the illustrations. This, of course, is a visualization of a familiar creative method—the technique of plotting backwards, such as Poe describes brilliantly in writing of his own literary practice. Tarkington worked from the illustration of a climactic scene, whereas Poe first conceived imaginatively his denouement. Both writers planned in advance the outcome of a story and arranged all details to lead inevitably towards a prepared ending. As Tarkington abandoned drawing, he shifted from his pictorial procedure to Poe's actual *modus operandi*. Then in mid-career he discarded plot-logic for character-logic, and the mutations in his creative process finally ceased.

Shortly before *John-a-Dreams* expired, Tarkington had drawn for the magazine an illustration showing two men in early eighteenth-century clothes facing each other over a gaming table. One was large and irate, the other young, dapper, and French; and in the background lurked several indistinct figures about a doorway. He fell sick before he could send off the illustration, and during his convalescence, as he glanced over all his drawings on hand, this particular picture caught his imagination. He then created a story to go with the drawing, but when Sloss' magazine suspended publication, the tale went begging. It eventually appeared in print under the title *Monsieur Beaucaire*.

Tarkington, however, still was two years away from the end of his apprenticeship, and the fate of this new story at first was the familiar one of editorial rejection. He sent the manuscript to one of the monthly magazines, but it came back unerringly, and after revising it, he put it away. The editor who turned down *Monsieur Beaucaire* lost an opportunity to buy a manuscript that quickly reached the best-seller lists after McClure published it, and thereafter continued to prosper. Eventually it provided Richard Mansfield and Lewis Waller with plays, British and American companies with operettas, Rudolph Valentino and Bob Hope with movies, at least eight anthologists with selections, and countless readers with a pleasant story that never has been out of print.

Monsieur Beaucaire is a young man's story, written, as Tarkington later said, "in the fashion of the time" when "a romanticism somewhat sentimental" was the mode. The familiar story, laid in Bath during the reign of Beau Nash, describes the adventures of the Duke of Orleans, disguised as a barber, among the English nobility at that famous spa. How the young Frenchman exposes the duplicity and baseness of the Duke of Winterset and the snobbery of the beauty of Bath, Lady Mary Carlisle, provides the burden of the tale. Even though Tarkington in his maturity disparaged his early fiction, the story was a deservedly popular and well-constructed example of its literary genre, the costume romance; and its charm lies not only in the evocation of eighteenth-century England but also in the employment in its plot of the always appealing underdog who comes out on top. The story has won many admirers, one of whom—the hard-bitten Damon Runyon—wrote in 1937: " 'Monsieur Beaucaire' is ever green. It is a little literary cameo, and we read it over at least once a year."

During the last months of his apprenticeship Tarkington occasionally interrupted his work to visit his sister and her children on Lake Michigan in the summer, to take part in weddings of friends, fall in and out of love, and to renew friendships with former classmates. But for the most part, despite his discouragements, he continued writing, and in the spring of 1898 he once more took from his desk the manuscript of his unfinished Indiana novel. From time to time in the previous four years he had added a sentence or two without being able to get the story going again, and he even had revisited Marshall, Illinois, to refresh the inspiration of his childhood; but still the novel would not budge. All the while, however, the characters and plot were in his mind undergoing a subconscious alchemy.

In December, 1897, an event had occurred that had a profoundly moving effect on Tarkington. His closest college friend, John Cleve Green, died in Philadelphia. Throughout their two years at Princeton the two young men had been David and Jonathan to one another. They had belonged to Ivy together, sung in the Glee Club together, and visited each other at holidays during and after Princeton. To his friend, Green had been a hero—a model of tact and charm, an arbiter of taste, a hater of cant—in short, a gentleman in all the best senses of the term. Now Tarkington knew what he wanted to do with his novel. John Harkless, the gentleman, had been modeled after Green all along, though perhaps Tarkington had not realized fully the source of his inspiration. In all events the book would be a memorial dedicated to his friend. During April, 1898, he pulled out the manuscript for a new try, discarded the incomplete draft of the story, and began over. He suddenly discovered that the tale was in his mind ready to be set down on paper as fast as he could write. From spring to autumn he worked with inexhaustible energy, writing furiously and abundantly but revising slowly and carefully as he went along. By the time he completed the task a remarkable turn had come in his literary fortunes—brought about in part by the irrepressible optimism of his sister.

Mrs. Jameson, a woman of great energy and moral courage, never had doubted the ultimate success of her brother. She already had been responsible for sending his play to a New York agent, and three years later she felt that the time was ripe to strike another blow for recognition. *Monsieur Beaucaire,* which Tarkington subsequently dedicated to her, was Hauté's favorite of all his languishing manuscripts, and the editorial blockheadedness that could not see merit in the tale incensed her. When she happened to visit New York near the end of 1898, she carried with her a letter of introduction to McClure and the manuscript of the story—both without the knowledge of her brother. She promptly called at the offices of the S. S. McClure Company, left her note and *Monsieur Beaucaire* for the publisher to read, then returned some days later for the verdict. John Phillips, treasurer of the firm, tried to reject the story, but as Tarkington reconstructed the scene in his memoirs, the following dialogue took place:

"Did he [McClure] read it?" my sister asked.
"Well—no," the associate [Phillips] admitted. "I read it."
"You did?" my sister said. "Didn't you think the poetic quotations at the heads of the chapters quite good?"
"Oh, very," he told her, for he wished to be as kind as he could. "The poetic quotations were excellent."
"There aren't any," she said. "Where's Mr. McClure?"

Making his entrance on this cue, McClure emerged from the inner office to rescue Phillips, agreed to read the story, and asked Mrs. Jameson to call back later. After he had read the tale, however, he was not immediately charmed with it and equivocated when Mrs. Jameson returned once more for a decision. At that point Tarkington's sister told McClure of the Indiana novel that was nearly finished, and the publisher, being a shrewd judge of public taste, scented a manuscript that might have real possibilities. The result of this interview was a telegram from Mrs. Jameson to her brother instructing him to rush *The Gentleman from Indiana* to McClure. Surprised, since he had not been privy to his sister's plans, he mailed the novel, but as usual he nursed gloomy thoughts of rejection. Too often his sister had been sure that his stories were going to captivate editorial hearts, and after five years of continuous failure he had learned resignation. Two weeks passed. Then out of a clear sky came a letter in a strange hand, not from the publisher but from Hamlin Garland. It began: "Mr. McClure has given me your manuscript, The Gentleman from Indiana, to read. You are a novelist."

Garland had been a successful writer for nearly a decade since leaving the Iowa prairies to go east, and as a literary protégé of Howells he seemed to Tarkington in 1899 one of the favored mortals who already had scaled Parnassus. The thrill of that letter never died, and Garland's praise echoed and re-echoed within him to the very depths of his soul. In 1920 when Garland wrote him of his election to the American Academy of Arts and Letters, Tarkington reminded his friend that the earlier letter had been his "first laurel leaf" and added: "Now you come with another leaf, and I begin to think that if I stick to your trail long enough the leaves may increase till they go clear round my head." Even four decades after his first novel was published, Tarkington in a posthumous tribute to Garland recalled vividly the letter "that changed everything for me" with its four dumfounding words: "You are a novelist."

> I couldn't imagine anybody's saying such a thing, and last of all could I have believed that an accredited novelist would ever say it; but after I came to know Hamlin Garland I found that nothing was more typical of him than his stopping work to

write such a letter to a groping, unknown youth dismally mystified about himself and the art of writing.

To the incredulously happy young man the next mail brought from McClure a business letter that required action. "We accept your manuscript to be published in book form," wrote the publisher, "and we are considering it for serial publication in the magazine, though for this purpose you would have to cut it almost in half. If the idea interests you, perhaps you'd better come to New York as soon as you can." Tarkington, dazzled but eager, left Indianapolis for the East a few days later to begin the great adventure.

Booth Tarkington, drawn by himself,
just before sailing to Capri in 1905

FOUR

"THE MOST FAMOUS YOUNG MAN IN AMERICA"

On THE THIRTIETH OF JANUARY, 1899, Tarkington boarded a train in Indianapolis for his final trip east as an obscure young man from the provinces. Upon arriving in New York, his five years of apprenticeship ended abruptly, as if he suddenly had stepped through the looking glass into an exciting new world inhabited by authors, editors, and publishers, all eager to serve him. His letters home during the late winter and early spring of this memorable year fortunately have survived, and on each page they record the undisguised delight of a young man who scarcely believes, but thoroughly enjoys, his good fortune. Tarkington must have felt himself living in a dream that might dissolve in an instant, leaving him once more in his brownstone boardinghouse with an ink bottle and an unpublished manuscript; yet when he returned home in May, he was the author of a serial already appearing in McClure's widely circulated monthly magazine.

After a sleepless night on the Pullman, Tarkington treated himself to a four-dollar room at the Everett House on Union Square. Then he called his college roommate "Big" Murray, and while the two old friends had dinner together, they discussed the meeting scheduled for the next day with McClure. The following morning at eleven, knees knocking together uncontrollably, Tarkington entered the elevator that carried him to the publisher's office and a moment later in a fainting voice gave his name to the receptionist. Then for a few seconds he sat in the outer office fumbling with his gloves and stick, waiting to be announced. Presently a brisk young man, a sub-editor who had read his manuscript, appeared beamingly and ushered him into the office of McClure's chief of staff, August Jaccaci, who rose with a "joyous & polite howl" and kept repeating: "We haf waited for you!" and "So it iss you." Almost at once Jaccaci whisked him into still another office, where a crowd of busy people suddenly melted away, as if on signal, and Tarkington found himself at last face to face with the head of the firm. McClure jumped up energetically and greeted his visitor with overpowering enthusiasm—as though his main function in life were to welcome new authors. "You are to be the greatest of the new generation, and we'll help you to be," he declared emphatically. Tarkington barely could stammer his thanks when the publisher added that *The Gentleman from Indiana* was to run concurrently with a novel by Kipling and that a manuscript by Anthony Hope (author of *The Prisoner of Zenda*) had been turned down to make room for the Indiana serial.

Then the people who had been in the office when Tarkington arrived began returning. He met Garland, whom he had interrupted in the midst of telling F. N. Doubleday the plot of his latest novel, and he was introduced to the distinguished woman journalist Ida Tarbell, to whom McClure said: "This is to be the most famous young man in America." When Tarkington reported the extravagant prediction to his parents, he wrote: "I felt like a large gray Ass!—and looked like it." Soon McClure and Jaccaci turned to other business, leaving Tarkington alone with Garland, and the two men had a long talk together about books, authors, and the Midwest. Garland again praised the novel, and Tarkington thanked him humbly. The unforgettable morning ended at the Holland House where Tarkington lunched with Miss Tarbell, Jaccaci, and McClure, and after the group broke up, the new author floated back to his hotel in a rosy fog. In recounting the day's events to his family, he cautioned: "This isn't for publication."

When he relaxed at the Players Club on Sunday morning four days later, he caught his breath and sorted out his first impressions of a totally different New York that suddenly had opened to him. The night before he had been to the Century Club until 2:00 A.M. meeting Frank Stockton, "the yellowest—wrinkledest little man [who] ever lived," and Paul Leicester Ford, the brilliant scholar-novelist. Another of his Saturday

companions had been F. N. Doubleday, then a member of Mc-
Clure's firm, who already was becoming a close friend. Doubleday had entertained him at home on Friday, fascinated him
with editorial reminiscences of George Meredith and James
Barrie, and even told casually how he once almost had rejected
Stevenson's "Dr. Jekyll and Mr. Hyde." As Tarkington surveyed his first real experiences of literary New York, he also
relived his overnight visit on Thursday to McClure's house at
Lawrence on the south shore of Long Island; and he planned to
return there Monday for a week or ten days to work on the serialization of his novel.

Three days later the task of trimming forty thousand words
from *The Gentleman from Indiana* was well advanced. Tarkington was installed in McClure's house in a large, comfortable room overlooking the stormy, snow-covered beach half a
mile away, and while his publisher obligingly kept an open fire
burning for him, he worked snugly at his manuscript. The Mc-
Clures made him feel at home, even to the point of providing
his customary midnight snack, and the work went smoothly.
In a week he finished cutting the manuscript and drafting the
connecting links; then he stopped to wait for typing before putting on the final touches.

The publisher and his new author immediately were attracted to one another. Tarkington had been at Lawrence less
than a week when McClure solicited his company for a European trip the next summer and also offered him an editorial
job at seven thousand dollars a year. Tarkington declined
both invitations with thanks, and writing his family that he had
no ambition to be an editor, he said he wanted only to write:
now that the way was open, he intended to flood the unsuspect-
ing public with stories and novels. He was planning to ask Mc-
Clure for a ten percent royalty on his book, and he further
hoped to receive five hundred dollars for his serial—one percent,
incidentally, of the sum that he one day would receive from the
Saturday Evening Post for the same amount of work.

Three weeks after reaching the metropolis, Tarkington felt
that nowhere else in the world could he find a more exciting
and satisfying life. When his mother begged him to return immediately, writing that she could not bear to have her boy
away from home, he replied patiently but firmly. He admitted

that his family still partly supported him, in recognition of which he had just moved to a boardinghouse at nine dollars a week; but he soon would be making money from his writing and besides, he wrote:

> I need the immense stimulus of the life here . . . at home *I* give the stimulus to people; I suggest things—*I* tell people things . . . here I get something from everyone I meet. . . . You'll have to accept this as the fact—I am very much wiser than when I came, three weeks ago—my mind has opened a great deal, enlarged to new perceptions, in so many and so subtle ways that I can't go into it here for lack of time and space—'twould be like trying to say what the world is like.

Then he interrupted his letter to attend a dinner at Double-day's where he sat with Mrs. Seton Thompson on his right, Mrs. Kipling on his left, her husband across from him, and Bliss Perry just beyond. When he finished the letter, his description of the evening gave point to his insistence that he must stay on until he felt ready to return home.

By the time he had been in New York a month, the first part of his serial had gone to the printer, and the artist Ernest Blumenschein had begun working on the illustrations. As each installment of the serial went to press, however, Tarkington experienced a mild attack of nerves, and just as the editors had been on the point of sending off part one, he had snatched it back for another revision. On March 6 he wrote: "The work goes on; I am taking a final leave of the second installment," but he added that he trembled over every word as he let the copy go. Nevertheless, by the middle of the month all six parts had been typed and a few days later were beyond recall. Spring then was approaching, and he began seeing more and more of his Princeton friends; but before he could take a break, he had another problem to contend with—his mother's fear that McClure would ruin him.

An Indianapolis acquaintance panicked Mrs. Tarkington one day by telling her that serialization of the novel would ruin the sale of the book. To his mother's alarming suggestion that the indomitable Mrs. Jameson be sent to New York to take the manuscript of *The Gentleman from Indiana* away from McClure, her son answered posthaste:

Can I never persuade you that I am a man of thirty—not only honest—but worldly-wise as well? You picture to yourself, always, the little, timid boy with the big nose and impertinent ears . . . being pitched upon and buffeted and torn by huge, designing men—but the reality is a "rather foxy" gentleman no longer in his first youth, who has had more experience of the world . . . than most people you know and who has studied his profession and the ways of getting on in it very hard.

He went on to explain to his mother that of course Bowen-Merrill would publish the novel now and so would Scribner's, "because it's been advertised as a serial for McClure's." That was why, he added, that publishers of wider reputation than Bowen-Merrill now were begging him to write for them. Finally, he declared: "Don't you know that all the publishers in the country are going to read that serial? And the serial is good, too—and *please* don't talk to people about it as you did . . . complaining of its having had to be cut." The next day, after rather sharply admonishing his family not to abuse McClure and Doubleday to him, he added: "N. Y. isn't a league of crime to persecute N. B. T." He further explained that the editors had let him write as he pleased and McClure even had insisted that he leave in one chapter he had planned to cut.

As April passed slowly, Tarkington impatiently awaited the May number of *McClure's Magazine* containing the first installment of his novel. Every few days he had to write his family explaining why he could not yet come home, and in between times he supervised the illustrations being prepared for *Monsieur Beaucaire,* which McClure would use in the magazine in December and January. He finished up his business early in May, and after a further round of dinners with writers, editors, and Princeton classmates, he returned to Indianapolis to see how the serial was faring at home. The May issue of the magazine preceded him by a couple of weeks.

Tarkington went back to Indiana a celebrity of minor magnitude. He did not awake one morning, as Byron did, to find himself famous, for public recognition accumulated gradually. He became the subject of newspaper interviews, laudatory editorials and within a few months found himself writing a newspaper book column. The pleasantest result of his new status, however, occurred at Culver City, Indiana, during the summer.

While vacationing at Lake Maxinkuckee, he asked a banker to cash a check but was refused for want of identification by a local citizen. Tarkington remained anyway to chat, for, he wrote McClure, "One doesn't often converse with a banker who is also cashier, teller, book-keeper and janitor." After a time the banker asked his visitor's name, and, continued Tarkington, "Behold, the money was mine one minute later—blessings be on McClure's! He was a Gentle Reader and opined that being as I was Booth Tarkington I could identify myself. . . . It was the most puffing-up thing that ever happened to me."

Public approval of the novel was overwhelming, but there was a minority verdict based on a well-established precedent. Both Eggleston's *Hoosier Schoolmaster* and Riley's homespun verses, on previous occasions, had irritated a parochial segment of Hoosier opinion; and early installments of the serial evoked some protests from country editors who concluded hastily that Tarkington was attacking the small town and painting Indiana landscape in colors too somber. The criticism, of course, served to stimulate book sales. Writing Dan Calkins, who had moved to the West Coast, Tarkington reported the novel's reception: "There wasn't [really] any criticism—four county-seat papers foamed at the mouth because they mistakenly thought I was sneering at Indiana. The [Indianapolis] *News* quoted their anathemas and I was tickled as well as everybody else. . . . The ire of the county-seats was a grand ad.—it kept the thing in talk." The city newspapers throughout the state reviewed the novel favorably and came to Tarkington's defense against the scattered attacks in the rural press. They took the detractors to task for not waiting until the story was completed and for being unable to stand criticism.

As time went on, however, Tarkington magnified the abuse in order to make a good story. He was fond of remembering in after years that the serial had drawn a storm of attack from thin-skinned Hoosiers who had misunderstood his intent. He recalled that he had been almost ashamed to go home, thinking he had spread the praise of his fellow citizens too thick, but he had been astonished to discover that he was a pariah in his home town. Because he had not made Plattville as large as Paris and its public buildings as imposing as the great pyramids, every newspaper in the state was heaping scorn on him. "I almost wonder," he quoted a friend as saying, "that you've had the courage to come back here." He even remembered that he was stopped on the street and accused of holding Indiana up to ridicule, and charged with assaulting the sacred altars of his people.

Tarkington's novel was inspired by a genuine desire to extol the virtues of his native state. When he had visited the homes of Eastern friends during his school days at Exeter and Princeton, he had encountered a disparaging attitude towards Indiana. He had been accepted, of course, but sometimes gratuitously insulted when people told him that he seemed more like an Easterner than a Midwesterner. With youthful tenderness and championship he set about to tell the story of John Harkless, stalwart young newspaperman who comes out of the East to settle in Plattville, Indiana. Buying a run-down newspaper that even the citizens of the town cannot praise, Harkless proceeds to make it a crusading organ of civic improvement and fights the good fight for honor, justice, and decency. In the course of his campaign he routs the hooligan Whitecaps, who live in a near-by shantytown, and by the end of the story he wins the heart of the beautiful Helen Sherwood.

Although it is sentimentally romantic, the novel is overlaid with a realistic patina deriving from the author's memories of Marshall, Illinois. The setting evokes an historical epoch, much as Mark Twain's Mississippi River locales hark back to his youth in Missouri, but the action is nominally contemporary, Harkless being a recent college graduate of the author's own generation. Part of the interest in the novel also lies in its use of the Whitecaps as the evil force against which the heroic Harkless is opposed. Whitecapping then was a perplexing problem, a manifestation of mob lawlessness that foreshadowed the organized virulence of the Ku-Klux Klan in Indiana two decades later.

The real popularity of *The Gentleman from Indiana*, however, rested on the manly virtues of the hero and feminine charm of the heroine. By snaring his readers through the attractiveness of his idealized characters, Tarkington produced a novel that he later held in low critical esteem. Inferior writers, he afterwards maintained, ask the reader to identify himself with the chief character and to enjoy a vicarious adventure. When most readers pronounce a story good or bad, they merely mean to say that they enjoyed their vicarious experience, and they do not pass a real critical judgment on the author's merits or faults. The novel really worth writing, he declared, "paints—reveals—and keeps to the *detached* view of the sheer artist. It can live with the reader only by virtue of its insight and its craftsmanship in revelation—in other words, by the distinction of its writing. Therefore its perceptive readers must be relatively few." Tarkington added that Henry James was the superlative practitioner of this kind of writing.

In addition to its romance and knight-errantry, the novel also owed some of its popularity to the freshness of the material. At the turn of the century local-color literature, though no longer new, still tapped the national curiosity about places remote from one's own purlieu. The exquisite Maine sketches of Sarah Orne Jewett, for example, still were popular, and early in the Nineties Garland had tapped a brand-new vein of regionalism in his tales of Iowa farm life. *The Gentleman from Indiana* contains authentic local color, an excellent example of which greets readers on the opening page:

> There is a fertile stretch of flat lands in Indiana where un-agrarian Eastern travellers, glancing from car-windows, shudder and return their eyes to interior upholstery, preferring even the swaying caparisons of a Pullman to the monotony without. The landscape lies interminably level: bleak in winter, a desolate plain of mud and snow; hot and dusty in summer, in its flat lonesomeness, miles on miles with not one cool hill slope away from the sun. The persistent tourist who seeks for signs of man in this sad expanse perceives a reckless amount of rail fence; at intervals a large barn; and, here and there, man himself. . . .

This is a notable start for a first novel, but there is little wonder that some country editors leaped to the barricades after reading the beginning installment.

During its first half century *The Gentleman from Indiana* brought prosperity to nearly everyone who handled it. Selling briskly from the start, it made the monthly best-seller lists twice in 1900, then lost momentum as other Tarkington titles began appearing; but it remained in steady demand for many years and never has gone out of print. It has been reissued and reprinted more than two dozen times, translated into at least six languages, made into a movie, and excerpted for anthologies. A financial bonanza, it suddenly provided a handsome income to supplement the modest stipend that Tarkington had been receiving from Newton Booth's bequest. Sales of the book reached one hundred thousand in its third year, a modest figure as best-sellers go, but the demand continued, and during the second decade of the novel's history, 1909-1919, Doubleday, Page and Company, then its publisher, disposed of an average of eighteen thousand copies per year.

One important result of Tarkington's new prominence as an author came a few weeks after the novel had been published in book form. The Indianapolis *Press* asked him to write a weekly book column for its Saturday supplement, which he did from January until May. His articles, twelve in all, furnish a reliable index of his mind at the outset of his literary career, for they range widely over books past and present and offer frequent judgments about art, life, and literature. It is clear that most of his tastes, attitudes, and preoccupations already were fixed by the time his first novel appeared.

His criticism was informal and largely subjective. He felt that few critics ever had spoken with lasting authority and that all criticism was a "house built on sand." The opinions of one generation, he maintained, are swept away by the next, and individual tastes differ about books just as they do about pie. His dislike of pretense and cant also show up in his weekly columns. He held a low opinion of cocksure critics who act as though the principles of writing were long ago settled and noted that every book finds at least one reviewer who hails it as the book of the year.

Tarkington's literary appetite, however, was both discriminating and hearty. He did not hesitate to tell his newspaper readers that Laura Jean Libbey did not write literature or to pronounce Shaw "possibly the most important, valuable, [and] suggestive writer at present employed in the composition of English prose." One week he praised the urbane output of James, while the next week he recommended the lusty autobiography of Benvenuto Cellini: "This memoir . . . is an actual slab of living flesh, cut from the breast of the sixteenth century, and flung upon the counter with the breath still in it." Other literary enthusiasms of the moment included Stevenson, whose Indiana-born widow he recently had met, Victor Cherbuliez, whose "lightness and beautiful finish" influenced at least two of his own novels, and "the master of all English humorists," Dickens, who wrote no book "wholly artistic except *A Tale of Two Cities."*

Perhaps the most interesting of all Tarkington's literary judgments are those which rank comedy over tragedy. Already his temperament fitted him to write comedy, and his attitudes towards life and literature were wholly consistent. The unhappy ending, he declared, is often a mere "exhibition of egoism on the part of the author," because in no way is "a reputation for 'strength' or 'power' more cheaply won than by writing a 'sad story.'" Young writers, he went on, are apt to write tragedy because it is easier than comedy, though they do not know it, and it is doubtful if any two writers of tragedy ever lived "who . . . did not regard themselves as geniuses." Pathetic or tragic denouements, nonetheless, are not illegitimate if the logic of events, as in Hardy's novels, demands them, but Victor Hugo irritated Tarkington by his "ridiculous catastrophes" and the second-rate Ouida infuriated him by perfecting "the trick of agony." The finest effect of all literature, he asserted, is a "pathos which only master craftsmen attain . . . tears, not of sorrow, but of delight. There are fewer tears of joy than of sorrow in life, and it is even harder to cause the former by something in a book than it is by an action of life." To make the reader feel himself "full of courage and the capacity for happiness in a brightened world" was the goal that Tarkington set for himself.

When William Allen White's Boyville stories were published, Tarkington wrote another column that cast a long shadow ahead. White's children, he declared, were like colts in a pasture kicking up their heels and coursing the length of the lot for no other reason than that the air is fresh and the sky is blue. They were by no means the artificial youngsters of the *St. Nicholas* or *Youth's Companion* magazines; they were the real thing, as Penrod Schofield also was to be later. Truth in art by then was becoming Tarkington's creed, though practicing this doctrine proved difficult.

His growing awareness of the superior merits of realism can be detected in his literary columns on a number of occasions.

Not only did he applaud White's fidelity to boyhood and attack the synthetic pathos of Victor Hugo and Ouida, but he also defended Kipling's right to describe the United States unflatteringly, as he himself had done at the outset of *The Gentleman from Indiana;* and he called for American writers to inject vigor and reality into American literature through the use of their native idiom, as Mark Twain had done in *Huckleberry Finn.* Finally, in his perceptive remarks on Shaw he detected the relative staleness and conventionality of Pinero, Jones, Thomas, and Fitch and discovered that Shaw was exciting because he searched for truth among the tough ethical problems of a changing society.

While Tarkington's theories looked forward towards realism, his practice also was moving slowly in that direction. One of his most curious works is *Cherry,* a burlesqued historical romance, which he laid in eighteenth-century Princeton and environs. When *Richard Carvel* appeared in 1899, it was "so rotten clumsy in the hero's telling what people said to him about himself" that it made Tarkington laugh and determine to satirize the awkward first-person narrative device. When *Monsieur Beaucaire* was in press following serialization, Tarkington sent *Cherry* to McClure, expecting the publisher to use it in the magazine, then bring it out in book form. McClure, however, thought the satire inferior to Tarkington's first two books and urged him strongly not to publish it—at least not until his reputation was established more firmly; but after giving his opinion, the publisher concluded: "If you wish to have us serialize it just let us know." McClure was determined not to lose his new author.

Equally determined to take advantage of McClure's lack of enthusiasm for *Cherry* was F. H. Sears of Harper and Brothers, who called on Tarkington at precisely the opportune moment. Sears capitalized on Tarkington's reluctance to force anything on McClure, wrote several enthusiastic letters about the novelette, and in the end secured the manuscript for *Harper's Magazine,* which printed it in January and February, 1901, and thus began a fairly extensive relationship between Tarkington and the house of Harper. Although Sears wrote after the first installment that the firm was getting favorable comments and did not doubt the story's success, nearly thirty-one months elapsed before the book version came out, and Tarkington by then had written his first real best seller.

" 'Cherry' will get by," Tarkington wrote later, "if taken on the ground of its intention—but if you read it as a *story* it's all off!" Since most readers were expecting entertainment, the serial attracted little attention, and the book version, even with extensive revisions, made no great splash. The protagonist of the tale is a priggish collegian, vintage 1762, named Sudgeberry, who had been suggested by a twentieth-century letter Tarkington once had read in a lonely hearts column. The letter had begun: "I am a young man of good habits, diligent and studious, and a member of the Y.M.C.A. My evenings are employed in the perusal of standard works recommended for their moral tone . . . can you tell me why it is that young ladies seem to prefer the flippant conversation of idle and probably dissipated nobodies?" Tarkington's mistake in *Cherry* perhaps lay in his effort to combine two disparate kinds of satire—satire of historical fiction and of priggish human nature. Had he placed his story in Princeton in 1893, he might have managed to create an amusing comedy of manners; but unfortunately, as he later realized, "No one ever saw what I was up to!"

About the time that Tarkington sent this manuscript to McClure, his correspondence with Helen Pitkin in New Orleans came to a climax. He visited Louisiana in March and soon became secretly engaged. He had been writing to Helen since her fan letter was forwarded from the *John-a-Dreams* office in 1897, and the two found many literary topics that were mutually interesting. They disagreed sharply on some matters, such as Tarkington's fondness for Stevenson against Helen's delight in Gautier, but on the whole the relationship was tinctured with the unforgettable memory of Tarkington's schoolboy passion. He recalled in middle age his youthful adoration: "I was fifteen —and she had the goldest hair and the scarletest stockings! She was the first girl I ever took to the theater—ever bought flowers for. . . . She was still there in '99 [1900 actually]—I went back to see! And one of the Beauties of the Southland—and literary!"

On her part, Helen recalled happily, as the correspondence began, that they had met in 1884 when Uncle Newton Booth took Booth Tarkington and Fenton Booth, to Louisiana on his way back to California. He had left the cousins in the care of a Terre Haute friend, and Helen remembered the good times they had spent together. She wished they were fifteen once more and climbing up the stairs of the customhouse to visit her father in his office. In his memoirs Tarkington also recalled the circumstances of his first trip to the South and his competition with Fenton for Helen's favor. His cousin then was more successful than he in winning Helen's attention and on one occasion even maneuvered Booth into escorting the girl's grandmother and sundry old ladies to a joint reading by Joaquin Miller and Julia Ward Howe, while he and Helen spent the evening shooting fireworks. At the end of 1899, however, Helen was completely charmed by Booth, and of all the girls with whom Tarkington corresponded during his bachelorhood she wrote the greatest number of letters over the longest period of time. When he published his first novel, he paid high tribute by naming for her his flawless heroine Helen Sherwood.

The visit to New Orleans occurred four months after *The Gentleman from Indiana* appeared in book form. Tarkington went to Louisiana to lay siege to Helen, who then was twenty-nine, tall, blue-eyed, fair-haired, and talented. She was a poet and short story writer of sorts and woman's editor of the *Times-Democrat*. In addition, she was an accomplished harpist and an amateur actress of unusual ability. The Pitkins were, moreover, a prominent though not old New Orleans family, and her father formerly had served as minister to Argentina. Helen's wit and lively personality were extremely attractive and swept Tarkington off his feet during the two or three weeks of his stay. She returned his affection, and the brief, informal engagement followed.

Yet the courtship came to a sudden halt under what Tarkington later described cryptically as "painful and awkward circumstances." Helen's maternal grandmother, the matriarch of the family, refused to consent to the match, giving only the specious explanation that Helen's health would not permit marriage. Helen apparently neither could defy her grandmother, who had raised her, nor alter the decision, and the engagement was broken in the summer. Why the grandmother objected so strenuously remains obscure, but the old lady was exceedingly hard to deal with. She made Tarkington promise not to write

Helen for several months and during the hiatus worked to undermine the relationship. Her machinations succeeded, for by summer Tarkington's enthusiasm had dimmed, and he was busily at work on a new literary project—the dramatization of *Monsieur Beaucaire.*

Even before his trip to New Orleans he had begun to plan a stage version of his eighteenth-century story of Bath. The suggestion first had come from a correspondent unknown to him, Mrs. Evelyn Greenleaf Sutherland, who introduced herself as a veteran Boston drama critic and the wife of a university dean. Moreover, she had written a couple of plays herself, she told him, and would be delighted to help turn *Monsieur Beaucaire* into a play. Acting on his first impulse, Tarkington told Mrs. Sutherland to try the project alone, but she wanted merely to act as editor of the script while he did the writing. This procedure eventually was followed in the collaboration that took place during the summer of 1900; but unfortunately for Tarkington, he signed away one third of his stage rights and thereby let himself in for trouble later.

At the end of March he was corresponding with Mrs. Sutherland about details of the dramatization, and it was she who insisted that the play must end with Lady Mary Carlisle in Beaucaire's arms. Perhaps that denouement was the only one acceptable to audiences then, but the original story, which ends with Beaucaire's return to France after exposing Lady Mary's snobbery, has proved more viable than the dramatic version. The difficulties in producing the play, however, did not result from the altered ending but from Mrs. Sutherland herself, who considered the dramatists' job done when the play went into rehearsal. Mansfield, who had taken a four months' option on the drama, had other ideas and insisted that the manuscript be shortened and rewritten. An impasse threatened: Mrs. Sutherland contended that Mansfield did not know a good play when he saw one, and the actor refused to go on with the production without extensive overhauling.

In October Tarkington received a distress signal from Paul Wilstach, one of Mansfield's staff, and hurried to New York to work over the dramatization. He knew that the play had to be tinkered with and went ahead with the chore, but Mrs. Sutherland bombarded him with letters, threatened litigation, and even had her lawyers write to remind him that she owned one third of the stage rights. It was a painful situation, but Tarkington replied patiently to his collaborator's letters, and eventually the storm blew over. Mrs. Sutherland received one third of the royalties from the play, but Tarkington and Mansfield were the real joint-authors. When *Beaucaire,* as the play was titled, could not be made ready for the current season, Mansfield renewed his option and scheduled the drama for an opening in Philadelphia the next October.

Tarkington spent nearly two months in New York that autumn, his first visit since his introduction to the literary life of the city a year and a half before. This time he realized an old ambition to become one of the cogs in the machinery of Broadway. Wilstach sponsored him for membership in the Players Club, where the spirit of Edwin Booth presided behind the brownstone façade on Gramercy Park, and soon he met John Drew, Joe Jefferson, and, of course, Mansfield. When Mansfield gave a dinner for the visiting French actor Coquelin, Tarkington was present and sat dumfounded as the host made his after-dinner speech to the guest of honor in French. Then when Drew arose and addressed Coquelin as *"cher maître,"* Tarkington felt "that alone made life worth living."

After the dinner Mansfield offered Tarkington a seat in his carriage to the Holland House where both men were spending the night. On their way uptown to the hotel Tarkington thanked the actor for the pleasure the evening had given him. When he said he had felt himself at an exhibition of portraits of great men, Mansfield asked, "Didn't you think you were the greatest man there?"

"No; not precisely!" answered Tarkington.

"You should have," replied Mansfield, who then became expansive and said that he always did. "That's the way you always ought to feel."

Some time after that first dinner, when the play was in rehearsal, probably the following autumn, Tarkington entertained Mansfield. There were just three in the intimate party in the deserted dining room at the Players Club: the actor, A. M. Palmer, his manager, and the playwright. As coffee was brought in, Wilstach and another member of Mansfield's staff joined the diners. Tarkington's party was going smoothly, and

Mansfield was affably holding the center of the stage when into the room came two noisy Englishmen, one an actor, the other a London broker. The intruders insisted on drawing up chairs, and what was worse, remembered Tarkington, they stole the spotlight from Mansfield. The British actor began bragging, for the benefit of "you American boys," of the royalty he had met. On one occasion he had bumped into the Prince of Wales in the wings of a London theater, and the Prince had apologized to him. On another occasion he had been invited to dinner by Louis Napoleon.

Tarkington shuddered as he saw disaster overtaking his carefully planned evening. Mansfield sat "poisonously coiled—in his corner. . . . his contracted eyes glittered like the points of two bright stilettos." The British actor drank copiously, puffed, panted, and gurgled; then his unctuous voice continued, as he described the dinner he had attended at the Tuileries: "The Emperor took my father's arm to conduct him to the magnificent table, and *I*—I myself, gentlemen—I who am sitting with you here to-night . . . *I* had the honor to conduct the Empress Eugenie to dinner! I was not nahvous—" At this point Mansfield struck, Tarkington remembered: "He leaned slightly toward [the Englishman] . . . and his expression remains in my memory as one of the most interesting things I've seen in a lifetime of considerable duration. 'What about the Empress?' Mansfield asked. 'Was *she* nervous?'" Then the atmosphere marvelously cleared, and Tarkington's party went out with Mansfield beaming because he had played such a beautiful climax.

Beaucaire opened in Philadelphia at the Garrick Theater on October 7, and when Tarkington was interviewed in his room at the Hotel Walton, he paced the floor restlessly and chain-smoked as he talked about his hopes for the play. Later the first-night audience was enthusiastic and called for the author, but Tarkington with characteristic diffidence fled from the building. The Philadelphia reviewers praised the play, and so did the Boston critics, who also saw the production before it was taken to New York. When *Beaucaire* reached Broadway, however, the reviewers liked Mansfield but did not care for the play, and after a few weeks at the Herald Square Theater the company went on the road for the rest of the season. The play

was considerably more successful abroad where Lewis Waller
as Beaucaire toured England and the Continent for several
years.

After Mansfield opened in *Beaucaire,* Tarkington returned to
Indianapolis to write another novel, his first important new
work since McClure had accepted *The Gentleman from Indiana.*
From October through March he labored at the big drawing
board which served him as a writing table throughout his life.
He still lived with his parents on Pennsylvania Street a few
doors from his sister and her family, and when he was not busy
with the novel, he raised a glass with friends at the University
Club or played the role of an eligible bachelor. The story
which emerged from the drawing board was *The Two Vanrevels,* his last obeisance for thirty years to the "incredibly
prevalent . . . entertainment for the 'tired businessman' "—the
historical romance. Like Maurice Thompson's *Alice of Old
Vincennes* (1900), it made use of Indiana history and was a
popular success and best seller.

Laid in Terre Haute (Rouen in the novel) at the time of the
Mexican War, Tarkington's new story drew its inspiration
partly from his mother's memories of her schooldays at St. Mary-
of-the-Woods. The heroine of this romantic tale, who is named
Elizabeth for his mother, returns home from St. Mary's as the
story opens, and her experience with the world outside the convent walls provides the plot of the novel. Just as his mother had
fallen in love with a young lawyer, Betty Carewe loses her heart
to an attorney, Tom Vanrevel; but there the parallel with
family history ends.

In the Terre Haute of his mother's girlhood French culture
struggled against the inundating tide of Yankee and Southern
migration. Tarkington had a chance to write a novel of manners, for Robert Carewe, father of the heroine, represents the
old social fabric, while Vanrevel is spokesman for the new. The
city, however, provides merely the setting for summer evening
serenades and other romantic trafficking, and the novel is a
sentimental melodrama in which Betty's tyrannical father carries on a bitter but unsuccessful feud with his daughter's lover.
The story, moreover, uses an elaborate case of mistaken identity
and a cold-blooded murder to sustain the reader's interest. Yet
Tarkington's selection of material capable of supporting a

novel of manners indicates perhaps the transitional nature of the story. He gradually was working himself out of the stereotypes of the historical romance and laying the groundwork for his later studies of contemporary Indiana life.

When his engagement to Helen Pitkin was broken off, Tarkington became once more the popular escort of Indianapolis belles. Since college days he had enchanted feminine acquaintances wherever he went, being naturally thoughtful and courteous to all women, attractive or unattractive. "I never knew another man of such infinite tact," a friend reported; "I never knew of Tarkington ever hurting the feelings of a man, woman or child. His manners are exquisite. . . . He can make a young girl feel that she is in the seventh heaven, by his thoughtful and delicate attentions to her, while he completely wins the hearts of the matrons." This trait sometimes proved a source of embarrassment when girls mistook his intentions and fell in love with him without any real encouragement.

There was more to Tarkington's personality, however, than good manners: he was really different from the average young man a girl encountered among her partners at a ball. The usual chitchat was missing from his conversation, and when he sat out a dance, the talk was likely to explore the depths of his partner's mind. When the bottom was not too shallow, the effect on the partner often was exhilarating. A St. Louis girl who returned home considerably agitated from a visit to Indianapolis explained to Tarkington the effect he had produced on her: "To be honest I am a little afraid of you. . . . No one has ever understood me as you seem to. . . . I was told that you were a singular man, a—genius?—very eccentric—easily bored, loving variety (especially in girls), incomprehensible. To me you are altogether different—possessing, what I admire above all things—a broad mind." In a subsequent letter she thanked him "for playing Dominie" and said that she would henceforth "try for a deeper understanding of the things I read and talk about."

This St. Louis visitor was Irma von Starkloff, who often came to see a Hoosier cousin and long had been acquainted with the Indianapolis "set." She had seen Tarkington sitting in his backyard strumming a banjo years before she ever met him, and when the meeting eventually took place, it occurred at a spelling bee. She misspelled a word, and he came to her rescue, gallantly asserting that her orthography was perfectly logical. Then he began calling on her and taking her for walks along the secluded river bank, a daring thing for her to permit, because Tarkington's habits—his nocturnal working, daytime sleeping, and incessant smoking—were censured by many people. He was by far the most superior person she had encountered, but their association was "brief, turbulent, and intense" before they were "torn assunder by rigid and disapproving relatives." When Mrs. Tarkington called on the cousin's family to meet "the girl for whom my Booth will get up out of bed," she already had been packed off to St. Louis. Irma von Starkloff later became Mrs. Edgar Rombauer, author of that superb vade mecum—*The Joy of Cooking*.

After eight post-college bachelor years, however, Tarkington was ready for marriage. When the Indianapolis *Sentinel* covered the opening of *Beaucaire* in Philadelphia in October, 1901, its report gave the society gossips a tempting morsel of news. Among the visitors in the first-night audience, noted the paper, was Miss Louisa Fletcher, who had accompanied Mr. and Mrs. J. S. Tarkington from Indianapolis. The thirty-two-year-old novelist-playwright, who often had been a groomsman but never a bridegroom, was becoming serious. He was soon to end the bachelor activities he previously had described to Dan Calkins: "I have tipped a bishop with infinite grace. I have toasted brides more prettily than you could dream; I have ushered with notable éclat and put the cooks of distant relatives in the pew reserved for the groom's mother oftener than any man you know. And I have the weddingest clothes you ever see!" but at that writing, he added, no girl for him had appeared.

Louisa Fletcher was not an old friend, nor even a contemporary, but Tarkington had been seen squiring her about during the preceding spring and summer. Returning from Smith College after her graduation in 1900, she had become editor of that year's *Flower Mission Magazine,* in which capacity she had solicited successfully an article from Tarkington. Then she had joined the Indianapolis Dramatic Club and in the autumn was cast by Mrs. Jameson for a part in T. W. Robertson's *David Garrick*. Tarkington, after visiting New York to revise *Beaucaire*, returned in time to play the title role when the club presented the Robertson drama just after the Christmas holidays. From this beginning Miss Fletcher gradually began to receive more and more of Tarkington's time; but until she accompanied his parents to Philadelphia, there had been no talk of an engagement. By March, however, as Tarkington was writing the closing chapters of *The Two Vanrevels,* rumors of a betrothal reached the papers, and a few weeks later an announcement confirmed the speculation.

Louisa Fletcher was the daughter of Stoughton J. Fletcher, Indianapolis banker, and the granddaughter of an Indiana pioneer. Her grandfather, also Stoughton Fletcher, had come from Vermont in 1831, following his brother—Louisa's granduncle—Calvin, who had begun practicing law in Indianapolis when the city first was laid out in 1821. The Fletchers at the turn of the century were already an Indianapolis dynasty, and Louisa's brother Stoughton, the third of that name, carried on the family tradition. This Stoughton, who became Tarkington's brother-in-law, amassed a fortune, built himself a baronial mansion, and after the First World War went broke. Louisa, a slender, fair girl ten years Tarkington's junior, was interested in art, music, drama, literature, and wrote poetry. She, too, found Tarkington utterly fascinating.

The last two months before the marriage were a busy time for Tarkington. The weeks were filled with dinners for distinguished visitors, public appearances, legal harassment, and short trips. Soon after he finished his new novel in early April, he gave a party at the University Club for Woodrow Wilson, then about to become president of Princeton, and a few days later entertained Mansfield, who brought his *Beaucaire* company to Indianapolis for a short run. On the opening night of the play at English's Theater Tarkington made one of the two curtain calls of his career; then on the last day of May he performed on the same stage with other Hoosier authors—Riley, Ade, Major, Wallace, Nicholson, Catherwood, and G. B. McCutcheon —in a benefit reading for a memorial to Benjamin Harrison. As if he were not busy enough, between his two public appearances a suit was filed against him, as the owner of a building housing a bakery, for maintaining a nuisance, the baker's next-door neighbor alleging that new ovens and the mass production of doughnuts had made life intolerable. Finally during the last month before the marriage, Tarkington visited New York on business and Lancaster, Pennsylvania, to usher at a Princeton classmate's wedding. He returned with scant time to arrange his own bachelor dinner at the Country Club.

After an intermittent courtship of about a year and a half Louisa Fletcher and Booth Tarkington were married on June 18, 1902. Only relatives and close friends were invited to the ceremony, which was performed by the Reverend Louis Brown of St. Paul's Episcopal Church in the library of the Fletcher home on East Ohio Street. An orchestra hidden behind potted palms furnished appropriate music for the service and wedding breakfast, after which the bride and groom entrained for the East. Their honeymoon itinerary included a sojourn at a mountain resort, a round of receptions and dinners in New York, a visit to Quebec, and a stopover with the O. B. Jamesons at Mackinac Island.

Sketch of Booth Tarkington, by himself, from a letter to Dan Calkins written in November, 1889

FIVE

IN THE ARENA

Dᴜʀɪɴɢ ᴛʜᴇ sᴘʀɪɴɢ ᴏꜰ 1902 Tarkington not only made plans for his marriage but also entered the political arena. After he had delivered *The Two Vanrevels* to McClure, Phillips, and Company, his urge to write romance had pretty well vanished, and he needed new experience to stoke the fires of his creative impulse. Indianapolis, as the capital of the state, provided a rich potential source of new material in its biennial legislative sessions and continuous governmental operations. Tarkington, like many other Hoosiers of his social and economic group, had grown up in an atmosphere of political activity. His father had been in politics for many years, having served as a gubernatorial secretary, judge of the circuit court, and member of the legislature; Cousin Fenton Booth was in politics; and Uncle Newton Booth's career as Governor of California and later senator was the brightest page in family annals. Moreover, Benjamin Harrison had been a close family friend, and Tarkington knew both of Indiana's senators, Charles W. Fairbanks and Albert J. Beveridge.

A sense of civic responsibility, which caused writers like Tarkington, Sandburg, and Brand Whitlock to enter politics as young men, prevailed over the corrupt actuality of representative government in the early years of the century. That was a period when political machines were powerful, particularly in the Middle West where the cities had grown so fast that large masses of immigrants and emancipated Negroes had yet to be educated and assimilated. That was also a period when the rottenness of municipal governments, so shockingly revealed by Lincoln Steffens in *The Shame of the Cities,* was a national

97

disgrace. Believing in the Jeffersonian idea of a natural aristocracy, Tarkington felt it the duty of good citizens to run for
office and was easily persuaded to file for the state House of
Representatives in the primaries that took place on March 14.
This step proved to be an important factor in shaping his
literary career, for it began an experience that provided
laboratory conditions for studying human nature in its less attractive moments. It revealed to him the vast fictional possibilities of contemporary life and inspired his first stories that
fall entirely within the precincts of realism.

Tarkington had experimented with political material before
he entered the arena, but without first-hand experience his efforts were unrewarded. When *Beaucaire* opened in Philadelphia, he was putting the finishing touches on a political play,
"The Man on Horseback," which he ultimately had to charge
off to experience. Although the protagonist, a Midwestern
United States senator up for re-election, could have been realistic, the setting was a resort hotel at Old Point Comfort, Virginia, and the plot was a melodrama of revenge and blackmail.
The play knocked about for years unproduced. Tarkington
offered it to John Drew, who considered the script a long time,
then turned it down. In 1907 as the play still languished, he
wrote resignedly: "That poor *ms* is still floating around somewhere—six years now, and not played yet, but I keep on hopefully trying to get somebody for it every now & then." Finally
James K. Hackett put it on for two weeks in San Francisco in
1912, but it was, wrote one reviewer, an unstable blend of sentimental romance and politics "destined neither for a spectacular success nor for tenacious life."

In his use of politics at this time Tarkington was moderately
successful only when he kept political matters on the periphery
of his fiction. Such is "The Old Gray Eagle," a tale which
sketches the career of a great man's son, using politics as the
incidental setting for a non-political character study. His taste
for politics also is demonstrated in a minor aspect of *The Gentleman from Indiana,* for not only does John Harkless at the
end of the novel get the beautiful Helen Sherwood, but he also
wins his party's nomination for Congress.

The political sympathies of Indiana, then as now, fluctuated
between the Republican and Democratic parties. As the son

of a Civil War veteran, Tarkington inherited his politics and
ran on the Republican ticket as a matter of course. Most of
his neighbors on the fashionable North Side of Indianapolis
also were Republicans. Yet there was a strong Southern tradition in Indiana, and some of Tarkington's oldest friends were
Democrats. Even his father had been a Democrat before joining the Republicans to follow Lincoln, and two or three friends
were Socialists. Throughout his life, though he kept up political interests long after his active participation ended, loyalty to
his friends never depended on political conformity, not even
during the successive terms of Franklin D. Roosevelt. Sometimes Tarkington's amiability in his old age was put to a severe
test by the conflicts of political philosophy within his circle; but
in 1902 the Republican Roosevelt was in the White House,
and the G.O.P. was accustomed to flattening the opposition on
election day.

Tarkington entered the primary almost surreptitiously, and
because he was busy writing a book, he conducted no campaign
at all. His name on the ballot was all that he needed to win his
nomination, and he learned with astonishment that he had led
nineteen Republican candidates from Indianapolis and Marion
County for seven places on the November ballot. Having received 10,733 votes, four thousand more than he needed, he told
a reporter the day after the primary that he could not account
for his success, although he had heard a reasonable explanation
attributed to a Washington Township farmer: "We voted for
him as a sort of experiment," the farmer explained; "the paper
said he's a play writer and some kind of an actor, and we just
want to see what sort of a gosh derned fool he'll make of himself in the Legislature." The farmer's observation became one
of Tarkington's favorite anecdotes about himself, and throughout his life, whenever he could not avoid making a speech, he
usually recalled this incident. As time went on, he added further embellishments, until finally his political career sounded
like a mere vagary in his literary life. But he actually took his
public office seriously—more so even than the party managers
wished.

His easy nomination, however, insured a light-hearted approach to the general election in the autumn. His wedding
journey kept him busy all summer, but when the political cam-

paign opened in September, he still was nowhere in evidence. Two weeks before the balloting, he was vacationing with his wife at Lake Maxinkuckee, where he had been for several weeks. The absence of the party's best-selling novelist-candidate created resentment among members of the Republican City Committee, who demanded that Tarkington come home. Nevertheless, he stayed away as long as his conscience would let him, and when he did return, he was reluctant to campaign. "I would as soon be sent to jail," he said, "as to have to make a speech."

Yet he made five short appearances and four shorter speeches during the last week of October. When he agreed to exhibit himself, the party scheduled his maiden address in the obscurity of a fire station, and the afternoon papers obligingly buried a brief announcement of his ordeal in the back pages. He was an attraction, however, and a capacity crowd jammed the engine house to eat free apples and listen to various candidates. Reporters assigned to the meeting noted that Tarkington was a success as a hand-shaker but a failure as a speaker. His performance suggested to them a schoolboy's first piece. "My position as a public speaker," Tarkington began, "reminds me of the bad actor who was playing Hamlet. Some of his friends asked him if he was called before the curtain and he replied that they not only called him before the curtain but they dared him to come. They dared me to make a speech and here I am."

Speaking to residents of the Second Ward, Tarkington embarrassedly urged them to do their duty as voters and citizens. First he would "stammer out a sentence, laugh at the effort and then fall headlong into another sentence." He held his hat before him to serve "as a comforter in a moment of peril," and when he groped for a word, he shoved his hat ahead of him to notify his audience that it was coming. The burden of his remarks, which lasted a scant two minutes, was "Get out and vote." The more seasoned campaigners discussed the issues and the party platform.

A few minutes later Tarkington repeated his appearance farther downtown in another fire station. On his second try reporters timed his performance at one minute and twenty-two seconds, although he claimed that he had given the same speech. Again he urged apathetic voters not to stay at home on election day, and again he left the serious campaigning to his colleagues. Luckily for Tarkington, when he completed his talk, the fire bell rang, and as the firemen scrambled for their apparatus, he retreated towards the street to keep his own horses from breaking away in the confusion.

When he again took to the hustings four days later, he noted happily that there was no advance notice in the papers. He then talked briefly to a group of voters on the banks of the canal and later crossed town to a meeting at which Congressman Overstreet was the principal speaker. The press agreed the next day that Tarkington at least seemed more at ease in the role of political orator, though there was some doubt about his effectiveness. One amused reporter, who timed him at three minutes and twenty-nine seconds, took down the speech in part. Even if one allows for some journalistic retouching, the address still is a pretty remarkable document:

> I have just come from a meeting which kept me awful late, and I hoped to get here sooner. I am no public speaker, as you know. The issue of this campaign is to get out the vote. I met a Big Four [New York Central] man today on the street, and I asked him to be sure and vote, and he wanted to know when the election day was. He didn't know there was going to be an election. There are too many that are that way. There are a good many businessmen who will have more time to vote next time if they don't know when to vote this time. There is the high price of beef, and I have wondered how high it would be under a democratic rule. The great issue is to get out the vote. Vote early but not often. The indifferent voter is a worthless sort of cuss. He is not a very good man. You have got to make him vote. If you get enough of them the result will be the same. I remember a story of an old . . . man and his boy who went fishing at a dam, and the boy fell into the swirling water which soon took him under. A bystander asked the old man why he took it so hard when his boy was a worthless fellow. "Why, he had the bait," said the old man. That's the way with the apathetic voter. We need him in our business. If he realizes what his right means, he will vote. The Hanna meeting the other night [Mark Hanna had just visited Indianapolis] roused the people. You should rouse them.

This speech resulted in another of Tarkington's prized personal stories, for his remarks attracted comment from William

Jennings Bryan, who shortly before had begun publishing his weekly periodical, *The Commoner*. In the first issue after election day Bryan, summarizing the campaign for the Indiana legislature, noted that Tarkington in his initial appearance had been attacked by a severe case of stage fright and had been virtually unable to speak. Remarking on what Tarkington actually had managed to say in his second appearance, Bryan observed: "It would perhaps have been better for Mr. Tarkington if he had been stricken with stage fright on his second effort."

When he finished his campaign on the last Friday before the balloting, Tarkington arrayed himself in brown frock suit, gay waistcoat, and green topcoat to visit a farm auction on the outskirts of the city. He drove to the site in his fancy trap with Lew Shank, an auctioneer turned candidate for county recorder. He had planned to wear a silk hat to show his respect for his farmer constituents, but friends protested that such garb would ruin the entire Republican county ticket. After they reached the farm gathering, auctioneer Shank slapped backs and shook hands like a seasoned campaigner. He went through the crowd "like a big dog scampering in a pile of fallen leaves, and was quite impossible to follow." It took him about twenty minutes to shake the hand of everyone there and distribute most of his cigars, and when that was done the place looked like a burning hayfield. Tarkington simply stood aside marveling at the born politician in action, and when his legislative experience was concluded, he put Shank, who later became Mayor of Indianapolis, into a political article for *Collier's*.

Tarkington also learned a lesson that morning in voter psychology. He found that his small ten-cent cigars were far less popular than the big, cheap stogies that Shank passed out. He carried off this *faux pas*, however, by admitting that while his cigars were little, he after all only was running for an unimportant office. The mistake was no great calamity; in fact, it earned him at least one vote from a farmer who tried unsuccessfully to light his tiny cigar, which barely protruded from beneath an abundant mustache, like a pitchfork handle from under a load of hay. After bringing the match up to his mouth, he decided that the effort was too dangerous; but he conceded that at least the candidate who gave him such a "durned little cigar" was economical and would be a safe man in the legislature.

Tarkington's cavalier approach to his campaign was justified by the easy confidence of the Republican Party as election day approached. Although the Democrats maintained that they could and would win, the Republicans were concerned chiefly with estimating the size of their majority. When the ballots were counted, as events turned out, the G.O.P. state ticket polled fifty-six percent of the vote for an easy victory. Tarkington was so little excited on election day that he stayed in bed till noon and later cast his vote as the *News* headlined: "Candidate Tarkington Slept Peacefully While the Ballots Fell." By the next morning, November 5, through little effort of his own, he was Representative-elect Tarkington.

During the next two months, while he waited for his term in the legislature to begin, he visited New York on business and while there attended a birthday dinner for Mark Twain. In early January, as the start of the General Assembly drew near, he turned out to meet other new representatives on their arrival in the capital. Then on the eve of the opening session the amiable Tarkington, too polite to cope with the situation, was besieged by office-seekers referred to him for a joke by his colleagues. When the legislature at last convened on January 8, he was in his seat for the opening gavel and thereafter attended the sessions daily until the assembly adjourned in March. No one expected strenuous political activity from Tarkington, but almost immediately he jumped headlong into legislative problems. Idealism instantly clashed with political expediency, and within a week he was fighting the most powerful politician in the state—the Governor himself—Winfield T. Durbin.

The legislative session was a sobering and eye-opening experience for Tarkington. All the tales he had heard of politics and the exposés he had read could not equal the impact of one first-hand encounter in the political arena. He listened attentively to the Governor's opening address which painted a glowing picture of the "peace, happiness, and contentment" then prevailing throughout the state of Indiana. The Governor even said: "It should be the constant aim of all right-thinking men to encourage, by every possible means, the growth of tolerance between man and man." In reality, however, Tarkington found himself in a legislative body that even the Republican *News* conceded was the most lobby-ridden in recent years and the Democratic *Sentinel* charged with extravagance and "gross betrayal of the people's interests." Serving the electorate turned out to be more than a mere matter of voting as conscience dictated for or against proposed legislation. There were, to contend with, pressure, misrepresentation, reprisal, and downright dishonesty. The session was disillusioning, but at the same time it was a valuable period of practical education.

Early in the session one of the Governor's men introduced what seemed an innocuous bill to reorganize the state reformatory at Jeffersonville. The measure was not so innocent as its title seemed, however, and Tarkington, perhaps because he was a freshman representative, quickly saw it for what it was. The bill proposed to oust the reformatory board (which somehow had incurred the Governor's wrath) so that the chief executive could in retaliation appoint a new panel. Ironically, the Republicans in their campaign had pledged themselves to keep state institutions out of politics. With unpolitical candor Tarkington announced his objections and set out to fight the Governor. He did not fancy himself Jack-the-Giant-Killer: the Governor's proposal simply would be a rotten thing to enact, and any decent person ought to oppose it.

What began as a routine legislative session soon turned out to be a fight to the finish. Luckily, the newspapers were delighted to support Tarkington's stand against a bad bill, for without some powerful backing the contest would have been hopeless. The Governor's faction resorted to character assassination, threats of political reprisal, and promises of patronage. They rammed their measure through the senate first, then turned to the house. The odds against Tarkington at first were huge, and veteran politicians warned him that he could not beat Durbin. Even the Democrats were not interested in helping but sat happily by, hoping that civil war among the Republicans would wreck their two-to-one majority. Tarkington worked hard to marshal the timid opposition and to enlist additional help. For days the issue was in doubt. When the Governor's henchmen circulated rumors that Tarkington was buying votes, he threatened libel suits against those who impugned his motives. He was learning politics fast, commented the *Sentinel*.

Finally, the Governor conceded defeat and sent representatives to meet with Tarkington and his supporters. In a smoke-filled room at English's Hotel on January 27, the Governor's men agreed to a face-saving bill that gave Durbin no powers he did not have already. On the next day the harmless "compromise" measure was brought up in the house and passed. Tarkington was the man of the hour. The *News* congratulated him for his notable accomplishment: "From the first he saw the question in its true light, and he has had the courage and independence to stand up for what he believed to be right." The *Sentinel* ran on page one pictures of both Tarkington and the Governor as the chief opponents in the Reformatory Bill fight. Tarkington won the respect of Democrats and Republicans alike and the enmity of the Governor. After the legislature adjourned, Tarkington wrote in the *News* significantly that the *sub rosa* influence of the Governor on the legislature had been one of the most surprising and disquieting things he had learned about lawmaking. The Governor's influence, he declared, was "extraordinarily pervading" and "exceedingly difficult to counteract."

Before the Reformatory Bill was disposed of, Tarkington took part in another event that had little intrinsic importance but wide personal ramifications: he made the only speech of his legislative career—the nomination of Charles W. Fairbanks for re-election to the United States Senate. The Republican leadership chose Tarkington to place Fairbanks' name before the lower house, while a colleague sponsored him in the upper branch. Even prior to the assembly's vote on the nomination, as the federal Constitution then provided, there never was any doubt that the Republican majority would elect its man. The selection of Tarkington as party spokesman, however, packed the visitors' gallery of the house. His speech, which lasted about six minutes once the introductory applause died away, devoted itself merely to eulogizing Senator Fairbanks, whom Tarkington knew both socially and politically; but despite its brevity the address cost Tarkington a great deal of effort. Nearly a week before the nomination the *News* reported that he was already at work on the speech and suffering from stage fright.

After Fairbanks was re-elected, Tarkington quit public address and restricted his activities to committee work and private discussions in the Capitol cloakrooms.

Although he later laughed about his nominating speech, recalling particularly his ridiculous efforts to use gestures, his appearance before a large audience was a profoundly disturbing experience. He never again addressed a crowd, and the number of speeches of any kind that he made during the rest of his life can be counted on the fingers of one hand. As he won more and more distinction through his writing, he became less and less willing to make public appearances. After Columbia University awarded him an honorary doctor of letters degree in 1924, he even stopped accepting academic honors because he hated to appear on commencement platforms, and in 1938 he had a bad case of nerves just from addressing a Chicago gathering by telephone in Indianapolis. By that time he had given up all public appearances, even theater attendance, following a series of eye operations that aggravated his nervousness.

Usually Tarkington excused himself from making speeches by inventing a polite lie, but occasionally to close friends he explained his real feelings. In 1920, after receiving from Garland a compelling request for a speech, he wrote:

> In 1916 the Lotos Club gave me one of their kindly celebrative dinners . . . If they hadn't sent a committee down to Princeton to see me, I'd have wriggled out of it somehow. But they did, six weeks before the dinner, and there just wasn't *any* way out . . . I was trying to work, but had to stop at once . . . and the six weeks that ought to have been a time of industry shifted to a prolonged fit of shivers. That was my last "appearance." It's not only a mental horror with me—it's physical: I "run down," and I can't work *afterwards* for a long time. If I knew now that I *had* to "read" to—or address—seven or more people next March, I couldn't do a lick of work before MAY!

This dinner was the last time he ever accepted an invitation to speak, and for the final thirty years of his career, he studiously avoided any public occasion that would interfere with his writing. Yet he had begun his career as an amateur actor of considerable talent and even in old age amazed his friends with a physical transformation when he played charades. If the chance had presented itself in the Nineties he might have become a professional actor, for footlights and grease paint were powerful attractions in those days. Throughout his life, however, he was always available to a large circle of friends. He loved people in small, intimate groups and gave generously of his time to friends and sometimes even to strangers. Newspaper interviewers were always welcome; biographers of friends, also dissertation-writers, always received courteous and, when possible, detailed answers to their requests for data; even autograph-hunters found Tarkington obliging.

But to return to 1903 and the legislature. The bill which created the greatest public controversy in the Sixty-third General Assembly was a plan to legalize Sunday baseball. Although Tarkington had no direct part in the legislative fight, he collected literary material from the resultant wrangle. This measure caused no furore in the house where it passed easily, but a real battle developed in the senate. Before the Senate Public Morals Committee could approve the bill, the opponents rallied their strength, and when the bill came up for a final vote, its enemies were ready. The galleries were filled with spectators, the floor overrun with lobbyists. Members of the house watched the tumultuous senate session with intense interest, and for Tarkington, the writer, the events of that day wrote themselves into "Mrs. Protheroe," a tale of the struggle to legalize Sunday baseball.

In contrast to the Reformatory Bill, which was fought bitterly behind the scenes, the Sunday Baseball Bill exploded the liveliest fireworks seen on the floor of the senate in years. For two weeks petitions for and against were circulated throughout the state, while a barrage of pulpit oratory denounced the proposal. Before the measure came to a vote, the opposition leader, Senator Ogborn, fulminated against the bill in an obvious play for the gallery, and as the roll call began, a singular scene took place. Tarkington remembered: "Senator O'Brien sat white-faced and refused to vote while the clerk shouted at him for an hour." When the tumult died down, the measure failed to carry by one vote. Later it was reported that O'Brien had promised his wife not to vote for the bill but could not bring himself to vote against it.

The action of the senate was a source of disappointment to

Tarkington, who wrote frankly about it when he later reviewec for the *News* the work of the legislature:

> . . . it requires a reckless humor or a superior species of moral courage to stand against the "church element" in a matter of principle. You are personally proclaimed as of the damned by the particular authorities on damnation! You may buck the machine and get hard fighting, a lot of rough handling, and have some pretty fancy tricks played on you, but when you are looking for real trouble follow your sense of right when it conflicts with the ideas of a Sunday-school superintendent.

Tarkington thought that Sunday baseball was an excellent proposal, since Indianapolis then offered little besides saloons for week-end recreation. He also believed that the legislature had no right to "set up a moral code for the entire population" and gave this opinion flatly to a delegation of Indianapolis women who visited him during debate on the bill. The General Assembly, however, did not legalize Sunday baseball in Indiana until 1909.

"Mrs. Protheroe," the story of Sunday baseball, owes its provenance to more than the effort to repeal one particular blue law. The captivating lady lobbyist of· the tale had a real-life prototype in Letitia Gallaher of Evansville, who staged a one-woman campaign—not for Sunday baseball—but for a deaf and dumb asylum. Between the debate over legalizing Sunday baseball and the efforts of Miss Gallaher to win approval for her project, Tarkington found his story materials. Mrs. Protheroe in the story is a charming but devious young woman who works for Sunday baseball with disinterested words but not disinterested motives (she owns the ballpark). She charms young Senator Alonzo Rawson of Stackpole, Chairman of the Committee on Drains and Dikes, so effectively that he reverses his original opposition to the bill; but in the end her efforts fail.

The real Mrs. Protheroe, attractive Miss Gallaher, came to Indianapolis to lobby on behalf of her father, who was principal of a private school for the deaf in Evansville. The bill that she promoted so vigorously should have caused no controversy in either house, and her motives were pure. Her measure slipped past the house quietly but stuck in the senate, although it only authorized the Evansville school district to divert its own funds for the education of the deaf and dumb. But apparently Miss Gallaher was one lobbyist who could be ignored with impunity by a senate that was unable to pass any bill opposed by powerful corporate lobbies, and her bill was eventually defeated.

One of the strongest assailants of the harmless measure was Senator Ulrey, who perhaps inspired Tarkington's own Josephus Battle, leader of the fight in "Mrs. Protheroe" against the "Sabbath-Desecration Bill." He thundered against the "baldheads and beardless youths" of the senate who had been captivated by the "sweet, fascinating smiles and five-cent posies" of the beautiful lobbyist. If the bill is passed, boomed the Senator, expressing sentiments that Tarkington thought antediluvian, "we will have every county in the state running its own deaf and dumb asylum or every home in the state that has a dumb child looking to the county for help." Tarkington regretted the defeat of this bill and later wrote that it is the duty of the state to look after its unfortunates.

He learned during his term in the legislature that the most useful members devoted themselves to a few specific projects —the killing of three or four bad bills, the passing of two or three good ones, or the defending of the treasury. In practicing what he learned, he was only partly successful, for while he blocked the Reformatory Bill, he failed to put through two other measures that he had sponsored. His experience with these bills was discouraging but again, highly educational. He learned practical lessons in political skulduggery and legislative reprisal, though at the same time two worthy measures were lost.

One of these proposals brought down on his head the wrath of the insurance companies. A plan to bar rate-fixing, to insure competition, and to force lower premiums, the measure was motivated by the same anti-trust impulse that already had produced much governmental restriction on powerful corporations. Yet the insurance bill marched down the familiar legislative cul-de-sac: it passed easily in the house but was blocked by the lobbies in the senate. The house, apparently because it was too large to control easily, was more independent than the senate, which unhappily became the graveyard for bills opposed by strong corporate interests.

Tarkington was astonished by the downright trickery of his opponents when the insurance bill reached the senate. His friends had to force the bill out of committee, then contend with its disappearance from the printing office. For twenty-four hours the document was "lost" while the legislature was rushing towards adjournment; and when the bill did come up for a vote, there was filibustering. That tactic failed, but the opposition then amended the measure, virtually assuring its failure: there was no time left to iron out house and senate differences. As the frustrating conclusion to this melodrama, the senate finally defeated the bill by two votes.

Tarkington probably realized that the Governor would have vetoed any measure that he backed. In such a way could the Governor retaliate against his enemies in the fight over the Reformatory Bill. After the adjournment Tarkington found himself the apparent victim of just such a reprisal on a relatively trivial measure, a bill to educate blind adults who had no trade. In response to pleas from blind persons who did not want to live on charity, Tarkington had introduced a bill (costing the state only $2,080 annually) to train a limited number of blind persons in broom-making. The bill, opposed by scarcely anyone in either the house or the senate, went to the Governor with a special recommendation for its approval from Helen Keller. Yet the Governor turned it down and said in his veto message that the measure would set a dangerous precedent "for the establishment of innumerable institutions of similar character, thereby imposing upon the tax-paying public a burden they would not and could not assume in justice to themselves." Although Tarkington was incensed at the Governor's lack of humanity and his pettiness, he admitted that many of his colleagues had said to him: "Oh, Durbin will veto your bill all right."

When the legislature adjourned in March, Tarkington was in politics up to his neck. He retreated to French Lick Springs for rest and recuperation, but he looked forward to future political activity. He ended his first term of office with only a partially satisfied sense of achievement and with a real desire to continue his crusade for good government. In his review of the legislative session he urged good citizens to get into politics, and the deeper one gets in, he declared, "the more he feels the need of other good citizens to be with him." As the session ended, Tarkington was mentioned as a possible candidate in the approaching Indianapolis mayoralty race, but he wanted next to try a term in the state senate. If he could not get that, however, he was willing to return to the house.

At the end of his first term of office he definitely was a political maverick, though he certainly had not been a Socialist as he sometimes maintained in after years. He was, however, a humanitarian, perhaps most attune to progressive Republicanism of the La Follette variety, and he would have joined forces with any political group to keep politics clean and honest. Typical of his spirit throughout life is his old-age memory of Eugene Debs, with whom he shared no practical solutions but was drawn to by a kindred humanity. Some years after he left politics, Tarkington fell into conversation in a smoking car with Debs, whom he then never had met, and the two men talked from 7:30 A.M. till noon, when Debs got off the train:

> I've never been more interested in a chance acquaintance. To begin with, I liked his face and his voice and his quiet dispassionate manner. Moreover, I liked everything he said, his opinions and his analyses of people and of events. It seemed to me that I'd never encountered a sounder or more steady-minded, fair and profoundly intelligent patriotic American citizen.
>
> From the first there was something that seemed faintly familiar to me about him; yet I was pretty sure, and rightly so, that I'd never before seen him, and yet, as a perception of his mental and moral stature grew upon me, together with the strong impression that I was talking with a remarkable man who was also profoundly good, a wholly upright citizen who looked upon all the world with Christian kindliness and yet was blinded to none of the evils in the world, I felt that I must surely know who he was if I could only think. Such a man must surely be Somebody.
>
> Then, perhaps half an hour before we reached Cresline where he was to leave the train I recognized him. . . .
>
> I didn't mention that I'd identified him and I saw that I was certainly anonymous to him. We shook hands as he left the compartment and both of us said that we hoped to meet again, but we never did.

I still [January 10, 1945] have the impression of him I had that long morning on the train, something over thirty years ago. . . . Politically and generally I'm an old Republican . . . and yet among the highest respects in my life is that which I still retain for the memory of Eugene Debs.

While vacationing with his wife at French Lick in March and April, Tarkington began the literary use of his political experience. Although he modestly doubted his ability to write a political novel based on his recent term of office, he set to work immediately on two of the short stories that eventually grew into the collection *In the Arena* (1905). One was "Boss Gorgett," a tale of machine politics in a mayoralty campaign, which Tarkington began but did not finish until summer. This story concerns the unsuccessful efforts of a reform candidate to oust the boss who has been mayor for four terms. When the reformer discovers a plot to stuff the ballot boxes and threatens to expose the boss, the wily mayor quickly silences the opposition by uncovering in his rival's private life an extra-marital flirtation. This is a neatly plotted and well-spun little comedy using politics effectively as background coloring. Quite different, however, is "The Aliens," the other story written at French Lick, for it is a small, unrelieved tragedy, "a story of politics in a tough precinct," in which Tarkington's observation of ward politics at their slimiest produced a work of naturalistic fiction.

The aliens of the tale are Pietro Tobigli, young Italian immigrant, and his fiancée Bertha, a German waitress, both representative of the polyglot minority of Indianapolis in 1903. A hard-working chestnut vendor is Pietro, who saves his money to buy a fruit stand and some day, in his beloved adopted country, hopes to own an entire store; but in his innocent loyalty to the Republican Party he becomes a pawn, expendable in the game of politics. Because he persists in supporting his party, the Republican committeeman Frank Pixley, who has sold his precinct to the Democrats, coldbloodedly sacrifices him and his little bloc of Italian friends by having them quarantined in a smallpox-infested tenement. Pixley then delivers his precinct to the Democrats, but Pietro, despite his sanguine hopes for Bertha and himself in the new country, contracts the disease and dies anonymously in the pesthouse.

The slum locale of this tale was unfamiliar ground for Tarkington, but he observed shrewdly and the tale has the ring of truth. Characters like Pixley, "a damp-looking, soiled little fungus of a man," he had met during his brief foray into politics; and in his study of the structure of machine organization he had found at the bottom these ward-heelers from whose office led "an upward ramification of wires, invisible to all except manipulators," which extended to higher levels. Usually, however, the Pixley was "a deep-sea puppet," wholly controlled by the wires that ran down to him; but there were times when the Pixley gave forth "initial impulses of his own" that occasionally altered the upper surfaces. Such was the double cross by which the naïve Pietro was victimized. A similar type, too, was Sam Arbaugh, an elusive ward boss who fixed the cops and bought the votes. He occupied a higher place than Pixley in the subterranean mechanism and was a power to be feared and paid off. This unsavory character sat for another non-fiction sketch that Tarkington contributed to *Collier's*.

Tarkington's most direct use of his term in the legislature was in "Mrs. Protheroe" and "The Need of Money," both stories which were not written until some months later. Although the latter is inferior to "Mrs. Protheroe," "The Need of Money" creates in Uncle Billy Rollinson a simple-minded country lawmaker who sells out to the railroad lobby without knowing that he has been bribed. A story of real pathos, the latter tale undoubtedly was inspired by Tarkington's first-hand observation of his legislative colleagues. During the legislative session there were nine members of the house who offered no bills and remained inconspicuous and inarticulate, one of whom perhaps served as a model for Tarkington's character. Moreover, the sordid dealing of the railroad lobby, which had been active during the session, was taken directly from the author's experience. He had served on the Committee for the Affairs of the City of Indianapolis and in that capacity had fought unsuccessfully to force the railroads to elevate their tracks through Indianapolis.

One of the most ardent admirers of *In the Arena* was Theodore Roosevelt, who read the stories while they still were appearing serially. Tarkington discovered this a few days before Christmas, 1904, when he was summoned unexpectedly to

Washington to lunch at the White House. He went to the capital thinking that Mr. Roosevelt wanted first-hand information about Hoosier politics—and his guess was right—but at the same time he learned with astonishment that the President had read his work. He wrote his father that during luncheon the President made "a long & generally favorable comment" on his stories. "Of course," he added, "I just sat & purred—too pleased to eat." It was also at this luncheon, Tarkington remembered, that the President delivered a tirade against gentlemen in their clubs who would not dirty their hands with politics, and Tarkington recalled that the President hoped good men would not be deterred from entering politics by such stories as "The Aliens." *In the Arena* then was in press, and a few weeks after it was published, Roosevelt wrote a flattering commendation, particularly praising the Preface which urged all responsible citizens to take part in politics. "I like all the stories," added the President; "Mrs. Protheroe does not come within the ken of my own experiences, but the other comedies and pitiful tragedies are just such as I myself have seen."

After Tarkington had been at French Lick for a month, both his writing and his plans for further political office suddenly were cut short by a severe case of typhoid fever. Fortunately he managed to get home in the early stages of the disease, but the attack was so virulent that it nearly killed him. Two months later, when he was still so sick that the sound of wagons rattling past the house disturbed him, his father had half a block of Pennsylvania Street covered with sand to deaden the sound. By July, however, he was well enough to travel, though eighty pounds lighter, and the doctor prescribed "the healthiest place in the United States . . . Kennebunkport, Maine." There he spent the balance of the summer, breathing salt air sieved through pine woods, eating Maine seafood, and building himself up, and while he was in Maine, he made plans to spend the following year recuperating abroad. Although he had left the Indiana legislature with a record of worth-while accomplishment and hoped to serve again, he was too far away from his political experience by the time he returned from Europe and too deeply involved in his literary career to pick up the threads of his former life in Indianapolis.

SIX

WANDERJAHRE: 1903-1906

WHEN TARKINGTON BOOKED PASSAGE for Europe, he reserved space for a party of four—his mother and father, his wife and himself—and soon after the middle of September the four Tarkingtons, in holiday mood, embarked for England on the *Blücher* of the Hamburg-American Line. Their itinerary for the next eleven months included a short stay in London, a longer visit to Paris, and a leisurely trek southward towards Italy via Switzerland. After stopovers in Verona, Venice, Florence, Rome, and Naples, they planned to spend a month on Capri and to return to the mainland for the winter. In the spring the tourists would travel north through Germany and the Low Countries, then back to Paris before sailing for home at the end of July. The schedule avoided winter weather and provided a maximum of sunshine for rebuilding Tarkington's run-down constitution.

In London Tarkington primarily was interested in the theater, for Lewis Waller's production of *Beaucaire,* in its third season, still was running, and as playwright he found himself the object of flattering newspaper attention. He reciprocated London's approval by noting that the British stage was in some ways superior to the American. He observed that English theatrical companies had better casts, were not plagued by the star system, and in general had more distinguished actors than their American counterparts. But also during his brief stay at the Dysart Hotel on Cavendish Square Tarkington was pleased to be recognized as a novelist, for *The Gentleman from Indiana, Monsieur Beaucaire,* and *The Two Vanrevels,* already were available in British editions. He left England for France comfortably aware that British royalties were helping make possible his delayed grand tour.

Paris in early October charmed Tarkington at once, as it later was to captivate American writers of Hemingway and Fitzgerald's generation. It drew him back again and again until he almost became an expatriate later in the decade. Having learned French history from his mother's reading and the language in school, he felt a congeniality in Paris that he never experienced elsewhere in Europe, even though in Italy he spoke the language and loved its art and in England was a popular author and dramatist. He delighted in all things Parisian and tirelessly followed his Baedeker from one memorable place to another. After growing up in the raw, mushrooming Midwest, he was fascinated by the permanence of Paris. From his first glimpse of the city on a rainy night at the end of September, "a picture of moving fiacres reflected upon the wet surface of the boulevards," until his last visit to Paris in 1925, it was the spot outside of the United States that he loved best.

The attraction of the French capital began immediately through an introduction to the ever-enchanting Gallic sense of humor. Upon his arrival in the city, he had to declare his trunk before a middle-aged customs inspector at the Gare du Nord, and when that official asked perfunctorily if his luggage contained any tobacco or liquor, Tarkington tried out his French. Although he could read the language easily, he never had spoken it, and he blurted out the information that his trunk contained three hundred thousand cigarettes.

"*Trois cent mille?*" asked the official. "*Impossible!*"

Realizing his error, Tarkington tried to explain that his spoken French was faulty, that he had gotten mixed up, that he had meant to say three hundred cigarettes; but again he said three hundred thousand.

"Go away!" said the customs official wearily. "Go away from me, if you please. Immediately! I am a good citizen and I have an excellent mind; but I shall have none at all if you continue talking to me." As he chalked the trunk, he added that it was better for the French government to lose the duty than for him to go mad.

Parisian humor was infectious, and Tarkington's letters home from his first trip abroad are full of lively displays of wit, burlesque descriptions, invented legends, and observed incongruities. Most of his letters went to John and Donald Jameson, his sister's boys, of whom he was especially fond, and throughout the journey southward he tantalized his nephews with references to Christmas presents that he was buying for them. In Paris he wrote that each boy was to receive a "lovely, calf-bound hymnal," and he added: "But that is not all. Perhaps I shouldn't tell you so far ahead . . . but I can't resist. Each of you is to have a fine woodcut engraving of the Apostle Peter!" Later from Capri, continuing in the same vein, he promised the boys additional gifts, which included a "handsome big door mat with 'Wipe Your Feet' in large attractive letters" and a splendid edition of *Lives of the Saints*. He also promised that some embroidered mottos would be included, such as "Virtue Is Its Own Reward," "Haste Makes Waste," and "Honor Thy Uncle."

When Tarkington visited Florence, he was enchanted by a multilingual guide who claimed to speak English but who described thus the tomb of the Medicis: " 'Ere ve haf il tombeau de Lorenzo le Magnifique and Allesandro his fratello. Zis grand mausoleum costed trois million pound und it is der grösten arbeit of dat kind in il mondo." And in a subsequent letter from Rome Tarkington reported that they were all becoming pious: "I doubt if a single day has passed since we landed that we haven't been to church." After visiting the catacombs, he drew for the benefit of his nephews a small, solid black square which he labeled "a little sketch I made of the interior for you. I'd have drawn the exterior, too; but there isn't any." Scraps of Roman history, even a complete nonsense legend about the Tarpeian Rock, adorned his letters from Rome, and his nephews were highly diverted when he reported visiting the Palatine Hill where Romulus and Uncle Remus had founded the city. The boys' parents also enjoyed the letters, especially his comparisons of things Italian with things Hoosier. When he visited the cellars of the Capuchin Church and saw two thousand skeletons on exhibition, he remarked that "truly the legislature is nothing beside it," and a little later he observed that Lucrezia Borgia, whose villa he had just seen, had "poisoned more people than Sherman's Restaurant."

Tarkington traveled through Italy collecting impressions and dispensing largess like a potentate. He carried so much copper in his pockets, he said, that if he ever fell in the water he surely would drown. He still enjoyed the novelty of having a large income and did his sightseeing in style—to the delight of all the hotel proprietors, guides, and livery stable owners who served him. But his popularity with the operators of the tourist industry rested on more than his munificence, for he was neither the rich American who fawned over titled Europeans nor the wealthy businessman who saw Vesuvius only as an appalling waste of unharnessed power. His generosity was not patronizing, and he enjoyed everything he saw. The French, German, and Italian that he had taken in school and college finally were useful, and if his study of modern languages had prevented his being a degree-candidate at Princeton, at least it enriched his European travels.

Not all of his letters home were written to amuse or to instruct his nephews. At times he was so carried away by the things he saw that his descriptions served as an outlet for his own enthusiastic response. One such time followed a trip from Sorrento to Amalfi along the winding road that hugged great precipices overlooking the incredibly blue Mediterranean. The late November day was bright; the air was clear; the sun was hot. Tarkington, his wife, and parents rode in two open victorias and marveled at the contrast with Midwestern landscape. As they climbed the backbone of the Sorrentine Peninsula, thousands of orange trees loaded with ripening fruit nodded over brown stone walls, while far below and behind them was the blue Bay of Naples and the smoking cone of Vesuvius. The sky was equally blue, "like a big bowl set over the mountains and islands and sea," and the hills, neatly terraced with miles of grape vines and lemon trees, rose above them like endless green tapestries.

After returning from Amalfi, they crossed over to Capri for a month and rented a suite of rooms that once had been the apartment of the munitions-maker Krupp. Tarkington, enjoying himself thoroughly, visited the grottos, rambled over the places associated with the Emperor Tiberius, and almost daily hired a girl donkey-driver named Paloma and her temperamental beast Michelangelo. The small American colony on the island welcomed the Tarkingtons, and two painters in particular, Charles Coleman and Elihu Vedder, became friends. The latter then was building, high on the saddle of the island, an elaborate villa that Tarkington later was to rent for a short time. The ancient lineages of the Capriotes, many of whom had lived in the same houses for two thousand years, impressed Tarkington deeply and furnished him with the text for a brief sermon to his nephews on the vanities of ancester worship by Hoosiers inordinately proud that their families had lived in Indianapolis for three generations. A day or two before Christmas they left "the loveliest spot in all the world" to return to Rome for the winter.

Throughout his life Tarkington was an art collector—interested in painting, sculpture, tapestry, furniture, and all sorts of *objets d'art*—and his acquisitions began during his first trip to Europe. He made his early purchases tentatively in Venice, Florence, and Naples, but when he settled down in Rome for the winter, he found that the antique shops were impossible to stay out of. One day in early January he went out for air, but instead of driving in an open *vettura,* as he would have preferred, he thought that he ought to economize a little and walk. Soon he passed a shop window displaying antiquities, stopped to admire the contents, and could not resist entering. A moment later he was lost. Writing his sister of the experience, he admitted that his economical walk had cost him a thousand francs ($200), but he rationalized his purchases in a thoroughly characteristic manner: "We so often mistake money for value. Beauty is better than shekels." Throughout his life he regarded money as only a means to an end, and later when everything he wrote commanded fifty cents or more a word, the end might be a Gilbert Stuart or a Sir Joshua Reynolds, but his attitude towards beauty did not change.

No art object bought in a lifetime of collecting, however, thrilled him more than the acquisition he made that morning in Rome. A day later he wrote: "Then I came to a big modern shop and stopped, hypnotized. In the window, against a solemn drapery of old green, was a bust of a laughing faun. He was of the finest Parian, the eyes half-closed in lazy merriment, big leaves and grapes entwined in his hair, and so happily sylvan that I gave up to him wholly and stood grinning like an idiot in the street." The faun stood over six feet on his pedestal, which Tarkington later learned had been cut from a column that Hadrian had ravished from Egypt. "I had to tell myself that *Beaucaire* was still running in London, yet I believe I *must* have had him anyway! He really belonged to me. No antique comes near him, to my mind and heart." In a sense this "woodland, vineland, dreamland humorist in marble" captured Tarkington's own mood at this period in his life. Relaxed, gay, confident, and healthy again, he looked forward to a happy, successful career in the well-ordered world of 1904. He put the bust in the salon of his Roman apartment overlooking the Borghese Gardens, and every time he passed, he imagined such a faun lying languidly in the ancient forests of the Campagna, wine cup in hand and smile on his lips.

At the end of the mild Roman winter the Tarkingtons began their trek northward to Paris with home as the ultimate destination. They traveled leisurely through Germany and the Low Countries as they awaited the July 30 sailing of the *Noordam*. In Belgium they made an excursion to the battlefield of Waterloo in two automobiles rented from an agency in Brussels, an expedition which was Tarkington's introduction to motoring. Although he later became an ardent motorist, on this first automobile trip, as he bounced along at forty miles per hour over the old cobble road that Wellington's troops once had followed, he marveled at the stimulation provided for his spinal ganglia by the solid rubber tires and throbbing, two-cylinder engine. It is a great sensation, he wrote his nephews, "if one doesn't get nervous prostration." When the time finally came to leave Europe, Tarkington embarked for America well satisfied that his grand tour had been worth while; but he also was eager to get back to writing.

For personal reasons, however, he no longer wanted to return to Indianapolis. Marital storm warnings had appeared on the horizon, and he realized that friction could not be avoided if his devoted mother and sister and his equally demanding wife were to be neighbors once more. To forestall trouble, he stopped off in New York on his arrival in August. He and Louisa planned some day to build a house in Indianapolis, but in the summer of 1904 they had no domestic establishment to draw them back to Indiana. They took an apartment in the Beverly Hotel, west of Central Park, and by the end of September were well settled. As soon as their European purchases cleared the customs, they began entertaining friends, among the first of whom were the S. S. McClures. Another early guest was George Ade, who came to New York for the opening of *The College Widow,* a play about Purdue, which Tarkington saw on the first night and "wept with laughter all through." Meantime, Tarkington was being courted by publishers, especially Colonel George Harvey, head of Harper and Brothers, who soon invited him to dine at the New Astor Hotel with Mark Twain. While McClure, Phillips, and Company prepared *In the Arena* for book publication, Colonel Harvey talked Tarkington into promising Harper's a novel for the following year, perhaps to make up for *Cherry's* lack of success.

Despite a great deal of social activity Tarkington resumed work soon after settling down in New York. Although he had written two or three of his political stories in Europe and had described a visit to the Vatican for *Harper's Monthly,* his eleven months abroad had been a fallow period in his literary life. During the following autumn, however, he wrote one or two short stories, four articles, and dramatized *The Gentleman from Indiana.* His first task was *The Beautiful Lady,* a two-part tale suggested by an incident of his Paris sojourn. In it an American couple encounters the bizarre figure of a man sitting under a café awning with a theater advertisement painted on his shaven head. Tarkington had seen such a person and was excited by the chance to imagine a story explaining the weird sight.

He made the protagonist of the *nouvelle* an impoverished Neapolitan gentleman named Ansolini, who in desperation takes the humiliating job of "headlining" a popular musical review. As he sits in the Paris café, the beautiful lady of the title sees him, instantly senses his shame, and earns his gratitude for her sympathy. Using a plot that anticipates his play, *The Man from Home,* Tarkington concocted a pleasant story in which Ansolini exposes the fortune-hunting of a rascally halfbrother and saves the beautiful lady from making a disastrous misalliance. At the same time, Ansolini, who becomes the traveling companion of a young American also pursuing the lady, helps his employer win the girl. The story, which is cleverly done in Tarkington's earlier manner of elaborate plotting, took advantage of interest, then current, in the international novels and stories of James, Howells, and Wharton. It pleased the readers of *Harper's Monthly* where it first appeared, but it remains a minor though diverting work.

The major work of the autumn was a dramatization of *The Gentleman from Indiana,* a project that began a long and ultimately profitable relationship with the producer George Tyler. Tarkington had not intended making a play out of the novel; in fact, he had sold an option on the dramatic rights at the time the novel appeared. But five years later when no satisfactory script yet had been fashioned from the book, he tried his hand at the task. During all of November and part of December he worked on the dramatization, and when it was finished, Tyler was delighted with the script. So were Eugene Presbrey, his stage director, and Eugene Morgan and Julia Dean, who were cast in the leading roles; but after the play had been put into production, Tyler remembered, "We found it had only read well—it just plain wouldn't rehearse." The drama opened in Indianapolis in late February before a large, friendly hometown audience and critics from several Midwestern cities. But in spite of all the interest that the play created both the critics and the author's friends were disappointed. Tarkington was forced to agree with Percy Hammond of the Chicago *Post,* who said that the play needed a thorough overhauling. Yet subsequent tinkering could not save the production, and after another tryout in Boston in April, with Clara Bloodgood replacing Julia Dean, the play finally was dropped. Tyler was able to recoup his losses, however, when he produced a second Tarkington play two years later.

Tarkington recovered quickly from his disappointment over the play's failure, and 1905 actually was a prosperous year for him. The big monthly magazines at last were so eager to publish his work that he had more requests for stories and articles than he could fill. Although he wrote industriously, some of the solicitations he answered by digging into his earlier accumulation of rejected manuscripts, and during the year following his return from Europe he contributed to *Collier's, Cosmopolitan, Everybody's, McClure's, Metropolitan,* and *Harper's Monthly.* He was especially proud of being a *Harper's* writer, for that periodical enjoyed great prestige, even though its contributors did not take home the biggest checks. He had yet to win the critical approval of Howells, but he was appearing beside the "dean" in *Harper's Monthly,* along with Mark Twain, Edith Wharton, and other prominent authors.

Tarkington's residence in literary New York began during the golden age of the mass-produced monthly magazine. After the invention of the linotype machine and the halftone engraving, the quality literary journal of the post-Civil War decades was succeeded by magazines like *Munsey's, McClure's,* and the *Ladies' Home Journal,* all of which built up circulations in the Nineties of hundreds of thousands. The sensational exposés of the muckraking movement in the first years of this century further swelled their audience, and for every periodical that achieved half a million readers there were a dozen less successful ones competing for a share of the fast-growing magazine public. In 1907 in New York alone there were forty-five monthly magazines devoted to belle-lettres, most of them priced at ten cents. Although some of these journals were short lived, many were competently managed and alert to the opportunities of an expanding demand. They promoted their interests vigorously through an influential trade organization, the Periodical Publishers Association.

Tarkington came into direct contact with this trade association during the months he lived in New York. Each year the publishers sponsored an annual dinner for authors and other important persons in some secluded resort hotel. They chartered special trains from New York and Philadelphia to take their guests to the selected retreat for wining, dining, and merrymaking, and the next day they returned the grateful recipients of this largess to their original points of origin. The 1905 dinner at Lakewood, New Jersey, was an occasion that Tarkington remembered vividly for the rest of his life, because there he shared a suite with Harry Leon Wilson, George Horace Lorimer, and David Graham Phillips. Wilson was to play an important part in Tarkington's literary career, and during the overnight trip to Lakewood the two men laid plans for a playwriting collaboration that resulted in ten dramas. The relationship thus begun with Lorimer was equally important, for the brilliant editor of the *Saturday Evening Post* became a warm admirer of Tarkington, and as he built his magazine's circulation to three million in his thirty-eight-year editorship, he published more of Tarkington's work than any other editor. Phillips, whom Tarkington knew as an expatriated Hoosier and Princeton alumnus, became on that occasion an even closer friend and remained so until his tragic murder in 1911.

For other more frivolous reasons, too, the Lakewood dinner was an experience that some guests of the Publishers Association did not forget easily. In one of the rare altercations of his life Tarkington exchanged hot words with novelist Morgan Robertson, and when he was called a gilded youth who cared too much for fashion, he pushed Robertson's silk hat down over his ears. Jesse Williams separated the disputants and led off the infuriated Robertson, who departed muttering threats of revenge. Tarkington next met Colonel William Mann, editor and columnist of the *Smart Set,* greeted him cordially, and proceeded to lecture him on the vileness of his publication. Aghast at the enormity of this indiscretion, friends urged Tarkington to go to bed, but while Phillips, Lorimer, Williams, and John Corbin (then drama critic of the New York *Sun*) argued with him, they awakened Cyrus Curtis in a room across the hall. Curtis poked his head indignantly into the corridor and demanded quiet. At this unreasonable request Corbin became so outraged that he poured a bottle of champagne into a pair of shoes left for the bootblack outside Curtis' door. Corbin, so the story goes, had persuaded his wife to let him go to Lakewood expressly to meet and make a good impression on Curtis. After a good bit of dalliance, Tarkington finally agreed to go to bed to please his friends, but as soon as he was left alone, he got up, dressed, and sought out Wilson, and together the two new friends held a long talk with an interested stranger about their future playwriting plans. A week later both men received notes from this unidentified person, who had thought over their persuasive arguments and had decided to go with them to Capri for the next two years.

The return to Capri was actually a serious plan that Tarkington carried out with Wilson in the autumn, but first he had to complete a novel already begun for *Harper's.* This was *The Conquest of Canaan,* an Indiana tale that combines elements of both *The Gentleman from Indiana* and *The Two Vanrevels.* Like the former, the action is contemporary and embroidered with local color, and like the latter, the hero is a self-made lawyer in a town reminiscent of Terre Haute. There are, in addition, touches that come from Tarkington's year abroad and his growing interest in art, for the novel introduces a Paris-educated heroine and her artist grandfather. The plot of the story perhaps was suggested by Victor Cherbuliez, for whom Tarkington, like Henry James, had great admiration. He had read most of Cherbuliez and later acknowledged that the French novelist once was the "most persuasive" influence on him. There is a superficial resemblance between the motivating idea of *L'Idée de Jean Têterol* and *The Conquest of Canaan*. Both are tales of poor country boys, driven away by the hostility of their native towns, who return as adults to conquer; but the parallels cannot be pushed very far.

Joe Loudon, the protagonist of Tarkington's novel, who is regarded by the "best" people of Canaan as a juvenile delinquent, is forced from the city by the hardness of its citizens' attitude towards him; but years later, after putting himself through law school, he returns to Canaan, and through his industry, skill, and championship of the underdog builds up a large popular following. Eventually he triumphs over the rich but unscrupulous Judge Pike in the climactic episode of the novel. The story gives an extra fillip to the poor-boy-triumphant theme by providing the heroine with a history similar to Joe's. Ariel Tabor, who dazzles the local belles after her return from France, begins the tale as a hoyden scarcely thought fit company for the "nice" girls. She and her grandfather, a frustrated artist, inherit money and go off to Paris; he to paint and she to be educated. It is inevitable that Ariel and Joe share a common destiny in the resolution of the novel's complications.

For the first time, Tarkington allowed a novel to begin its serialization before he finished it, and two months after the first installment appeared, he had yet to solve some technical problems posed by the plot. The story required complicated legal manipulations, which Tarkington asked both his father and John Thompson, an Indianapolis attorney, to help him work out, and from May through July he wrestled with these unfamiliar details. On August 18 a few days after finishing the novel he wrote his father: "Never again a lawyer hero for me, though

I do hope I've got this one straight—thanks to your coaching." By then half of the eight-part serial had appeared.

When the book came out in the autumn, the reviewers were favorably disposed towards it, the public eager to buy it, and Tarkington again made the best-seller lists. Harper sold seventy thousand copies in the first six weeks, and paid the author a handsome twenty percent royalty; but despite the popular success of the story, Tarkington later disparaged it along with his other early works. When Harper brought out a new edition in 1935 and asked him to write an introduction, he found only a few passages that were bearable, and on the whole the novel seemed then "a pretty jejune performance." He regarded it, however, as an honest book written in the realist-romantic spirit of its time and perhaps worth reprinting as a period piece picturing some extinct types of people and their ways of thinking. Artistically, he felt, Judge Pike was too black a villain to be very credible, and the plot was spiced with more melodrama than he later allowed himself. Actually, the novel still is very readable and has its moments despite creaky psychology and excessive plot.

The same letter that announced completion of *The Conquest of Canaan* also broke the news of Tarkington's imminent return to Europe. He told his parents that the cost of living in New York had become so high that the outgo always seemed to match the income, and he added in further explanation that the social distractions of the metropolis made working extremely difficult. The trouble that he encountered in finishing his last novel suggests that social demands on his time supplied the stronger motivation to go back to Italy. The relative isolation of Capri perhaps seemed in the summer of 1905 the perfect answer to his need for uninterrupted quiet to work; but he undoubtedly was thinking, too, about matters of expense and future responsibility, for by summer he knew that his wife was expecting a child in midwinter.

Before sailing, Tarkington visited Indianapolis to see his parents and while at home told a newspaper interviewer that he planned soon to write a play for David Warfield. He further added that he had a second play in mind which he hoped to work up during his stay abroad. The lure of the theater was becoming irresistible, and after finishing his third novel, he was determined to give playwriting a thorough try. The next six years, in which he produced only one novel, were to be a period of intense preoccupation with the stage. He was getting farther and farther away from the Indiana scene, which eventually was to furnish him with material for his most significant accomplishment.

The arrangements for sojourning on Capri did not aim at perfect seclusion but rather at a controlled privacy. Harry Wilson and Tarkington, who were fast friends by summer, planned jointly to rent Elihu Vedder's magnificent new villa and to combine pleasure and playwriting under what seemed ideal conditions. Before mid-September they sailed directly to Italy accompanied by their wives, by Nora and Lucy Taggart of Indianapolis, and the Mark Lee Luthers (another writing couple). The ship, with "deck like a street in a prairie town," made a smooth crossing under skies that were all "sunshine & amber breezes." After a two years' absence Tarkington again found the island perfect. There were no newspapers, no autos, no subway, and no telephones to break in upon the tranquility, he wrote an old friend. Also to be enjoyed were the wonderful wines of the island and the dreamlike landscape that earlier had attracted such connoisseurs as Augustus, Tiberius, and Caligula.

Tarkington, however, made a miscalculation when he thought that he could work in the communal establishment he and Wilson had planned on Capri. He discovered that he was unable to write at all, and during the entire calendar year of 1906 he published nothing. "I pumped the cistern dry last year, I suppose," he explained to his parents four months after going abroad. Yet life at Villa Torre Quattro Venti was extremely pleasant, and his letters do not reflect any real concern over his inability to work. "We're rich again," he wrote home in describing the excellent sales of *The Conquest of Canaan,* and if writing was impossible, at least life on Capri was healthful. Tennis throughout the afternoon, then a cold bath, rough rub, and a walk, he reported of his daily regimen and added: "Thank heaven the waist-bands of my trousers are getting perceptibly loose." By this time the American colony also had been augmented by the arrival of two more couples, the illustrator Lawrence Mazzanovich and his wife and the Julian Streets. Mrs. Street was a former Smith classmate of Louisa Tarkington, and her husband, who had abandoned journalism for creative writing, was something of a Tarkington protégé.

The Harry Wilsons, with whom the Tarkingtons shared their villa, were a strangely matched couple. Wilson was excellent company, a good-natured, modest humorist whose rugged exterior belied a sentimental heart. He formerly had been editor of *Puck,* the comic weekly, and later would write such contemporary successes as *Bunker Bean, Ruggles of Red Gap,* and *Merton of the Movies.* Tarkington saw in him an artist who neither talked art nor took himself seriously and was greatly attracted to him. His wife, the illustrator Rose O'Neill, creator of the Kewpies, on the other hand, was a strange individual—difficult, exasperating, unpredictable. As Wilson's exact opposite, she was a huge pink-and-white, two-hundred-pound blonde, the largest Kewpie of them all, who talked baby talk. Wilson had been fascinated by her, and the Tarkingtons during a July visit to Kennebunkport with the Wilsons had found her rather charming. Living with her for an entire autumn, however, was a different matter, and even Wilson gradually became disenchanted as the weeks passed in the villa on Capri.

According to the tradition among Tarkington's friends, trouble resulted from prolonged exposure to Rose O'Neill's speech affectation. Julian Street, after listening to all he could stand, began, whenever Rose started her baby talk, to excuse himself, go to the balcony overlooking the garden of the villa, and pretend to be sick. After a while the baby talk began to lose its charm for Wilson, and he issued an edict against it:

"Rose," he remarked one day, "if you ever say 'woses' again, I'll divorce you."

The Wilsons remained on Capri several months longer than the other couples, and, though domestic relations apparently were somewhat strained, Rose curbed her baby talk for the time being. Months later in Paris, however, after the Wilsons and the Tarkingtons had settled down in separate establishments, the uneasy calm was broken one morning. Rose, who was a teetotaler and early riser, came into their apartment, all dewy and fresh, with a bouquet of flowers in her arms and shoved the blossoms under the nose of her husband, who was silently breakfasting and enduring the agonies of a hangover.

" 'Mell my pitty, pitty woses!" she cooed.

As the story goes, Wilson at this point folded his napkin, straightway packed his bags, and walked out on his wife; but they were not divorced immediately. Tarkington and Wilson subsequently maintained apartments close to each other, while Rose had a studio where she painted and sketched and occasionally entertained her former associates. Tarkington filed away for future reference the unique image of Rose O'Neill, and none of his friends ever doubted that she furnished the inspiration for the insufferable Lola Pratt in *Seventeen*.

Louisa's approaching confinement cut short the Tarkingtons' stay on Capri, for the superior medical facilities of Rome made the Italian capital a better place to be when the baby came. There both an English doctor and nurse could be engaged and a modern apartment rented. By Christmas the Tarkingtons were in Rome getting settled in a penthouse establishment on the top of the Palace Hotel. The apartment was high and quiet —four rooms and bath—all shut off from the rest of the building and opening onto a large balustraded section of roof, which served as a terrace and was equipped with marquee and chairs for sunbathing. Rome was again the attractive place it had been two seasons before, a city full of arresting colors, sights, and sounds. The schools of gray girls and blue boys passed by daily; the sandled brown Capuchins scuffled through the dust; gowned students kicked footballs in the Borghese Gardens; the band played on the Pincian Hill; the Triton again blew water from the green shell; nothing seemed changed.

Tarkington also found that the native charm of the city was enhanced that winter by the presence of a good many traveling Americans. While the Wilsons stayed at Capri watching the great 1906 eruption of Vesuvius, the Luthers and the Streets preceded and followed the Tarkingtons to Rome, George Ade soon arrived with a companion from home, and the Taggart sisters, whom Tarkington described as "strong in kindness and robust of heart," rounded out this congenial circle. In addition during this winter Tarkington sometimes saw Robert U. Johnson, co-editor of the *Century Magazine,* also a Hoosier by birth, and he at least made the acquaintance of Thomas Nelson Page, Virginia novelist, who later became American Ambassador to Italy. Another pair of wandering Americans, two of special importance, were Stoughton Fletcher, who came to see his new granddaughter, and his traveling mate, Jim Stutesman, a former member of the Sixty-third General Assembly of Indiana.

Laurel Tarkington was born uneventfully on February 11, and four days later, at the insistence of her grandfather, all traveling Hoosiers in the area were summoned to the Palace Hotel for the baptism. Besides Fletcher, Stutesman, and the elated parents, there were Jack Thompson, Joe Sharp, and the Taggart sisters. Lucy Taggart officiated as godmother, and Stutesman acted as best man for Fletcher. When Stutesman slipped a bank note into the hand of Dr. Nevin of the American Church in Rome, Tarkington wondered, as he later queried his father: " 'That sort of thing' never COULD have had anything to do with 'infant Damnation'?"

After joining the American colony in Rome, Tarkington found that the necessary quiet for writing still was unobtainable. The birth of Laurel added new responsibilities and complications to his routine and was accompanied by many distractions. Tarkington had to wait until later in the year before he could get down to serious work again. But even though his Pegasus was balky, he still was not interested in harnessing himself to a formal contract, and when his old college friend Jim Barnes offered twenty thousand dollars a year for all his work, he rejected the proposal flatly. Barnes, then an editor for D. Appleton and Company, traveled all the way from New York to see him but went home empty-handed after several days of arguments. The royalties from *The Conquest of Canaan* continued to roll in, and Tarkington let himself enjoy Rome with his friends.

One of the popular diversions for the Romans that winter was Buffalo Bill's Wild West Show, which then was touring the Continent to the huge delight of European audiences. Tarkington one day invited George Ade and Julian Street to go to the show with him. On the same occasion Victor Emmanuel III and his queen also decided to attend, but the royal party unfortunately gave the management insufficient notice, and when its request for tickets was made, the best seats already had been sold. Although Ade, Street, and Tarkington had choice seats, they arrived late and discovered that their box, which was next to the King's, was occupied by part of the royal entourage. The three Americans took in the situation at a glance and tried to defer to the visiting royalty, but their uninhibited Nebraska usher, one of Cody's employees, would have none of it.

"*You* got the tickets, ain't you?" he asked insistently. Then he tapped one of the trespassers on the shoulder and proceeded to order the Italians to leave. A shocked Italian usher rushed up uttering stricken apologies to his royal compatriots.

"Tell them people to git out o' there an' tell 'em to hurry," continued the Nebraskan.

"Imposs-s-sible!" replied the Italian usher. "It is the Prince and Princess di ——."

The Nebraskan cut him off contemptuously. Tarkington, Ade, and Street began a hasty retreat greatly embarrassed at the attention they were attracting. The unabashed American usher, however, became indignant at their unwillingness to insist on their rights and would not let them leave. An impasse seemed unavoidable. The Italian usher, fortunately, had the presence of mind to bring some extra chairs, and the problem was solved to the satisfaction of everyone but the Nebraskan, who was reluctant to accept a compromise in Rome that he would have rejected in Omaha.

After the Wild West Show Antonio Ansovini, Tarkington's private hackman, undoubtedly was waiting to drive the three Americans back to their lodgings. How Tarkington acquired a personal chauffeur in Rome is a story of considerable interest, for it illuminates character quite as much as events of greater intrinsic value. The faithful Antonio threaded his way through the fabric of Tarkington's career for more than a generation, but he was only one of many employees whose loyalty was complete and unwavering. Tarkington had a real talent for inspiring loyalty in those who worked for him—especially his drivers. Previously there had been Peg Hamilton, Indianapolis hack-man, who had attached himself to Tarkington about the turn of the century, and after Antonio there would be Francis Mulberry Chick, his chauffeur in Kennebunkport. Both Hamilton and Chick named their sons Booth in honor of their patron, and Antonio surely would have done so too, if his son had not been christened already.

The relationship with Antonio began one day in 1904 when Tarkington came on a crowd gathered around a horse that had collapsed between the traces of "the most disreputable rig in

Rome." Taking charge of the situation, he sent to near-by shops for wine and castor oil (why, he later could not explain), and while he was trying to administer this prescription to the beast, the horse passed out. He concluded that the animal was dead, gave Antonio a gold piece, and left; but the horse eventually revived, and the hack driver attached himself to Tarkington as his exclusive driver. Later the old horse died, and Tarkington bought the Italian another, an act which made Antonio his vassal for life.

Within twelve hours after his *signore* returned to Rome in 1905, Antonio somehow learned of the arrival and again presented himself to claim his old office, bringing with him the new horse Romulus, who "looked at me askance," reported Tarkington, "& knew me not!" More than three months later when he was packing to leave Rome, Tarkington was touched by Antonio's sorrow at the prospect of his departure and wrote his mother that he was tempted to take the Italian with him. By that time the driver not only was hauling Tarkington about but also was wearing his livery—an old Mackintosh that once had belonged to Tarkington *père* and trousers and hat that formerly had been worn by Tarkington *fils*. Into the hat Antonio had thrust a decorated line-drawing of his patron cut from a magazine.

By the time Laurel was six week old the mild Roman winter was over, and Tarkington grew impatient to move northward. At the first signs of spring he made plans to take his menage to Paris for an indefinite stay. Warm weather soon would return to the Bois and the boulevards, which he remembered so well from two years before. The Taggart girls, still in Rome, agreed to travel with them, and the baby's nurse also would accompany the expedition. Accordingly, early in the afternoon of April 4 they left the Italian capital by train for Paris, and by the next evening they reached the Hotel Regina where the Tarkingtons had stayed two years before.

Paris that April, however, was in the throes of political unrest. The state's long struggle to control the Church had reached its final round, and the streets were full of marching troops, patrolling cavalrymen, and machine guns mounted in positions commanding the bridges and boulevards. "You might think you were in Petersburg," wrote Tarkington after a particularly annoying encounter with the government's security measures. He had engaged his hotel rooms well in advance, but one day the manager announced that he would have to move because his suite had been rented to someone else. He indignantly took his family to the Hotel Continental after rejecting the Regina's offer to give him more expensive quarters at the same rate. Then somewhat chagrined he realized that the government undoubtedly had requisitioned his suite, the only corner one with a balcony in the entire hotel. All over the city such vantage points had been commandeered.

But if Paris was full of troops that spring, the surrounding countryside was as lovely as ever, and soon after reaching the French capital, Tarkington, the Taggarts, and Gamin, his French poodle, made an auto circuit of two hundred miles to Fontainebleu Barbizon, and other points southeast of Paris. It was a far more pleasant trip than the bumpy ride from Brussels to Waterloo two years before. From this time on Tarkington became a confirmed motorist, though he never learned to drive, and soon bought "an idle, roaring Fiat," which was as noisy as "an itinerant battle" and nearly as dangerous. Although it was a superb-looking machine, the Fiat was entirely intemperate, and when it was not in complete repose in the repair shops, it was in complete action. It terrified its owner as it charged down hills in the country at sixty miles an hour and only by the greatest of miracles in Paris avoided slaughtering pedestrians, who in 1906 had not yet acquired nimbleness in dodging motor vehicles. At night when he went to bed, recalled Tarkington, "that half-awake interval preceding sleep would be crowded with pictures reproduced out of the events of the day . . . terrified peasants escaping dimly into clouds of dust beside the road and crossing themselves . . . open-mouthed children screaming as they ran from our path . . . scared women with baby carriages trying to go both ways at once . . . pompous fat men outraged by the necessity to leap backward . . . faces in every distortion of fear and fear's close companion, hatred." When he could stand the strain no longer, he disposed of the Fiat and the daredevil Victor, whom he incautiously had hired as chauffeur. Selling the car, however, was easier than sacking Victor, he reported to his father: "I never discharged anybody before, & at the last moment, Louisa seeing my miserable anticipations of the final interview . . . bravely took it off my hands."

In May Tarkington leased a villa on the outskirts of Paris at Champigny-sur-Marne where he spent the next seven months and for the first time in a year was able to write. Known as Colline-des-Roses, the house stood on a hilltop from which Paris could be seen a dozen miles away. Often in the early evenings Tarkington watched spellbound from his balcony or terrace as the profile of the city became silhouetted against the setting sun. It was a beautiful place and came staffed with a full complement of servants, to which he added Laurel's nurse; and all summer the gardens supplied strawberries and fresh vegetables, the grounds ripe fruit, and the flower beds and arbors a wide variety of blossoms. But before settling down to work, Tarkington made three more short trips, one to London with the Luthers, the second through the châteaux country along the Loire, and the third to Normandy.

The tour of Normandy was especially significant because it covered ground that Tarkington was to use for the locale of his next novel. He traveled by automobile with two visiting friends from Boston, and both his new Bayard-Clement car—"very handsome and silent in running, like a swallow"—and new chauffeur—"half-cockney, half Parisian"—behaved beautifully. He was so delighted with automobile travel by this time that he thought he would bring the machine home with him, for he could not think of ever again being without a car. On the way back from Normandy he lunched at Dives at the William the Conqueror Inn, where he met a Princeton friend, then continued to Trouville and Le Havre.

The only disappointment of the entire trip was the famous bathing beach at Trouville. There the weather was warm, and he ran gaily down to the water in his bathing suit only to be stopped by a guard in a gray beard and red sash. He reported his adventure to his mother:

"Say there! [ordered the guard] You must keep to the left. You can't come into the water here."

"Why not? Can't I go into the water where I please?"

"Such ignorance! What strange place do you come from that you do not know that you can only go into water allotted to

your own bath-house, FROM that part of the beach allotted to
your own bath-house."

I entered as per regulations and was wading out with still
undampened bathing-suit and anticipations, when another pi-
rate bellowed at me from a row boat: "Say there! Where are
you going?"

"I'm coming out where it's deep enough to swim."

"Go back! You have passed the limit regulated."

"But I'm not knee-deep."

"Brigand! Have you no respect for regulations? Do you wish
to be arrested?"

I had to go back; and to get really moist all over was forced
to lie flat in a puddle. The French love it. Hundreds of people
were excitedly wading, ankle-deep. The ironical part of it is
their taking the trouble to wear bathing-suits.

When Tarkington once more began to write, his first production was a two-part story, *His Own People,* written at the urgent request of *Harper's.* Again making use of his European
sojourn and the international theme, he told the story of an
American youth who goes to Europe to learn about LIFE.
While the story was still in progress, he described it as a novelette about a prig with Rome for a scene—"surreptitiously a
satire on the Hump. Ward-Wharton-James style & point-of-view
—but that must never be known." The story turned out well
enough, although Tarkington had his doubts as he sent it off.
"I have at last completed," he wrote, "& sent off to *Harpers*
a novelette (they asked for a short story) and my conviction is
that it is AWFUL! I doubt their printing it." This prediction
proved to be accurate, for they did not publish the tale; but
their objection was moral rather than aesthetic, a reaction that
both astonished and annoyed the author.

He refused to revise the story to meet the objections of Henry
Mills Alden and F. A. Duneka, Harper editors, and cabled the
magazine to send the story back. Duneka wrote that they would
publish it in *Harper's Weekly* but were afraid to print it in
the monthly. Tarkington next offered the tale to Robert U.
Johnson, who replied that if Alden found the story frightening,
the *Century* probably would shy away too. Some months later
George Lorimer had the good sense not to be shocked at
Tarkington's story and printed it, without revisions or reper-

cussions, in the *Saturday Evening Post*. It was the first contribution Tarkington sent Lorimer, but it began a relationship
with the *Post* that outlasted Lorimer's editorship. In another
respect, too, Harper perhaps regretted their rejection, because
F. N. Doubleday happened to visit France at the time the story
was hunting a publisher and jumped at the chance to bring it
out in book form. Thus Doubleday, who no longer was Mc-
Clure's partner, re-entered Tarkington's life and ultimately became the exclusive publisher of his books.

His Own People is the story of Robert Russ Mellin, a callow
Midwestern youth, poet and real estate clerk, who accumulates
a bit of money and goes to Rome on a holiday. As the story
opens in the magnificent dining room of the new Excelsior
Hotel, Mellin sees in the brilliantly clothed cosmopolitan crowd
assembled there the people he most wants to live among—his
own people. Subsequently, he is dazzled by a French countess
who turns out to be the partner of two professional cardsharp-
ers. The burden of the story is the shattering of Mellin's smug
naïveté—accomplished by the loss of his money at an alcoholic
poker party in the countess' apartment; and the moral objection
was a kiss that the inebriated young man planted on the shoulder of a second woman accomplice during the bibulous fleecing.
Tarkington described the story to Johnson: "No young girl has
a baby in it . . . nor is anybody remotely threatened with a baby
. . . people sit up all night . . . a young American *kisses* a middle-
aged and horribly bored Englishwoman. . . . It's a serious study
of an American boy . . . who's accumulated some common
enough ideas of the 'World,' of 'Society,' and 'Life'—come over
here, where he doesn't belong (but thinks he does) and is cured,
morally and mentally—and suddenly."

Tarkington turned to other work even before learning that
Harper's would not print *His Own People* and invited Harry
Wilson to come out from Paris to begin the long-planned play
collaboration. Together the two men worked over the ideas
that became *The Man from Home,* beginning perhaps in the
middle of September and finishing in less than a month. On
the twenty-first Tarkington wrote: "We mull & roil & toil &
moil it over & over: we take long walks in the country & seem
to make some progress." Twenty days later he reported that the
play was finished except for revision, which he expected to be

tedious; but before polishing up the manuscript, he was going to take another motor trip, this time to Rheims and Compiègne.

While the play was in progress he took a day off to entertain the children from an orphanage in Champigny. The owner of his villa customarily had allowed the children to picnic on his grounds once a year, and the new tenant was happy to continue the tradition. He abandoned, however, the usual practice of confining the picnic to one part of the estate and allowed the children to have the run of the place. They climbed the fruit trees, picked the strawberries, and tramped through the flower beds. The gardener complained, but the children had probably the first unregimented day of their lives, and when the happy occasion ended, Tarkington summoned his chauffeur to return all the children to the orphanage by automobile. The distance was only about six blocks, but each child had the thrill of riding, and Tarkington remembered, as he watched their awed faces, a similar experience from his own youth. Years before, he had driven children from the Indianapolis Orphanage up and down the institution's grounds in the family carriage while his mother and Mrs. Benjamin Harrison were inside on business. It had been the first time in his life, he remembered, that anyone ever had called him mister.

At the end of December the lease on Colline-des-Roses expired, and Tarkington had to make new arrangements for his household. When his parents urged him to come home, he begged off by saying that he dreaded a winter Atlantic crossing, but he promised to make a trip home in the spring. He did plan to return the next year when his play opened, but he had decided to make Paris his home for the present. Accordingly, he took a three-year lease on an apartment in a famous quarter of the city at twenty Rue de Tournon on the Left Bank and near the Luxembourg Palace and Gardens. Leaving Champigny caused a real pang, and Tarkington wrote on December 30 that at twilight "we took our last walk along the hill-road and saw the moon rising rosily over the snow, and the white villages and flat white meadows below the ridge, cut by the long blue crescent of the Marne—and felt quite melancholy to be leaving this beautiful place, where we've had six months of health and rest and country-life at its best."

SEVEN

PERIPATETIC PLAYWRIGHT

Wнем Tarkington moved into his new apartment in the Rue de Tournon, he plunged suddenly into the pages of French history and literature. Even though the street was so short that the houses barely exceeded twenty, each had a story to tell, and he discovered that the "history of any spot, however small, in Paris, is the history of the whole of occidental civilization." The Rue de Tournon was a case in point: Molière had acted in the Condé Palace across the street from number twenty; Daudet had lived impecuniously in a little room at the top of number seven; Renan and Balzac once were tenants of the short thoroughfare; and John Paul Jones, died in lodgings at number twenty-one.

"Our front windows," wrote Tarkington, "look down into the courtyard of the Luxembourg: THAT goes back in history to the day when a Roman camp stood there." Meantime, looking to the right from the same windows, he could see the corner of the Rue Cassette "where on a better than merely historic day" two hundred and eighty-three years before "four well-known gentlemen met to fight 'the most dramatic & delightful duel in fiction.' Their names were Athos, Porthos, Aramis [*The Three Musketeers*], & d'Artagnan." The neighborhood moreover, was pregnant with the history of the French Revolution. Danton's and Desmoulins' revolutionary society, the Cordeliers, had met there, and municipally the quarter had been the Section Marat. "I shouldn't have cared to know THAT ward boss if we'd been here then," concluded Tarkington; "a prettier thought is the romance of Desmoulins & his Lucile," which began in the Luxembourg Gardens.

The Rue de Tournon not only evoked the riches of the past, but it also lay in the midst of the pleasant contemporary life of the Left Bank Bohemia. Tarkington joined the international colony of writers and artists about him, and when he was not writing spent memorable hours with his friends in the *bistros* and sidewalk cafés. In the afternoons he often dropped into the Café du Dome on the Boulevard du Montparnasse for a convivial hour, and when he wanted to have a party, he reserved a table at the Restaurant de la Tour d'Argent, the oldest and most famous eating place in the city. He also lunched weekly near the Gare St. Lazare with the Wednesday Club, which consisted of American newspapermen, among whom were Vance Thompson and William Hereford. Wilson, Street, and Luther, who already had settled down in Paris in near-by apartments, formed the nucleus of his American circle, but his friends of this period included, in addition, several artists, two of them being Blumenschein, who had illustrated *The Gentleman from Indiana,* and James Montgomery Flagg, who later became a summer neighbor in Maine.

As Tarkington sat at the sidewalk tables on the boulevards, he never tired of watching the endless stream of traffic. From all countries the multitudes came: exhausted Americans whose feet were killing them, Chinese princes in silk, swarthy Antillean dandies, ruddy English and pallid English, Europeanized Japanese, burnoosed sheiks from the desert, Sudanese Negroes in frock coats, Italians, Turks, and Spaniards. These added color to the native main stream: somberly clad burgesses, rich men who rode past in limousines, cripples who flopped by on hands and leather pads, students in velveteen, shabby young priests, sober workmen, and vendors of questionable wares. And then the women: rich ones in fine furs, poor ones also in fine furs; worldly women bedizened in electric landaulettes, and wordy women trundling carts of cut flowers, women in rags and tags, and women "draped, coifed, and befrilled in the delirium of maddened poet-milliners and the hasheesh dreams of ladies' tailors."

In the Paris restaurants and the cafés Tarkington acquired the reputation of a wag and wit. Among the American expatriates in Paris he became something of a legendary figure, about whom grew up a folklore of extravagant deeds. Although the details of these exploits may have stretched in the telling, they are rooted in actuality and more abundant than one can relate. Typical is Julian Street's record of a scene laid at Maxim's where Tarkington was dining on a particular occasion with a friend newly arrived from Chicago. When he asked his visitor if Maxim's was not a pretty gay place, the guest complained that the restaurant was overrun with Englishmen. Gravely considering an instant, Tarkington said he could fix that and then disappeared outside for a moment. He returned with a borrowed gendarme's cape, cap, and stick and made the rounds of tables occupied by British patrons. Soon the English diners began calling for their checks and departing, all except one argumentative group which wanted to know why they should leave. To these individuals Tarkington explained in his best broken English that a murder had been committed upstairs and that anyone not leaving immediately would be held for the coroner's inquest.

On another occasion, after dinner at the Taverne du Panthéon, Tarkington, Wilson, and Street (who reported the incident) were seated at an outdoor table while the crowds milled past. A young Frenchman accosted Tarkington and asked if he could not join the group in order to practice his English pronunciation.

"Why, of course," said Tarkington making room for him and introducing himself: "My name is Tarkington. If you will tell me yours I will introduce you to these gentlemen." The Frenchman dug in his pocket and pulled out a hunting license which he passed over to Tarkington.

"This is my *permis de chasse* with my name."

Tarkington looked at it intently, turned to Street and Wilson and said: "Gentlemen, allow me to introduce the Minister of Agriculture."

"But no, monsieur," protested the young man. "My name is here, above."

"But you pointed to where it says Minister of Agriculture."

In vain the Frenchman protested that he had pointed to his own name on the license, not to the printed signature of the Minister of Agriculture, but Tarkington refused to understand. Then Wilson, who apparently had been watching the passers-by, joined the conversation.

"You are a very young man to be Minister of Agriculture," he said politely.

"No, no, monsieur! I am not! I am not!"

"You aren't? You certainly look young."

Again the Frenchman protested that he had been misunderstood and tried to explain the mistake to Wilson. Wilson turned to Tarkington: "Didn't I understand you to say he was Minister of Agriculture?"

"That's what he told me."

By this time the Frenchman was gesticulating wildly and waving his hunting license in the faces of Wilson and Tarkington.

"No, no, no, no! I never say such thing! . . . I tell you I would not make such story! I am honest Frenchman!"

"You mean," asked Wilson gravely, "that the Minister of Agriculture is not honest?"

The conversation went on for some minutes while Tarkington and Wilson continued the comedy, but finally an onlooker declared audibly, *"Quelle blague"* and the excitable young man overheard the remark. Tarkington then admitted it was all a joke, and the Frenchman subsided.

The comedy, however, seldom subsided for long when Tarkington was around, and everywhere he went he continued his personal mythmaking. This was particularly true in New York at the Lambs and Players clubs, which he frequented each autumn when he returned to the United States to supervise production of his plays. One time at the Lambs he demolished a checkroom full of derby hats in perpetrating an elaborate joke, and another time at the Players John Drew looked out of the window and saw him in checked suit and chamois gloves on the curbstone quietly handing out oranges and bananas to pedestrians.

Even more fabulous was a third exploit involving Tarkington's passion for fruit and the help of a fellow prankster, comedian Jacob Wendell. The two men were returning home early one morning after a late party when they passed a huge display of fresh fruit somewhere adjacent to Madison Square. The weather being mild and the park benches well occupied, Tarkington had an idea as he surveyed the peaceful scene. Together he and Wendell bought armloads of fruit and entered the park. Working in relays, one member of the pair walked up to a sleeping bum, roused him, and announced: "Good morning, sir. A fine bright day. And here is Meadows with your breakfast." The other then stepped up with a contribution of fruit.

Hoosiers, too, were not exempt from his jokes, although Tarkington was an infrequent visitor to Indiana during his Paris years. On one occasion, however, when George Ade's comedy, *Father and the Boys* (1907), had its première in Lafayette, both Tarkington and Wilson happened to be in Indianapolis. They drove to the play's opening in two touring cars, Tarkington and friends in one, Wilson and companions in the other. The leader of the two-car cavalcade, Tarkington, stopped in towns along the sixty-mile route and informed villagers that Senator Beveridge and Charles W. Fairbanks, then Vice-President of the United States, were in the car behind him. When the second vehicle passed through the towns, Wilson, whose rugged features had earned him the nickname "Old Ironface," smiled and bowed benignly to the people.

If neither Wilson, Street, nor members of the Players Club were on hand, the comedy went on anyway with casual acquaintances playing the "straight" roles. Such was the case when Tarkington occasionally visited Old Point Comfort, Virginia, and used his guest membership in the Fort Monroe Officers Club. There one blustery spring day in 1910 he hailed young Lieutenant Frederic Price, who was propelling himself very casually by rope ferry across a fifty-foot channel from the officers' quarters to the club in the Casemates.

"Come back and pick up a landlubber," Tarkington called.

Lieutenant Price returned, and Tarkington climbed aboard the tiny boat, which then rocked and tipped and shipped water. Halfway across the ridiculously narrow channel, he ordered:

"Stop the ship, sailor. I want to offer a prayer," and while the six-foot craft lay to, securely fastened to both banks by ropes, Tarkington invoked divine guidance in "this wild storm at sea." Then he turned to his pilot:

"Pull for the shore and let's see if Keeny has forgotten how to make a real mint-julep."

Unfortunately, Tarkington offered his prayer on the wrong voyage, for not long afterwards he embarked again on the ferry-boat with another young artillery officer and a retired naval captain weighing 285 pounds. "The Old Salt casually leaned his ponderousness against the starboard rail," Tarkington later recalled, "and the three of us immediately entered the water, feet last. The uproar that followed was caused by the Artilleryman's indiscretion: he called out to inquire if the Naval old party could swim, and such language as ensued has seldom been heard anywhere."

But to return to Paris in the spring of 1907. If members of the American colony thought that Tarkington was an idle boulevardier, they were mistaken. He not only found time to eat and drink with many friends, show visiting Hoosiers about Paris, and to entertain George Tyler, but he also began work on a new novel, which he completed in four months. On April 15 the new story was one fifth done, and on July 22 he completed it at four o'clock in the morning, five days before he was to sail for home. During the writing of the novel, the last that he would produce until 1912, he kept what he called early hours: in bed by two and up at nine, with only rare nights out for the opera and theater.

The new story was *The Guest of Quesnay,* which he later regarded as a failure; but in several ways it is the most interesting of all his early works. This is the novel that shows most strongly the influence of Cherbuliez and perhaps Henry James, although the flavor of James may have derived independently from the common interest that both novelists had in the French romancer. *Samuel Brohl and Company,* which was one of Tarkington's favorite novels, suggested the plot and part of the technique for *The Guest of Quesnay.* If James had any direct influence, it may have been to provide further refinements in the narrative method, for the story is told through the device of a minor character who observes the main action from a vantage point. Reminiscent of James' *Madame de Mauves,* this tale is related by a painter-narrator fortuitously "on location" in the Normandy countryside where the plot is laid.

Samuel Brohl and Company is a brilliantly narrated story of an obscure German Jew who passes himself off as a Polish count and nearly succeeds in marrying a French heiress before being exposed. The duality of the character Samuel Brohl-Count Larinski is known to the reader throughout the tale, but the novel's fascination comes from the adroit manipulation of the plot. Cherbuliez, wrote Tarkington, had the ability to "construct the most delicately ingenious plots of his time." But even more impressive to Tarkington, as to James, was Cherbuliez' technique of revealing character by degrees. The heroine, observed Tarkington, "is never painted in detail at her first entrance; we are presented with a quick sketch more of her significance than of her looks; it is only at the end that we find we have realized her." In his novel Tarkington portrays his heroine, Louise Harmon, in this manner, creating the artist-narrator as the person through whose eyes she can be revealed gradually. *The Guest of Quesnay* also uses a dual character, Larabee Harmon-Oliver Saffren, who is cut from cloth similar to Cherbuliez' Brohl-Larinski. Just as the low-born Brohl is unacceptable to rich Mlle. Moriaz, so is Harmon anathema to his lovely estranged wife. There are important differences, of course, and Tarkington's story belongs to its time and place, just as Cherbuliez' did a generation before.

At the outset of the tale, Larabee Harmon, the most profligate rich American in France, is involved in an open affair with a notorious harlot, the Spanish dancer Mariana. Presently the dissolute pair is critically injured in an automobile accident, after which Mariana disappears and Harmon, following a long period of slow convalescence under the care of a famous psychiatrist, returns to the world as Oliver Saffren. The main plot element is the reconciliation and rematching of husband and wife. The husband does not know the identity of the woman he meets and falls in love with in the Normandy woods, and the wife, although she recognized her husband, forgives, takes him back, and fights both friends and enemies to hold him. The emotional climax of the story occurs when Mariana discovers Harmon-Saffren's whereabouts and flings herself before him in a desperate effort to win him back. This complication is resolved rather melodramatically in favor of the wife, but the denouement is justified by the logic of the situation.

Tarkington's experimentation with theme and symbolism makes this novel something to speculate about. He stated the motif as the "emancipation from sin by the power of good-will," but in a larger sense the story works out the Christian theme of redemption and treats symbolically the admonition: "Except man be born again, he cannot see the kingdom of God." The automobile accident is a cataclysm violent enough to provide an opportunity for the spiritual rebirth of the most miserable of sinners, Larabee Harmon, for he survives the crash only as Oliver Saffren, a penitent seeking salvation. The instrument of his redemption is the faithful wife Louise, who like the Virgin never abandons her errant child, and when he comes back contrite, she receives him gladly and provides the bulwark "between him and the destroying demons his own sins had raised to beset him." Reinforcing the Christian analogy, the artist-narrator observes that she is "not only wife but mother to him" as well.

Another significant character is Dr. Keredec, who serves Harmon-Saffren as priest and whose faith that his patient can be saved makes possible the redemption. Also as spokesman for the author, Keredec states the theme and its ramifications following the emotional crisis of Mariana's return. If a man shakes off his sin, says the doctor, the sinner then "stands as pure as if he had never sinned." But the consequences of the sin can never be effaced completely, "for every act, every breath you draw, is immortal, and each has a consequence that is never ending . . . though you are purified, the suffering from these old actions is here, and you must abide by it. Ah, but that is a little thing . . . compared to what you have gained, for you have gained your own soul!" To the theme of sin and redemption Tarkington has added a trace of Calvinistic determinism—filtered down to him perhaps from his New England ancestors.

As in his earlier stories, Tarkington again allowed his imagination to shape actual observations and experiences. The Amédée of Les Trois Pigeons Inn was drawn from an employee of Foyot's Restaurant in Rue de Tournon where Tarkington frequently ate. The inn itself probably was suggested by the William the Conqueror Inn at Dives, which he had visited during his tour of Normandy. When a newspaper interviewer asked later if the protagonist was taken from life, he replied that Larabee Harmon was a "composite of a thousand dissipated, dissolute young Americans who disgrace their country abroad. I have seen many of him."

Tarkington had misgivings about the story as he finished it. Although he had promised it to *Everybody's,* which began its serialization in November, he wrote his father a few hours after completing the manuscript: "I don't know what it is, at all— 'symbolism' in its way, perhaps . . . very different from anything heretofore of mine." Years later he believed that there was "no vigor in . . . 'The Guest of Quesnay,'" and he wrote reminiscently: "I was perishing, I think, and hardly knew I had anything in me that *wasn't* perishing." Yet the novel is more provocative than *The Conquest of Canaan,* its predecessor, and was reprinted in at least ten editions down to 1925. Tarkington suspended the writing of novels after finishing *The Guest of Quesnay* because he was more interested in the theater; and two or three years later when he perhaps wanted to write additional fiction, he found that his domestic relations were too unsettled for sustained creative effort.

Tarkington returned to the United States early in August for the first time in nearly two years, bringing with him his newly completed novel, his rejected novelette *(His Own People),* and the jointly written comedy, *The Man from Home.* He also brought Harry Wilson, his collaborator, and when the *Nieuw Amsterdam* docked in New York, George Tyler already was preparing for an autumn production of the play. During Tyler's spring visit to Paris Will Hodge had been cast in the leading role of Daniel Vorhees Pike, a Kokomo lawyer, and the title had been decided upon. Although David Belasco originally had asked Tarkington to write a play for Warfield, by the time the manuscript was finished more than a year later the producer already had found something else for his star. Tyler saw real possibilities in the play and was eager to produce it, although he first offered it to Nat Goodwin, who could not see himself as the Hoosier lawyer. When Hodge accepted the part eagerly, he was the third person to have a chance at the role of Pike.

This successful play, which occupies a comfortable niche in theater history, is familiar to anyone who was a theatergoer before the First World War. The second largest money-maker that Tyler ever produced, it netted six hundred thousand dollars during its five-year run in New York, Chicago, and on the road and paid Tarkington an average of two hundred dollars a week for the entire period. The play first set a Chicago record with 375 performances; then it was taken to New York where it ran for more than a year before going on tour. In some ways the success of the drama was unfortunate, because it kept Tarkington writing plays for the next three years, with diminishing results and with increasing frustration.

The play was a genuine collaboration between Tarkington and Wilson, each of whom contributed what he could do best. "There is no spot upon which either of us could lay a finger & say, 'This is mine,' " wrote Tarkington when the play was in progress, and later he declared that the plot was two thirds Wilson's and the character development two thirds his. "I can write plays," he added, "but I could not have written *this* play, nor half of it, without his collaboration." Into the drama both men inserted the characters and situations that they had observed during their foreign residence: unmarried American heiresses traveling abroad with more dollars than sense; unprincipled European aristocrats preying on American naïveté; homespun tourists from the Midwest aping the irreverence of Mark Twain's innocents.

Two Hoosiers in particular contributed to the character of Pike—Jim Stutesman and Stoughton Fletcher, visitors to Rome in 1906. Stutesman, the lawyer-politician from Peru, Indiana, was perhaps the more useful of the pair. "[He] has," reported Tarkington, "the most delicious *unction;* a most happy burlesque when burlesque is appropriate—& his solemnities, when he is 'deeply impressed,' *really* send me into risible ecstasies." Moreover, one of Stutesman's actual adventures with Lord Lascelles, attaché of the British embassy in Rome, wrote itself into the play. Tarkington overheard Stutesman one day telling Lascelles that if he ever came to America, he should not miss seeing Indiana. The young peer wanted to know where Stutesman lived, and when he heard the name Peru, he confused it with the South American country. Then he asked how the shooting was in Peru, and Stutesman, rising to the occasion, replied that it was great, the big game animal being the Inca, which was becoming scarce but still could be found in the remote mountain fastnesses of Indiana. Fletcher, the Indianapolis banker, supplied something of Pike's American point of view, though his distaste for things European was considerably more extreme than Pike's. Tarkington had to bully him into sightseeing in Rome, for he maintained: *"I* ain't going round smelling dead monks!" and he was generally contemptuous of European inefficiency and, particularly, Italian *dolce far niente*.

Tarkington and Wilson did not realize until the play opened just what they had created in Daniel Vorhees Pike. The character's response to Europe, especially his bragging about his native state, they had thought comic, and they had worked into the play "bits of stalwart patriotism" that they believed would amuse their audiences. When Pike was not being laughed at, however, the authors made him as agreeable as they could and gave him a melodramatic comedy triumph at the end. He was the guardian of two foolish but rich Americans about to throw away their patrimony by marrying predatory titled Europeans, and the burden of the plot was his successful mission to Italy to save his wards from their folly. Tarkington and Wilson expected their audiences indulgently to forgive Pike his nonsense when he complained of Europe and bragged of America, but the reaction was a complete surprise: "When our young man announced from the stage that he wouldn't 'trade our State Insane Asylum for the worst ruined ruin in Europe' they didn't laugh at him forgivingly, they applauded thunderously. In all such matters they felt as he did."

This miscalculation of the audience's response did not spoil the play, for it still was a good comedy whether the spectators laughed at Pike or applauded his provincialism. This unexpected reception probably insured the play's long runs in Chicago, New York, and on the road. The critics were as surprised at the applause for Pike as the authors, and Tarkington remembered that he and Wilson were accused of planning it that way. When *The Man from Home* reached New York in 1908, it was an immediate success, though some reviewers complained that it was full of nonsense and stupid attacks on European culture. From the very beginning—during three nights of tryout in Louisville—the comedy played to enthusiastic crowds and mostly sympathetic reviewers, and by the time it reached Chicago via Dayton and Columbus, actors, producer, and playwrights knew that they had a hit. After the Chicago opening Tarkington and Wilson, plus Ade and Street, who were on hand for the occasion, held a gay celebration lasting most of the night. But the really important event connected with the play's opening occurred during its one-night stand in Dayton where Tarkington met Susanah Robinson, the woman who was to become the most important person in his life.

No playwright ever enjoyed his trade more than Tarkington. Having been stage-struck since 1882 when he dramatized the story of Jesse James in his father's stable, he delighted in all aspects of a theatrical presentment. Casting, rehearsing, directing, and costuming were perennially fascinating, and during the initial stage of any play's production he worked eagerly with the actors and director. He mastered the craft of play-making perhaps better than any of his novelist contemporaries because he regarded the author as only one third of the team which created the drama. When competently urged by actors and directors, he never objected to changing lines, rewriting scenes, or adding business.

A young dramatist's initiation into the mysteries of play-production is depicted ably and no doubt autobiographically in the short novel *Harlequin and Columbine* written after Tarkington ended his 1907-1910 period of playwriting. Here Stewart Canby, whose first play is accepted and produced by the great actor Talbot Potter, finds that his precious manuscript is only a point of departure. Potter lectures him on the real nature of a play: "It won't be a play at all . . . unless the public thinks it's a good one. A play isn't something you read; it's something actors do on a stage; and they can't afford to do it unless the public pays to watch 'em. If it won't buy tickets, you haven't got a play; you've only got some typewriting."

On still another occasion Tarkington described the gulf which sometimes exists between the playwright's concept and the stage reality. When the author visualizes a love scene in a moonlit garden between a handsome hero and a golden-haired leading lady, Tarkington wrote, the dramatist sometimes has to alter his dream. He may find that "the harvest moon for his moonlight love-scene must be discarded because the moon-machine is creaky" and the audience can hear the moon go up, or he may discover that the heroine must play her part as a brunette because she does not like to wear gold wigs. Then, too, the playwright sometimes finds that the pathetic father role must be given to a "comedian who 'gets a laugh' upon all of his heart-rending speeches."

Tarkington accepted as truth Talbot Potter's view that the

playwright alone cannot create a successful theatrical illusion. For that reason he regarded the novelist's art, practiced alone and independently, as infinitely more subtle and difficult than the playwright's, for if the novelist is capable of realizing his conception, his characters will stay put and the dream will not suffer from the exigencies of staging. Yet Tarkington loved play-writing and approached the stage sensibly like a man trying to solve a difficult equation. What the actors could do must be equated with the technical limitations, and what the producer was capable of accomplishing must be reconciled with the public's taste. What the public would not patronize in New York, it would accept in Scranton, and against all of the other imponderables were the prejudices and preconceptions of the critics.

Hence it was a thrill to discover that *The Man from Home* was a play that people would go to see in large numbers night after night; but he was under no illusion that it was great art and years later wrote that it was full of typed characters and coincidental impossibilities "long since become stock stuff in the general discard." As much as he enjoyed being a successful playwright, moreover, he never took himself very seriously as a dramatist. On one occasion, he recalled, Wilson had said to him in Chicago where they had a hit running, perhaps *The Man from Home:* "Come on and go listen round the box office and hear something pleasant." They frequently loitered in theater lobbies to gather comments and on this occasion expected to hear patrons talking excitedly of the play about to be performed; but the first person they overheard stepped up to the box office and said: "Give me three seats for tonight; I never miss anything by George Ade, if I can help it."

During the next three years Tarkington and Wilson continued their collaboration, writing six more plays of varying merit. As soon as the success of *The Man from Home* was assured, they were besieged with offers to write plays, and they kept at the partnership long after their stock of usable ideas, characters, and situations ran low. In 1908 they turned out two plays and in 1909 four, but never again could they duplicate their initial smash hit. Three of their subsequent productions, *Cameo Kirby, Your Humble Servant,* and *Getting a Polish,* played on the road for one or two seasons each after short runs of two months or less on Broadway. The rest included "Cinderella of Tompkins Square," which was discarded by the authors, *Foreign Exchange,* a failure, and *Springtime,* which achieved moderate success.

Tarkington was largely peripatetic during his playwriting period. Sometimes he lived in his Paris apartment; occasionally he visited Indiana; but frequently he bivouacked in New York or other towns where his plays were being produced and tried out. On some occasions his wife and daughter stayed in Indianapolis while he traveled with his plays; on other occasions Louisa followed him about but left Laurel in Indianapolis. This life was not conducive to unruffled domestic relations, and as time went by, tensions developed; and as marital difficulties grew, Tarkington drank to obtain relief. In the spring of 1908, however, he was back in his apartment in Rue de Tournon with his family and Wilson and at work polishing up *Cameo Kirby* and writing *Foreign Exchange.*

When Nat Goodwin turned down the chance to play Daniel Vorhees Pike, he had asked Tarkington and Wilson to do another play for him, and thus the role of Cameo Kirby, Mississippi River gambler, was created. The veteran actor was delighted with the part, and Tyler produced the play the following autumn, but the romantic melodrama lasted only twenty-four performances in New York. Audiences could not see the aging Goodwin as a romantic lover and stayed away in large numbers. When Dustin Farnum was substituted for Goodwin, the road company packed the theaters along its route, and the faltering play began returning a profit to its authors and producer. But *Cameo Kirby* provided better material for the movies than for Broadway, and the hard-boiled gambler with a sentimental heart (derived perhaps from Bret Harte's John Oakhurst) became a favorite for Hollywood directors. The play was filmed three times in the old silent picture days, and as late as 1945 Twentieth-Century Fox, which had made it twice as a silent movie, paid twenty thousand dollars for sound rights.

Cameo Kirby is a romantic melodrama of the type brought to perfection and popularity before 1900 by theatrical craftsmen such as Bronson Howard and William Gillette. It is a story of the ante-bellum South laid in New Orleans and a near-by plantation, and its title character is an honest gambler falsely charged with ruining the leading lady's father. The real villain of the piece, who poses as the protector of the heroine, ultimately is exposed by Kirby, who then restores to the lady the deed to her father's plantation. The play, of course, was not so stereotyped in 1908 as it became after numerous motion picture treatments, but it belongs nevertheless to a defunct stage genre. There is some good theater in the play, however, particularly one effective scene reminiscent of Shaw's *Arms and the Man* in which Kirby escapes pursuit by coming in through the window of the heroine's town house and asking for protection. The New Orleans locale, which had delighted Tarkington during his courtship of Helen Pitkin, made a good background for this romantic story, and he liked the Louisiana and Mississippi River settings so much that he returned to them twice before quitting the theater.

During this period of non-stop playwriting, while Tarkington was a transatlantic commuter, his mother died suddenly of a heart attack in Indianapolis on April 17, 1909. Although he had not lived at home for half a dozen years, he had been a devoted son, and the death was the first of a member of his immediate family. Only hours before she died, his mother had said goodby to him at the train in Indianapolis when he left for a vacation at Pinehurst, North Carolina, but almost as he reached the southern resort, he received the news. The shock of her passing was profound, and he hurried home to be with his father and sister. Then after two weeks of emotional readjustment he called Wilson, who had been with him in Pinehurst, to come help him work off his grief. Wilson responded promptly and the two men plunged into a therapeutic playwriting session that lasted several weeks. Tarkington found that he could lose himself in work, a faculty he was fortunate to possess years later when his daughter died under tragic circumstances.

By June Tarkington and Wilson were back in Paris at work on another new play, this one *Your Humble Servant*, a drama commissioned by Otis Skinner, whom Tarkington first had met during his literary apprenticeship in 1895. Skinner supplied the idea for the play, discussed it with Tarkington and Wilson, and arranged to visit Paris in the summer to go over the first draft. The product of this three-way collaboration was a comedy that Skinner played enthusiastically for a year and a half and which was revived successfully by the Pasadena Playhouse in 1943. It was expertly tailored to the talents of Skinner, then fifty years old, who played the role of Lafayette Towers, an old-time actor. As Skinner remembered, it concerned "an actor of the old bad school—one of those simple fellows given overmuch to 'sound and fury,' whose mental horizon was bounded by backdrops, wings and footlights. I had known so many of them!"

Tarkington and Wilson devised a story for Skinner that involved a master-pupil relationship between a young actress on her way up and the aging Lafe Towers, a has-been. The heroine, Margaret Druce, is the orphaned daughter of an old actor-comrade who has entrusted the girl to Lafe, and during the play Margaret becomes a star while Lafe ends his career. In the denouement the actress, realizing that Lafe is more to her than teacher and protector, rejects a socialite pursuer and marries her guardian. The play was too sentimental for the taste of the New York critics, but in smaller cities it charmed both audiences and reviewers.

Despite the unfavorable criticism, the play really is a skillful piece of theatrical craftsmanship and shows a shrewd sense of drama and timing. As an example, the first act is a well-managed glimpse behind the scenes of Lafe Towers' shabby road company which is playing Shakespeare to a small-town audience. The action takes place "off-stage" as the sheriff of Weedsport, New York, sits on a costume trunk that will be seized on the closing curtain in payment of the company's debts. From the wings at intervals Lafe can be heard declaiming the speeches of the Duke of Buckingham in *Richard III,* and the actors make their entrances and exits from the fictitious stage to the real one. The stage-within-a-stage setting, of course, was not original, but the device was ideal for the sort of comedy edged with pathos that Skinner excelled in. At the end of the act when the sheriff carts off the company's costumes and personal effects, Skinner brought down the house and his overcoat, which was suspended among the backdrops for just such an emergency.

Skinner records in his memoirs an illuminating picture of Tarkington and Wilson as collaborators during this period. When he arrived in Paris in July, the playwrights had finished their first draft on schedule; and Tarkington read the manuscript one evening in his apartment, while Skinner listened and Wilson paced the floor. From time to time Wilson made a mild suggestion; then he progressed to acid criticism. Finally when an impasse was reached, he began protesting fiercely, and Tarkington, by that time aroused, answered Wilson's outbursts in kind. Skinner finding himself in the midst of a loud wrangle, wondered if he would have a play or not, and after the evening session ended, he spent a sleepless night at his hotel. Early the next day, however, both Tarkington and Wilson came to his quarters "buoyant, hopeful, smiling, declaring that last night's session had been one of harmony and understanding."

Skinner opened in *Your Humble Servant* the following autumn, by which time Tarkington and Wilson had written or revised four additional plays: *Springtime, Foreign Exchange, Getting a Polish,* and "Cinderella of Tompkins Square," the last of the quartet being the one rejected by the authors. They concluded rightly that "Cinderella" was a wooden piece of melodrama which should not be staged, and had it been produced, there might have been justification for the New York *Tribune*'s critic who wrote peevishly of *Your Humble Servant* that it was "one of those harmless but inevitable Tarkington-Wilson plays which fall of late upon the stage like autumn leaves in Vallombrosa." The other three plays were staged in the fall of 1909 and with Skinner's drama made four new plays by Tarkington and Wilson produced during a single season. In addition, Will Hodge's company and a number-two troupe were playing to capacity crowds in *The Man from Home,* and Dustin Farnum was touring in *Cameo Kirby.* Two of the plays, however, *If I Had Money (Getting a Polish)* and *Foreign Exchange,* did not get beyond a tryout at that time, and the latter never achieved more than a test presentment.

Foreign Exchange reads much better today than one would expect of a total failure. Although it degenerates into melodrama at the end, the first two acts treat seriously an American girl unhappily married to a French nobleman. The play represents Tarkington's last use for many years of the American-abroad theme and bears slight resemblance to *The Guest of Quesnay.* Again the scene is the French countryside near the English Channel; again there is an American painter who plays a minor role in the story; and again the action ends in a flight to a near-by port. The basic conflict in the play, reminiscent of the stories and novels of James, is between the moral codes of the Old World and the New, as represented by the unhappy American wife, Nancy Baxter, and her profligate French husband, Victor de Savergne. The play was unsuccessful, perhaps, because the material is better suited to the novel than the drama, and the playwrights could not fashion a romantic or comic melodrama out of a situation that was neither romantic nor comic. To increase the problems confronting this drama, there were casting troubles, and two months after *Foreign Exchange* had been tried out in Chicago, Tarkington wrote that no acceptable actress to play Nancy Baxter yet had been found.

Springtime, a happier experience for everyone concerned, utilized the fragile, elfin talent of Mabel Taliaferro. Again Tarkington and Wilson placed their action in Louisiana in the early nineteenth century, making their heroine this time the seventeen-year-old daughter of a stern planter of French descent. The heroine, Madeleine de Valette, falls in love with Gilbert Steele, the unwelcome son of a neighboring planter, elopes with him, and is disowned by her father. Meantime, the War of 1812 is blazing in New Orleans, and Gilbert subsequently is reported killed in battle. Madeleine loses her mind temporarily, although in the end when Gilbert comes back unscathed, she recovers, and her hard-hearted father is persuaded to forgive her. Reduced to its bald outline, the play sounds like a modern version of *Romeo and Juliet* with a happy ending; but the playwrights gave Mabel Taliaferro a story that she was able to make convincing. The critics were divided in their over-all reaction, but many of them were enchanted by the scene in which Gilbert and Madeleine fall in love at first sight and melted by the pathetic chapel scene in which the father lights candles to signify the "death" of his daughter, while Madeleine, who has sought sanctuary in the church, looks on in horror.

Getting a Polish underwent a good many vicissitudes before Tarkington quit the theater and cost more time and energy than it was worth. By the time the final curtain fell on it, he was weary from too much barnstorming and play-carpentry, and the law of diminishing returns was in full operation. This play

was first written as "Mrs. Jim's Romance," then produced unsuccessfully as *If I Had Money,* and finally overhauled by Tarkington alone and given its last title. It is a burlesque comedy
of manners somewhat in the vein of *The Man from Home,*
though the contrast is between the Far West and New York
rather than between America and Europe. Mrs. Jim, keeper
of a boardinghouse in Yellow Dog, Montana, and her deceased
husband's partner, John Blake, strike it rich, then go off to
New York to get a polish. After many adventures in New
York society, most of them concerned with the rapacity of various Easterners for the riches of the Yellow Dog gold mine, Mrs.
Jim and Blake find that they are really meant for each other
and go back to Montana. If this play had been created when
the Tarkington-Wilson partnership first was formed, it might
have succeeded as well as *The Man from Home,* but the play,
as it was written in 1909, lacks the sparkle and vitality of the
earlier hit. *Getting a Polish* ultimately ran a season in New
York and on the road with May Irwin as Mrs. Jim, but its
limited triumph was a Pyrrhic victory and left Tarkington
nearly exhausted.

At the end of 1909, after helping launch four new plays,
Tarkington was weary of the theater and tired of being a part-
time expatriate. Having so many plays on the stocks at once
had kept him in New York most of the fall and winter following his mother's death, and when the lease on his Paris apartment expired, he did not renew it but had his furniture and
art collection shipped home. He wrote Dan Calkins from
Indianapolis: "I'm tired of crossing back & forth, *more* tired
of N. Y.; if I can save a little I'm going to get a few acres in
the country near here, build a shack & settle down. I doubt
my capacity to *save* much, however. I make enough, heaven
knows, but it won't stay *by* me!" When another year had
passed, he was even more anxious for tranquility, but by then
his marriage was near an end, and domestic peace was nonexistent. The only work that he could do under the circumstances was to revise *Getting a Polish* for another production
in 1910, and during the following summer at Kennebunkport
he turned the play into pure farce, which then played forty-
eight performances on Broadway before going on the road.
Long fiction was out of the question during this unsettled

period, and the most that he could manage in non-dramatic writing was a revision and expansion to novelette length of *Beasley's Christmas Party*, which had appeared as a short story.

Tarkington's problems were formidable in this era, but he was not one to brood over them. He frequently found escape in the companionship of friends at the Lambs or the Players clubs where the company was always good; and when William Gillette, John Barrymore, Mark Twain, Howells, and many others—writers, editors, actors, producers—dropped in to drink or dine, he lived only for the moment. Tarkington always was the gayest of companions, an extraordinary storyteller, and when in his cups the most humorous fellow in any gathering. He regarded liquor as the source of infinite comedy, and his capacity for both was legendary. The limerick that Oliver Herford once made up for John Drew suggests something of Tarkington's great conviviality:

> There was a young feller called Booth
> Whose habits at times were uncouth
>   Once he sat a whole day
>   Drinking absinthe frappée
> Then tossed off six quarts of vermouth.

Underneath the frivolity, however, Tarkington was suppressing the accumulated anguish of marital discord, and as 1910 drew to its close, he was able, only with increasing difficulty, to drown his sorrows.

EIGHT

CRISIS AND RECOVERY

Tarkington touched the nadir of his physical and spiritual fortunes during the year 1911. Throughout the winter and spring the well of his creative imagination was as dry as dust, and in the face of marital difficulties he could write nothing. Two or three of his plays still were running, and his novels continued to sell modestly, but his future did not look bright. How many stormy scenes took place in private between Tarkington and his wife the record does not say, for he never complained of his troubles to his correspondents, and his friends only could make inferences; but in the summer, after nine years of increasingly tempestuous married life, a final separation took place. At the time of the parting no plans were made for a divorce, and Tarkington did not expect the break to be complete, but nonetheless Louisa brought suit in the autumn to dissolve their marriage.

The scandalmongers in Indianapolis were ready to pronounce the obsequies over Tarkington's literary career during this period of crisis. The detractors took his escape to liquor as cause rather than effect and saw only that he was drinking himself to death and no longer writing. As early as Christmas, 1907, he had shocked the pillars of the community by getting his name in the papers and police station records after a trivial scuffle with a reporter, and by 1911 he had not produced a novel for four years. Then, too, some of his townsmen looked askance at his living among the fleshpots of New York and Paris and were quick to condemn his cosmopolitan point of view and his easy familiarity with foreigners. These were the people who had delighted in *The Gentleman from Indiana* and

Monsieur Beaucaire and who believed that Hoosier authors, like George Barr McCutcheon, Meredith Nicholson, and Charles Major, ought to write at home while roaming imaginatively in time and space.

Tarkington, however, did not become permanently alienated from Indiana, and after his ordeal was over, he rooted himself in his home soil and regained the esteem of his community. Those who had counted him out were forced to admit that he had the vitality of Antaeus, for he bounded back to greater accomplishments than ever before. The decade which followed his physical and spiritual recovery was his period of most mature achievement, the era in which he wrote his enduring boy stories, his memorable tales of adolescence, and his Pulitzer Prize-winning novels. He also won a large amount of critical acclaim, academic honors, and a wide following of eager readers who bought his books in large quantities. But the man who produced *Alice Adams* in 1921 was hardly the same person whose personal difficulties threatened to end his writing career ten years before.

After the separation took place in July, Tarkington sought relief in another visit to Europe, his first in two years. This time he took with him his brother-in-law Ovid Butler Jameson and his nephew John, who had just completed the junior year at Princeton. As the party motored across France, he gradually left behind him the emotional turmoil of the marital break and conditioned himself for the final round of the unhappy contest, the divorce in November. He wrote Louisa regularly during the summer, but when she did not answer his letters, he wondered and worried about her silence, then probably guessed her intentions. She had written a conciliatory letter, which he had received on the ship before sailing, but there was no further communication from her until August. Then only after an urgent request she cabled him at Lucerne that she was well. In the meantime Tarkington played guide for his relatives over routes that he knew well from his years of *Wanderjahre*. Though Ovid Jameson had studied in Germany as a young man, Europe was a new experience for John. The tour, which began and ended in Paris, included three weeks in Switzerland and northern Italy and a leisurely trip through western Germany. The travelers were gone a little more than two months and returned to the United States about September 20 in time for John to begin his last year of college.

Paris was "hotter than Kentucky Avenue" in Indianapolis that July, and the tourists stayed there less than two weeks before hiring a car and chauffeur to take them to the mountains. When they reached Dijon after two days of motoring through France, Tarkington was glad to get out of the city, and the old delights of traveling by automobile came back once more. French roads, he reported, were such as "the Brunswick Balke Co. must have conceived to reward conscientious motorists." The travelers reached Switzerland on August 4 and after several days in the cool mountain air of the high Alps continued on to Stresa where they spent several days in a hotel overlooking Lake Maggiore. There Tarkington wrote: "We have a big balcony where John is stretched on a sofa . . . Ovid reading and I writing—a tropical garden below us bordering the lake, down to which the mountains run. Neapolitans sing & play for us in the garden as the moon comes up and it is Italy indeed." The former charm was there, but after a five-year absence he found that his command of Italian was growing rusty.

During the trip across Switzerland Tarkington regained his old gaiety one evening after an astonishing run of luck at baccarat in a Chamonix casino. Although he was not much of a gambler (only an occasional horse-race bettor), on that day in the famous town at the foot of Mont Blanc he played recklessly and could not lose. When he counted his chips, he had won four thousand francs. Sitting next to him, meanwhile, was a beautifully dressed woman whose luck was as bad as his was good. She had lost a large part of the money he had won and seemed greatly disturbed by her ill-fortune. Tarkington was distressed by the turn of events and without a second thought gave the woman a large part of his winnings. Having done that, he next invested the rest of the four thousand francs in a supper for nearly everyone present: the attractive stranger, the head of the casino, the manager of the hotel, the director of the theater, and a couple of actors. The woman who had lost at baccarat turned out to be the star of a vaudeville company then playing at Chamonix, and at the impromptu supper she sang her own songs and proposed toasts to the gallant Americans. Her fellow performers also recited and sang, and everyone joined in the camaraderie. It was "quite a supper," reported Tarkington, who added that he and John concluded the evening by teaching the entire group to say "to hell with Yale," which they all shouted in unison, standing. The theatrical members of the supper party promised their hosts that they always would interpolate the yell into every performance for the rest of their lives when they saw Americans in the audience.

Following the interlude at Lake Maggiore Tarkington took his companions to visit the Italian Tyrol, after which he planned to continue on to Germany by recrossing Switzerland, but when they attempted to climb the Stelvio Pass, torrential rains had closed the roads at the higher elevations. On the way from Tirano to Bormio the car came to a halt behind a string of vehicles drawn up at the edge of a swollen muddy stream that poured down a mountainside and spilled across the road. Although the water cascaded over the highway, it was not very deep, and Tarkington's chauffeur was willing to try fording the torrent; but just as the car pulled ahead of the less daring motorists, an avalanche broke loose above them. The chauffeur acted prodigiously to get out of the way and for a few seconds backed the car at top speed along the narrow mountain road. A boulder as big as an automobile, which barely missed them as they raced in reverse to safety, came along, reported Tarkington, "not tumbling over and over, but *skimming* like a shingle sliding into a sewer hole after a storm." After their narrow escape they retreated down the mountains all the way to Verona to wait until the lower Brenner Pass, also closed by floods, was reopened two days later.

The last leg of the summer tour was the drive through Germany via Innsbruck, Austria, to Munich, Nuremberg, Heidelberg, and Baden-Baden, a circuit that took ten days. Early in September Tarkington and his party crossed the German border at Strasbourg, then part of Germany, and encountered heavy troop concentrations. "We rolled not alone," wrote Tarkington; "batteries of light artillery rolled beside us; uhlans were seen riding on all the roads; and infantry regiments moved in the direction—toward Nancy—that we were taking." The military activity, they later learned, was a result of the Second

Morocco Crisis between France and Germany, an event which foreshadowed the outbreak of war three years later. As the travelers waited for the road barrier across the frontier to be lifted, they saw German uniforms lining the border for miles in both directions. Then after driving a few kilometers into France, they observed French troops also mobilized. Tarkington wondered at all the commotion but knew that war could not come between two enlightened nations in the second decade of the twentieth century. He remembered what a French engineer had told him only a few weeks before: "The German people . . . are busy and prospering; they are not so insane as to wish to ruin themselves and us with a war."

The ominous rumblings in Europe, however, were driven from Tarkington's mind soon after his arrival in New York in late September. He found out then why he had received no letters from his wife during the summer: she had determined to sue for divorce during the fall term of the superior court. Accordingly, in October she charged him with mental cruelty and asked for custody of Laurel. Tarkington had wanted to continue the unsuccessful marriage because of his five-year-old daughter, and his reaction to news of his wife's decision was chiefly sorrowful. He wrote his father that the family must hold Hauté down in her championship of him: "Louisa is, and always will be, dear to me, of course—and whatever she may do to me, so will I not do to her." He added that he did not want to return to Indianapolis for some time because "agitations make one talkative and belligerent. I was too close to it all—too much concerned, too much a husband, too little a friend." But a month later when his brother-in-law wired him to come home for a few days to attend to business matters, he changed his mind and returned to Indiana to stay.

Before the divorce came up for trial, news of the suit was impossible to keep quiet, and the newspapers headlined the story: "Tarkington charged with cruelty." Tarkington, who had remained in New York, recoiled from the publicity. "This will end my book-writing for a while," he told his father; "nobody would buy a book by a wife-strangler. . . . When Louisa told me she wished to change husbands, I agreed, but I thought the divorce 'charges' could be kept quiet." A paragraph later he said of Louisa: "She has been too much coddled. She loves

excitement & war (with everything on her side.) . . . Don't you
. . . be too gentle: she'll not be helped by that." And in another
letter he had written: "I can help her no more—my presence
had got to be a reproach to her . . . and she hated it."

Publicly he answered the newspaper story of cruelty by refusing to believe that his wife had charged him with the alleged
misconduct. He declared that the real trouble lay in his manner of life, which demanded much traveling about in the pursuit of his literary and dramatic career. To a woman who loved
a home and a quiet existence, he said, this nomadic life was
unbearable and who could blame her? He denied that he was
in the habit of making unexplained disappearances for a week
at a time, as the newspapers had reported, and vigorously asserted that Louisa could not have made such a charge: "She is
too fine a woman to have said it—for it is not true."

The divorce was granted on November 13 and the custody
of Laurel given to Louisa for eleven months of the year. Tarkington was to see the child at all reasonable times when they
were in the same city, and he was to receive prompt and regular reports on her health and details of life. He was particularly
anxious that Laurel should always keep his picture in her bedroom and never change her name from Tarkington, and these
stipulations were written into the decree. Then to clear the
air, Louisa signed a statement acquitting her former husband
of any "intentional unkindness to me" and declaring: "The
differences between us are of temperament and habit, and,
after nine years of effort, it is apparent to both of us that we
cannot reconcile our views of life."

Providentially for Tarkington during this period of emotional turmoil, Arnold Bennett arrived from England to make
a much-publicized tour of the eastern United States. No novelist since Dickens was given such a reception as Bennett received, and Tarkington took a hand in entertaining the British
visitor. The two men must have known each other in France
when Tarkington was living at Champigny and Paris and Bennett was writing *The Old Wives' Tale* at Fontainbleau. In all
events, Bennett looked up Tarkington in New York on November 2 and found him at the Princeton Club looking "rather
round-shouldered and ripe." Then two days later he accepted
Tarkington's invitation to attend the first Harvard-Princeton

football game in fifteen years. The visitor, amazed at the sight
of a college town during a football week end, noted in his
journal:

>   Nassau Club, Confusion.
>   Princeton Inn, Confusion.

And of the game he observed:

>   Naïve and barbaric! . . .
>   Left at half time.

Tarkington, however, shared all the enthusiasm of the under-
graduates over Princeton's 8-6 victory, and when a Princeton
back ran ninety-five yards for a touchdown in the second quarter, Tarkington was as excited as anyone.

Five days after the divorce decree was issued Tarkington entertained Bennett in Indianapolis. He invited the British
novelist to visit Indiana to see a typical Midwest city, and Bennett obligingly squeezed a week-end stopover into his crowded
schedule. While he was in Indianapolis, he met Meredith
Nicholson, Senator Beveridge, Mrs. Benjamin Harrison, and
Tarkington took him to call on Riley, who was recovering from
a paralytic stroke. Bennett enjoyed his brief visit but noted
objectively in his journal as he departed for Philadelphia: "Indianapolis just beginning to spend money. . . . Just beginning
to be sure that Indians aren't coming. . . . Even now it's rather
daring to buy a picture. Formerly you could spend money only
on a house, because that was solid and could be sold."

After Bennett left, Tarkington began a period of solitary
readjustment in the old homestead at 1100 North Pennsylvania
Street where he had not lived permanently since 1903. His sister, however, still lived across the street with her husband and
three boys, and his father and Linda, a much younger second
wife, also were close at hand. The old house, too, was a comfort in this period of crisis, for he was surrounded by "the kind-
est ghosts in the world." His mother, who had loved the place,
had lived and died there; he had grown up in the old home;
his maternal grandparents had spent a serene old age there; and
gay aunts and uncles had visited frequently. "It's the most
personal house in the world," he later wrote, and when he
finally returned home, it had seemed silent and reproachful
"like some one gently mourning an unkindness from a close
friend."

Tarkington's first problem at the beginning of 1912 was liquor. He had gone too far to reform himself into a moderate drinker and was slowly killing himself with alcohol. The only course was to give up liquor altogether, and one day early in the year, after a severe heart attack, he suddenly took stock of himself and his future and swore off drinking for good. His decision was unequivocal and proved to be permanent. He remembered for the rest of his life the instant that he made up his mind—9:40 A.M., January 16, 1912:

> I remember the exact time, [he reminisced to a newspaper interviewer in 1945] because it was then, right here in Indianapolis, that I suddenly decided I preferred to die sober. Got so I craved a drink before breakfast. . . . But as it turned out, it required surprisingly little will power to climb aboard the wagon. Couple of days later I was in the University Club and a fellow asked me to have a drink. I took one whiff and it smelled like kerosene. That was that.

Tarkington's old-age memory of the two-day period between his last drink and his return to the club, however, telescoped the time interval and oversimplified the ease of his physical rehabilitation. His essay "Nipskillions," written in 1916, more nearly recreates the situation as it actually occurred. There he describes the experience of a painter "friend," whose ordeal parallels his own. The painter on the morning of his fateful decision to drink no more goes back to bed to sleep until his nerves are somewhat quieted and stays there for ten days, after which he gets up a teetotaler. Tarkington actually remained in bed for several weeks under the care of his friend and physician Carlton McCulloch, then perhaps a month later returned to the club, sat with his friends during the cocktail hour, and sniffed the drink that smelled like kerosene. Although the painter of the essay becomes a "Nipskillion" (a reformed drinker who will not let anyone else drink), as Tarkington did not, he speaks for the author when he says: "I knew I couldn't 'drink moderately.' I didn't want to 'drink moderately.' I wanted to drink immoderately—enough for comedy, a hearty laugh, not a mere little smile of quiet exhilaration. . . . So I made up my mind, not that I would quit but that I *had* quit." Tarkington later wrote one more article on this subject, in which he declared that nothing is more foolish than being proud of an ability to drink more than any of one's friends, as he once had been able to do.' Yet the drinking problem was personal with him. He recognized that abstinence is necessary only for some people, and he became neither a Prohibitionist nor a host who denied his guests beverages they were accustomed to.

The strongest motivation of all in his physical recovery was a woman to whom he was tremendously attracted. His painter-spokesman in "Nipskillions" says: "I was anxious to marry a woman to whom I'd been 'respectfully devoted' . . . and when I asked her she seemed startled and compassionate, and rather shocked—as if a lunatic had proposed to her! Of course that did give me something of a jolt; I almost saw myself clearly that day." This statement, to be sure, exaggerates the actual situation, but Tarkington had become greatly interested in Susanah Robinson of Dayton, Ohio, and she did ask him to give up drinking. After meeting her at a dinner party in the home of his Princeton classmate Harry Daniels in 1907, Tarkington had seen her only once again, then quite by accident, before he began courting her; but she had made an indelible impression, and he went to see her soon after he was divorced. The influence of this charming lady, then, began dramatically early in 1912 and continued the rest of his life; for they were married ten months later and lived together in complete happiness for thirty-three years.

Tarkington's life breaks sharply at the critical date of January 16, 1912. After the emotional knots of the divorce had been unraveled and the physical specter of alcoholism conquered, he went back to his desk, and gradually the old delight in work returned; and with it came the old capacity to see and to do. Eight months later he was able to write: "Now I'm in condition as I was ten years ago, but with a very piquant realization of wasted time. . . . I want to make up for that time & have the energy to do it, & the 'stuff' stored. I don't want to lose any *more* time." He did not, for the amount of writing that he accomplished during the next ten years is prodigious, and its quality is uniformly high. A year later he advised Julian Street that to accomplish real work a writer must "go into training in the abstemious sense . . . give up gayeties and much enjoyable company, just as an athlete does. You have to make your mind do its calisthenics. Solitude is almost the whole of that prescription."

Soon after he returned to Indianapolis in November, 1911, he told an interviewer that he planned to get back to prose fiction by warming up with short stories. Playwriting and fiction are two very different types of work, he said, "and I feel that I am very far away from fiction now." Accordingly, he began with one of his best stories, "Mary Smith," a tale of a college sophomore on vacation, for which Donald Jameson, then in his second year at Princeton, provided the inspiration. This engaging story tells of the experiences of Henry Millick Chester on his way home at Christmas from an Eastern college to a Midwestern city. At breakfast in the dining car he sits beside a girl who charms him instantly, and after their meal together they retire to the observation car to carry on an inane conversation about the Great Topic—LOVE. Just as Henry reaches the point where he can hardly contemplate existence without this marvelous companion, the porter announces the imminent arrival of the train in Henry's home town. Panic seizes the youth, who realizes that he does not know the girl's name or address, and as the train slows down to enter the station, he begs the young lady to give him that information. She agrees, but only on the condition that he not open the sealed envelope containing the data until after he is off the train. He fulfills his obligation faithfully, but when his trembling fingers tear open the envelope, he reads: "Mary Smith, Chicago, Ill."

A first-rate story of adolescence, this tale foreshadows the better known *Seventeen*. Tarkington later recalled that his sophomore nephew had not been pleased with "Mary Smith," for it was, he reported quoting Donald, "an insult to every college man in the United States!" George Lorimer was delighted to receive the manuscript in June and wrote back promptly: "Mary Smith is a perfectly corking story." He ordered his treasurer to pay one thousand dollars for the tale, then wondered: "It is so long since we have had anything from you that I am not quite sure what your rate is now. . . . If this isn't entirely satisfactory, let me know." At last Tarkington was working with material close at hand and shaping it with a wonderfully acute comic sense. "Mary Smith" was the type of thing his talents best qualified him to write, for he was always the interested and sympathetic uncle who enjoyed observing and recording the activities of his nephews. His humorously exaggerated accounts of the problems of children and adolescents mirrored faithfully the comedy in American middle-class life.

Tarkington knew that he was following the right path in the work he had begun, and his next project was *The Flirt,* the first novel in his later manner. In it he abandoned elaborate plot, which had been his "stumbling block and curse for years," and let the characters make their own story. He recalled, after completing the novel, that he had smeared his early books with plot, and *"every* time it was the big flaw"; and he added: *"the thing I depended on to make a story* INTERESTING *was the* MOST *uninteresting thing about it."* Recommending his new method, he advised: "Think of them [characters] in their relation to one another and that's all the plot you should have. Your struggle should be against everything extraneous. It's unusual poignancy that makes a book unusual, not unusual plot." As he contemplated his literary career up to 1913, he concluded: "If I could, I would wipe out the books I wrote while I was *having* experience."

The Flirt is far from Tarkington's best novel, but he knew what he was doing when he wrote it, and the material develops leisurely and skillfully. "Nothing happens till the close," he explained: "It's just a slowly intensifying situation." Nominally, it is the story of Valentine Corliss, who returns to his Midwestern home town, after seventeen years abroad, intent on selling stock in a nonexistent Italian oil field. In the course of the tale he dupes Cora Madison's father into becoming an officer in the bogus oil company, swindles Cora's fiancé Richard Lindley out of fifty thousand dollars, and in the end is unceremoniously killed by Ray Vilas, one of Cora's rejected suitors. Despite the chance for melodrama, Tarkington underplays the short, violent ending, and in anticipating reader annoyance at a murder as unforeshadowed as in real life, he declared that "nothing in the world would have been easier than to split their [the readers'] gizzards with all kinds of thrills," if he had wanted to be sensational.

In several respects *The Flirt* was a proving ground for fictional materials that were subsequently to occupy a great deal of Tarkington's attention. Not only is it his first domestic novel, but it also is his first long fiction making significant use of a Midwestern city that is Indianapolis thinly disguised. The Madison family, moreover, belongs to the same submerging middle-class group that is treated later in *Alice Adams,* and the history of the Corlisses, who have been one of the city's great families, suggests the family dynasty chronicled in *The Magnificent Ambersons.* Cora, the flirt, is also the first of a good many selfish, egoistic women who make life a hell for their lovers and husbands in Tarkington's novels, and finally, it should be noted, Hedrick Madison, Cora's younger brother, is the earliest of Tarkington's juveniles, the prototype of Penrod Schofield.

Cora, the flirt, is Tarkington's most impressive creation up to this time. She is a terrifying beauty who actually is a far greater menace than the confidence man Corliss. Irresponsible, thoughtless, self-centered, she embroils her father and her fiancé in Corliss' schemes, blights her older sister's life, and then contemptuously dismisses Corliss, whom she also bewitches, because he can offer her only love without respectability. Yet when Cora finds that she has been made a fool of, she does not have to reap the whirlwind of her egomania; and after Corliss' bungling swindle fails, she skips town with still another of her submissive males, one who is willing to take her on the rebound with no questions asked. The reader ends the book feeling that life for Cora's husband will be, in the philosopher's words, "nasty, brutish, and short," before he is tossed aside for still another man. Cora is the *femme fatale* of literary history, a kindred spirit, certainly, with Circe, Becky Sharp, and Sister Carrie, and one of many such Tarkington ladies.

Tarkington's growing powers of narration and insight are nowhere better revealed than in a poignant sub-plot of *The Flirt* involving the bumptious younger brother and shy Laura Madison, Cora's older and quite different sister. In this episode the *enfant terrible* Hedrick, momentarily indiscreet, kisses a half-witted little girl who happens into the Madison backyard. When the defective child pursues the boy across the lawn, screaming for more kisses, Laura unfortunately witnesses the scene. Later Laura makes the mistake of telling Cora about it, and the thoughtless younger sister uses the story to blackmail Hedrick. The boy seeks revenge on Laura, ferrets out the hiding place of her diary, in which she has confided a secret passion for Cora's young man Richard, and sends the book to Richard. This terrible deed, which the boy sees only as a way of getting even, is cruelty beyond words for the sensitive older sister. Tarkington's evocation of Laura's anguish at the moment she realizes the enormity of her brother's act is a masterpiece of pathos.

One of the significant aspects of *The Flirt* for any historically minded reader is the fidelity of the Indianapolis setting in which the story is laid. As a perceptive observer of change, Tarkington noted with great interest the differences between the city of his young manhood and the Indiana capital of 1912, and the midland city of the novel is the same hot, thriving town that Tarkington returned to after years of living abroad. Corliss Avenue, which might have been Meridian or Pennsylvania streets, was long, straight and "still shaded by trees so noble that they were betrothed, here and there, high over the wide white roadway." Architectural transformations, however, staggered the exile, who remembered that Queen Anne once had dominated the street named for his grandfather. There since had been a revolution that had been a riot, and the evidences could be seen in the outbreak of Gothic, Tudor, Tuscan, and Moorish buildings that lined the avenue. Yet it was a pleasant street in spite of the changes and also in spite of the long, gray smoke-plume which crossed the summer sky and dropped an occasional speck of soot on Corliss' suit. Some of the houses, relics of the cupola and mansard days, remained as he remembered them, but the herds of cast-iron deer that once disported on the lawns had disappeared. "He wondered in what obscure thickets that once proud herd now grazed; and then he smiled, as through a leafy opening of shrubbery he caught a glimpse of a last survivor, still loyally alert, the haughty head thrown back in everlasting challenge and one foreleg lifted, standing in a vast and shadowy backyard with a clothesline fastened to its antlers."

The novel's weaknesses stem from a fundamental incongruity in the subject matter. The presence of a swindler in the circle of the commonplace Madisons is so incredible that the character of Valentine Corliss is never quite convincing. By the very nature of the story Corliss must be a major figure and share the center of the stage with Cora, but the confidence man is not Tarkington's forte, and Corliss remains only a *ficelle* by which the other story elements are manipulated. He is too smooth a villain at the outset to conduct his fraudulent scheme so clumsily at the end. Richard, moreover, is too faithful to the faithless Cora, too docile in his adoration, and too gullible in the swindle to be very real. Nevertheless, Cora and Hedrick emerge as vivid personalities, Laura and the Madison parents are authentic minor characters, and the midland setting is brightly sketched. The defects seem attributable still to Tarkington's old bugbear plot, and while the novel is imperfect, it looks ahead to greater things.

Not only was *The Flirt* Tarkington's first Indianapolis novel, but it also was a first in several other respects. After writing it in Indiana in the late spring and summer, he sent the manuscript to the *Saturday Evening Post,* and Lorimer accepted it eagerly as the first of Tarkington's many novel-length serials that subsequently would appear in the magazine. Then while Lorimer made plans to begin the story in December, Doubleday, Page and Company prepared to bring it out in book form in the spring. It was the first of more than thirty Tarkington titles that they and their successors ultimately were to issue. And finally, the new story would carry after its title page the first of many dedications to "Susanah."

During and after the writing of *The Flirt* Tarkington made several trips to Dayton to see the object of the dedication. Only an important reason could have kept him in Indiana during the dog days of the summer, and this he explained to his sister in mid-August: "I most exhaustively, earnestly, seriously, vehemently, and intrinsically desire to espouse Susanah Robinson, and should I ever find her of a mood to be persuaded . . . I will not give her time to change her mind. . . . I have worn all my best clothes and even got so low I had my nails polished, but without causing the lady any visible perturbation in my favor." Eleven weeks later Tarkington scribbled George Ade a short note to say he was rushing off to Dayton for an important engagement tomorrow, and he added: "the world is well with me." At the same time he wrote Street exuberantly: "I'm going

to marry Susanah tomorrow. Yes *sir!* You *Bet* I am! She's the
lady wot wouldn't hear a *word* of it till I stopped rum permanent and got to work at my own trade. She's my Susanah all
right, now I done it!"

Readers of the Indianapolis *News* on the evening of November 6 learned that Booth Tarkington and Susanah Robinson
had been married at ten o'clock that morning in Dayton. The
ceremony took place at the bride's home in the presence only
of close relatives—Susanah's sisters and the bridegroom's father
and sister. After the wedding the Tarkingtons left for a short
trip to Chicago, following which they returned to Indianapolis
to the old home at 1100 North Pennsylvania Street. Tarkington offered his wife the chance to live anywhere she chose, but
she wisely picked Indianapolis, which she found friendly and
congenial.

The vows hopefully exchanged in Dayton that morning en-
dured and strengthened during the succeeding decades. Both
husband and wife, having passed through the crucible of unhappy marriage, had emerged stronger and wiser for their experience. Each recognized in the other complementary
qualities upon which they could build a happy, tranquil, and
lasting life together. Prior to the marriage Susanah, under the
press of circumstances and without training, had gone into
business and made a success of it. She was a clear-headed, re-
sourceful woman who could meet problems without flinching.
She was in addition an able hostess, a vivacious conversation-
alist, and a wife whose devotion to her husband was unstinting,
unselfish, and shrewdly cognizant of his needs. To these feminine traits Tarkington added his own lightness of spirit, sweet
reasonableness, and unfailing thoughtfulness. After four years
the combination had proved successful beyond his fondest
hopes, and he wrote Street on his wedding anniversary in 1916:
"Sue and I have been married 4 years today. By golly, I'm
grateful! They've been 4 whopping years for me in every
last ole way I can think of, and Sue claims she's satisfied, too.
I haven't heard a cross word from her *yet*—and I don't believe
I ever *will*. Not that she hasn't occasion for 'em, but she doesn't
seem to *know* any—hopelessly vacant along that line! And if 'a
woman's as old as she makes a man feel' she's about 25!"

Tarkington's contribution to the marriage may be assessed

from the matrimonial theories that he expressed a dozen years later in an essay called "The Hopeful Pessimist." Although he modestly would have denied it, his own traits were those his spokesman lists as requisite for the ideal husband. His speaker, a forty-four-year-old bachelor engaged to be married, declares that the most important ingredient in matrimony is courtesy, and he goes on to explain that a man ought to be as polite to his wife as if she were a total stranger. Other considerations such as respect also play a vital role in keeping the union strong, he continues, for a husband must give his wife the opportunity to be proud of him by winning her admiration; and if he can win the esteem of others, so much the better, since community approval of a husband is the source of keenest pleasure to a wife: "He ought to find something that brings them upon congenial ground outside of their household and business routine" such as a "mild excitement over politics or the French Revolution . . . or music, or painting, or beetles and microscopes." In giving his prescription for the ideal husband, however, Tarkington at the age of fifty-five took exception to the view that early marriages are the most successful. Declaring himself a candidate for a successful match, the hopeful pessimist says: "I've got old enough to marry . . . if people under forty or fifty marry successfully they have a lot of luck. . . . the majority . . . come through all right in the long run, but it's usually after a good many anguishes that threaten smash-ups."

Susanah Tarkington became companion and manager for her novelist-husband, and if the first decade after their marriage resulted in a richly creative period, she was more than a little responsible. For years Tarkington had traveled here and there, lived in hotels and in clubs, and never was secure from the demands on him that his good nature could not ward off. His wife became the buffer between him and the thousand distractions that could keep him from his work. As the manager of the household she believed it her duty to make the domestic wheels turn so noiselessly that they could not disturb her husband. Since he worked at home on tasks requiring intense concentration, she had always to be on guard against interruptions, and in an establishment that was rarely without visitors, this sometimes presented a formidable problem. As time went on, moreover, and as Tarkington's reputation and income increased, the domestic management became increasingly complex; but she managed her houses in Maine and Indiana and directed the activities of half a dozen servants with the efficiency of a general and the tact of a diplomat.

Early in their marriage she also played a germinal role in the creation of her husband's best-known character—Penrod Schofield. One day during their first winter together she read Horace Vachell's *The Hill,* an English novel that moved her deeply with its tale of boylife at Harrow, and after suffering vicariously through the hazing of the small boys, she gave the novel to her husband to read. His reaction, however, surprised her. Although he readily admitted that the bullying by the older boys probably was authentic, he asserted flatly that no boy ever talked like the puppets in the novel. When his wife maintained that English boys were different from their American counterparts, he held his ground and repeated his contention that the story was false. "Why don't you write about boys as they really are?" she then challenged, and he answered that maybe he would. Since he already had experimented with a boy character in *The Flirt,* this exchange proved to be the motivation that sent him to his desk-drawing board for two or three weeks of steady work. He refused to say what he was writing, and when he knocked off work in the afternoons to walk across town to the University Club, he would only admonish: "Wait until I've finished." Then one day he called his wife into his workroom and read her the story he had been writing—"Penrod and the Pageant," the first of the Penrod adventures and Tarkington's first real bid for a permanent place in American literature.

Tarkington actually had been preparing all his life to write the Penrod stories. An abundance of usable material was stored up within him, and all he needed was the time and place for concentrated effort and something to precipitate his experience. "I know what makes Penrod because I've been years on the job," he later wrote when the stories were being dramatized; and the truth of this assertion is evident, for *Penrod* is compounded of two elements: Tarkington's own memories of childhood and his observation of his three nephews. The original story, the tale of the pageant, evoked his own childhood sufferings as a pinned, powdered, bewigged, and involuntary actor in charity entertainments gotten up by his older sister. Like the author, Penrod submitted rebelliously to the parental ukase that sent him forth dressed as the child Sir Launcelot in tights devised from old silk stockings, trunks fashioned from worn-out red flannel underdrawers, and a doublet made from a discarded silk dress. Tarkington also remembered and used in *Penrod* the distasteful dancing classes of his boyhood, the annual visit of the circus, the feud with his fourth-grade teacher, the shows staged in the stable loft, and the narratives he wrote as a schoolboy.

His own recollections constantly were refreshed and reinforced by the spectacle of the Jameson children, who frequently were in his thoughts and almost always under direct observation. When he went to New York after McClure's acceptance of *The Gentleman from Indiana* in 1899, for example, the sleeping car rocked and jolted so much that he was unable to sleep, and he wrote home after arriving: "I dreamed that Jno. & Don. were dancing on the roof and making my room shake so I couldn't work." A few years later when he served in the legislature and lived in Indianapolis, John and Donald were the age of Penrod; and by the time he began the actual writing of the stories Booth Jameson was approaching the same age. Daily Booth and his friends played in the old stable that still survived behind the Tarkington house and in the adjacent alleys and yards. Tarkington remembered later that Booth Jameson probably supplied the dominant note in Penrod's complex personality, but he added: "A number of boys in that neighborhood who played in our back yard, unconsciously were writing themselves into that book." A case in point was the creation of one particular member of Penrod's circle—the model boy. During the writing of the stories, recalled Tarkington, he asked Booth Jameson one day what he thought of a certain small contemporary, a little boy who seemed somewhat more civilized than the rest of the gang. "We call him the Little Gentleman," answered the nephew; and thus was born Georgie Bassett, the saintly boy whose perfect conduct is a continual reproach to Penrod.

The genre to which *Penrod* belongs, the realistic boy story, had a well-rooted tradition in American literature by 1913, and Tarkington himself traced the type back to Mark Twain, who created the first boy story in which "the hero was recognizable *as a boy* throughout the whole narrative." Until *Tom Sawyer* was written, he added, "nearly all the boys of fiction were adults with a lisp, or saintly infants, or mischievous eccentrics or merely the sturdy 'young gentlemen' who fought with the butcher's boy before going to Eton in the English novels." In addition to Mark Twain *Helen's Babies,* John Habberton's amusing tale of a bachelor uncle who "baby-sits" with his nephews, belongs in the sequence of realistic children in literature; and to these books, both published in 1876, he added William Allen White's Boyville stories (1899) and Stephen Crane's *Whilomville Stories* (1900). He completed the list finally with the Lawrenceville stories and *The Tennessee Shad* of Owen Johnson, which appeared shortly before the Penrod stories were written.

Tarkington had firm ideas of what boy life really was like and relegated most stories of children to the limbo of claptrappery. Both *Tom Brown's Schooldays* and its American derivative *The Story of a Bad Boy,* he thought, belonged in the bogus tradition of the boy story that imposed on its children an adult moral order in miniature. In both Thomas Hughes' English novel and Thomas Bailey Aldrich's American story, for example, the hero at the proper moment thrashes the bully so that virtue triumphs conventionally over vice. This Tarkington regarded as artificially contrived and didactic, and while there is a bully who gets trounced in *Penrod,* the difference between the two methods of handling the same topic is significant. There is in Tarkington's story no manly exchange of blows according to Marquis of Queensberry rules or even a David and Goliath encounter in which craftiness in single combat overcomes brute strength. Instead, Herman and Verman, Penrod's Negro playmates, both assault Rupe Collins with savage frenzy and an arsenal of garden implements, and the bully from across the tracks flees precipitately from combat too rough even for his own free-wheeling standards. Tarkington's boys are young savages whose battle is primitive in its ferocity and refreshingly amoral.

The difference between Tarkington and Aldrich or Hughes, whose children were either naturally noble or depraved, lies in a different concept of child psychology. The creator of Penrod was an environmentalist who believed that the child was forced into the rigid patterns of adult behavior only through the long and relentless pressures of parental and social discipline. The child, he believed, relives the entire story of mankind in his growth from infancy to maturity. To illustrate this theory, Tarkington described a day in the life of one Harvey Pringle, age eleven, who might have been Penrod, Sam Williams, Booth Jameson, or himself. During this eventful day Harvey wakes up the neighborhood, creates havoc in the kitchen, draws a chalk picture on his father's overcoat, fights with a passing boy, carries off new lumber from a building site, pushes a little girl into the fish pond, slings mud at a passing wagon, plays dangerously in the framework of a new house, and breaks his collar bone by falling into the cellar. Harvey's day was an encapsulated survey of man's history: he obeyed the primitive urges to draw, to attack strangers, to appropriate unprotected property, to woo in caveman style, and to engage in personal combat. "I began to see," wrote Tarkington, "that, just as in his embryo man reproduces the history of his development upward from the mire into man, so does he in his childhood and his boyhood and his youth reproduce the onward history of his race, from the most ancient man to the most modern."

Although *Tom Sawyer* and *Penrod* have much in common, Tarkington was not imitating Twain. There is little similarity in the boy activity of the two books, and their disparity may be detected in the full titles: *The Adventures of Tom Sawyer* and just *Penrod*. "Tom and Huck," wrote Tarkington, "are realistic only in character. He [Twain] gave 'em what boys don't get, when it came to 'plot.' All that the boy, Sam, had wished to happen, he made happen." Tarkington's only concession to plot is a characteristic exaggeration of the commonplace incidents of his literary material: Penrod always has the last word. When Penrod breaks up the pageant of the Round Table by slipping the janitor's overalls over his humiliating costume, he achieves, of course, an unrealistic triumph over the adults who rule his life; but the irony of the ending turns the literal transcript of boy life into humorous art. Another episode illustrating the same point is the tar barrel scene, in which Penrod goes berserk when his friends taunt him with Georgie Bassett's epithet "Little Gentleman." His revenge, a tar-daubing of all his tormentors, is the sort of dream adventure that a child might have, but it is keyed low and made of routine play. Far more spectacular is the equally unreal triumph of Tom, Huck, and Joe Harper, who run away to Jackson's Island when they are not appreciated at home and subsequently witness their own funeral. Most of *Penrod*'s effects are subdued, and the book succeeds through the abundant use of accurately observed detail which is episodic in arrangement rather than continuously narrative. "The detail—*not plot*—is what has made it," wrote Tarkington to George Tyler when the latter wanted to have the Penrod stories dramatized.

Both *Tom Sawyer* and *Penrod,* neither of which was written especially for children, are able to evoke realistically American boyhood because their boys are real people. "Penrod has been a success," said Tarkington, "because it has kept to *true* boy and avoided book-and-stage boy." Any man can get back his boyhood from *Penrod,* moreover, "unless he lived in the east side of New York or went yachting out of Newport." This is not literally true, but for millions of Americans who grew up in urban surroundings, at least until recently, it is an accurate statement. The insurance broker's son in Yonkers, the merchant's boy in Evanston, or the lawyer's offspring in Indianapolis—each could have been Penrod Schofield or perhaps another of Tarkington's characters—Sam Williams, Georgie Bassett, Maurice Levy, Roderick Magsworth Bitts—when he was twelve.

Tarkington skillfully particularizes the typical and often prosaic experiences that are common to most children, and through his genial but observant eyes adults who somehow have managed to grow up normally can see themselves passing through the rigors of childhood. Tarkington knew that most of his friends had, and most of their children would, turn out satisfactorily, and he was perfectly aware that acute indigestion or a broken collar bone was about the most serious consequence of an escapade that an average boy like Penrod probably would suffer. Like Howells, Tarkington was interested in the commonplace material of everyday life rather than in the exceptional event. He could have made *Penrod* melodramatic without departing from his own boyhood experiences, for he remembered events more extraordinary than he used. He recalled in his memoirs the story of Chase Walker, a friend who accidentally shot himself and nearly died of blood-poisoning because he concealed the wound, and at another time he cited the unforgettable experience of seeing in the alley back of his home a Negro couple, Bob Philips and his wife, the one with "his throat imperfectly cut" and the other with "her head *almost* off."

Tarkington was in full mastery of his literary medium when he wrote *Penrod*. His style, which is supple, articulate, witty, is equal to all the demands he makes of it and succeeds simultaneously in entertaining children and delighting adults. His management of detail is so deft and subtle that the juvenile reader enjoys vicariously the activities of Penrod and his gang and the adult takes pleasure in Penrod's *"suffering and* his mental processes, not what *happens* to him." Tarkington's episodes have traces of the tall tale, but in essence they are everyday incidents in which style and arrangement of detail are everything. The successive chapters detailing Penrod's secret authorship of "Harold Ramorez the Roadagent or Wild Life among the Rocky Mts." and the humiliating actualities of the Round Table are a brilliant juxtaposition of humorous irony; and the linking of Penrod's schoolroom dreams with the realities of arithmetic is a similarly effective stroke. The language of the boys, too, is fresh and the situations avoid triteness. *"One* main thing is to keep out . . . hand-me-down boy humor," warned Tarkington when the dramatization was under way, and he added: " 'Boy-writers' depend on 'Gee, fellers' and 'Say, kids' and 'kid nicknames'—if you'll notice I have utterly avoided this stock stuff . . . even though most boys actually do say 'kids' & 'Gee.' "

The Penrod stories were an instant success when they began appearing serially in 1913 in *Everybody's Magazine*. The *Cosmopolitan* soon outbid other periodicals for the tales and published, at several thousand dollars each, all that Tarkington cared to write, then begged for more. "My prices astonish me," he wrote Street at this time; "they've climbed steadily, by offers, until I'm rather sorry for the magazines that pay 'em. I've really never asked any particular price: the thing has somehow just done itself." When the stories were brought out in book form the next year, they began sales that eventually passed the half million mark and have not yet stopped. The book and its successors, *Penrod and Sam* and *Penrod Jashber,* still are in print and still circulate in school and public libraries. As soon as the first of the tales appeared, Harry Wilson wrote enthusiastically: "These two stories are the best since Stephen Crane's. . . . Only you and he have done anything real with the boy at the age when he's the hardest to get. . . . I wouldn't dare touch one at twelve. Haven't enough Zola in me for the realism, and the realism has just got to be ruthless."

Tarkington, in addition to critical approval, began receiving fan mail from *Penrod* readers. Whole classrooms of children sometimes were directed to write to him in the sort of captive performance that Penrod himself would have loathed. Tarkington recalled one particular letter which he often laughed over and quoted in its entirety: "Teacher told us we must each write you a letter and she will send the best one. Well, how are you? Yours truly." The sheer desperation of the boy delighted Tarkington, for he was Penrod in life.

NINE

THE MAJOR PHASE

WHEN TARKINGTON RETURNED to Indiana to live, he found that his roots still were deeply planted in Midwestern soil. After eight years of wandering he remained a midlander under his cosmopolitan exterior, and the fertile flatlands surrounding Indianapolis always would be home. As he paid off his cab driver and stepped to the sidewalk—no longer a traveler—he felt "unexpected stirrings" within and knew that he had come back to stay. For the rest of his life he regarded himself as a resident Hoosier, even when he later built a house in Maine that he occupied from May through December. A multitude of old friends and memories drew him back to Indianapolis each winter, and late in his life, when he looked back on several decades of semi-annual moves between New England and the Midwest, he admitted that he liked Maine better than Indiana, but "Indianapolis," he explained, "is sort of a *person*—my uncle or somebody."

Long foreign and Eastern residence, however, gave him a new point of view about his home and made vivid the contrast between Indianapolis at the turn of the century and on the eve of the First World War. Much had happened, it seemed, during his absence, and little by little he became disenchanted with his native city. No longer could he appraise Indiana uncritically as he once did in *The Gentleman from Indiana,* for he saw with alarm that everywhere about him people worshipped materialism, bigness, and speed. The sedate, well-mannered, and self-contained society that he remembered in Indianapolis in 1900 had crumbled before the irresistible force of big business and the vast complexities of an industrial democracy. The life

181

he formerly knew had been succeeded by a frenetic rat race in the grimy maze of his once relaxed and friendly city. To the returned exile the feverish tempo of the new era was astonishing and a little frightening.

When Tarkington resumed his fiction-writing, nevertheless, he withheld judgment on the great changes that had taken place in his absence. During his first year home he was concerned with physical rehabilitation, and throughout the second he was preoccupied with the novelty of marital happiness. When he wrote *The Flirt,* he was chiefly interested in character development and noted only briefly the physical disparities between his home town before and after his years away. In the Penrod stories that followed he placed his action nostalgically "in the days when the stable was empty but not yet rebuilt into a garage" and did not have to grapple with either the tangible or intangible problems of the change.

Then early in 1914 he wrote *The Turmoil,* in which he indicted angrily the great despoiler, business. Once he had begun scrutinizing the social and economic life of his native community, the impulse continued for ten years and three more novels: *The Magnificent Ambersons* (1918), *Alice Adams* (1921), and *The Midlander* (1924). Intrinsically, these are well-made novels written in the tradition of commonplace realism as pioneered by Howells, and taken as a whole, they represent Tarkington in his major phase. All four are Indiana family chronicles against a business background, and together they paint a valuable picture of the urban Midwest during the early decades of this century. When the time comes that American life of this period must be reconstructed from documents, Tarkington's tetralogy will be immensely useful to the social historian. It is also worth noting that Tarkington was attacking American materialism a decade before Mencken and Sinclair Lewis discovered the "booboisie."

To a fastidious man who believed that beauty was more important than money the change from the old Indianapolis to the new was symbolized shockingly by smoke. Tarkington's old home already was on the fringe of the industrial center of the growing city, and the noise and dirt grew more appalling each year. In his youth central Indiana had been blessed with abundant supplies of natural gas, but the gas had given out about the time he first went to Europe, and the old industries as well as the new ones now were nourished by soft coal. The sooty pall hung over the city like the foul breath of the industrial giant beneath it. Under the blighting smoke panted the monster whose voice (in *The Turmoil*) seemed to repeat the single theme of the city's worship: "Wealth! I will get Wealth! I will make Wealth! I will sell Wealth for more Wealth! My house shall be dirty, my garment shall be dirty, and I will foul my neighbor so that he cannot be clean—but I will get Wealth!"

As Tarkington looked from his doorway up and down Pennsylvania Street during the winter months, the ravages of the smoke were dreadfully apparent. Even newly built or freshly painted houses that should have shown a cheerful appearance were as stricken as the rest. Each succeeding snow had turned black with the everlasting soot, "and this soot-snow, melting to a thinnish ink, had flowed and trickled, and congealed again" until the bedraggled buildings looked like "negro minstrels in a half stage of make-up." But the houses lacked the gaiety of minstrels and rather looked like patients "not yet convalescent after racking illness." And they stood in "leprous enclosures of besooted bare earth where lingered a few patches of sparse grass not yet slain by the acids in the smoke." The choking, corrupting, and defiling smoke became the dominant symbol in *The Turmoil*.

"Commercialism is the savage of the world," Tarkington wrote a friend while the novel was being serialized; "it's that stinking dirty brute I'm after, with what entrails I have, in 'The Turmoil,' which is written much more feebly than I'd like." To a Harper editor he equated commercialism with "the stage of *greed* this country is passing through." From the greed of his compatriots derived the desire for bigness, and from bigness came ever-increasing riches. Everyone wanted money, money, money, and cared little how it was obtained. They worshipped Bigness because it created Wealth, and they demanded that the city constantly increase its size to produce more riches. There was no reckoning of the price that had to be paid in spiritual and human values. The universal cry was: "We must be Bigger! Blow! Boost! Brag! Kill the fault-finder! . . . Bigness is patriotism and honour! . . . Bigness is Money! We want Bigness!" And sheer size they got, as people from the four corners of the earth were bribed, coaxed, and swindled into coming to the mushrooming cities on the plains. Money they got too, at the expense of ugliness, squalor, and damaged lung tissue.

Tarkington was profoundly shaken by the haste, waste, and insensitivity of the society he had come back to. The attitude of James Sheridan, the self-made millionaire in *The Turmoil*, was typical. He loved the smoke, and when soot fell on his cuff, he only chuckled. "It's good! It's good!" he said and smacked his lips in gusto. "Good, clean soot: it's our life-blood, God bless it!" In fact the smoke was one of Sheridan's great enthusiasms, for he saw it as the symbol of his fortune and the growing wealth of the city. When a smoke-abatement committee of women visited him, asking aid in ridding the city of its blight, he told his callers jovially: "Smoke's what brings your husbands' money home on Saturday night."

Equally distressing to Tarkington was the human misery and license brought by the greedy worship of Bigness. The teeming center of the city festered with slums where the producers of the wealth huddled in unsanitary poverty. As the city piled itself high in the center, tower on tower for a nucleus, and spread itself out over the plain, mile after mile, the blighted vitals remained with all the saloons and hells that cities always shelter. "Temptation and ruin were ready commodities on the market . . . highwaymen walked the streets at night . . . snatching thieves were busy everywhere in the dusk . . . housebreakers were a common apprehension and frequent reality." Life was somewhat safer from intentional destruction than in medieval Europe, but death or mutilation from vehicular accidents lay in ambush at every crossing.

Municipal services, like police and health protection, also lagged behind the acceptable minimum standards, even though the tax rate was always going up. "It was no part of a business administration," wrote Tarkington, "to waste money trying to keep streets clean from September until May." When a citizen walked up the best residential avenue in winter, a gust of wind might cover him with "flinty particles, bacilli, hairs from dead cats and rats and dogs, shreds of feather and bits of dead birds," and everything else that had lain on the pavement since the sanitation department had gone into its annual hibernation. Only if some citizen made a specific complaint, added Tarkington, would the bodies of dead animals be removed from the public thoroughfares.

The politicians as well as the businessmen worshipped Bigness, Commerce, and Wealth, and let nothing interfere with their cult. They regarded lawmaking as a harmless pastime and gave the people all the statutes that were asked for. There were laws on the books forbidding dangerous speeds, shoddy workmanship, and sharp practices, and more marvelous still, there were laws forbidding smoke. The politicians made laws for all things and forgot them immediately, though sometimes the rumblings of discontent spurred them to pass new ordinances providing for the enforcement of the old ones. But, said Tarkington, "wherever enforcement threatened Money or Votes—or wherever it was too much bother—it became a joke. Influence was the law."

Though Tarkington pulled no punches in attacking the scramble for wealth and its attendant ugliness, he believed that the problems of industrialization eventually would be solved. He tempered his indictment with the knowledge that other Midwestern cities—Columbus, Chicago, St. Louis, Omaha—also were dirty, insanitary, corrupt, and he recognized that all were involved in the historic process of growth. He knew too that "the kiln must be fired before the vase is glazed and the Acropolis was not crowned with marble in a day." Tarkington lived to see a measure of this predictable change take place, and if he seemed to mellow in his attitude, particularly after 1923 when he moved uptown thirty-two blocks away from the blighted center of the city, he was not without justification. Even if he never was to see the obliteration of Midwestern slums, his lifetime did parallel a steady amelioration of many ills that he diagnosed in his socio-economic novels.

The Turmoil is the story of an ascending family, first-generation makers of the wealth. James Sheridan at the outset of the novel is the owner of the biggest skyscraper, the biggest trust company, and the biggest manufacturing works in the city. Having come from the country in his youth, Sheridan, like Howells' paint manufacturer in *The Rise of Silas Lapham,* has risen to wealth but not to social position. His success in business has not prepared him for success in human relations, and while he possesses a Midas touch, his acquisitive genius is no more able than the fabled king's to buy happiness. The conflicts in the novel arise from his efforts to run his family like a financial and industrial empire. He kills his favorite son as a sacrifice on the altar of business. He dismisses an unacceptable suitor, only to have his daughter elope. He forces a second son into the business and watches the boy crack under the double strain of parental coercion and marital trouble. Sheridan wins his main contest, however, which involves his youngest son Bibbs, a fragile, poetic young man who wants no part in the family enterprises. Bibbs ultimately suppresses his own desire to write and by an act of will makes himself into the image of his father. In doing this he succumbs to the historic force that always bends the creators in society to the will of the acquisitors, and thus Tarkington anticipated the problem posed by Van Wyck Brooks in *The Ordeal of Mark Twain* (1920) and O'Neill in *The Great God Brown* (1926).

The Sheridans in *The Turmoil* are a composite of many families who rose to positions of affluence and power in the Midwest during the early years of the century. The father is the high priest of Bigness, who all his life has "struggled and conquered, and must all his life go on struggling and inevitably conquering, as part of a vast impulse not his own." He is a convincing character, though his material values and domestic bullheadedness do not inspire affection. Bibbs also is a real creation, as Howells wrote flatteringly when the novel began to appear in *Harper's*. He recalls something of Tarkington's own attractiveness during the Nineties, and under different circumstances Tarkington himself might have lived the part he created for Bibbs.

The transformation of this character from poet to industrialist comes close to tragedy, though the extent of Bibbs' frustration is no more than implied. Howells thought that Tarkington was purposely not specific about Bibbs' fate, perhaps because it is "too dire for consolation." But Howells may have read more into the story than was intended, for Tarkington holds no tragic view of life and sees his character merely as fulfilling an inevitable role in capitalistic society. He never suggests that society can be reorganized so that the artists may preserve integrity against their predators. When Bibbs forswears poetry for business, the act rings true as a gesture of family sacrifice. One knows that in reality reluctant sons like Bibbs sometimes have felt compelled to follow his example. In Tarkington's fictional world, as in life itself, all characters are involved in the lives of each other, and "no man is an island entire of itself."

Tarkington compensates Bibbs for his renunciation by supplying him with a charming heroine, Mary Vertrees, daughter of a declining "old family"; and through his use of a sub-plot romance he manages to further another of his objectives in the novel—the portrayal of urban society in a state of flux. As the heroine's family goes down in the world, the Sheridans go up, and ultimately the old and the new are joined in a matrimonial alliance. The character of Mary Vertrees provides, in addition, a mellifluous obbligato as counterpoint to the strident turmoil that is the novel's chief concern.

Tarkington wrote *The Turmoil* in sixty days of semi-perpetual work from January to March, 1914. During this period he toiled long hours over his drawing board, sometimes from breakfast until after midnight. He followed a system he had worked out the year before in which he lived in bathrobes and was shielded from all interruptions by the vigilant Susanah and the servants. "About two o'clock," he explained, "they bring me beef tea and coffee [on a tray to the workroom]. I put on pants, jacket and stock at six, 'dressing for dinner,' *don't eat heavily,* and am back at seven, bathrobe again." Each morning he sharpened up a handful of pencils and wrote all day in a large, flowing script on legal-sized paper. On days when the story poured from his brain most freely, the long sheets dropped from his pencil beautifully crisp and clean and without need of much revision. After the manuscript was completed, he sent it to Harper's, who published it both serially and in book form.

Although Tarkington was immensely flattered by the novel's brisk sale and wide critical approval, he was pleased most of all by the praise of Howells. When the older author first wrote him about *The Turmoil*, Tarkington replied humbly: "Any writer in America would rather have a word from you than from any other man. . . . It has helped my self-esteem as nothing else could . . . you are responsible for whatever . . . good . . . we produce." Later he told George Ade that Howells was the "only critic alive worth pleasing." He considered himself quite definitely as a perpetuator of the decorous realism that Howells had ably written and critically championed for more than a generation.

About the time *The Turmoil* began appearing serially Tarkington and George Barr McCutcheon, who also was summering in Maine, drove to York Harbor to call on Howells, only to find the older novelist away from home. The next summer, however, after Howells had written two letters and two "Easy Chair" columns praising the novel, he invited its author to have lunch with him. Tarkington accepted and found Howells alone in his summer home with Thomas Sergeant Perry, "another good old soul, a relic of the great Boston period," and both older men talked enthusiastically about the novel. Tarkington, who was forty-five at this time, felt, in the presence of his host and Perry, "a sprig and a too sporty one; too prosperous also, arriving in the long shiny car," and he wrote afterwards that he was afraid they "let me talk too much." But he enjoyed hearing the old men speak familiarly of "Harry James" and other distinguished authors they knew intimately, and discuss books from a vast and cosmopolitan literary background. During succeeding summers Tarkington followed up his visit to Howells, and a warm personal relationship developed. When the old man died in 1920, Tarkington felt a keen sense of loss, for Howells had been a "strong and gentle" teacher who "knew how to make true things" and had led him, among others, "out of a wilderness of raw and fantastic shapes where many of us dallied, making childish and romantic figures in imitation of the falsities we found there."

Having preached against materialism in *The Turmoil*, Tarkington next demonstrated his versatility by returning to comedy. The lode that he had struck in "Mary Smith" remained rich and unworked, and he soon created in Willie Baxter in *Seventeen* a character almost as well known as Penrod. Sub-titled "A Tale of Youth and Summer Time," the new novel appeared serially in the *Metropolitan Magazine,* which previously had published three Penrod stories and the theater novelette *Harlequin and Columbine.* Readers of the magazine got their first taste of the new story in January, 1915, when Tarkington wrote a brief Foreword including Willie Baxter's poetic effusion "Milady." The installments began the following month and continued in nine of the next thirteen issues, after which Harper collected them in book form.

The sufferings of William Sylvanus Baxter during the summer that Lola Pratt visits May Parcher are too well remembered to need much recalling. Few booklovers have neither suffered with Willie nor laughed at him during the tortures of his adolescence; and his amorous yearnings towards the baby-talking Miss Pratt, who is beyond doubt one of the most insufferable women in all literature, are the stuff from which enduring comedy is made. Willie's family, of course, does not understand that he has reached man's estate: his mother sends him on a humiliating errand carrying a wash boiler across town with the handyman Genesis; his younger sister Jane embarrasses him before his friends by her appalling indiscretions and childishness; his father cannot understand the son's need for a dress suit to wear in the ineffable presence of Miss Pratt. One indignity after another is heaped on Willie as he struggles manfully against his family and the fierce competition of Joe Bullitt and Johnny Watson, two contemporaries who also have succumbed to the charmer. In the end, when Lola goes home leaving May Parcher's irascible father in peace, Willie is somewhat closer to being grown up and looks ahead to the imminent beginning of his freshman year of college.

It is hard to write objectively of a book that evokes so powerfully one's own high school days. *Seventeen* is a nostalgic tale that was compounded from the author's memories of adolescence when he was Willie Baxter and Bush Browning and Horace Hord were Johnny Watson and Joe Bullitt. It also derives, like "Mary Smith," from Tarkington's observations of his own nephews, John and Donald Jameson, when they were some years younger. It is one of the superb comedies of adolescence and one of the happiest moments in Tarkington's literary career. Its viability may be judged from its many printings, movie and stage productions, and translations. In trade and reprint editions it has enjoyed a sale of something approaching eight hundred thousand copies, a figure that compares favorably with the several Penrod books. Since it first was put to paper in the winter of 1914-1915, it has gone through various dramatic versions, none of which Tarkington had a hand in: silent movie, stage play, musical comedy, talking movie, and again in 1951 a new musical.

Although most readers liked *Seventeen*, approval at times was given grudgingly, as in this observation: "*Seventeen* is Mr. Tarkington's high water mark. It is farce, without passion, without poetry, palpably insincere and shallow—but it is hilarious. Baxter never comes alive, but he is nonetheless a creation with his calf-love, his sighs, his fastidious scorn for the mere business of living." This critic was right in judging *Seventeen* a rollicking good comedy, but to say that it was insincere or that Willie did not come alive revealed as much about the commentator as about the book. *Seventeen*, of course, was comedy, but the exaggeration for humorous effect did not distort the basic authenticity of awkward adolescence. To the many readers who saw their own youth reflected in the novel, Willie was not only a creation but also a reality. There is no doubt that Tarkington, and also the Jameson boys, had been Willie, but at the same time, to be sure, Willie was not every American adolescent of 1915. Ernest Hemingway, the Oak Park doctor's son, who then was seventeen, certainly never was; but American life has been varied, and Tarkington, as any honest artist must, wrote only what he knew. He always admitted candidly that life contains many facets, and he neither could nor would illuminate more than a few.

Because *Seventeen* appeared at a time when writers were discovering a larger latitude possible in the fictional treatment of sex, Tarkington began receiving abuse from a new generation of critics who condemned his biological reticence. When Willie Baxter falls in love with Lola Pratt, his physiological reaction is a frequent blush, an inability to concentrate, a vacancy of expression, and a desire to write poetry. This, contended some detractors, ignored the realities of life, for Willie and Lola only talk vaguely about love, not procreation. They sit on the front porch looking calf-eyed at each other instead of studying anatomy in the spiraea. But Tarkington had been perfectly honest in his treatment of puppy love, for Willie never knew that his suffering was due to the awakening of sexual desire. He only knew that Lola Pratt was pretty and that he had to spend as much time as possible in her company.

Tarkington usually ignored the critics, but sometimes he

bridled if he was accused of dishonest writing. When Heywood Broun charged him with glossing over sex, he wrote the columnist a letter of protest. Broun contended that Tarkington was not being candid because he skipped over sex problems in dealing with adolescents. He should have tried, said Broun, to capture some of the torments that come to the young through their first recognition of sex; but Tarkington replied vigorously: "I don't see it. I never knew a youth who had that sense of torment under the circumstances depicted in 'Seventeen.' Willie didn't recognize anything." Then he went on to warn Broun that "you young men make the same mistake about us older ones that we made about those who were older in our own youth. We are not necessarily ignorant of what we ignore in art."

This exchange with Broun was typical of Tarkington's attitude towards sex in literature. Sometime before, in a New York *Times* interview, he had explained himself further, saying that he never wrote of sex simply because he did not think about such things. His preoccupations were with other human emotions such as egoism, selfishness, ambition, jealousy, all of which passions aroused his interest far more than the relatively uncomplicated sex drive. Furthermore, he deplored the modern fashion of " 'French post-cards' in the form of novels" (a phrase he used in writing to Garland), but he wanted no part in censorship. He was not in the least flattered when a self-appointed guardian of public morals named him as a writer who was successful without being salacious. He declared that censorship was probably always wrong and cited the earlier banning of Shaw's *Mrs. Warren's Profession* as a case in point. "There was nothing indecent in that play," he said; "it was a mistaken judgment that ordered its suppression." The root of the whole problem of sex in literature, he felt, lay in a breaking down of taste: "I've never thought of it as a question of morals." When the matter came up on a later occasion, he urged Kenneth Roberts to cut certain passages from *Arundel* and quoted Howells to the effect that decent people do not make love on park benches.

Besides creating Willie and his contemporaries, Tarkington introduced into *Seventeen* Penrod's female counterpart in Jane Baxter. *Penrod* had contained a sugar-and-spice little girl in

Marjorie Jones, a latter-day Becky Thatcher, but *Seventeen* exhibits in Jane an engaging young hoyden. Her childish lack of inhibitions and her inability to understand the problems that confront Willie furnish superb moments of situation comedy and humorous irony. Any adult who once had a brother or sister five or six years younger experiences frequent promptings to memory throughout this novel. So successful was Jane that she appeared later as Florence Atwater in *Gentle Julia*.

Tarkington wrote more Penrod stories, another novel, and returned to playwriting in the next three years, then produced in *Gentle Julia* the same type of comedy that had made *Seventeen* popular. The characters in this story are reminiscent and the locale is familiar: children, young lovers, and long-suffering parents—all living in the informal urban intimacy of large, rambling houses with verandas overlooking shady lawns. Thirteen-year-old Florence, the spark plug of the novel, is created with consummate skill and a real understanding of pre-adolescent girls. To show her off to best advantage, Tarkington provides two male contemporaries, her cousin Herbert, and Henry Rooter, both of whom she annoys and outwits hilariously. Tarkington captures deftly the emotional and mental lag between boys and girls of this age, and in the episode of the *North End Daily Oriole,* where Florence "muscles" into Henry and Herbert's newspaper enterprise, Tarkington used his memory of a summer in Marshall, Illinois, when his cousin Fenton Booth had been a newspaper publisher.

The young lovers in *Gentle Julia* are not so young as in *Seventeen,* but their parents have the same problems. Florence's Aunt Julia, who lives across the street, is a twenty-year-old beauty whose charms have attracted a circle of admiring males, one of whom is Noble Dill. Although the Dill boy is the least promising of the lot, Florence unaccountably undertakes to promote his interests, and thereby hangs the tale. Then, too, just as Mr. Parcher suffers from the fatuities of Willie Baxter, Joe Bullitt, and Johnny Watson, so does Julia's father undergo the tortures of having a ravishing belle in the family. His *bête noire* is the Orduma Egyptian Cigarettes that Noble Dill smokes incessantly; and here one detects another autobiographical note, for Tarkington, who had been a heavy smoker since preparatory school days, certainly encountered similar prejudice against his cigarettes from the fathers of Indianapolis daughters.

Co-equal with Tarkington's human characters in *Gentle Julia* is the woolly black clown Gamin, the French poodle who turns even Julia's ill-tempered father into a dog-lover. After using Booth Jameson's nondescript Trixie as a model for Penrod's dog Duke, Tarkington followed this precedent by giving Julia a replica of his own comical poodle. Always fond of dogs, Tarkington had bought Gamin in France during his first trip abroad and had laughed at the dog's antics until Gamin was run over in 1911. When this pet died he was succeeded almost at once by Lorenzo the Magnificent, known as Wops, who also lived eight years, then died suddenly of a heart attack in 1922. The night he died Tarkington wrote George Tyler: "I don't think I'll want another; it hurts too much"; but he did, after a long interval, acquire Figaro, who captivated and made a poodle fancier out of Alexander Woollcott.

By the time Gamin and Wops had been succeeded by Figaro, Woollcott was a periodic visitor to the Tarkington household, and on one occasion in 1935 a lecture tour took him to Indianapolis. All through luncheon, Woollcott remembered, Figaro sat pensively in a windowseat looking out of doors; but the arrival of coffee apparently was a signal, and the dog leaped down and faced his master expectantly. When Tarkington asked Figaro if he were feeling pious, the dog ran to the painting of an Italian madonna and planted his forepaws on a chair beneath the picture. He kept looking about, however, until reproved; whereupon he buried his black head deep in his paws:

> "Are you a miserable sinner?" Tarkington asked. A faint moan came from the woolly arc. "Are you"—much louder this time—"a miserable sinner?" A considerable groan from Figaro. *"Are you a miserable sinner?"* This final repetition elicited a very wail from an humble and a contrite heart. "Amen!" at which cue Figaro came bounding from church and was rewarded with a cracker.

The chapters of *Gentle Julia* dealing with the acquisition of Gamin (a gift from Noble Dill) are pure delight to a dog-lover. Tarkington regarded a man's affection for a dog as evidence that he was highly civilized, and French poodles were the natural bit players in the human comedies that Tarkington was peculiarly fitted to write. He had seen his first French poodle on Fifth Avenue in New York during a preparatory school vacation and had been just as startled as Kitty Silver, the cook in *Gentle Julia,* who exclaims: "Listen to me, dog . . . Is you a dog, or isn't you a dog?" A moment before, Gamin had risen incredibly to his hind legs and walked beside her on the leash. But she is captivated, as everyone else is, when the dog looks up at her with his bobbed tail wagging and his garnet eyes sparkling through a black chrysanthemum. French poodles, wrote Tarkington on another occasion, "are made of black sunshine . . . the friendliest humorists in the world."

A long friendship with Woollcott began when the novel was published in book form in 1922. Woollcott wrote that he first had read of Gamin's antics in a "Y" hut in France at the end of the First World War, had wanted to write then, but somehow did not. When he returned to Europe for a visit three years later, he took along a copy of the book, just published, and enjoyed again the stories that had delighted him when they first appeared in *Collier's.* He wrote from the ship that he had finished the novel before the vessel had cleared Sandy Hook, "chuckling and wheezing away in the smoking room to such an extent that I started this trip surrounded by passengers all under the impression that I was a deranged American being shipped overseas by his family to be rid of him."

The huge success of Tarkington's stories of children and adolescents, plus a return to the theater, kept him for three years from continuing his social and economic studies of Midwestern growth. Then early in 1917 he began his first Pulitzer Prize novel, *The Magnificent Ambersons.* Where he had built *The Turmoil* around the rising Sheridans, he picked a completely opposite group, a descending family, for his next novel. In it he creates an Indianapolis dynasty whose patriarch, old Major Amberson, has returned from the Civil War and built a fortune during the Gilded Age; in the course of the tale the old man's wealth gradually is dissipated by the second and third generations. The Ambersons, therefore, typify the "old," socially prominent but declining families, like the Vertrees in *The Turmoil* that James Sheridan climbs roughly over in his quest for wealth and power. The ugliness and power of the growth are illustrated in the former novel, while its social destructiveness is shown in the latter.

Tarkington had observed that American families sometimes went from rags to riches and back to near rags again in three generations, and he wrote *The Magnificent Ambersons* partly to document this phenomenon. The process, he found, moved in a sort of spiral, rather than a circle, for the gradual movement was upward, and the great families eventually regained their vitality before touching bottom. Howells had noted the same pattern in American life in *The Rise of Silas Lapham* and had given the Back Bay Coreys a history similar to the Ambersons. Just as Tom Corey, grandson of a Yankee merchant, begins the rehabilitation of his family, so does George Minafer, Major Amberson's grandson, initiate the upward turn of the Amberson fortunes. The cyclical progression of the Ambersons was perhaps not so usual a case history as the steady rise of the Sheridans, but both patterns were typically American.

While this novel is thoroughly American in character and setting, it bears a slight resemblance in structure to a Thackeray novel, as Tarkington slyly indicates by naming George's horse Pendennis. The irresponsible young George Minafer has a good many traits in common with Arthur Pendennis: both are selfish, conceited, arrogant young gentlemen who eventually land on their feet. The heroine of Thackeray's novel, Laura Bell, who ultimately marries Arthur Pendennis, presents another point of comparison, being, like Lucy Morgan, loyal, patient, forgiving, and, moreover, the daughter of a former lover of Pendennis' mother. Finally, Isabel Amberson resembles slightly Helen Pendennis, Arthur's mother, in her great devotion to her son and in her blindness to his many shortcomings. Thackeray, however, was not one of Tarkington's masters of style and narrative technique: the Englishman's old-fashioned authorial asides and moralizings were objectionable, and in one specific characterization (Henry Esmond) Tarkington thought there was "too much niceness." Yet in his mid-sixties when he rediscovered Thackeray, he found him "a true giant."

The story of *The Magnificent Ambersons* focuses its attention on the old Major's grandson, George Minafer, who is introduced as a nine-year-old terror. Completely spoiled and undisciplined, George conducts himself like an arrogant young lord and gains the cordial dislike of the entire community. Everyone hopes that some day he will get his "comeuppance." As he grows up, he begins to dominate his indulgent mother, the beautiful Isabel, who unhappily has married a nonentity in Wilbur Minafer, and when his father dies, he refuses to let his mother marry the man she once had loved, Eugene Morgan, now a widower. George also quarrels with Lucy Morgan when she objects to his idleness, and together mother and son go off to live in Europe. By the time they return to their midland city some years later, Morgan has become a wealthy automobile manufacturer, and the Amberson fortune has vanished. George's mother then dies of a heart attack, and the spoiled youth finally comes up against the realities of life with neither money nor position. George also finds that he must reap the universal hostility that he has been sowing all his life. But as the novel ends, he begins the family comeback by going to work in a factory (the only thing he could do) and starts his personal regeneration by asking Lucy to forgive his follies.

The Magnificent Ambersons is a book to conjure with, for Tarkington not only told a good story against the social and economic background of Indianapolis, but he also worked out appropriate themes to give the novel significance. George is the victim of the dead hand of tradition, which is represented by the inherited self-esteem of the Amberson clan and rests on no firmer a foundation than the physical accumulation of wealth. The imposing mansion that the old Major builds in Amberson Addition symbolizes the unsubstantial nature of the family's magnificence, for the house cannot remain a monument in a dynamic, expanding society, and as the city spreads beyond the house and the industrial center encroaches on it, the Major's proud creation becomes an anachronism, then is razed for a tenement. When the family fortune finally is dissipated and George has to go to work, the moral rebirth of the Ambersons takes place and the family begins to grow again. In Tarkington's moral order, work was the cornerstone.

Allied with the theme of work and regeneration is another interesting motif represented by the mother-son relationship. Isabel is a possessive mother whose smothering love leaves her son incomplete. In fact, it reduces him to moral idiocy and results in the destruction of her romance, her subsequent death, and the near ruin of George's own life. One critic, Robert Morss Lovett, wrote: "There is something very powerful in Mr. Tarkington's working out of this theme—the love of Isabel for her son . . . but it is clothed in a garb so usual, so domestic, that we do not recognize it. . . . It is the fate of Greek tragedy in an American home." Tarkington did not need to go to Greek tragedy for this theme, however, because he had experienced himself the perils of over-protective maternal affection.

Isabel's love for her son also is closely linked to George's regeneration, although its connection at first glance is paradoxical. When Isabel's love makes her its chief victim, its memory watches over and protects the son so that he emerges at the end stronger and better for it. It was both the cause of his damnation and the instrument of his redemption, and here again, as in *The Guest of Quesnay*, woman's love is revealed as an ennobling and purifying force. Tarkington believed implicitly in the subtle and pervasive power of women, for good or ill, on the character of men, and as Lovett also pointed out in his review, Tarkington gives an answer to Henry Adams' query in *The Education*: why is the power of woman unknown in America when she once was supreme in medieval Europe? "It is to Mr. Tarkington's credit as an artist," continued Lovett, "that he fits this theme perfectly into the American setting and handles it with reserve and proportion, in good faith and without cynicism. . . . He gives us spiritual values according to American standards, and professes his own artistic belief in them."

Old Indianapolis residents made a parlor game out of matching Tarkington's fiction to the history and physical features of their city. They noted that Amberson Addition with its large homes and cast-iron statues had been modeled after Woodruff Place, although liberties had been taken with the city's geography. Present-day readers can see, relatively unchanged, the locale of this novel, for Woodruff Place still is a residential enclave close to the industrial heart of Indianapolis. Having survived the ravages of the soft coal era and the trek to the suburbs, the Place remains somewhat as Tarkington knew it a generation ago. The Amberson mansion, however, was put in Woodruff Place by artistic license, as the author explained to a *Life* editor in 1942 when Orson Welles made a movie of the novel.

The old Major's monument actually had been drawn from the house which still exists as headquarters for the Knights of Columbus on Delaware Street near the center of the city. Perhaps even more interesting than the identification of places is Tarkington's use of Indianapolis economic history in the character of Eugene Morgan, the pioneer automobile manufacturer. His rise to wealth and position was taken from life, for the Indiana capital once rivaled Detroit as an automotive center. Nowadays Hoosiers are reminded of this fact once each year when the Five-Hundred-Mile Race is held at the Indianapolis Speedway on Memorial Day.

Although the novel appeared in book form during the unsettled autumn of 1918, it was an immediate popular and critical success. The following year it won the Pulitzer Prize and since then has enjoyed an active history of reprintings and translations. Moreover, it has been excerpted for anthologies, published in Braille, condensed, broadcast and filmed twice. But one of the most satisfying aspects of its reception was another letter from Howells, who wrote: "I thought you could not do another book as great as *The Turmoil,* but I believe your *Magnificent Ambersons* is even greater in certain ways. It is very *even,* very close, very equal. . . . there is no weakness in the Ambersons. George and his mother are no truer than the rest, but they are wonder-true, and they are marvelously managed. . . . I hail you again triumphant." To this Tarkington replied, characteristically: "There is no other reward, for me, like a word from you."

While the years from 1914 to 1918 were a richly creative period for Tarkington the novelist, they were a time of action for Tarkington the propagandist. As a man, he could not escape the demands of his social conscience, and the cataclysm which began at Sarajevo in the summer of 1914 immediately engaged his emotions and soon his energies. His strong French ties aligned him with the Allies long before most Americans troubled themselves over the issues involved in the war, and in the Midwest where isolationism was strong his outspoken support of France and England was especially conspicuous. Indianapolis, moreover, like other Midwestern cities, offered a special problem with its large German-born population whose sympathies had to be neutralized before American support of the Allies could be marshaled effectively. During the thirty-two months between the outbreak of hostilities and America's entrance into the war, Tarkington wrote at least ten magazine and newspaper articles vigorously upholding his convictions. He also associated himself with like-minded individuals, first in the Indianapolis branch of the American Rights Committee, then looking ahead, in the League to Enforce Peace.

Tarkington watched the conflagration with growing alarm during its first winter, and after the *Lusitania* was torpedoed the following May, he no longer could stand aside quietly. "I'm a little crazy about the whole thing," he wrote Jim Barnes. "Can't think of other things. I've written to Woodrow [Wilson]!" His letter had urged immediate training and arming of one million men and the passage of gigantic appropriations for army and navy. But at the moment, he said, any strong posturing at Germany by this country would be like "my threatening to twist Jack Johnson's wrist." He realized early in 1915 that the United States could not remain on the sidelines and ought to be getting ready. He published these ideas in the *Metropolitan Magazine* in July, and when the Indianapolis *News* attacked him, he defended himself spiritedly.

Throughout the following year Tarkington leveled his sights at the large pro-German element in the United States and for their benefit refuted claims that the war had been forced on Germany. His arguments were calm, logical, and deadly earnest, and although he seemed uncomfortable in the role of foreign affairs analyst, he expressed himself strongly and forthrightly, not hesitating to attack anyone who opposed his views. "Joining the German-Americans [who oppose preparedness]," he wrote, "are the pacifists and the followers of Mr. Bryan and the kind of Republicans in the Congress who are willing to injure their country for the sake of embarrassing a Democratic administration, and also . . . the political trimmers who are afraid of the German vote."

A year later, less than a month before America entered the war, Tarkington no longer was able to argue dispassionately. He then took as a point of departure for bitter satire Wilson's charge that a "little group of wilful men" had rendered the

United States "helpless and contemptible." Tarkington flayed these "wilful men" in Congress and their followers who opposed American preparedness and specifically the arming of our merchant ships. In terms almost Swiftean, a highly unusual performance for Tarkington, he traced the history of the war and American relations with Germany from the viewpoint of an arrogant German who is convinced of English and French treachery and contemptuous of American passivity. Entitling his article "Laughing in German," he described with heavy sarcasm the merriment produced in Germany by the spectacle of an American Congress voting to accept docilely German piracy on the high seas.

As American-German relations gradually deteriorated, Tarkington went beyond the mere writing of articles in an effort to help swing public opinion behind policies that the United States had to adopt. He joined a local committee sponsoring a mass meeting to protest the deportation of Belgians to Germany for forced labor and wrote a bare-knuckled letter to the editor urging support for the rally. "Whoever goes to that meeting," he declared, "is a voice—one more voice lifted in protestation against slavery . . . being actually and increasingly brought into existence in the year 1917 by the order of the German government." Two thousand persons turned out for the demonstration, for by then the United States was less than three months away from war. At the end of March Tarkington called a local meeting of the American Rights Committee, of which he was the Indianapolis chairman, and sponsored the adoption of a resolution urging Congress to enact compulsory military service legislation.

During the nineteen months that America was in the First World War Tarkington wrote twice as many articles supporting the war effort as he had written urging preparedness in the two and one-half years before, and in addition he added to his propaganda barrage a short story and a novel. Once the United States had entered the war, he shifted his polemics to meet the altered circumstances, and instead of attacking German-Americans and the lack of preparation, he tried both to allay the suspicion against German-born citizens and to solidify American acceptance of the war. He filled all requests for articles, whether or not the suggested subject lay within his compeency. When the Secretary of the Interior asked him to support he U. S. School Garden Army, he made Penrod a victory gardener, though he wrote a friend that he knew nothing about vegetables except on the table. Later he admitted, after producing a solicited article on wartime economics, that he was writing on subjects about which "I know not a damthing; but I'm an old fox at that—I won't get caught at it!"

Tarkington's wartime pamphleteering was a compensation for his inability to serve more actively. He recognized that a writer's chief function in time of war is the production of propaganda, but even so, he often felt that words were inadequate. "I wish they'd find me good enough for something besides writing," he explained on one occasion, "[but] it's all I can do." Another time he stated his attitude more fully, in a letter to George Ade: "I have a feeling of shame . . . that I'm not carrying a gun . . . EVERYTHING's been said and said . . . I want my limber joints and good wind and dependable heart of twenty years ago . . . I don't want to argue . . . I want to call 'em bastards and move toward the brick pile."

While Tarkington was turning out propaganda with indefatigable zeal, he wrote the story "Captain Schlotterwerz," which treated fictionally the German-American conflict of loyalties. For this tale he created a German-born wholesale grocer and his daughter from Cincinnati and described their gradual disillusionment with the Fatherland. Their awakening takes place during a wartime visit to Mexico where they meet a German relative, Captain Schlotterwerz, who is engaged in espionage. The Captain first shocks them by casually admitting that German propaganda is deliberately mendacious, and when he goes on to promulgate a master-race theory and to argue that war is ennobling, they turn from him in horror. The grocer and his daughter return to Ohio clear in their allegiance to democratic ideals and their adopted country. The story was sent first to *Collier's,* which turned it down as too patently propaganda, and when Tarkington recovered from the surprise of his first rejection in eleven years, he placed the tale in the *Saturday Evening Post.*

The novel which Tarkington wrote early in 1918 was *Ramsay Milholland,* an imaginative exposition of the reasons for America's war participation. Tarkington used all the skill that he had learned in *Penrod* and *Seventeen* to create a youth whose story was both a tribute to the men who fought and a justification for their sacrifice. He pulled the reader emotionally into the conflict by the gradual involvement of Ramsay, whose enlistment while still in college furnishes the denouement of the novel. Ramsay is first shown at the age of Penrod, then at the age of Willie Baxter, and finally as a college student. He represents, Tarkington told a friend, "the 'average young fellow' I saw turning into a soldier in Indiana in 1917—the boy who got in at the first." That Tarkington loved this boy is apparent, but the novel suffers artistically because of its didactic content; yet he designed it as a work of siege merely, and it served a temporary purpose. The only other memorable character in the tale is Dora Yocum, Ramsay's studious classmate who grows up to be a disarmingly pretty pacifist. She serves the author's end as a mouthpiece for ideas that he refutes, but he cannot help sympathizing with her spiritual anguish when war comes, and he makes her a credible individual of a recognizable type—the idealist in a pragmatic society.

During the last six months of the war Tarkington was completely absorbed in pamphleteering. He wrote frequently for the National Security League's campaign for patriotism through education, and his articles were distributed by the League to newspapers from coast to coast. He urged the buying of Liberty Bonds, with tireless repetition of the same arguments, and solicited funds for the Red Cross with equal diligence. In the midst of these voluntary labors he reported that his hand and eyes were bothering him from trying to write fiction already contracted for as well as war propaganda. He added, however, that he planned nothing but the war work from then on, and at the end of April he wrote: "I've long since dropped all work of my own." He was even selling war bonds on the University Club team, he said, and when he observed that old clothes and patched shoes had become fashionable, he added: "I'm wearing patched shoes myself—first time since I was about 14, and feel able to survive the shame of it as once I *could* not!"

When it became apparent that the Allies would defeat Germany, Tarkington began thinking and writing about postwar policies. In June Albert Beveridge, former Indiana Senator, attacked the League to Enforce Peace, and Tarkington, who was a member of the organization, wrote a sharp reply. He argued boldly for a League of Nations that would have real power to outlaw war. When Beveridge charged that the United States would have to go to war with other nations to enforce orders of the League, Tarkington replied that we must dare to do exactly that. When Beveridge argued that the League was not American in origin, Tarkington answered that neither were the Pilgrim Fathers. Finally, Tarkington concluded: "[If] you are opposed to a safe world you are opposed to the principles of the league. You may think the thing can't be done, but you can't think it oughtn't to be done."

Tarkington had been deeply and exhaustingly engaged in the dual role of creative artist and propagandist during 1917 and 1918. With splendid energy he finished *The Magnificent Ambersons* as the war engulfed the United States and put another play on Broadway while the conflict was going on. Moreover, he produced a wartime novel in *Ramsay Milholland*, supervised a collected edition of his works in 1918, and turned out an astonishing number of ephemeral pieces to support the Allied cause. Yet three weeks before the Armistice was signed, he already was planning important new work which would carry on his renewed interest in the theater.

TEN

BACK TO BROADWAY

W HEN TARKINGTON RENOUNCED THE THEATER in his moment of physical and spiritual crisis, he thought his retirement would be permanent, but he soon discovered that the habit of writing plays was inveterate. In 1915 he returned to Broadway and subsequently divided his ripest creative years between fiction and drama. Though he regarded the theater as merely a hobby, when he finally burned his last footlight behind him at the age of sixty-one, the four years after 1911 turned out to be the only hiatus in his theatrical career. Even after 1931, the year he decamped from Broadway, he took an active summer interest in the Garrick Players of Kennebunkport, rewriting two of his plays for them, and gave winter encouragement to the Indianapolis Civic Theater, which was named for him after his death.

After his interest in the theater revived, Tarkington wrote thirteen additional plays, more than he had turned out earlier for the amateur and professional stage combined, and in this renewed burst of dramatic energy he wrote with and without the help of a collaborator. Four times he tried with Harry Wilson to recapture the old gaiety of *The Man from Home* but failed each time. Usually he went it alone, and while he achieved his greatest theatrical success in this fashion, he also bore the responsibility for several complete failures. As before, Broadway exerted an irresistible pull, and he seldom could turn down a producer or an actor who begged him to do a play.

When Tarkington decided to try the drama once more, he wrote Otis Skinner: "I am beginning to have a feeling that I'd like to write another play, and that I'd like to write it for you." He wanted to create a *"Beautiful* man," he said, although he was not sure just how he would do it. At various times before writing, the "beautiful" man was banker, farmer, electrician, and policeman, but Tarkington finally drew inspiration from Antonio Ansovini, the hack driver he once had employed in Rome. He called the play *Mr. Antonio*, made his title character a wandering organ-grinder, gave him for companions a jackass and a half-wit, and provided him with faith in humanity and *joie de vivre*. After pondering the characters and action for about two weeks, he wrote out the play, almost exactly as it was produced, in another three weeks. "I get what I want now, the first time I do it," he wrote Tyler.

Skinner saw the manuscript in May, 1915, when Tarkington invited him to visit Kennebunkport for a reading. "Never was a more engaging, lovable Dago than *Tony Camaradonio*," the actor recalled later in his memoirs. From the start he was charmed with the play and captivated by Tony, who became a favorite role. For three seasons after the opening night in New York in September, 1916, he toured the country as Mr. Antonio and while the war was going on sold Liberty Bonds, during curtain calls, in the broken English of the organ-grinder. "There is scarcely a city of importance in the country," wrote Skinner, "where this son of Sorrento has not appeared. Several of our little jackasses grew weary of the burden . . . but still *Tony* went on his way grinding out THE TOREADOR and ON-WARD, CHRISTIAN SOLDIERS from New York to California."

The play opens in Tug's European Café on Third Avenue in New York where Mayor Jorny of Avalonia, Pennsylvania, is sleeping off the effects of a three-day spree in the city. Jorny discovers that he has been robbed of his money, watch, and overcoat, and just as the bartender is about to throw him into the street, Tony drops in, gives him a coat, and loans him a dollar to wire home for money. Tony performs his Good Samaritan act fully recognizing Jorny as the blue-nosed Mayor who the year before had caused his arrest in Avalonia for playing his hurdy-gurdy on Sunday. But Tony believes in returning good for evil and bets the skeptical bartender that Jorny will be grateful.

The play then shifts to the Mayor's town, which Tony purposely visits some weeks later in his annual wanderings. He soon finds that Jorny is a pious hypocrite at home. As Tony arrives, the Mayor and the village minister are energetically persecuting June Ramsay, a hired girl caught sneaking out at night for a date. Tony, championing June, reminds Jorny of the New York escapade, but the Mayor is incapable of a generous act and tries to destroy Tony to avoid forgiving June. Stung by this duplicity and ingratitude, Tony is about to unmask Jorny when he realizes that exposure is not worth the effort. The organ-grinder then turns his back on Avalonia and taking the girl with him goes off to continue his summer roaming. He grieves that his estimate of Jorny was mistaken, but he will not brood over man's inhumanity to man.

Skinner rightly observed in his memoirs that *Mr. Antonio* was "the expression of all that is tender and imaginative in Tarkington." He might have added that the character of the organ-grinder was in part a projection of the playwright's own personality, for Tony is a genial, optimistic humanitarian who is unwilling to pass judgment on people and reluctant to believe in human depravity. "Dees worl'," says Tony expounding a philosophy of laughter, "she can do wot she like to me; I am goin' to *laugh!* If a man 'e do me some ugly trick, I am goin' laugh in 'is face! . . . I laugh w'en I wan' to laugh an' I laugh w'en I wan' to cry!" If one insists on making a noise in the world, the Italian adds, one should laugh rather than cry, for laughter is the pleasanter sound and pleasant people get on better.

Because the play reached Broadway at a time when the theater was ripe for the naturalism of O'Neill, Tony's Christian ethics did not please many of the Broadway critics and theatergoers. "Poor Mrs. Tarkington & Mrs. Skinner," wrote the playwright after the opening, "wept over the anvil chorus in the next day's papers"; but notwithstanding, *Mr. Antonio* ran six weeks in New York before going on its long, successful tour. The reviewers liked Skinner, but they thought the play was loaded with stereotyped characters unworthy of the creator of Penrod and Willie Baxter. They especially thought the small Pennsylvania town was artificially contrived. Tarkington's disappointment was somewhat mitigated by *Harper's* request to serialize the play, and he wrote Tyler: "If you happen to suggest to any critic that he might understand it better by reading it in *Harper's* I shan't be hurt." He added that the magazine never had published plays, except the one-act farces of Howells; hence the editors' desire to print *Mr. Antonio* was "a very pretty compliment and rather an answer to the 'critics.'"

Although the New York critics were unimpressed, the play was not regarded as a stencil in the smaller cities that it visited. During the road tour its criticism of human failings sometimes touched sensitive spots. On one occasion a clergyman charged that the village preacher, who was drawn, like Jorny, as a sanctimonious bigot, slandered the ministerial profession. Tarkington replied that his purpose had been to satirize individuals, not to attack occupations or types. "It is dangerous," he wrote in rebuttal, "for an individual to assume that any attempted work of art . . . actually is what it appears to himself. I have known a child to assume that his grandfather, kneeling for family prayers, was a horse to be mounted and ridden." To George Ade he explained that the play was "meant to symbolize the inwardness of the Good Samaritan who was a good pagan, lover of beauty and spirit—didn't care for gratitude or ingratitude either."

Two months after Skinner visited Maine to read the manuscript of *Mr. Antonio,* Tarkington began work on a second play, this time a comedy in collaboration with Julian Street. After he had written a play for Skinner, George Tyler also wanted one and suggested a variation of *The Man from Home.* He thought that a female counterpart of the Kokomo lawyer could be created and put into a similar situation. Tarkington was agreeable: "I get your idea of sex-reversing 'The Man from Home' and it can be done successfully, I feel sure." The result of this three-way partnership by producer and co-authors was *The Country Cousin* (originally *The Ohio Lady*), which places an Ohio girl, Nancy Price, in amusing juxtaposition with a passel of sophisticated Easterners. The play eventually became one of Tyler's more successful presentments, but before it reached Broadway in 1917 it had to be overhauled. Tarkington did the remodeling, taking infinite pains to get every scene, situation, character, and line right, but even when the early version was hardly recognizable, he insisted that Street still receive half of the royalties.

Tarkington and Street, though not exact contemporaries, had

been friends a long time, and the comedy's joint authorship resulted from Tarkington's desire to give his protégé some experience in the theater. Tarkington originally had persuaded Street to quit journalism for creative writing and during the intervening years had dispensed much literary advice and encouragement. Street admired and loved Tarkington, relied heavily on his literary judgment, reckoned him his favorite novelist, and was a frequent correspondent. When Tarkington was temporarily blind in 1930, Street organized the compilation of a "golden book" of Christmas greetings from scores of prominent statesmen, writers, and old friends. For Street there always was a "kind of magic" about Tarkington and however much one admired his writings, he said after his friend's death, "the man was greater than anything he wrote."

The Country Cousin, a farce-comedy of manners, is full of amusing lines, humorous situations, witty characterization. The fun begins when Nancy Price goes to New York from Ohio to rescue her rich, foolish cousin Eleanor Howitt, whose divorced father has taken her off to see LIFE in the East and, incidentally, to support him. One of his friends is George Tewksberry Reynolds III, a rich young snob, who is divested of his smugness and then captivated by the redoubtable Nancy. The play ends with two missions accomplished: the repossession of Eleanor and the reformation of a rich, eligible young man.

Tarkington and Street turned out the first draft of the play easily in July, 1915, when Street visited Kennebunkport. After several days of hard labor Tarkington wrote Tyler: "Finished Act 1 last night at two—and Julian all in. Calls me 'Simon Legree,' and is evidently having a new experience. My way of plug-plug *straight* on is hard on him—and he's hollow-eyed and weak-voiced. . . . First act looks pretty fair." The collaborators soon finished the remaining three acts, then polished up the manuscript and sent it off to Tyler for casting.

During the production of the play Tarkington and Tyler resumed their old relationship. Although they were direct opposites, they got along well together and remained friends as long as they lived. Tarkington once more gave Tyler the first chance at most of his plays and got so accustomed to Tyler that he eventually began to feel himself on insecure and unfamiliar ground whenever anyone else produced his work, "like

a Princeton undergraduate wandering in the Harvard Yard."
After he had known Tyler for thirty years, Tarkington put him
into a theater novel, *Presenting Lily Mars,* and there drew his
sharp but sympathetic portrait as the producer George Hurley,
"the most uneven-tempered man in the world." George Hurley is neither the cold-blooded, statistically minded promoter
nor the P. T. Barnum kind of showman, the young playwright
in the novel tells his mother: "Managing is really an art for
him, not a business; he rages at the stage, wails that he hates it
and all the time has a passion for it. That's why he's so difficult."

Tyler, for his part, not only was attracted to Tarkington as
a friend but also was indebted to him as a dramatic adviser.
When Tyler had an anemic play on his hands, Tarkington
often would drop what he was doing and suggest ways of in-
jecting new vitality into the languishing drama. "Nobody will
ever know how much he helped with many of our big successes," wrote Tyler in his memoirs; "he's always been the most
generous man I've ever known." Sometimes Tyler, to his regret, rejected the advice, such as when Tarkington urged him
to give George Kaufman and Marc Connelly a typewriter and
a free hand and not to trouble himself further about lack of
plot in their plays. But Tyler could not resist meddling, he
remembered, and ultimately lost the playwrights he had discovered.

Tyler was impulsive and often tried the patience of his associates by rushing ahead with productions that needed
recasting and revising. After *The Country Cousin* failed in its
tryout at Columbus, Street wrote Tarkington that the next
time they collaborated on a play they ought to make Tyler
outline explicit staging plans at the beginning or have their
play put on by producers who "don't slap things on in too
much hurry, and who don't live in perpetual hysterics during
production." Yet Tarkington never lost his temper with Tyler
and assumed a large share of blame for the early failure.

During the play's long period of incubation Tarkington took
an active interest in production details. "I know your anxiety
to cast rightly is greater than mine," he wrote Tyler a month
before the play was tested in Columbus; "but I want to be a
prop to your elbow. . . . Don't yield to the temptation to take

the best the market affords if that best isn't *right!* . . . Don't put it on at all if you don't get THE 'George.' If he isn't right, we haven't a smell." Tarkington also wrote frequently of the necessity for getting exactly the right person to play Nancy, suggesting at various times Janet Beecher, Marjorie Rambeau, Elsie Ferguson, then wishing "there were some fascinating creature entirely or almost new to the public." He went on to specify: "She must be fresh-looking, *youthful,* not a kid, but young womanhood." Earlier he had declared that the "girl to play it will be the one who's crazy about it." Above all, he cautioned Tyler, "there's no hurry."

When the play finally reached Broadway in September, 1917, Alexandra Carlisle and Eugene O'Brien were cast in the roles of Nancy and George, a happy combination that insured a successful New York run. After the final rewriting Tarkington had advised Tyler: "I've completed the 78th or *1*78th remodeling (I forget which) of 'The Country Cousin' and, while I think there was the *ms* of a very respectable and probably successful play before, I'm inclined, for the first time, really to chuckle over this new edition." But again the Broadway critics found fault and damned Tarkington's efforts with tepid enthusiasm. Yet they admitted that the duel between Miss Carlisle and Mr. O'Brien was superb and might carry the play if the basic incredibility of the "crude moving-picture plot" could be swallowed. The comedy never caught on as *The Man from Home* had, though it became one of Tarkington's four or five most successful plays. Fortunately, the opening-night reaction of the critics was partly offset by an old Tarkington admirer, Theodore Roosevelt, who occupied a box with Street at the première and by popular demand made a curtain-speech praising the play.

The most memorable aspect of *The Country Cousin,* however, was not its production but its result. When Eugene O'Brien left the company at the end of its New York run, Miss Carlisle nominated his replacement for the road tour. The young man she suggested only recently had come to New York and had just played his first small part on Broadway. She had been greatly impressed with his talent and persuaded Tyler to engage him for the tour. When the road company visited Boston later, Tarkington, full of misgivings about losing

O'Brien, went down from Kennebunkport to see it. The fencing between Miss Carlisle and O'Brien had been the great thing in the play, and it seemed impossible that an inexperienced youngster could manage the role. Hence Tarkington had no confidence at all in the evening's success when he scanned the program and saw opposite the part of George Tewksberry Reynolds III the name of an unknown actor—Alfred Lunt.

Backstage, after the performance, however, Tarkington delightedly congratulated Lunt on playing a perfect George to Miss Carlisle's Nancy. Greatly impressed, he invited the young man to have lunch with him the following winter when *The Country Cousin* visited Indianapolis. He had decided on the spot that he wanted to write a play for Lunt, and all summer he mulled over ideas for a comedy that would show off best the youngster's personality and ability. In October, 1918, he wrote Tyler: "Let me write a play for Lunt of my own kind. . . . You don't have to take it, but you['ve] got to let it go on my way if you do take it—only keep a hold on Lunt so we can get him. He's *it*."

The next month Lunt arrived in Indianapolis for a week at English's Theater and called on Tarkington, as he had been asked to do. After lunch (Lunt still recalls that they had artichokes with Hollandaise sauce, lamb chops, and au gratin potatoes) the two men retired to the study to discuss the play that was taking shape in Tarkington's mind. When the session broke up hours later, an exuberant young Lunt slid down the banister and exclaimed to Mrs. Tarkington: "He's going to write a play for me! I'm made! I'm made!" The play was *Clarence,* which gave Lunt his first starring role on Broadway and began a warm friendship between the two men. "I should have worshipped Mr. Tarkington even if he hadn't written a play for me!" writes Lunt; "he was, and still is, my idea of a great American gentleman."

Although the play was written for Lunt, *Clarence* also made theater history by featuring another of Tyler's discoveries—Helen Hayes—in one of her first grown-up parts. Tarkington had Miss Hayes in mind as well as Lunt when he worked up material for the play. In the same letter that urged Tyler to hang on to Lunt he had said: "Let me make your fortune for you—about next year, perhaps . . . [with] LUNT and a girl like

Miss Hayes." Several months later when the play was half written, he again wrote, this time emphatically: "*Got* to have
Helen Hayes. . . . This is the best girl or woman part I ever
managed to write . . . and needs just that one young genius-
person H. H. to play it." The actress had come to Tarkington's
attention in 1918 when she played her first adult part as the
older sister Margaret in E. E. Rose's dramatization of *Penrod,*
a play that had the bad luck to reach New York about the time
the influenza epidemic closed public places to children. When
Clarence was cast several months later, Helen Hayes was just
eighteen and available for a part, but already she had been on
the stage for ten years and had played fifty roles.

Between the closing of *Penrod* and the opening of *Clarence*
Miss Hayes played Margaret in Barrie's *Dear Brutus,* giving a
performance which more than ever convinced Tarkington that
she had extraordinary capabilities. He wrote Tyler again:
"Lovely pictures of Helen Hayes in 'Current Opinion'—con-
firming me in *my* opinion of her at first sight that she could be
the coming first lady of the stage." The part of Cora that he
wanted her to play in *Clarence,* he added, would give her a
chance to do the opposite type of character from Barrie's Margaret, who is a "dream" girl—"the sort of daughter a bachelor
thinks he'd have. 'Cora' is what would really happen with
average luck." His young woman, he continued, was a feminine Willie Baxter, silly and foolish because of "adolescent
longings and glamorings combined with inexperience." The
part of Cora overplayed, he warned, would be idiotic. "There
must be a kind of funny sweetness about 'Cora'—and Helen
Hayes would strike that note center."

After he had been to the play's opening, Tarkington wrote
Tyler that his most retained picture was "that *darling* Helen
Hayes sitting on the floor at the end. Golly, what an inspired
wonder she is! She's one of the few perfect things one sees
in a lifetime—and her performance of 'Cora' doesn't leave a
look, gesture or intonation that could possibly be imagined as
different." Miss Hayes, too, found the relationship with Tarkington completely satisfying, and after she had left the *Clarence* company to star in *Bab,* she wrote him: "There will never
be another 'Clarence.' I don't believe you realize the happiness

you have given with that play—not only to the public but mostly to the actors in it."

Clarence was the one perfect instant in Tarkington's dramatic career. He wrote it exactly as he wanted it, and Tyler staged it just as it was written. Perhaps the most remarkable thing about the entire venture was that the play opened in September with scarcely a line changed from the manuscript that Tarkington had delivered to Tyler in the middle of June. Frederick Stanhope, who directed the production, never had seen a play so little revised in his twenty-five years of theater experience. After watching the Atlantic City try-out, Tarkington rewrote a ten-word speech near the end of act one; then in the third act the director himself later transposed a speech with the playwright's permission. There were no other significant alterations or cuts: the play was a felicitous combination of inspiration and technical control at Tarkington's most creative moment.

With characteristic modesty Tarkington gave complete credit to the cast. In a good play, of course, Lunt and Miss Hayes could not have failed to score a hit, but Tarkington included everyone in his note of appreciation tacked by Tyler on the call board at the Hudson Theater: "Please express my gratitude to all of the 'Clarence' Co. & tell them to note how nicely a play goes when the author keeps away from it." And, he added, the cast is so good it could "play the Telephone Directory and make a hit with it." To Tyler privately he said: "Perfect casts are once in ten years, and you've about got one."

The play ran three hundred performances on Broadway and delighted everyone. Even Heywood Broun and Woollcott, who had maintained loudly that Tarkington could not write a play, publicly retracted their previous opinions. Woollcott wrote in his review that *Clarence* was "as American as 'Huckleberry Finn' or pumpkin pie. It is as delightful as any native comedy which has tried to lure the laughter of this community in the last ten seasons." On opening night when the first call came and the curtain went up, the entire house was standing and "remained that way up to about twenty-five curtain calls." People tore up programs, used them for confetti, then threw hats and handkerchiefs. Not only did the play storm New York triumphantly, but the Chicago company, which opened four months later, received much acclaim and gave its cast, which included Ruth Gordon and Gregory Kelly, a moment long to be remembered.

Clarence is a play that still reads and acts well. As the curtain rises, its title character, a recently discharged war veteran who looks like "Sad Sack," waits patiently in the outer office of a busy industrialist named Wheeler to ask for a job. He is an ex-private, whose uniform does not fit, whose manner is inept, whose appearance is utterly undistinguished. In the course of the play, moreover, the audience learns that Clarence never saw action, did not even get overseas. He spent the war driving mules in Texas (somebody, he explains, had to drive the mules), and his only wound was sustained during target practice. While Clarence waits, one agitated member of Wheeler's family after another comes in. Cora Wheeler is in love with a married man and resents her governess' interference. Violet, the governess, cannot control Cora and has to seek advice from Wheeler. Mrs. Wheeler is jealous of Violet, and Bobby, the adolescent son, not only has been expelled from preparatory school but also has been caught kissing the housemaid. Clarence, unnoticed, is privy to all the Wheelers' domestic problems, and when he finally gets to see the magnate, Wheeler gets rid of him by hiring him as a social secretary for his home.

The rest of the comedy keeps pace with this skillfully managed opening. When Clarence takes off his badly tailored uniform, he turns out to be a person of amazing charm and ability. He soon begins to attract Cora, who forgets her infatuation with the married man. He tutors Bobby in math in order to get him back in prep school, and he charms Mrs. Wheeler out of her jealousy. He also diverts Della, the maid, so that she forgets about blackmailing Bobby, and he entertains everyone by playing the saxophone. Later in the play, after the hilarity has gone on for three-plus acts, Clarence is revealed as a distinguished entomologist, an authority on potato bugs, who is working for the Wheelers only until a professional appointment begins.

The critical response to *Clarence* was one of the major surprises that Tarkington experienced in a long life. Two weeks before the play was to open, the critics mercilessly flayed the initial performance of *Up from Nowhere,* a new play written with Harry Wilson. Although Skinner had been offered and had rejected this drama, Tarkington was not prepared for its complete failure and blamed the critics' *idée fixe* that novelists could not write plays. This stereotyped judgment had plagued the openings of *Mr. Antonio* and *The Country Cousin* until Tarkington had been convinced that he could not get an impartial hearing. "The newspaper notices of 'Up from Nowhere' let you know what to expect for 'Clarence,'" he wrote Tyler; then he added: "These play-lice will never go back on their own verdict until I slip a name over." *Clarence,* however, was produced under Tarkington's name despite his impression that "a dramatic critic entering a theater to see a play of mine . . . would be unable to see it except as another demonstration of his previous pronunciamentos in my favor as a novelist." When the critics surprised themselves and confounded Tarkington by greeting *Clarence* with unrestrained enthusiasm, he wrote several weeks later: "I have not yet recovered from the astonishment natural to this occasion—a pen name would have made no difference at all."

The success of *Clarence* helped to assuage the disappointment of four failures that occurred during its preparation and long run. First there was *Up from Nowhere,* which closed just as *Clarence* opened. It was about a self-made millionaire, George Washington Silver, and his problems in adjusting to wealth. Woollcott found it "a somewhat languid and only spasmodically interesting comedy." Then Tarkington and Wilson tried again in an anti-Communist propaganda farce, *The Gibson Upright,* which dealt with labor relations in a piano factory. Stuart Walker produced this play in Indianapolis in July, 1919, but it never got to New York, and even reviewers in Tarkington's home town called it "decidedly amateurish." Yet after the *Saturday Evening Post* published the drama, it won a measure of approval as a reading play. The Eastman Kodak Company published a special edition to distribute to its employees, and the *Plumbers Trade Journal* asked to reprint it. Far greater discouragement, however, attended the failure of two plays that Tarkington wrote without collaboration and wanted greatly to succeed, *Poldekin* and *The Wren.*

Poldekin was a serious attempt to combat the spread of Communism by attacking the specious propositions of Marxist dialectic. As early as 1919 Tarkington saw clearly the threat to democratic institutions posed by the Russian Revolution and sounded the alarm. Spurred by the same patriotic motive that guided his propaganda output during the war, he wrote the play to make people think about the basic freedoms that Americans take for granted. In an attempt to get his message across Tarkington tailored the drama to the talents of George Arliss, who he felt could give the "purely intellectual performance" that the play required; but all his efforts to make a success of *Poldekin* failed, and the play ran only forty-four performances on Broadway.

It is difficult to judge fairly today an anti-Communistic play written a generation ago when the ideological struggle was new and different. Tarkington's motive in creating *Poldekin* was wholly admirable, and his vision was unclouded; but the play is dated because the nature of the problem has changed. When *Poldekin* was produced, Communistic dogma was a more subtle poison than now, though the physical fact of Russia was negligible. Now that this situation is reversed, Tarkington's simple revolutionists, who know only a few Marxist slogans, are hopelessly ingenuous compared with present-day agents of the Kremlin. Yet the basic idea of the play remains sound: the conspirator Poldekin, who comes to the United States to foment revolution, learns the meaning of America and in the end rejects the Communist Manifesto in favor of the Declaration of Independence. Tragically, when Poldekin "finds" America, he is liquidated by the other revolutionaries.

Although the play sacrifices action to ideology, Tarkington was not wholly responsible for its early demise. Errors of judgment by the producer and star, the hostility of the critics, and the apathy of the public insured the failure. When the play was tried out in the spring, it became obvious that the theatergoers were not much interested in Communism and unresponsive to an intellectual appeal. Tyler and Arliss then tried to capture the audience through its emotions and to make the play into a melodrama. They insisted that the shot fired at Poldekin in the last act had to miss so that the play could end happily. When this suggestion, already put into effect, was relayed to Tarkington, he wired: "Play end as I wrote it." Then by letter he explained that the New York critics would not stand for that kind of ending. He had tried a missed shot in *Mr. Antonio* and had not gotten away with it. "I decline," he continued, "this ticket entitling Booth Tarkington to be hit on his nut by the *same* sledge hammer. . . . If the play is kept a tragedy, at least the NY critics will have to say there was no concession made to the happy ending." Tyler and Arliss ultimately had their way, however, and Tarkington rewrote the ending so that the shot did not injure Poldekin fatally.

Even if the final scene had not been altered, some of the critics still would have been unfriendly for ideological reasons. After reading the opening night reviews, Tarkington wrote Tyler: "My feeling is one of some bewilderment . . . as if one spoke to a gathering of ordinary human beings . . . what one knew to be the truth . . . and suddenly the human faces became masks of bestial mockery, screaming 'Fool!' 'Liar!' 'Jackass!' . . . Some devil of perversity must have been at the Park Theater on the 9th." Tarkington attributed this hostility to the Socialistic bias of several influential critics whom he regarded as the bellwethers of the newspaper reviewers. To one of them, Heywood Broun, who read into the play ideas that were not there, he wrote in protest. The play says nothing, he asserted, about the American form of government being the best possible system: "It says that to any man inclined towards individual freedom what we have is more pleasing, and seems to work for more progress than what the Bolshevists offer us at a price of bloody revolution." And he went on to suggest that Broun discriminate between the best system that can be devised and the best system that can be practiced.

The critics, however, had the last word and attacked the play on artistic as well as ideological grounds. They accused Tarkington of creating bungling Russians who were straw men set up for easy knocking down, and they complained that so much economic theory had been crowded into the play that it really should be called "A Night on a Soapbox." Against these adverse judgments, public pronouncements in its favor by such eminent citizens as Nicholas Murray Butler could not keep the play going. Tarkington never again tried to combine polemics with either fiction or drama, although he rewrote

Poldekin in 1939 as *Karabash* for the Garrick Players in Kennebunkport and simultaneously let his agent offer the revision to Broadway producers. After his first feeling of bewilderment over the play's reception, he counseled Tyler philosophically: "We mustn't take this debacle too hard: in one way it is a fearful kind of joke on us—we expected people to understand. . . . We instantly got shot for trying to be . . . benefactors. . . . Well, be damned to 'em, and let it go at that."

Although Tarkington's head was bloody after *Poldekin* closed, he still was defiant and did not wait long before writing another play, *The Wren,* his first important work with a Maine locale. His bad luck continued, however, and this play failed too, though it was unsuccessful for reasons that still are hard to explain. *The Wren* was written expressly for Helen Hayes, and Tarkington poured into it all the skill that he could command. Tyler brought Leslie Howard over from England to play opposite Miss Hayes, and during the tryout the drama seemed destined for success. The New York critics, however, did not like it, and the play had to close after three weeks. Yet it contains much sparkling dialogue, a rich Maine flavor, and several excellent characterizations.

The weakness of *The Wren* apparently lay in the subtleties of its plot and character development, for though it treats a triangle situation, it does so with neither melodrama nor titilation. Laid in a Maine summer boardinghouse, *The Wren* dramatizes a low-keyed contest between Seeby Olds, the quiet daughter of an invalided sea captain, and Clara Frazee, a neurotic city boarder, for the affections of Roddy, a young artist guest. At the start of the play Clara has managed to charm Roddy, but presently her husband arrives unexpectedly to break up the flirtation, and by the end of the second act he gains the upper hand over his errant wife. From that point forward it is apparent that Seeby is going to win Roddy, and in the last two acts the romance between the Maine girl and the painter blossoms with minor complications and a minimum of action. When the Boston *Transcript* reviewer called the play an exquisite miniature with "some excellent subtleties in character and dialect," Tarkington replied that he intended it to be a little play and added: "it's taken me 30 years to learn how to make 'em little."

The part of the Maine sea captain's daughter was exactly what Tarkington thought Helen Hayes was ready to do in 1921. He wrote Tyler in April: "My feeling about her is this: it isn't time for her to play a *'great'* part (tragic end part). She mustn't be *cutely* funny again [as in *Clarence*], and the part *mustn't* be 'too sweet.' What's most wanted is something as fairly truthful as possible, with perhaps a bit of oddity and certainly *pathos*. But not deliberate pathos or obvious pathos." Her portrayal of Seeby Olds was expertly done as the playwright had imagined it. Giving her the chance to be more than the gay comedienne, it raised her acting to a higher plane than before. She was the mild, canny mistress of her father's household, at first shy and wistful in the face of Clara's superior competition for Roddy, then gradually radiant as she began to win the man she already had fallen in love with.

During the spring before the fiasco Tarkington enjoyed every minute of the play's composition and in the summer invited Miss Hayes to visit Maine. Kennebunkport, of course, is the play's locale, and the actress spent a week there in August to get the flavor of a seacoast village. Tarkington worked on the play with her, took her swimming and motorboating, and exposed her to authentic Maine vernacular. After she left Kennebunkport, he wrote that he had conducted himself towards her "not inconsiderably like a nervous old hen with a young and irresponsible duckling—especially when she went in the surf." He felt a little guilty about keeping her away from the summer colony, for after all she was only twenty. "She *ought* to have been taken to a boat-club dance of *young* people, Saturday night," he wrote Tyler. "Instead we spent the evening—till eleven—with a retired sea cap'n only 86 years old! Rest of the time working over the script, being lectured on it by a warp-faced old party [the author] with a big nose and spectacles, and motoring about Seeby's coast with the same and another aged 89! She ought, as a treat, to be taken to the birthday party of somebody four years old!" Then warning Tyler to watch her cold, "though it seems to be better," Tarkington concluded: "We all love her, of course—she's dearer everytime we see her."

When the play opened in Boston, Tarkington wrote that "Helen was touchingly appealing & it was a triumph for her. I don't see how either Boston or N. Y. could deal very unkindly with us, but one never knows." A month later when he went to New York (two weeks after the play's opening), he reported: "I never saw anything like it: a failure played as if it were a 'million dollar success'—with such *nerve* . . . and sprightly smoothness—and before an audience . . . that was beamingly delighted." The only thing wrong, he added, was the half-filled house, and he sadly concluded that the play simply did not strike the mood of the first-night audience: "We offered a pretty dish of good Maine apples and 'they' were tired and bored . . . didn't want *anything at all*." Woollcott, in his review, had called the play a lettuce sandwich, finding it insubstantial fare for a hungry man; and Tarkington admitted ruefully to Tyler that *The Wren* was "lettuce in the mouth of a chap who's fed daily on 'high' meat, fried Bull and gin."

Shocks did not come singly in the autumn of 1921, and as the critics helped destroy the play, Tarkington's emotions again were wrenched, under far different circumstances, in Washington, D. C., where he soon went on additional theater business. In the capital he witnessed a real-life drama, unexpected and unrehearsed, as moving as anything he ever had seen on the stage. He felt as if he suddenly had stepped unawares into the living pages of a modern Plutarch's *Parallel Lives,* into a scene entitled "The Leader Triumphant and the Leader Defeated." The first tableau took place early on the afternoon of November second when he joined a group of writers in a call on President Harding at the White House. Having recently been propagandists for war, Tarkington and his colleagues proposed to offer their services again in the cause of peace. They found Harding in an expansive mood and glad to see them. He had been President only seven months, and none of the troubles that later beset his administration were yet disturbing the surface. The President chatted amiably, recalled his start in life as a journalist, and singled out Tarkington for a special, and embarrassing, salute as the interview ended. Tarkington left the White House strongly impressed with Harding's physical aliveness and vibrant personality and reported later to his father: "He is a very large, very handsome man: a man who *looks* a President; and he seemed splendidly vigorous, full of quiet power—equal to anything." Harding was the triumphant leader.

A few hours later, however, in another part of Washington the Plutarchian contrast was completed. While the crowd dispersed after the Wednesday matinee of *The Intimate Strangers,* Tarkington saw with equal vividness the defeated leader:

> Coming toward me, from the door to the boxes, slowly walked a tall straight, proud woman in fine black, and behind her, leaning upon an old negro and a cane, another tall figure—that of a man in black with his face shadowed under a great black soft hat;—there was in every line and movement the expression of something remarkable, of something that had been vast, and was now unutterably shattered. His progress was tragically slow—painfully careful. He stopped, thirty feet from me, and though it's nine years since he saw me last, and though I never meant much to him in any way, he knew me at once. 'Tarkington,' he said, in a voice that was broken, too, like his body. It was Woodrow Wilson.

The sight of the physically and spiritually blasted statesman, whom Tarkington had known for thirty years as teacher, university president, and wartime commander-in-chief, was profoundly disturbing. Nothing ever effaced the indelible impression made on the playwright-novelist that afternoon in 1921 by the broken Wilson and the ebullient Harding. When both men died within two and a half years, Tarkington again had cause to reflect on the Plutarchian parallel and the vanity of human wishes.

ELEVEN

FROM BURKE TO BURR

THERE WAS NO TIME TO MOURN the untimely death of *The Wren*. Its abrupt withdrawal after twenty-four performances did no injury to Miss Hayes' career, and Tarkington already was busy not only writing but also directing a lively new domestic comedy starring Billie Burke. The new play, *The Intimate Strangers,* opened for a trial week in Washington as *The Wren* closed in New York. It was a moderate success and provided a full season of employment for its company, which included not only Miss Burke but also Alfred Lunt, Glenn Hunter, and Frances Howard. Tarkington seemed to have gained his second wind after the previous failures, and while *The Intimate Strangers* was neither as successful nor as good as *Clarence,* it was an amiable comedy in the best Tarkington vein.

Although Florenz Ziegfeld produced the play for his wife, it originally was written for Maude Adams, who had planned a return to the stage. She had written Tarkington in February when he was mulling over ideas: "I want more than anything to have you feel free and unhampered. I am so proud that you will consider writing a play for me and I should think it not only presumptuous but foolhardy to send you my chest measurement and length of skirt, back and front." She only stipulated that she could not abide Griseldas or martyrs. Tarkington avoided both and wrote her a play that was well suited to her talents, but she did not go back to the theater then; and after she had visited Kennebunkport in July to talk over the play, Tarkington reported that he did not know if she would take it or not. She has to feel it, he said,

222

Beebe Booth, maternal grandfather, who fought in the War of 1812 and then migrated to Indiana.

Mrs. Beebe Booth, maternal grandmother of Booth Tarkington.

Group picture of Joseph, Booth, and John S. Tarkington, three generations, probably taken in 1882, when Booth was 13.

Uncle Newton Booth, Governor of California and later Senator, the great man of the family for whom Booth Tarkington was named.

Sister Hauté, about the time of her marriage in 1886, to Ovid Butler Jameson.

Booth Tarkington at the age of three, taken in California in 1872, when he visited his Uncle Newton, the Governor.

Booth Tarkington at the time he went to Phillips Exeter Academy, 1887-1889.

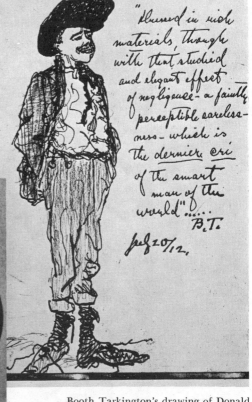

To Donald Ovid Butler Jameson, junior at Princeton on Vacation.

"Dressed in rich materials, though with that studied and elegant effect of negligence - a faintly perceptible careless-ness - which is the dernière cri of the smart man of the world"......
B.T.
July 20/12.

Booth Tarkington's drawing of Donald Jameson, his nephew. It was made just before publication of "Mary Smith," a story about a college sophomore on vacation, which Donald claimed was an insult to every college man in the country.

Booth Tarkington, Princeton '93, as Cassius (on the right) in *The Honorable Julius Caesar*, produced by the Princeton Dramatic Association, 1893. Tarkington wrote the book and directed the production, which was repeated the next year as the first show of the Triangle Club. (The Dramatic Association changed its name to the Triangle Club in the spring of 1893 when Tarkington was president.)

Booth Tarkington, his mother, nephew John Jameson, and unidentified dog, taken during the late Nineties, during Booth Tarkington's literary apprenticeship.

Booth Tarkington and Billie Burke, taken at the time *Rose Briar* was produced, December 25, 1922.

Exterior view of Seawood with Tarkington in the foreground. A late picture, taken in the early Forties.

Drawing by S. J. Woolf of Booth Tarkington at the age of 70.

The Floats, which Booth Tarkington and his neighbor William Trotter used for a clubhouse, on the Kennebunk River, with the *Regina* in the foreground, a retired fishing schooner that Tarkington bought for atmosphere.

Booth Tarkington and Wops, his second French poodle, at 1100 N. Pennsylvania Street in 1916. The car is a Hudson.

Booth Tarkington about the time *Alice Adams* was published in 1921.

Portrait-sketch of Susanah Tarkington by Robert Reid, made in 1914 during the second year of her marriage to Booth Tarkington. It is owned by Mrs. Tarkington and reproduced with her permission.

and at first reading the comedy had not captured her imagination. Her visit, however, was a stimulating experience, though Tarkington recalled "there's a kind of eager sweetness about her that makes it a strain to be with her for hours at a time on first acquaintance." Her manner was "like a gentle woman of the world who's seen everything and everybody without a hint of surfeit." When Maude Adams decided not to come out of retirement, Ziegfeld took the comedy for Billie Burke and engaged Lunt to play opposite her.

The Intimate Strangers is laced with sparkling repartee and develops a situation that has a rich comic potential. It opens with one of the best single acts that Tarkington ever wrote and, moreover, introduces a lively pair of adolescents reminiscent of *Clarence.* The brilliant first act is laid in an isolated railway station where Isabel Stuart, spinster, and William Ames, bachelor, are stranded by floods that have interrupted the train schedules. After Ames shares Miss Stuart's lunch, a middle-aged romance gets timorously under way, and by night when the two go decorously to sleep on separate benches in the deserted depot, they are virtually engaged. This situation, reported Percy Hammond in the New York *Tribune,* is "one of the most sweetly sophisticated interludes of Mr. Tarkington's achievements as a playwright."

Although the suceeding acts do not keep pace with the first, Isabel's niece Florence and her neighborhood Johnny soon are introduced with a great deal of animation. The youngsters rescue Ames and Isabel by auto the morning after the flood, and while Ames pays an impromptu visit to the Stuart home, young Florence sets out to fascinate him. Ironically, Ames the night before has expounded at length on the moral deterioration of the younger generation, but he is, nonetheless, susceptible to Florence's charms. When he also registers shock at meeting Isabel's other *niece,* who is well over sixty, he begins to wonder how old Isabel really is, and she tantalizes him by pretending to be of very indefinite age. She talks of the Hayes-Tilden election as though remembering it vividly and shows Ames daguerreotypes of Uncle Charles, who was a colonel in the Mexican War. Ames finally realizes that his leg is being pulled, and when he gets over his momentary infatuation with

Florence, he is reassured to learn that Isabel is the child of a very late second marriage.

Both Billie Burke and Lunt were eager to play in a new Tarkington comedy. The former had been off the stage for several years and was anxious to act again, while the latter had just finished his extended triumph in *Clarence*. After Lunt was told that Tarkington wanted him in the new play, he wrote enthusiastically: "The idea of playing in something of yours again was unbounded joy and Mr. [A. L.] Erlanger's saying you had suggested me—simply clinched the matter. . . . I still feel that you are under some illusion about my acting ability."

When the play went into rehearsal, Ziegfeld and Erlanger, joint-producers of the comedy with Charles Dillingham, insisted that Tarkington direct the production, which he did with a good deal of enthusiasm. Miss Burke remembered that as director he was "as happy as a clam at high tide," a phrase, incidentally, that she learned from him. "He directed his plays expertly, claiming to have learned how at Princeton," she further recalled. Tarkington found his leading lady eager, willing, and terribly anxious to get the part exactly as he wanted it. "Miss Burke," he wrote his father, "was lovely at rehearsals: I coached her line by line—& she was as submissive as a gentle, bright child: I never knew a star like that before! Then when she gained confidence, it was pretty to see how she built up the part for herself." Lunt, of course, needed little help from the playwright; nor did Glenn Hunter, who had been in the *Clarence* cast as Bobby Wheeler, Helen Hayes' brother.

When the play opened, the critics were unable to agree on a single verdict; but in general they were favorably disposed, and the show was able to run nearly three months in New York before going on the road. Some reviewers did not think the play was much, but they liked Billie Burke's performance; others were diverted by the play but not charmed by the leading lady. All were unanimous, however, in praising the adroit first act, though they differed widely on the merits of the succeeding acts. The critics and theatergoers in cities visited on tour were far more appreciative than New Yorkers, and when the play reached Buffalo in March, Lunt summarized for Tarkington the delighted response encountered outside the metropolis: "Audiences love the play & never once has a hat gone on before two curtain calls."

When Billie Burke returned home from the road tour, she found her husband infatuated with another woman and registered strenuous objections. But even the resultant stormy summer of marital wrangling could not dampen the enthusiasm of both Ziegfeld and his wife for another play by Tarkington. They asked him to write a new drama, found him agreeable, and the result was (in the view of one critic) "a brightly witty, good-natured bit of fluff as light as thistledown" called *Rose Briar*. Tarkington shaped this play for the special abilities of both star and producer, making Miss Burke a cabaret entertainer, which gave her a chance to sing, and laying one act in a night club, which gave Ziegfeld an excuse to stage the play extravagantly.

Rose Briar is a comedy of manners that brings into conflict the cabaret singer Rose and rich, pampered, selfish Fannie Valentine. Rose, despite her night club calling, which the socialite Mrs. Valentine scorns, is the moral and intellectual superior of the two and in the course of the drama demonstrates her pre-eminence in a contest of her rival's own choosing. Fannie Valentine is the sort of woman who goes in for all the latest fads in interior decoration, treats her husband abominably (though he still loves her), expresses her soul-thoughts in verse that she publishes herself, and imagines that she is in love with another man. When her much-abused husband turns to Rose for sympathy, Fannie concocts a plot wherein she will hire Rose to compromise her husband and thus obtain grounds for divorce. The singer accepts the proposal but does not go through with it, and Fannie's underhanded scheme backfires. In the ensuing scene Rose cuts the obnoxious Mrs. Valentine to ribbons in a magnificent verbal duel that is the high spot of the play. In the end, Rose humiliates and subdues Fannie, takes the man Fannie thought she wanted, and thereby brightens the prospects for Valentine's future domestic relations.

The role of Fannie Valentine is a good but unsympathetic part, and Julia Hoyt gave it an extremely competent performance. Although the audience sides with Rose Briar, Tarkington knew better than to make Fannie out of strings and pasteboard; and in the contest between the two women Rose bests a formidable adversary. By making the conflict real, Tarkington intended his comedy to have something serious to say about marital relations, for Fannie (like Cora in *The Flirt*) belongs in the considerable company of selfish, destructive women that Tarkington impaled on his pen during his literary career. She is an early specimen of a type that he enjoyed creating to give tension to his studies of domestic situations. The germ of *Rose Briar* came from a story by Henry James about the hired co-respondent in a divorce case.

The idea of this play interested Tarkington so much that sixteen years later he returned to the same situation, with modifications, in "Otherwise Kitty Swift," a magazine serial never reprinted. Although the night club singer Kitty Swift in the story is not actually hired as a co-respondent, the rich, selfish wife plots similarly to compromise her husband and Kitty in an effort to get rid of an unwanted spouse and simultaneously to take another man away from the cabaret girl. The ending is somewhat more realistic than the play, for the selfish wife gets the man she wants and Kitty Swift is left at the end to console herself with the discarded husband. Tarkington felt that in the later treatment he had worked out a better development of the situation confronting the main characters.

Although "Otherwise Kitty Swift" is one of Tarkington's lesser works, it throws interesting illumination on his mature creative process. On two occasions many years apart the question which had fascinated James, "What about the other woman?" stimulated Tarkington's mind—first because the query opened an exciting avenue of speculation, and second because he thought he could improve on his original use of the material. Just as *The Flirt* was the original pattern for *Alice Adams*, *Young Mrs. Greeley* (1929) the model for *The Lorenzo Bunch* (1936), and *Harlequin and Columbine* the proving ground for *Presenting Lily Mars*, so Tarkington at widely separated intervals reworked similar material. He was rather like a painter, he told Woollcott, "who takes another go at the same landscape after a period of reflection"; and as always his fiction and drama grew out of situations which fertilized his imagination. In retrospect, the basic situation of both *Rose Briar* and "Otherwise Kitty Swift" seems better suited to 1922 than 1938, for by the latter year it was hard to make plausible the social distinction between a night club singer who was instinctively a lady and a socialite who was not. The psychological conflict still was credible, but the material no longer could be successfully molded from the original clay.

The summer of 1922 when *Rose Briar* was written was a happy time at Seawood, Tarkington's Kennebunkport home. As always, Laurel, then sixteen, was allowed to spend the summer with her father. Between motor trips, boating excursions, and entertaining friends, Tarkington worked on the new play. Billie Burke visited Maine to cool off after her tiff with Ziegfeld and spent the summer, while the play was in progress, at near-by York Harbor in a cottage Tarkington found for her. When the manuscript was finished in the middle of August, he read it to her, and after he had finished act one, she reacted spontaneously: "I judged that I must be looking quite elderly enough to be safe," he reported, "for she kissed me!" Several weeks later while the play was being cast, Tarkington, at Ziegfeld's request, sat in the producer's office and helped pick the players, but that part of production was distasteful: there were always too many actors who needed jobs, and there was no ruthlessness in Tarkington's make-up.

When *Rose Briar* opened on Christmas night, it charmed the critics and audience, and Tarkington apparently had another hit. One of the reviewers, Brett Page, thought it "perhaps the best example of polite American comedy we have had on Broadway in a season or two," and Woollcott, who liked the show next to *Clarence,* found it "adroitly fashioned" and well cast. But the play closed after eighty-eight New York performances and did not go on tour. Bille Burke's volatile husband Ziegfeld, not reluctant patrons, was the cause this time of the short run. He was in Palm Beach having a good time, and Miss Burke, worried about what he was doing there, shut down the show and hurried to Florida to take him in hand. Tarkington recalled later that the play was doing about eleven thousand dollars' worth of business a week at the time it closed and probably could have done even better in a tour of the large Eastern cities. Again the theater turned out to be exasperating and completely unpredictable.

Tarkington's interlude with Billie Burke and Florenz Ziegfeld, however, did not exhaust his enthusiasm for the theater, and his next venture was *Tweedles,* a comedy staged and acted by Ruth Gordon and Gregory Kelly. Having started its career as "Bristol Glass," this play, which is laid in Maine, originally was written and laid aside by Tarkington and Wilson, probably in 1919, when they collaborated on *The Gibson Upright* and *Up from Nowhere.* Subsequently, the failure of *The Wren* frightened Tyler from trying another production with a Maine setting and characters, and he declined *Tweedles* when Tarkington offered it to him. Miss Gordon and her husband Kelly were eager to have the comedy, but production and casting difficulties kept it from reaching Broadway until August, 1923. Miss Gordon, who had played Lola Pratt in a successful dramatization (by Hugh Stange and Stannard Mears) of *Seventeen,* long had been a Tarkington fan.

Tweedles is a well-constructed comedy of manners which seems potentially as mirthful as *Clarence,* though in production it never realized its apparent possibilities. The fun of *Tweedles* lies essentially in bringing together a proud old Pennsylvania family and an equally proud New England clan. The scion of the "Main Line" Philadelphians, Julian Castlebury, falls in love with Winsora Tweedle, whose people have been "Maine Liners" themselves for nearly three hundred years. The Castleburys, immensely conscious of their social position in Philadelphia, pale at the thought of allying themselves with the Tweedles, humble Maine folk whose purpose in life, they think, is to serve the summer colony. In a marvelously funny scene the Castleburys confront the Tweedles with the wish, tactfully expressed, that the budding romance be nipped. To their surprise the Tweedles, proprietors of the village antique shop, are just as eager as the Castleburys to break off the match. They agree perfectly that the barrier of social position cannot be bridged successfully. Then each side discovers that the other thinks itself too good for the alliance; whereupon general indignation prevails. The Tweedles, who founded the State of Maine, want nothing to do with a family of transients who come from God knows where, and the Castleburys shudder at the thought of a connection with a tribe of shopkeepers. After Tarkington aims some sharp barbs at the sin of family pride, Julian and Winsora (who had met over the display of Bristol glass) take matters into their own hands, defy both sets of parents, and go off on their first date.

The play deserved a better fate than it suffered, for it is a delightful comedy based on an authentic knowledge of the summer resort social structure. It survived only ninety-six performances in New York, even though it pleased several reviewers, one of whom was Woollcott, who wrote that Ruth Gordon's portrayal of Winsora Tweedle had been glowing, while Donald Meek and George Farren had played other members of the Tweedle family to perfection. Woollcott also thought that the recognition scene, in which both families discover their mutual contempt for the other, was a great bit of comic writing. When the play was forced to close, Tarkington wrote disgruntledly to Kelly that theatergoers would patronize the "flesh-shows" and plays "involving seduction or street-walking . . . but we are too *mild* for them." The boy and girl in the play obviously were adequately sexed, but they did not seem, in Tarkington's later phrase, "to have just excitedly made the discovery, as the curtain went up, that they were not neuter." Yet the production was not really a failure. In the days when a play could be produced for a few thousand dollars, a Broadway run of eleven weeks was not to be despised; and at the end of *Tweedles'* career the comedy was the seventh oldest play out of fifty current New York productions.

A run of five weeks, however, was a different matter, and Tarkington had the unhappy experience of writing a play that opened and closed in New York while *Tweedles* still was playing. The failure was *Magnolia,* which had its première in late August and its demise at the end of September after forty performances. After this show had faltered, Tarkington once more was sated with the theater and ready to quit writing drama. He wrote Tyler two days after the play opened: "I gather the critics are not enthusiastic over 'Magnolia'. . . . 'Well anyhow,' it's my last play for a long time—likely forever."

But he could not give up the stage, even though he renounced it for the second time in his career after the 1923-1924 season. Two years later he let Stuart Walker revive *Magnolia,* and in 1927 Tyler tried unsuccessfully to resuscitate *The Man from Home,* which Tarkington obligingly revamped for him under

the title *Hoosiers Abroad*. In 1928 at George Arliss' request
he wrote his last drama, a play about Aaron Burr, and the following year, less than a month after the stock market crash, another intrepid producer staged forty-seven performances of
How's Your Health?, a labored comedy about hypochondria that
had been gathering dust ever since Wilson and Tarkington
had written it ten years before.

Magnolia is another play that failed through no apparent
fault of the playwright and was an unconscionable length of
time in being produced. It reads well, starred a competent
actor, and received—despite Tarkington's impression to the con-
trary—favorable notices from several influential critics at its
Broadway opening. Yet it did poorly during the first two weeks,
and Erlanger scheduled another play to open in the same theater on October 1. When the production subsequently began to
attract large crowds during its third week, no theater was available to house it through a long New York run, and the company was forced to go on the road. Although the play starred
Leo Carillo, it originally had been written for Lionel Barrymore, who had outlined the story to Tarkington about 1919
and commissioned the work; but when the manuscript was finished, the role of "Kunnel Blake," as the drama first was called,
seemed to Barrymore too young a part for him, and he rejected
the play. Tarkington then suggested to William Harris that
he produce it with Lunt in the title role. Such plans were made
tentatively in 1922, but for some reason, unfortunately, Lunt
never played in *Magnolia,* though he thought it a play which
"should have been a success."

Tarkington tried in *Magnolia* to "make a little parable
founded on a poem of Wordsworth's" and "to amplify it in a
comedy built round that picturesque recollection, the Mississippi River Gambler." The lines that inspired this play come
from the ode, "Intimations of Immortality." They lie close to
the heart of Tarkington's philosophy of life and often are implicit in his work:

> Though nothing can bring back the hour
> Of splendour in the grass, of glory in the flower;
> We will grieve not, rather find
> Strength in what remains behind. . . .

Two of Tarkington's most enduring books, *Penrod* and *Seventeen,* for example, nostalgically evoke "the hour" but without regret, and therein lies their strength and charm. Like Miniver Cheevy, Tarkington "loved the days of old/ When swords were bright and steeds were prancing," but unlike E. A. Robinson's character, he did not sigh "for what was not." He accepted life as he found it, though his acceptance did not carry unqualified endorsement.

The story of *Magnolia* is laid in the ante-bellum South, Mississippi, 1841. At the outset Tom Rumford, who has been raised by a Quaker uncle in Philadelphia, returns to his plantation home after an absence of fifteen years. Having grown up with books and Quaker ethics, Tom finds himself an alien in his home. His father is a hard-drinking, hard-fighting, hard-gambling planter who disowns his son when Tom refuses to fight a duel. Tom then leaves home and in the second act wanders into Orlando Jackson's gambling dive at Natchez-under-the-Hill, the toughest place on the River. There he is "educated" in the code of his father and emerges after a suitable apprenticeship as the notorious "Kunnel Blake," a fire-eating devil with a reputation the length of the River. When he returns home in act three, he bullies his parents and woos his former sweetheart in cave man style.

There are some wonderful things in this play: idyllic passages of adolescent stirrings in the first act and a marvelous gambling-dive scene in the second. When Tom first returns home, he falls in love with his cousin Lucy, and together they read Wordsworth among the magnolias of the Mississippi plantation. This is exquisitely nostalgic and delicately satiric, capturing perfectly in the manner of *Seventeen* the evanescent quality of youthful dreams. In contrast is the second act where Tom learns from the scoundrel Jackson how to get along in a world that despises poetry and perverts the word honor. Early in Tom's initiation Jackson shoots two trouble makers before breakfast, and while his guns still are smoking, he turns to his octoroon slave girl and orders: "Now, damn you, get me some ham and eggs!" Tom, at the end of the act, after killing the vicious Captain Blackie and becoming himself the most feared man on the River, repeats Jackson's line as the curtain rings down.

Not many people saw *Magnolia* for what it really was—a parable within a comedy. They thought rather that the play satirized (as one reviewer put it) "certain gaudy habits of the South before the war" and liked or disliked it according to their attitude towards the South. Tarkington protested vigorously that such had not been his intent. He might have laid the play in California in 1849, he said, or any place where "the people are not greatly emerged from a state of backwoodsiness." He was not, he added, dealing with the " 'Warringtons of Va.' or 'Col. Carter' or 'Marse Chan.' " He used the backwoods locale to give contrast to the "brave ideals of youth" expressed when Tom first returns home, and he used the South and the Mississippi because of "a fondness for the river, left over from boyhood." Tarkington's greatest mistake in *Magnolia*, perhaps, was his expectation that audiences would catch the serious motif behind the humor.

If Tarkington hoped to retire from playwriting with one final success, he was bitterly disappointed over the debacle of *Colonel Satan*. The theater already was reeling from the impact of the movies when Arliss asked him to do a historical drama about Burr, and though he had planned to write no more plays, Arliss' request unlocked a secret desire. He had been interested in Burr ever since he had impersonated that historical figure in a charity pageant at the age of seven, and he could not resist the temptation to do just one more play. Again bad luck stalked his efforts. Before the drama reached Broadway in 1931, Arliss had declined to act the role, and the depression was threatening to administer the *coup de grâce* to the already prostrate theater industry.

Tarkington put the play away for a year after writing it, because Arliss was "the painter who would give it the color of life, he and no other." Dealing with Burr in his old-age exile after the Hamilton duel, the play chronicles his shabby panhandling, political intriguing, and unromantic gallantry against the background of Napoleonic Paris. Arliss perhaps had misgivings about the love-making, although, said Tarkington, it was not real: "Burr's success with women . . . was principally due to his treating them as if they were 'souls' instead of 'bodies.' . . . They fell for him violently because this so immensely flattered them." Arliss' lack of theatrical gallantry, Tarkington thought, was just right for the part. All he had to do was to speak the romantic lines to get exactly the right effect.

Tarkington never should have allowed Tyler to produce *Colonel Satan,* but his old friend was eager to do it, and Tarkington was anxious to help him recoup the losses of two bad seasons. When he let Tyler read the manuscript, the producer wrote back: "Best romantic play I have read in many years— very likely the best I have *ever* read." He suggested Douglas Fairbanks for the role of Burr, a recommendation that appalled Tarkington, who knew the play only could be successful if produced "with realism instead of a romantic *manner.*" The only person that Tarkington was willing to have do the part outside of Arliss was Lunt, but the latter was under contract to the Theatre Guild and unavailable. When the play finally was staged, the leading part went to McKay Morris, who did it like a Valentino rather than a Mansfield. Tyler simply did not understand the subtleties of the part Tarkington had created, for *Colonel Satan* is really a drama contrived with great skill.

Despite its excellence, however, the play did not suit the temper of the Thirties, and apparently it needed pruning that Tarkington could not give it because of ill health. These obstacles, added to the romanticizing of Burr, resulted in unrestrained critical condemnation and a run of only seventeen performances, a dismal low record in the annals of Tarkington's dramatic career. Typical of the unsympathetic reaction was this commentary: "From the first rising curtain to the last falling one you wish that Mr. Alexander Hamilton had been quicker on the trigger and of better aim. . . . Mr. McKay Morris begins to speak along about nine and only pauses to change his trousers between that hour and eleven." Yet when Tarkington told an interviewer that he would write no more drama, he meant only that he would write no more for Broadway. "It isn't fair to the producer," he declared; "I don't know the taste of New York and unless a play pleases there it hasn't got a chance." About the same time, he wired Tyler cheerfully that both of them now were free to retire to the woods to live on roots and birchbark.

Like the child of a father's old age, *Colonel Satan* held a special place in Tarkington's affections, and he lived to have it produced twice more in the years after the New York fiasco.

When the Garrick Players of Kennebunkport held a Tarkington festival in 1938, he rewrote the play under the title *Aromatic Aaron Burr,* and they produced it along with the dramatization of *Seventeen.* Then again in 1943 when the Pasadena Playhouse put on a cycle of eight Tarkington plays at their annual Midsummer Drama Festival, he picked *Colonel Satan* to be one of them. The other plays that he selected for the California revival spanned the entire period of his connection with the professional stage, beginning with *Beaucaire* and including *The Man from Home, The Intimate Strangers, The Country Cousin, Mr. Antonio, Your Humble Servant,* and *Seventeen.* All of the plays except the Burr drama, he said, seemed at that late date "to have been written by a total stranger" rather than himself. The revival of the plays was a great success, and the 1943 Pasadena series broke all previous attendance records for eight earlier festivals.

The enthusiastic reception of the Tarkington play cycle was a suitable valedictory for a career long devoted to matters theatrical. Not only had Tarkington written tirelessly for the professional stage, but in addition he had produced a handful of one-act plays for amateurs, a fair amount of radio drama, numerous movie scenarios, and a half-dozen pieces of theater fiction. He always was alert to new media of communication, eager to try his hand at all dramatic forms, and if he had lived another five years, he no doubt would have written plays for television. He had anticipated as early as 1933 that when television came it would probably be "intensely interesting to the audience," but he warned, "progress doesn't always make us happier . . . often it doesn't even improve us."

Tarkington wrote nine one-act plays during his career, including two that he fashioned in his apprenticeship in the Nineties and two that he wrote late in his life exclusively for radio. The other five, all of which first appeared in the *Ladies' Home Journal,* were reprinted in book form and enjoyed many successful productions by amateur groups. Several are reminiscent of the light-hearted farces that Howells wrote for *Harper's* several decades earlier. *The Trysting Place,* for example, is laid in a summer hotel and involves much humorous trafficking among several sets of furtive lovers who simultaneously pick the same rendezvous, and *The Travelers* concerns the escapades of a night when several American tourists, frightened by stories of bandits, are forced to stop at a remote Sicilian inn. Still another, *Station YYYY,* makes use of early radio broadcasting, the period in which fans spent their evenings twisting dials and logging distant signals, just as Howells once had employed Pullman cars, elevators, and phonographs when those inventions were new.

Although the Penrod stories were turned into radio scripts by other hands, Tarkington in 1933 tried radio writing for himself, creating a juvenile serial which originated three times a week from WJZ in New York. In this series he dramatized part of *Gentle Julia,* particularly the sections dealing with the youthful activities of Florence and Herbert Atwater, and he rechristened the sequence "Maud and Cousin Bill" after Maud and Bill Ricketts, a pair of children he had invented for still another group of stories. Aunt Julia, Noble Dill, and Kitty Silver, all from *Gentle Julia,* also are characters in these radio dramas. The new medium of radio, he found, made heavy demands on the playwright, because each performance was a first night; but he enjoyed experimenting with the "free suggestiveness of sound" unhampered by sight.

He also liked working with the free suggestiveness of sight unhampered by sound in the silent motion picture. Although his relationship with the movies was barely tangential, he frequently was asked to write scenarios, and during the years immediately following the First World War he heeded several of Hollywood's blandishments. In 1919 he turned out a dozen short scenarios for an "Edgar Pomeroy" series of boy adventures reminiscent of *Penrod,* and in the early Twenties he wrote sketches for three full-length pictures. Two of these were unimportant, though they starred the popular Thomas Meighan, but the third furnished Tarkington with his one really pleasant movie experience.

This picture was *Boy o' Mine,* a serious domestic comedy involving troubled relationships between a boy and his father and between the boy's parents themselves. When the film was released by its producer, First National Pictures, in 1922, Tarkington thought that the motion picture industry finally had come of age. Upon his agreeing to write for Hollywood, he had told a newspaper reporter that "those who work in pictures so far—rapid as the advance has been—are the pre-primitives" and that the motion picture is "the possible means of a new art." He was agreeably surprised to find that *Boy o' Mine* had been directed, just as he had wanted, without bad taste or overacting. The marital triangle, which gives density to the narrative, had been handled so subtly that only a perceptive viewer would see it at all. "The Moviers," Tarkington wrote a friend, "have actually represented two decent people decently in love and feeling deeply for each other without any heavings—and *being* so decent that they can set their feeling aside without visible suffering. . . . I was flabbergasted when I saw the film." Produced by William Beaudine, with Irene Rich and Ben Alexander in the cast, the picture also impressed the critics, who thought it a "splendidly produced and brilliantly acted" story which bubbled along with just the right blend of comedy and pathos.

The success of the movie, however, put in motion a fantastic lawsuit early in 1925. Just as Tarkington was packing for a return visit to Europe, the U.S. Marshal knocked on his door with a summons to appear in court in Los Angeles to answer the complaint of Maude Greenwood of Palestine, Texas, who claimed that he had stolen her story in writing *Boy o' Mine*. Mrs. Greenwood, as Tarkington explained to Kahler, had taken a correspondence course in scenario writing, had turned out a story called "My Dad," and had mailed it to First National Pictures. Some time after her manuscript was rejected, Mrs. Greenwood and the "12 other ladies of the Acorn Club," the "most intellectual ladies" of Palestine, saw the picture and unanimously voted it had been stolen from her scenario. They urged that legal measures be taken, and Mrs. Greenwood sued Tarkington for half a million dollars. There was a similarity in plot, Tarkington noted, for the boy in both stories was misunderstood by his father and ran away from home. The defendant, however, turned the matter over to counsel, went on preparing to sail for Europe, and told Kahler: "If not in jail, we leave [the] 3rd [of January]." The case was thrown out of court later in the month without Tarkington's appearance.

His enthusiasm for motion picture art gradually diminished as technical growth outdistanced aesthetic development. He remained a moviegoer during the Twenties, but by the time that sound was added, dimming eyesight had ended his days of theater attendance. He did not miss motion pictures, however, because he had by then given up hope for Hollywood. His own novels and plays continued to be filmed, but Tarkington took no part in turning his literary output into movies. He sold motion picture rights and let Hollywood do what it wanted with its purchase. The movies, he felt, were an inferior but ephemeral sort of entertainment and would have no effect either to preserve or to destroy the books they were based on. He had neither the energy nor the interest to give to feeble dramatizations which he knew in advance would ignore his meticulous details of character and setting. He developed an attitude of disillusioned neutrality, which is summed up in his reaction to Rudolph Valentino's 1924-version of *Monsieur Beaucaire:* "I don't know what Mr. Valentino was doing, but it certainly wasn't what I intended."

Even after he passed through a center of indifference towards Hollywood, he sometimes cavalierly accepted writing commissions from insistent picture companies. Occasionally he wrote scenarios which prodigal producers discarded unused, and once he did the dialogue for a talking picture, *The Millionaire,* starring George Arliss. Perhaps to salve his conscience after refusing to play in *Colonel Satan,* Arliss stipulated to Warner Brothers in 1930 that Tarkington must do the dialogue for the picture. Tarkington agreed, provided that he did not have to go to California to do it, and the producer sent a man to Kennebunkport to explain the technicalities of the project. "When I saw what the job was," Tarkington wrote a friend, "I realized I could do it in about 8 hours." The man from Hollywood knew it too, but said pleadingly: "It'll take about three weeks, won't it? . . . This is an awful nice healthy place and *so* restful after Hollywood." Tarkington took his movie emissary out in the motorboat every day for three weeks; then in a couple of evenings at the end of that period he wrote the dialogue for the picture. His Hollywood guest took the script back to California, "a new man." For this task, reported Tarkington, Warner Brothers paid him enough to buy four pictures for his collection.

Ultimately Tarkington's relationship with Hollywood deteriorated beyond recall, ending ironically in protracted litigation with Warner Brothers. When the movie company produced a picture in 1938 called *Penrod and His Twin Brother,* Tarkington's family and friends discovered indignantly that the film had no connection with the Penrod stories except in the similarity of names. It was all stock boy material, which Tarkington studiously had avoided in *Penrod,* and worst of all, Tarkington wrote Carl Brandt, it was based on "the most obvious steal from 'The Prince and the Pauper.' Naturally," he added, "I don't enjoy planting the idea in people's minds that I lift my studies of youth out of Mark Twain."

When Warner Brothers ignored his protests, he sued the company on grounds that his exclusive right to use the character Penrod had been infringed upon. There was no question of the right to film the Penrod stories, for Warner Brothers owned those movie rights; but two Penrod pictures previously had been made, and the original material apparently had been exhausted. At this juncture Tarkington felt obliged to act for the protection not only of himself but also of other writers. Besides the indignity of having inferior work palmed off as his own, if he could not control the use of the character Penrod, then other producers could similarly exploit the fictional creations of other writers. By purchasing the rights to one story in which a character appeared, they could continue using the character indefinitely. What could stop the producer, argued Tarkington, from making a picture of Penrod as a bank robber at the age of thirty or a movie in which Penrod was guilty of even worst crimes?

Although Tarkington had a strong case, he won only a Pyrrhic victory, and that not until litigation had dragged on for three years. Diligent sleuthing by Warner Brothers' lawyers turned up a copyright flaw in the original magazine publication of the Penrod stories, and though this discovery was entirely irrelevant to the principle involved, Tarkington's case was jeopardized, and his lawyer could not risk letting the suit go to trial. The company then settled out of court, paying token damages and agreeing to submit future Penrod scripts to Tarkington for approval before filming.

Another important ramification of Tarkington's long interest in the stage was the fictional by-product. The unfinished theater novel that he wrote during his apprenticeship was followed from time to time during the next forty years by three

short stories ("The Property Man," "Francine," " 'Thea Zell"),
two novelettes *(Harlequin and Columbine,* "The Divine
Evadne"), and one novel *(Presenting Lily Mars).* In all of these
works Tarkington uses theatrical settings with obvious affection and excellent verisimilitude. The smell of grease paint,
the heat of the footlights, the backstage confusion, the opening-
night tension are reproduced with an authenticity that makes
credible for lay readers the arresting personalities of the theatrical characters. Not only is Tarkington the rare novelist who
can write plays, but he is the playwright who can tell a convincing story of the stage.

One of his early fictional uses of the theater was *Harlequin
and Columbine,* written in 1913 during his five-year absence
from playwriting. Portraying well the stage before the First
World War, the story details the production of a neophyte
dramatist's first play. Superficially at least the young author is a
projection of Tarkington himself about the time he dramatized
Beaucaire. The glittering protagonist, the actor-manager Talbot Potter, who is the center of all eyes when he walks up Fifth
Avenue, might have been Mansfield, Drew, John Barrymore, or
a composite of various actors Tarkington knew during the early
years of the century. Potter in this story dominates the play
completely: he changes scenes, alters lines, and revises the stage
business—to give himself the spotlight all the time. Only one
other character in the production has a chance to shine with
Potter, and she, ironically enough, is a stand-in, Wanda Malone, who suddenly is called on to play the ingenue role. She
captures the imagination of Potter, who proceeds to expand her
bit part to show off her talents. Between Potter's temperamental egoism and Miss Malone's sudden elevation to prominence
the young playwright, Stewart Canby, has to stretch and pad
and rewrite much of his play. Later when Potter finds that
Miss Malone is secretly married to his stage manager, he flies
into a great rage, threatens to call off the show; but after the
volatile actor cools down, he goes on with the play as though
nothing has happened. The playwright, of course, suffers
acutely during the vicissitudes of the rehearsal period, and although the story is a bit melodramatic, Tarkington undoubtedly
had watched actual outbursts of temperament as astonishing as
Potter's.

While Tarkington was writing plays in the years after 1915, he produced no theater stories; but in the mid-Twenties he returned to the fictional stage and wrote " 'Thea Zell," the story of a woman of mediocre talent whose stage ambitions bring her a lifetime of misery. This tale, a brilliant characterization of a complete egotist, is one of Tarkington's most skillful stories. 'Thea Zell, when first seen, is a child whose foolish mother pushes her into all possible public performances and lays the foundation for the later tragedy. After the girl grows into a supremely self-centered woman, she marries a substantial young man but cannot settle down to domestic routine. As an actress in local amateur productions, she at first leads her husband an exasperating life; then she runs off to New York, leaving husband and children, to go on the stage. Completely unable to evaluate her own ability, she falls prey to a shabby promoter who visits her midland city to direct a charity show and glibly promises to put her on Broadway. He cannot do it, of course, and 'Thea is forced to struggle desperately with only a modest talent in a highly competitive business. She is last seen several years later when she returns to her home city as a bit player in a third-rate stock company. She is deeply moved—a tragic figure—when she sees her children, meets her happily married sister, and realizes what a ruin she has made of her life. But there is no turning back from the path she has chosen, and she goes away again with the stock company. Tarkington was in perfect command of his art when he wrote " 'Thea Zell."

The character Wanda Malone from *Harlequin and Columbine* returns, with suitable modifications, for top billing in *Presenting Lily Mars*. The idea of thrusting a brilliant new ingenue into a play already cast barely was explored in the early novelette, and the problem of what might happen under such circumstances set Tarkington going in the later work. Again he laid the story in that period of theatrical history when "the depot hack still struggled against the station taxicab and extinction," and once more a young playwright, such as Tarkington had been, provides a point of view for the author. Particularly effective in this novel is the detailed account of opening night in Somerville, a city that might have been Atlantic City, Wilmington, New Haven, or any of the many places where Tarkington's own plays were tested.

The novel begins in a city such as Indianapolis where Lily Mars is a stage-struck youngster of no experience but real talent. Through a connection with the playwright's mother, who lives in the same city, she gets a chance to act for the producer George Hurley (George Tyler) when he brings his latest production to her midland city for a week's run and plans simultaneously to begin rehearsing his new play there. Hurley explodes in anger when he finds himself part of a captive audience at the playwright's home, but the girl makes a powerful impression, and soon afterwards when the ingenue hired for the new play proves unsatisfactory, he decides to gamble on Lily. The company then goes to New York for rehearsals, and she turns out to be a real discovery, though temperamental and unpredictable. She flirts with the leading man, who previously has been the property of Isabelle Hedrington, the leading lady, and nearly wrecks the play before it opens. Then in the tryouts she steals the show with her small part and again incurs the jealousy of the star. The cast becomes too small to hold two prima donnas, but in an off-stage drama Lily is outplayed by the veteran Isabelle; whereupon Lily quits the play and goes home. The producer, who has been completely charmed, goes after her, not to bring her back to the cast but to marry her.

When reviewers who knew little about the theater complained that Lily Mars was incredible, Tarkington had no difficulty in defending the reality of his creation. Looking back on more than half a century of stage history, he recalled that Mary Anderson, whom he had seen in *Romeo and Juliet* at the age of seven, never had appeared except as a star, and he remembered that Julia Marlowe also began as a star when very young. Glenn Hunter and Helen Hayes, he declared, in small parts could take the audience away from everyone else on stage. Maude Adams was made by being herself in a small part; Bernhardt and Duse did "Lily Mars" things; and the history of the Comédie Française was full of such bits. He wrote Street: "I saw Clara Bloodgood, up to then an amateur, really take the play away from Annie Russell. . . . Cissie Loftus, at sixteen, a month out of a convent, tore London wide open. Lily's built of facts, as I've known them; but when you describe an exceptional thing in *fiction* you're likely to encounter doubts in readers who haven't an experience of the exceptions."

TWELVE

"IN NATURE ALL IS CHANGE"

Dᴜʀɪɴɢ ᴛʜᴇ ʀᴏᴀʀɪɴɢ, postwar Twenties, when American society seemed to be changing beyond all recognition, Tarkington in his fiction recorded dispassionately the amazing transformation. His attitude towards the Jazz Age was summed up in Carlyle's comment when Margaret Fuller once declared that she accepted the universe as it is: "Gad! she'd better." Though Tarkington might deplore privately America's lost innocence, as a novelist and social historian he knew better than to grieve for what was irretrievable. And if he did not mourn the past, he also did not agitate for a different present. He cherished his memories of a happy childhood and youth, lived actively for the moment, and hoped for a better future.

Although he accepted change as inevitable and not undesirable, he did not mean to suggest that this is the best of all possible worlds. Philosophically, he held a mid-position between the Calvinistic determinism of his New England ancestors and the frontier-nurtured faith in man's infinite capacity to implement his own will. Life, he knew, is full of cruelty: "Misfortunes fall upon us inexplicably," and "even in the safest of civilizations, when we part with a friend for half an hour we cannot be sure of ever seeing him again," but he could not look on himself as a creature caught in the inscrutable web of mechanistic circumstance. His own career was sufficient evidence that industry and resolve are vital factors in shaping human destiny.

True enough, he was born on the right side of the tracks, but the subtle chemistry that precipitates pessimism or optimism from American experience is not to be explained satisfactorily

242

by environment alone. Temperament and personality act mysteriously despite favorable or unfavorable surroundings. One cannot say for sure that the polar development of the two most important Indiana novelists of this century resulted entirely from a difference in background. Although Theodore Dreiser was born into a depressed social stratum while Tarkington was growing up in a comfortable professional family, poor boys often grow into staunch idealists, and rich boys become pessimistic determinists.

However it may be accounted for, Tarkington was by nature or by experience an optimist who appraised the world affirmatively and interested himself in it. During his fifties he recalled once attending a dinner at which Mark Twain, discussing with Howells the essence of happiness, had maintained that "happiness . . . is merely a person's unconsciousness of troubles that he really has." But this negative opinion of Twain's bitter old age was incompatible with Tarkington, who thought that one is happy if he thinks he is and that external reality is nonexistent. If a man believes that he has no troubles, asserted Tarkington, he does not have any. This relativist view of man's emotional responses, shaped both by personality and environment, fitted well into Tarkington's acceptance of a physical universe in which nothing was fixed. He saw the broad sweep of history not in terms of a two-dimensional cyclical movement but as a three-dimensional upward progression; for there is no absolute, and "in nature all is change." Yet change is not an evil, and Tarkington placed a sanguine interpretation on his philosophical and historical perspectives: "Looking forth upon the examples apparently set by the rest of the universe, we are encouraged to surmise that the world moves, not as a pendulum, but in an ascending spiral."

Because of his philosophy and temperament Tarkington found himself, in the Jazz Age, an old liberal who had become a conservative. When the rebels of the Twenties grabbed the spotlight, he refused to join their act, though he kept a close eye on developments. He was perfectly aware of his position among the new writers of the "lost generation" and made no attempt to conceal his disapproval of their sex-frankness in literature and their negative view of American experience. He continued working calmly in the literary tradition of Howells

and James, which he regarded as positive and enduring. He let
Lewis, Mencken, Dos Passos, and others hurl their thunderbolts
at American culture or lack of it and remained interested, as
it seemed to him, in the main current of American society
rather than in the eddies and backwashes of the shallows.

While F. Scott Fitzgerald illuminated in his novels some of
the gaudier aspects of the Twenties, Tarkington maintained in
his fiction a consistency with his work of the preceding era.
With Cather, Glasgow, Wharton, and other older novelists still
active he went on recording honestly the life he observed from
his somewhat detached vantage point. He had begun his even-
tempered criticism of American materialism six years before
Main Street was issued, and he continued this theme in various
ways throughout the Twenties. Since he was neither rebel nor
reformer, he viewed his surroundings hopefully and concluded
that on the whole the United States was a dynamic, viable society which was likely to last for a long time. He was always
the eager recorder of change and far more interested in reporting than in preaching.

The unifying factor in Tarkington's writing of the Twenties
is his strong sense of historical movement. Implicit or explicit,
it appears in most of his fiction and nonfiction and even slips
sometimes into his titles. When he collected his trilogy of
family chronicles, all set against the socio-economic background
of Indianapolis, he called the single volume *Growth,* and when
he published a volume of autobiographical and reflective essays,
he named it *The World Does Move.* The changes during his
lifetime indeed had been startling: immigration, industrialization, mechanization, urbanization had transformed the world
of his youth. As an experienced, perceptive, and articulate observer, a bystander with a memory capable of almost total recall,
he had watched fifty years of American history speed by "with
time condensed," like a fantastically accelerated motion picture.
Summing up the era between the Civil War and the First
World War, he wrote:

> That had been a great railroad-making and railroad-breaking
> period; the great steel period; the great oil period; the great
> electric-invention period; the great Barnum-and-Bunkum pe-
> riod; the period of "corrupt senators"; of reform; and of sky-
> scrapers thirty stories high. All this was old now, routed by a

newer and more gorgeous materialism. The old had still its disciplines for the young and its general appearance of piety; bad children were still whipped sometimes, and the people of best reputation played no games on Sunday, but went to church and seemed to believe in God and the Bible with almost the faith of their fathers. But many of these people went down with their falling houses; a new society, swarming upward above the old surfaces, became dominant. It began to breed, among other things, a new critic who attacked every faith, and offered, instead of mysteries, full knowledge of all creation as merely a bit of easily comprehended mechanics. And in addition to discovering the secret of the universe, the new society discovered golf, communism, the movies, and the turkey trot; it spread the great American cocktail over the whole world, abolished horses, and produced buildings fifty stories high.

Tarkington began the new decade with *Alice Adams*, his tenth full-length novel. Written in the summer of 1920 at Kennebunkport and published the following year, it is very likely the best work of his entire career. He planned it as a significant story of American middle-class life and executed it with complete artistic control in a thoroughly realistic manner. The heroine is a well-drawn, complicated, and recognizable human being, a charmer despite her vanity, self-dramatization, and pretension. Although the novel was intended to be the third volume in the *Growth* trilogy, it does not fit precisely into the theme developed by *The Turmoil* and *The Magnificent Ambersons*, being more the story of an individual than a family. Tarkington later wrote *The Midlander* to complete his observations on half a century of Midwestern history and let *Alice Adams* stand as a separate study of individualized mediocrity.

Yet *Alice Adams* is a further probing of the materialism amid change that Tarkington saw about him in the years following his *Wanderjahre*. The desire for money, which seemed the universal motivation in 1920, pursues the characters in the story like an avenging fury. It makes a monster out of Alice's mother, wrecks her father's life, physically and spiritually, corrupts her brother, and blights her own youth. With the corroding mania for riches goes the foolish longing for social position, which money can buy; but the Adamses are not an emerging midland family like the Sheridans or the Morgans and are destined not to rise above the surface. Because they are unimaginative, unsuccessful, and average, damaged by the false idol of materialism, they are left at the end with nothing to compensate for their loss of self-respect. The story is both depressing and comic when stripped to its thematic content, but Tarkington is an adroit storyteller who keeps his ethic well concealed. Alice alone emerges from the ordeal with the mental and physical resiliency to adjust herself to the realities of life. For all but her the story is low-keyed tragedy.

Alice Adams takes place in the midland city of the Sheridans and Ambersons at a time contemporaneous with the novel's composition. As the story opens in late April, Virgil Adams, fifty-five years old, recuperates at home from a serious heart attack. Alice, his twenty-two-year-old daughter, prepares for a dance at the home of Mildred Palmer, her last remaining wealthy and socially prominent friend, and Mrs. Adams, who lives solely for her daughter, slaves over her sewing machine to remodel an old dress for Alice to wear to the party. The Adamses live in a small frame house "already inclining to become a new Colonial relic," which they built a decade and a half before; but "fifteen years is a long time to stand still in the midland country," and people like the Palmers already have moved into grander houses farther away from the center of the city. It is the great sorrow of Mrs. Adams' life that her husband has remained a faithful employee in the drug business instead of becoming a prosperous employer. Daily she reproaches him for failing to make the money which would give Alice all the social advantages that Mildred and other former childhood friends now enjoy.

Alice's appearance at the fashionable dance is her last one, for the kind-hearted Mildred finally has been convinced by her mother that Alice is "a very pushing little person" and plans to drop her. She is snubbed by the matrons, ignored by the other young women, and thoroughly discomfited by wearing the only white organdy dress so early in the season. Her brother, moreover, has to take her to the dance in a hired "tin lizzy" when everyone else goes in a cab or limousine, and she is further humiliated by being conspicuously a wallflower.

The dance episode is one of the supreme moments in Tarkington's fiction, a perfect example of humor blended with pathos. Alice is a silly creature living in a dream world, but she also is a pathetic figure as she sits bravely on the sidelines trying to pretend that she is waiting for a partner who will return at any moment. One cannot help smiling when fat Frank Dowling defies his mother to dance with her, but when Alice surreptitiously disposes of her home-made corsage, wilted violets that she picked herself in the city park, the reader feels only sympathy.

The one happy event of the dance is meeting Arthur Russell, Mildred Palmer's cousin, who dances with her late in the evening. He follows up this encounter with frequent calls during the succeeding months, and before the summer is over, the two are in love; but the romance is a summer interlude only and flourishes as long as the couple confine their activities to front-porch tête-à-têtes and walks in the park. The time comes, however, when Arthur must meet the Adams family and learn the reality behind Alice's dramatization of herself and her family. This unhappy occasion takes place when Mrs. Adams insists on inviting him to dinner one hot summer night. It is to be his first appearance inside the dingy little house with its heterogeneous collection of rocking chairs, plush furniture, steel engravings in baroque frames, and one huge photograph of the Colosseum, which Alice thinks of as "the only good thing in the [living] room."

The dinner scene, another triumph of Tarkington's narrative skill, brings Alice's last effort to enter the *haut monde* to a disastrous conclusion. After lunching with his relatives in their large, cool, perfectly appointed house, Arthur goes to dinner at the Adamses'. Alice's mother has recruited a cook and waitress to put on what she thinks will be an elegant and impressive meal, but the weather turns blindingly hot during the afternoon, and the heavy, inept menu in the steaming little house is unendurable. In her foolish effort to promote her daughter's interest Mrs. Adams reveals the appalling meanness of a modest family pretending to something grand. Alice's simple-hearted father is acutely uncomfortable in dinner jacket and unaccustomed manners trying to please his wife, and Alice realizes during the awful dinner that Arthur never will come to see her again. The scene is a painful experience for the reader, who

can only perspire and squirm his way through it, amused by
the absurdity but embarrassed and saddened by the spectacle.

After the debacle of her social aspirations Alice comes out of
the make-believe world she has inhabited so long. She learns
at the end to accept the universe as it is and to adjust herself
to her surroundings. She loses the chance to marry into the
Palmers' circle, but she gains her soul. Tarkington ends on a
note of ironic realism by sending Alice into Frincke's Business
College to learn typing and shorthand, a denouement that she
always had looked on "as the end of youth and the end of
hope." But even as she climbs the stairs to register at the
school, she thinks of a French romance she once read and sees
herself as the tragic heroine who took "the veil after a death
blow to love."

While the story of Alice is comedy freighted with pathos,
the parallel life of Virgil Adams is tragedy caused by weakness
of will and love for his daughter. At the outset of the novel
he is the devoted employee of J. A. Lamb, a merchant prince
of the midland city, and after a quarter of a century of faithful
service he has risen to a place of minor responsibility in the
drug business of Lamb and Company. He is able to provide
modestly for his family, but his foolish wife nags him endlessly
to make more money. Because he loves his daughter and wants
to give her a more abundant life, he is persuaded by his wife
to quit his employer. He tries to go into business for himself,
but the effort is beyond his financial and physical capabilities,
and he fails about the time the disastrous dinner finishes Alice's
romance. Moreover, Adams is shattered morally by the break
with his venerated employer, for his wife goads him into ap-
propriating an unpatented formula that he had developed as a
member of the drug firm. At the end of the story Adams is a
broken old man forced to become a pensioner of his wife and
daughter. His vainglorious wife is served with ironic justice,
however, by having to turn her home into a rooming and
boarding house.

One other character who plays a small but important part is
the brother Walter, a youth with a sense of values as false as
Alice's. His story, however, takes a much different turn, for he
is a young scapegrace who dishonors his family in their bitter
moment of social and financial downfall by embezzling money

from his employer. Tarkington uses him not only as a fearful product of Mrs. Adams' wrongheadedness but also symbolically as mocking fate. Alice's dream world and Mrs. Adams' pretensions are shrilly penetrated at critical intervals by the uninhibited scorn of Walter. When Alice boldly acts as though she belongs in the fashionable world at the Palmers' dance, Walter is found shooting dice in the men's room with the help. When she walks in the moonlight with Arthur, she meets Walter with a tart. When Virgil Adams gives in to his wife's insistence that he begin his own business, Walter contemptuously refuses to have any part in the enterprise. He is a thoroughly bad creature, mediocrity debased by inauspicious environment.

An immediate critical and popular success, *Alice Adams* won the Pulitzer novel award for 1921 at the same time that Eugene O'Neill and E. A. Robinson were winning the prizes for drama and poetry. Although some readers complained that Alice did not get her man, they were the inveterate consumers of romance who liked nothing without a sugar coating. Tarkington felt after completing the manuscript that no one would want to read about such people as the Adamses, but his fears soon were allayed, for the novel was reprinted five times within the year and frequently afterwards. It later was anthologized, made into a talking book for the blind, translated several times, and turned into movies for both Florence Vidor and Katherine Hepburn.

The praise of literary colleagues whom Tarkington knew only by reputation swelled the chorus and perhaps pleased him as much as the applause from reviewers and friends. Sinclair Lewis, who had published *Main Street* the year before, wrote that he had been lecturing up and down the country on the younger generation of writers, but everywhere he had told his audience: "When you are considering the clever unknown youngsters, don't ever suppose that because he sells so enormously, Booth Tarkington can't write better than any of them." Ellen Glasgow also wrote to say that she had thoroughly enjoyed and admired *Alice Adams:* "You have achieved two things that I had believed almost impossible in American fiction— you have written of average people without becoming an average writer and you have treated the American girl without sentimentality. The end of the story is very fine and true—and it makes absolutely no concession to the ubiquitous devourer of the second rate." It was indeed a significant story of ordinary people reacting to the stimulus of a "more gorgeous materialism" in the changing society of the twentieth century.

There was no break for Tarkington after he had delivered his manuscript to the *Pictorial Review* for serialization. When Garland wrote him in February inviting him to attend the Howells commemorative meeting of the Academy of Arts and Letters, he replied that "this seems almost disastrously my busiest year." For three weeks a revenue agent had been with him, going over income tax returns and spoiling some of his best midwinter working time, and he added: "I'm in a bad way; for I have a series of eight stories, begun in January, to complete, three plays to begin & one to rewrite before July. These are contracted jobs; I simply daren't budge." To this Garland replied in some alarm: "Will you let a man of sixty offer a word of advice—and warning? Don't work the old subconscious self too hard. Instead of taking on contracts—work in leisure." But Tarkington was not worried about the quantity of writing that he had promised. He was doing his best work at this time and in full control of his creative talent. He wrote easily and could judge accurately how long a play or story would take him. He agreed with Garland that "it's a fearful big wheelbarrow-load of words"; but he added: "I'm more afraid of using up my eyes & right hand than the supplies of the mystic workman under the outer layers. I don't force that chap. . . . But when I *let* him be one, he's a Simon Legree driving *me*. . . . He *always* wants to go on: *wants* to use my strength to the last thimble of it."

Tarkington not only was at the peak of his creative powers in 1921, but he also was at the zenith of his fame. After he had won his first Pulitzer Prize, his alma mater Princeton had awarded him an honorary degree, and later he accepted additional honors from De Pauw, his father's school, and Columbia University before he began turning down chances to appear on commencement platforms. After 1924 his phobia against public appearances made him reject degrees from Bowdoin, Kenyon, Colby colleges, Butler and Indiana universities, and only Purdue managed to give him an additional degree by holding a special academic procession and presentation at his home in

Indianapolis in 1940. "What use is a collection of hoods?" he
asked Street after receiving notification that still another school
had voted him a Litt. D. "I wish I'd kept my old reputation . . .
I'm so darn dignified now that the only alleviating thing . . . is
the fact that most of the school children under the 7A grade
. . . think I'm the man that killed Abraham Lincoln."

Concurrently with academic honors, he began winning popularity contests held by various publications. When *Publishers'
Weekly* in 1921 asked booksellers to name the most significant
contemporary American authors, Tarkington led the list.* The
following year both the *Literary Digest* and the New York
Times held contests, and in the former publication Tarkington
was voted the greatest living American author, while in the
latter he was the only writer named in a list of the ten greatest
contemporary Americans. "Yes, I got in as last on the *Times*
list," he commented: "What darn silliness! You *can* demon-
strate who are the 10 *fattest* people in a country and who are
the 27 tallest . . . but you can't say who are the 10 greatest with
any more authority than you can say who are the 13 damndest
fools." Later, however, he was greatly touched to receive in
1933 from the National Institute of Arts and Letters the gold
medal previously awarded only to Howells and Wharton, and
in 1945 from the American Academy of Arts and Letters the
William Dean Howells medal awarded only once in five years.

Despite the midwinter interruption by the revenue agent,
he delivered as planned most of the material he had promised
before summer. He apparently eliminated one of the three
dramas, but the two new plays he did turn out were *The Intimate Strangers* and *The Wren,* both excellent creations, as we
have seen. He completed all eight of the stories he had contracted for and published them later in the year in the *Red
Book Magazine.* Comparable in quality with the plays and his
other works of this period, the tales (with one exception)
launched a new series, using a common dramatis personae,
which continued for six more episodes in the same periodical
during the next two years. The stories revolve about the com-

* Wharton, 2; Hergesheimer, 3; Van Dyke, 4; Atherton, 5; Churchill, 6;
Lowell, 7; Masters, 8; Cabell, 9; Lewis, 10. Others: Frost, 13; Dreiser, 14; Robinson, 16; Cather, 20; Lindsay, 21; O'Neill, 26; Zane Gray, 30; Kathleen Norris,
33; Sandburg, 39.

fortably placed Mears and Eliot families, each of which has a marriageable offspring and a lively pre-adolescent child. Renfrew Mears, just out of college, loves Muriel Eliot, woos her, and wins her, but not without a great deal of amusing domestic comedy and complications supplied mostly by his tomboy sister Daisy and Muriel's young brother Robert. These stories are reminiscent of the loosely plotted series that makes up *Seventeen* and *Gentle Julia* and are nearly as good. If Tarkington had not used four of them in *The Fascinating Stranger and Other Stories* (1923), he might have made a book of the sequence.

During the period 1921-1923 while he was heavily committed to the theater, he devoted his surplus time and energy to short fiction. Between writing *The Wren* and two one-act plays, writing and directing *The Intimate Strangers* and *Rose Briar,* rewriting *Tweedles* and *Magnolia,* he managed to produce sixteen stories. His regular work habits and unflagging industry accomplished these prodigies despite the loss of his father early in 1923 and the most profound emotional crisis of his life, his daughter's death the following spring.

A unique story among the eight written early in 1921 is "Jeannette," a tale that deserves more than passing mention because of its serio-comic treatment of twentieth-century change. It is in essence a parable of modern times, and in the case history of Charlie Blake, the protagonist, Tarkington projects his own attitudes and responses (with grotesque exaggerations) to the differences between 1904 and 1921. The story begins in Paris in the former year when the young, naïve Blake accompanies his worldly-wise older sister to the Folies-Bergère. The shock of seeing nude chorus girls deranges his mind, bringing on the delusion that he himself is naked, and the next morning he is found under the hotel bed fully dressed, wrapped in the bedclothes, and convinced that he has nothing on. After his mind snaps, Charlie spends many years in a mental institution, slowly regaining his sanity under the care of a skillful psychiatrist. Eventually his sister takes him home supposedly cured, but unfortunately for his delicately balanced mind the Jazz Age has begun, and he arrives at his sister's home just as his niece Jeannette, a bobbed-haired "flapper," is throwing a party.

The cacophony of the music and the intimacy of the "toddle" are too much for him. As he listened, the music "beat upon his brain with bludgeons and blackjacks, rose in hideous upheavals of sound, fell into chaos, squawked in convulsions, seemed about to die . . . leaped to life again more ferociously than ever." It reminded him of a youthful visit to a slaughterhouse, where he once had watched pigs screaming in terror as they were driven along chutes to the butchers' knives. Then he looked at the dancing humanity before him: "Partners in the performance below him clung to each other with a devotion he had never seen except once or twice, and then under chance circumstances which had cost him a hurried apology." Jeannette herself, with the upper half of her torso mostly bare and a skirt that barely reached below her knees, was unbelievable. "To find ancestors who would not be shocked at Jeannette," the author comments, "one would have to go back to the Restoration of Charles Stuart." As the result of this second traumatic experience Charlie loses his mind again and last is seen hiding in the cellar under the coal pile.

Like his character Charlie Blake, Tarkington himself held a low opinion of jazz and hated public displays of nudity and intimacy, but he regarded changing morals as inevitable. The younger generation of women, he explained, feel no more shame in discarding long skirts than their grandmothers felt in abandoning the bustle. Women simply had changed their ideas of modesty and the proper amount of clothing in order to cope with the challenge of their emancipation, and their elders would have to stand it. The new times were tolerable, concluded Tarkington, if one acclimated himself (as Charlie Blake did not) to the shifting mores. "Jeannette" is both a humorous comment on the change and a warning to accept the universe.

Another story of this period, a tale worth brief mention, is "The One-Hundred-Dollar Bill," which was reprinted in the *O. Henry Prize Stories of 1923*. It is not typical of Tarkington's major preoccupations, but it illuminates the somber mood that any sensitive optimist is certain to feel on occasion. This darker thread in Tarkington's work appeared as early as *In the Arena* (1905) when he wrote "The Aliens," the story of Pietro Tobigli, the expendable pawn of a corrupt politician; and there is a resemblance between "The One-Hundred-Dollar Bill" and the discordant husband-wife relationship in *Alice Adams*. The story concerns the uncontrollable web of circumstance which ruins a poor bill collector named Collinson. This unhappy character is nagged constantly about money by his wife and harassed by the philandering bachelor Charlie Loomis, who has dishonorable intentions towards Mrs. Collinson.

On the day that the collector takes in a one-hundred-dollar bill he plays poker with Loomis and several other friends. Unfortunately one of the players brings with him a lucky dollar, recently found, and both Loomis and Collinson want it. The rivals play for the coin, and as the stakes mount, Collinson, with reckless abandon (symbolically he is playing for his wife) risks and loses his employer's one hundred dollars. On the way home the defeated man sees a monkey on a stick in a shop window and ruefully recognizes himself as a similar captive mechanical toy. He concludes that he has no control over the events that brought him to disaster but is the victim of circumstance, unlucky in cards and unlucky in love. When Tarkington's story materials demanded naturalism, he used the uncongenial attitudes of pessimistic determinism.

Ironically, "The One-Hundred-Dollar Bill" was written in 1922 during a happy summer and early autumn, when Laurel was visiting her father in Maine, but the tale is more in the mood of the following winter. When Tarkington returned to Indianapolis, he knew that his father's death was not far off. He had written home every few days throughout the year, realizing that the old Judge was daily becoming more feeble, and in January John Stevenson Tarkington died. Although he had passed a serene old age, his death was hard to bear, for father and son always had been close to each other. "Papa John" had been a wise and understanding father, Tarkington later reminisced: "I don't doubt he worried unhappily over me at times; but only two or three times, after I was 15, did he ever so much as advise, and then he did it indirectly, gently and by mere suggestion. Seems to me he was right and wise." At the time of his death Tarkington wrote Garland that his father had been "always & always the blessing of the lives of all his family" and had reached the age of ninety "only in years." He was a gentle soul, kind, honorable, instinctively good, well beloved by everyone who knew him, and a powerful influence on his son's personality and sense of values. Finally, to make the winter even more distressing, Tarkington's sister Hauté was seriously, though not fatally, ill at the time of their father's death.

Bereavement did not come singly that winter: a few days after Christmas a strangely disturbed daughter arrived to visit her father for the last time. Following the previous pleasant summer at Kennebunkport, Laurel had returned to her boarding school at Norton, Massachusetts, excited by the thought that she soon would no longer be an only child; but when she went home to Boston for the holidays, anticipation and reality diverged sharply. A new baby occupied the household, and Laurel, after many years of being the single object of her mother's affection, felt herself supplanted by the infant. When she expressed her resentment extravagantly, her mother packed her off immediately to Indianapolis to visit her father. As quickly as that, the mischief was done, and she arrived in Indiana in a state of shock. Her heart was broken, for she fancied that she had been banished from her mother.

"I had one last night with her soon after she came," Tarkington wrote Street after the ordeal was over. "Somehow I knew it was the last, because the shadow had *appeared*—I never knew so strange a communion as that. We talked here in my workroom far into the night. She talked brilliantly, profoundly—it was a search for the meaning of life and death and God—she had always seemed a child, but that night she was a beautiful, brilliant, haggard woman." During the next three months Susanah and Booth Tarkington labored heroically to save the mind and body of the brilliant girl. Day and night they worked, talked, soothed, and reasoned, hours without end, often to the point of exhaustion; but the struggle availed nothing, and they could not restore the will to live, which Laurel had renounced. In mid-April when pneumonia set in, there was no resistance left to fight it, and on the fourteenth a weary, heartsick father wrote his old friend George Tyler:

> Yesterday afternoon, about five o'clock, Laurel had them call me in—and said "Goodnight"—
> It is over.
> Oh, such a brave and bright and gentle spirit!
> You see the *instrument* of the spirit had become maimed; the spirit could not endure to remain in the instrument after that.

But all day yesterday, which she begged us to let be *"her* day," her mind was clear again: she was Laurel.

Old friend, you must not grieve for her or for me. This was best. She came back to us for a day, and then went on. I think she went *somewhere* and that a day will come when I shall find her and she'll know all I've wanted so long to be to her.

The novel that Tarkington was writing that winter and spring was *The Midlander,* the third of the *Growth* trilogy. He planned to begin it in December when he got home from rehearsals for *Rose Briar,* but instead he had to undergo major dentistry. The "buzzing and chisel work began on our return and has gone on, every other day, until last week," he explained to Barton Currie, editor of the *Ladies' Home Journal,* in February. By then his father had died, Laurel was seriously ill, and the novel once promised for April was not delivered until mid-July. The project, however, was a salvation, for he wrote in May: "I must work: I must go on with this novel. If I shouldn't, I'd be wrecked, I think." Four weeks later again he reported: "This work has just about saved me from shipwreck. It's been hard to do it, but it would have been so much harder not to."

The Midlander is both a somber story reflecting the bleak events of its composition and the summation and conclusion which gives direction and significance to the phenomenon of twentieth-century change. By 1924, after he had been back in Indianapolis for twelve years, he saw that the ugliness and confusion, the dirt and materialism were moving somewhere and that its critics were "passing ephemera." He still condemned the turmoil and in addition cited the cost in human lives and happiness that the change exacted from its producers, but he now elaborated on his earlier suggestion that the kiln must be fired before the vase is glazed. He also kept the novel as realistic as possible, making it "undramatic, *un*pointed up" and killing off his characters as they die in real life—"at undramatic moments." He ended the story with the financial fall, marital smash, and death of his hero just as the protagonist's dream of the city beautiful is materializing. Although the story is tragic, Tarkington wrote Barton Currie that he did not feel it so: "Certainly it's no more tragic than almost the happiest *actual* life." He was chiefly interested in finding design in "what *seems* haphazard and almost ironically tragic," though he admitted that "we don't know, of course," what life really is.

The Midlander is the story of Dan Oliphant, an attractive young man with a vision of his city's future glory. When he comes home from college to enter business, the city's growth has not yet begun, but Dan is a born salesman and promoter and knows instinctively what the future holds. At the turn of the century, however, when he buys the Ornaby Farm for a subdivision, the city has not yet burst its Sixteenth Street boundary. Dan is regarded as a visionary and refused financial support by all conservative businessmen, but he goes ahead developing his property on a shoestring, and by 1905, or thereabouts, Dan begins to sell lots. Soon Old Hickory Shelby, the traction magnate, has to build a car line to Ornaby Addition, and by 1910 the boom is on. Dan ultimately becomes the general promoter of the city's growth, the founder of an automobile manufacturing company, a dabbler in interurban lines, and Mayor for a term. In the end, however, the hardshell bankers who lacked Dan's original vision take over his business empire, for Dan is a promoter, not an organizer, and always he has walked a financial tightrope.

Dan is a symbolic figure in Tarkington's study—both the creator and the victim of industrial America. Like the inventor and builder in Melville's "The Bell Tower," Dan is destroyed by the mechanism that he has fashioned. His Frankenstein monster is not satisfied, however, to smash only his business enterprises, and long before Dan dies of pneumonia, he has lost the boyish innocence that made him attractive as a young man. His single-minded absorption in building the city warps his personality and ruins his chances of making successful an unlikely marriage. Lena Oliphant is another of Tarkington's selfish, destructive women and totally unsuited to be the wife of a businessman. When she leaves him, taking their spoiled son with her, she and Dan long have ceased to love each other. Dan is a casualty in the growth of the city, and he finds no more happiness in his life than the millionaire automobile maker Dodsworth whom Sinclair Lewis created five years later. Whether Dan's sacrifice is worth while, Tarkington does not say. If the growth is to take place, his immolation is necessary; and if one regards the change as a good, Dan's death is not in vain. Elsewhere Tarkington argues that change is progress and hence beneficent, but here he does not feel obliged to pass explicit judgment on the inevitable historic process.

His conclusion that order and beauty eventually would follow the turmoil and ugliness came not only from rational analysis but also from personal involvement in the evolution. The year that he wrote *The Midlander* Tarkington himself moved to the vicinity of Dan Oliphant's Ornaby Addition. Finally deserting the home of his childhood, which by this time contained memories painful and pleasant, he bought a large house at 4270 North Meridian Street and moved away from the downtown smoke and noise. Leaving the old house caused a pang, and he did not sleep much the first night in the new: "It was as if the other, down there in the heavy smoke and noise and dirt, was . . . abandoned and betrayed." Long before he traveled north, his old home had been encroached upon by garages, office buildings, and parking lots, but when he moved into his new home, he saw that beauty had replaced the ugly defacements of subdivision builders like Dan Oliphant. The raw gashes cut across the once-pleasant countryside had healed over, and along the main avenues, such as Meridian Street, "the woodland was still there, so that one could hardly see the houses." Yet the cost of the growth could not be forgotten, for if one looked upward through the openings in the tall beech trees of the original forest, "the thinning end of a plume of industrial smoke, miles long, was visible" against the blue of the sky.

During the first winter that Tarkington spent on Meridian Street the contrast with the old homestead downtown was astonishing. He had bought a half-timbered Tudor house built eleven years before, remodeled it extensively, and decorated it to harmonize with his growing art collection. He paneled the dining room to enhance the tones of his eighteenth-century portraits, floored the sunroom in marble to show off his treasures, and erected in the drawing room a high terra-cotta fireplace copied from an admired European model. These and other improvements he carried out, so that when George Tyler visited the new house, the producer observed: "Well, if you *haf* to live in Indianapolis, this is certainly the way to do it!"

The house sat far back from the street on a large, well-

wooded lot that one of Tarkington's great-grandfathers once
had owned. When the Tarkingtons breakfasted in a green-
and-glass room they had made over the porte-cochère, they
could look out on the old trees laced with snow, while inside
their breakfast room they were surrounded by plants and gold-
fish, a green bronze faun and ivy in jars on antique gold columns. "We do enjoy this house—and the quiet of the life,"
Tarkington wrote Kahler in February, 1924, but he added,
slightly puzzled: "It's hard to realize I've written only one
single-act play and four short stories since we came home [in
December]. I *never* felt less like *work!*" Perhaps he was ex-
periencing a delayed reaction to the sorrows and emotional
stress of the preceding winter and needed time to rest and
savor his new surroundings. His lassitude continued into the
following summer, the laziest he ever spent, and it was autumn
before he was able to resume a full writing schedule.

Although he may not have felt much like working, his imagination was as fertile as ever, and the four stories he referred
to launched a new series, collectively entitled *Women,* inspired
by his removal to the north end of Indianapolis. The new
tales, which treat another phase of twentieth-century change,
deserve more attention than they have received, for they mirror perfectly the matriarchy of suburban America. Tarkington was fascinated by the daytime female world which had
come into existence in the outlying residential sections of urban
areas. During office hours, he noted, when the males were moil-
ing in the commercial heart of the city, a society flourished
made up of wives, teas, domestic servants, luncheons, children,
literary clubs, and Amazon warfare of a highly sophisticated
type. To catch the image of this world he used his well-tested
device of loose-plotting and common characters, heeding the
words of Lydia Dodge, one of his leading ladies, who explains
in the preamble that a novel about women should not "be cen-
tralized and bound down to a single theme, a single conflict, a
single heroine." Instead it should recount the thoughts and
acts of women in relation to their children, neighbors, "and
the people who casually walk into our lives . . . and out again."

There is not space to analyze these stories in detail, but the
first four chapters, which constitute the initial episode, are
typical of the whole and introduce the two main characters,

Mrs. Cromwell and Mrs. Dodge. The opening story characteristically shows Tarkington's subtle insight into feminine psychology and his ability to spin a tale, both true and humorous, out of the trivia of daily life. Its motivation is a "profound willingness to see a proud head lowered, particularly if that head be one that has displayed its pride," and its action catches a moment in the history of its characters when the normally calm surface of suburban life erupts. The plot is purposely slight, and the skill lies all in the telling.

"What could offer to mortal eye a picture of more secure placidity than three smiling ladies walking homeward together after a club meeting?" asks the author on page one; but he adds immediately that appearances are deceiving and goes on to illustrate the point. Two of the ladies, Mrs. Dodge and Mrs. Cromwell, are discovered busily congratulating the third, Mrs. Roderick Brooks Battle, on the sublimity of the paper, "Sweetness and Light," that she has just read at the club meeting. Mrs. Battle protests vigorously that it all was her husband's work: "I don't suppose I could write a single connected paragraph without his telling me how." This deference to the great Mr. Battle is a response the other ladies have heard before, *ad nauseam,* and on this occasion Mrs. Battle's everlasting praise of her architect-husband goads the slightly malicious Mrs. Dodge beyond endurance. "She thinks she's the only woman that ever got married," explodes that volatile lady after Mrs. Battle leaves her companions.

A few minutes later Mrs. Dodge and Mrs. Cromwell catch a glimpse of the paragon Battle showing a rich widowed client through her new house. The architect-husband seen from across the street appears entirely too ardent in his attentions to the befurred widow, and Mrs. Dodge determines that someone must tell Mrs. Battle how her husband is carrying on. "A sense of duty with gall behind it," reflects the kindlier Mrs. Cromwell after her friend's departure, "is indeed to be feared." But even vicious gossips cannot tell a wife to her face that her husband is philandering, and when Mrs. Dodge confronts Mrs. Battle with her tale, she tells it with a bit of circumlocution. The alert Mrs. Battle pretends to understand that Mrs. Dodge is confiding her own marital problems and is so effusively solicitous that the scandalmonger is routed.

In the final scene of the story Mrs. Dodge and Mrs. Cromwell again see the widow and Mr. Battle on the balcony of the new house, but as they watch, the mousy Mrs. Battle, dressed in her market clothes, arrives in her battered sedan loaded with groceries and before their eyes takes her husband away from the elegantly gowned rival. Mrs. Dodge then interprets the denouement as follows: "He [Mr. Battle] knows that between his . . . romance and his press agent he's got to take the press agent. . . . He mightn't be a great man at all without his press agent —and he'd rather keep on being a great man. And Amelia knows she's getting too skimpy-looking to get a chance to make a great man out of anybody *else;* so she wouldn't let me tell her about him, because she's going to stick to him!"

Tarkington collected the Dodge-Cromwell stories under the title *Women* late in 1925 during his fifty-seventh year. With it he completed his twenty-third volume of novels, novelettes, and short stories—all published in the quarter century since McClure had accepted *The Gentleman from Indiana*. But there was no happiness for Tarkington in anything but writing, and he went on using up his eyes and energy in unrelenting work for the balance of the decade. His total output of fiction eventually totaled forty-one volumes, plus dozens of stories and ten serials and story sequences that never were put into book form; and during the period between writing *Women*, January, 1924, and the end of the decade he wrote twenty uncollected stories. Some are excellent tales that ought to be gathered together, while others purposely were left uncollected because Tarkington decided they were not good enough to reprint. The best perhaps is "Stella Crozier," an O. Henry Prize story for 1926, which sketches brilliantly a rich female dilettante such as Tarkington later made the heroine of *Image of Josephine* (1945), and among those pieces left to the oblivion of the magazines is a serial about Belinda Dale, career girl, which occupied six issues of the *Ladies' Home Journal* in 1929 and 1930. At the end of 1924, however, Tarkington was temporarily weary and desirous of a long vacation. Accordingly, he planned for the following year his first Sabbatical leave from literature since he had settled down to serious writing and had produced *The Flirt* in 1912.

THIRTEEN

EUROPE, MAINE, AND AFFLICTION

WHEN THE TIME ARRIVED for his annual trek from Maine to Indiana, Tarkington varied his normal routine by going abroad for a six months' sojourn. After the usual summer and autumn at Kennebunkport he embarked from New York, with his wife, sister-in-law Louise Keifer, and the Howard Fishers, on his first foreign travels in fourteen years. He subsequently returned straightway to New England from his tour and thus remained away from Indianapolis for a year and a half, his longest absence from home since his days of Parisian exile. He had been mining the Hoosier lode extensively and needed a change both of scenery and literary materials. A return to Europe, which promised fresh vistas and additional literary ore, proved to be no disappointment. He came back in June, 1925, refreshed and stimulated, filled with new impressions, stirred by a few painful memories, and ready to write his next two novels, *The Plutocrat* and *Claire Ambler.*

The immediate destination of the trip was North Africa, where the travelers planned to motor from Algiers to Tunis before crossing the Mediterranean to Sicily. Later they intended to follow spring northward along the Italian peninsula, as Tarkington had done many years before, and to end their wanderings in Paris in May and early June. Their ship, the S. S. *Duilio,* sailed directly for Algiers and landed them in French North Africa after a rough January crossing. Although Tarkington was seasick for the first time in his life, he regained his composure when the ship paused at Gibraltar and then was utterly delighted with his first sight of Algiers. As an affluent, middle-aged American, he spared no expense to provide for creature comforts and on his arrival was greeted as if he had been the President of France. An Oxford-educated French courier met the Americans at the dock with an outsize Renault landaulet and took them to a gorgeous hotel suite which opened on a private garden of palms, orange trees, pansies, violets, and blooming vines climbing on whitewashed walls. "This is the most colorful city I *ever* [saw]," Tarkington wrote of his first impression of Algiers, and after touring the city, he was equally fascinated by the confusion of French, Arabian, Italian, and Spanish architecture sprawled over the crescent-shaped hills rising from the harbor.

The motor trip across Algeria to Tunis was a perpetual astonishment—unfamiliar landscape, strange people, an alien culture. "It's all incredible, picturesque and rather barbaric—but [a] continual delight," he wrote home from Bougie after two days on the road. When he reached Tunis, he felt as if he had stepped into the *Arabian Nights*. The bazaar, in particular, was beyond a "Ziegfeld dream of the Orient" with its shops "separated by marble pillars & columns, taken from the ruins of Carthage and painted in gaudy stripes . . . in long tunnels, reached by streets a yard wide." As he moved along with the crowds in the bazaar, a bare-legged, turbaned porter carrying his purchases behind him, he encountered robed sweetmeat sellers, unspeakable beggars, soldiers of the Bey of Tunis, Numidian Negroes, Turks, and merchants who tugged at his elbows as he passed. He was reluctant to leave Africa, which had proved more interesting than he expected, but plans had been made for hotels, couriers, and automobiles in Sicily, and the travelers went on to Palermo in mid-February to begin an eight-day motor trip around the island.

Returning to Italian soil after the strangeness of Africa seemed to Tarkington like "getting back to Kokomo." The bay at Palermo rivaled the harbor at Naples, Mount Etna was in eruption as Vesuvius once had been, and he again toured cathedrals and bought art objects. The Capuchin catacombs in Palermo, in addition, were even more horrible than their counterpart in Rome: Gustave Doré in his most "hellish mood" could not have drawn a suggestion of "this nightmare." He again enjoyed the blend of mountain scenery and seascapes as the Sicilian roads wound along the rugged coast. The drive from Siracusa to Taormina was particularly impressive, for though the day was rainy, the clouds occasionally lifted, and the tourists could look over palm trees and beyond lemon groves to see the fantastically shaped snowy ridges of Etna seeming only a hundred yards away. Taormina, just across the straits from the toe of Italy, was the terminus of the motor trip, and they stayed there several weeks before crossing to the mainland. The almond trees were in bloom, and on sunny days the weather was like late April or early May in Indiana.

The subsequent tour northward through Italy and France, which covered familiar ground and was relatively uneventful, included stops at Naples, Rome, Florence, Venice, and Milan. Tarkington was depressed in Rome, however, for Laurel had been born there, and the ghosts of old friends and old associations haunted him. He was glad to continue the trip after two weeks in the Italian capital, although he caught cold in Perugia and spent three days in bed in Florence. But when he reached Venice, it was fiesta time, and his last memories of Italy were gay. The great old banners were up on the masts before St. Mark's, the silk and brocades were hung from windows in the ancient fashion, a band played in the piazza, and serenaders drifted on the Grand Canal. Then in Milan he met George Tyler, also on vacation, and was persuaded to redo *The Man from Home*. After leaving Italy for the last time, Tarkington revisited Paris for five weeks, and on June 6 sailed once more for the United States, this time to stay. Age and affliction were stalking him, and his 1925 visit to Europe proved his last.

The trip was richly rewarding, however, and furnished "a long gallery of new memories . . . to take back with me." A week before leaving Europe he catalogued for Street his most indelible impressions:

Tanagra figures of Arabs in their flying robes, running to get sheep or camels or donkeys off the road before our honking cars should arrive; the golden stone [of] old houses on the mountain sides in almond blossom time in Sicily, and a peculiar, almost luminously gray stone type of house we saw between Agrigento and Siracusa—and Taormina; all of Taormina . . .; and Capri in the sparkling spring sunshine; the hillsides above Florence; the old fighting town of Perugia; the Byzantine mosaics at Ravenna; Venice in the rain, with carabinieri marching to St.

Mark's in the downpour; . . . the Little Trianon bosky and almost cheerfully ghostly in May sunshine; . . . arab Biskra in a
blue twilight—and that *Arabian Nights* town Sidi Ban Said, a
perfectly impossible sight in the twentieth century.

Another episode that he did not think worth reporting at the
time but which he recalled later was a chance meeting with
Ernest Hemingway, who then was still an obscure American
newspaper correspondent living in Paris. F. Scott Fitzgerald,
who also was in France, took Hemingway to see Tarkington,
but the interview was not very satisfactory, for the impeccable
Tarkington felt slightly affronted at the Bohemian appearance
of his visitors. About Hemingway, Tarkington later wrote:
"My impression . . . was of a Kansas University football beef;
but I rather liked him. Fitzgerald [a fellow Princetonian]
brought him up and was a little tight—took him away because
Hemingway was to have a fight that afternoon at three o'clock,
though I gathered they'd both been up all night."

Tarkington began using his new stock of memories in *The
Plutocrat,* which he wrote the next year in a renewed burst of
creative energy. The inspiration for the novel came from both
North Africa and his traveling companion Howard Fisher of
Pittsburgh. A Princeton friend and member of the Kennebunkport summer colony, Fisher had planned with Tarkington
the motor tours across North Africa and Sicily and during the
journey turned out to be an astonishing companion. His uninhibited response to things foreign and his unabashed Ameri-
canness, in primitive Arab villages as well as in luxurious
hotels, delighted Tarkington: "If we *have* a 'type'—and I'm now
convinced we have—he's it. You can't see it when it's a million,
but take one out of the million and set it among Arabs and
Pompeiis and English 'titled people' . . . and it sticks up like
Mont Blanc." Earlier he anticipated this conclusion: "Fisher
is an American Abroad all right. He shouts 'Eddie,' up and
down the hotel halls—for the valet de chambre; last night he
hired the hotel orchestra to play 'Yes, we have no bananas,' and
he calls our new courier 'Krauss'—the man's name being Ca-
ruzzo." Mark Twain's innocents, who in 1867 dubbed their
Parisian guide "Ferguson," were cut from the same cloth as
Tarkington's plutocrat.

Although Fisher served as model for the fictional plutocrat, he was not easily recognizable in the character of Earl Tinker. In the novel Fisher appears as a fairly uncomplicated piece of human machinery with a quite different background. "My fellow," explained Tarkington, pointing out that Fisher had been only a point of departure, "is a big, bragging, noisy Illinois manufacturer—he gets drunk, lies to his wife, chases women, makes himself a spectacle, and is a real show, I think." In addition he supports hospitals, employs five thousand persons in a business that he built all by himself, and is so completely good-natured, generous, and unpretentious that even his severest critic in the novel ends up liking him. Tinker is a superb creation, almost a legendary figure; but it is not the actual detail of Tinker's magnificent sweep across Algeria, showering silver as he goes, that is important. The significance of the book lies in Tarkington's concept of Tinker as a modern Roman. Tarkington saw America's impact on Western Europe in the twentieth century as similar to Rome's collision with Greek civilization at the beginning of the Christian era. Just as Rome had borrowed, diluted, and overwhelmed Greek culture, so was America repeating the process.

The view of America as a modern-day Rome is expressed for the author by Dr. Medjila, an archeologist who lectures to the American playwright Laurence Ogle on the Roman ruins at Timgad, Algeria: "America has so much that is the same as these dead people: the great Yawp, the love of health, the love of plumbing, the love of power, of wealth, and, above all, the worship of bigness. . . . What is strange, you find at the same time a great deal of common sense." Then the professor, who once lived at Rock Island, Illinois, adds that the one tourist he has encountered who best understands the Roman ruins is Tinker. The Tinkers of Illinois, as the Romans before them, are empire-builders, organizers, braggarts, and Rotarians. Tinker, explains the archeologist, instantly visualized the Roman city indicated by the scattered ruins, for he knew how to lay out a town, and the only difference between him and the founders of Timgad was his boast that he could have done it better.

Throughout the novel Tinker reveals himself as a twentieth-century Roman. Everywhere he goes in North Africa he insists on seeing, in addition to the usual tourist sights, the water works, the electric light plants, and the sewage systems, if any. When he comes in from a day's excursion on the desert, he rides a huge white camel at the head of a caravan of attendants, much as a Roman general might have returned from the Punic Wars. When he returns from visiting the native quarter of Algiers, he reflectively comments to Ogle: "Ain't this the dog-gonedest place you ever did see? Look at that sewer where we met you this afternoon, for instance. Why, the United States army ought to come over here and clean it up!" Tinker would have been delighted to know that the American army was to do exactly that, in parts of Algeria at least, during and after the North African campaign of 1942-1943.

At the tomb of St. Augustine, of whom he has never heard, Tinker reveals his appalling ignorance and cocksureness. With a splendid sense of comedy Tarkington depicts him staring at the grave and asking his guide for the third time:

> "Who'd you say he was?"
> "It is Saint Augustine."
> "What'd he do, John?"
> "He was the great ecclesiastical authority of the Fourth Century . . . the great religious power of his time."
> "Preacher, I expect. . . . What denomination was he?"

This question nearly stumps the guide, who manages with difficulty to explain to Tinker that St. Augustine lived before the Reformation; but when Tinker learns that the saint was responsible for the doctrine of original sin and infant damnation, he concludes: "Oh, *that's* it, is it? . . . Well, sir, that's just like my own father. *He* was an old-time Presbyterian." As the bedeviled guide protests the analogy, Tinker cavalierly disposes of the doctrinal similarity between St. Augustine and John Calvin: "Plum out o' date." Then he explains: "The only hell we worry about nowadays is slipping back in our progress; we got to show a bigger and better business this year than we did last year."

Tarkington's purpose in creating the plutocrat was to place, in the exotic setting that he had visited with Fisher, an interesting type, the American millionaire. While Tinker is a dynamic person, whom Tarkington admired in many ways, the plutocrat is drawn objectively and humorously. He is loud, crude, ignorant, and generous; but for all his grossness he is a twentieth-century fact. There is much good-humored satire in this portrait of Tinker, and Tarkington demonstrates his continued mastery of style and characterization. To the severest critics of American materialism, who could find nothing favorable to say about millionaires, the novel seemed apologetic, and to Tarkington's detractors it looked as if the author of *The Plutocrat* had cast his lot with the wealthy Philistines. Tarkington, however, denied before the novel's publication that he was glorifying the businessman, as perhaps an answer to Lewis' *Babbitt,* which, in fact, he claimed he had not read. In any event, *The Plutocrat* was not conceived of as propaganda.

Several years later Tarkington did defend the businessman when he wrote a magazine article called "Rotarian and Sophisticate." There he rallied about the Sheridans, the Oliphants, and the Tinkers more vigorously than ever before. The inescapable fact was, he declared, that the businessman had built America, though he admitted readily enough that the "boosters" and "go-getters" were often obnoxious and boorish. Tarkington himself had been accused of "knocking" his city a decade before when he first had begun his economic studies of the Midwest, but in 1929 his conclusion was that "the sophisticated satirists have made a man of straw and booster's phrases and put the label 'Rotarian' upon it; then, assaulting it, they believe the onslaught to be against something actual . . . their annoyance with sporadic cases of blatant 'go-getterism' has interfered with accuracy of observation; the condition is like that of a man who, disturbed by a rooster's crowing, swears that all eggs are bad."

Although Tinker is the most interesting character in the novel, and his activities the most amusing, Tarkington constructed a plot which also involves a skillfully managed French woman and the playwright Ogle. The story is loosely strung on a travel framework, beginning with the voyage from New York to Algiers and continuing with the automobile trip across Algeria to Tunis. The playwright and the plutocrat both succumb to the charms of Mme. Momoro, a highly sophisticated adventuress who might have interested Henry James, and compete for her attentions. Ogle provides a point of view from which a negative report on Tinker is made, but he does not represent the author's alter ego. Ogle himself is sharply satirized as an obnoxiously. vain aesthete and during the story is greatly humbled by Mme. Momoro's use of him to further her mercenary designs on Tinker.

Ogle is chiefly diverting as he reflects Tarkington's attitude towards one of the intellectual skirmishes of the Twenties, the controversy between the aesthetes and their critics. Tarkington takes pleasure in ridiculing the intellectual snobbery of Ogle and two of his friends, a modernist painter and an obscurantist poet who writes without capital letters or punctuation; and he makes the noisy but unpretentious Tinker, despite many shortcomings, a better man than they are. While Tarkington might have defended the aesthetes of 1904, he frankly preferred the Old Guard two decades later.

Tarkington's return to Europe not only furnished new material for his studies of the American businessman, but it also added to his gallery of feminine portraits. In this respect the literary result of the 1925 hegira was a combination of two earlier interests—the marriageable girl and the international novel. In *Claire Ambler* Tarkington revived a theme that Howells had used in *A Fearful Responsibility* (1881) and James in *Daisy Miller* (1878): the American girl, raised in innocence and without chaperones, flouting European social mores. In Howells' story Lily Mayhew from upstate New York strikes up an acquaintance with an Austrian army officer while she is traveling insufficiently chaperoned across Italy, and although no serious consequences ensue, Lily's unconventional behavior causes her guardian uncle, who is knowledgeable in European customs, a great deal of embarrassment. James's story is similar, though it has a pathetic outcome, for Daisy Miller dies of malaria after an unchaperoned walk at night in the Colosseum with an improper Italian suitor. But neither Lily nor Daisy is defiled in any way by her "shocking" behavior: their American innocence shields them.

So it is with Claire Ambler, who spends the winter of her twenty-first year at Raona (Taormina), Sicily. She always has been a belle, and when she visits the Italian resort, she captivates several Italians and develops a passion for a dying English war veteran. As in the earlier uses of the theme, Claire glides through her flirtations unscathed; but Tarkington gives a reverse twist to the Daisy Miller plot by making Claire the cause of a serious incident between her Italian suitors. One of them, an attractive young Italian prince from the North, a pro-Fascist, pursues Claire at the same time that she gives encouragement to the Bastoni brothers, native Sicilians of questionable character. She refuses to believe that playing fast and loose with the attentions of her Italian admirers can have any more serious consequences in Raona than in America, but when she snubs the anti-Fascist Bastoni in favor of the prince, the latter soon is waylaid and nearly killed by "unknown" assailants. Fortunately for the Englishman, who has only a few more months to live, Claire's infatuation cools off before his emotions are completely shattered by a hopeless romance.

Although most of this short novel takes place in Sicily, it opens and closes in America when Claire is eighteen and twenty-five respectively. She is first seen as a giddy debutante with a squadron of boys moored about her at a resort reminiscent of Kennebunkport. This section is superb social satire, which recalls *Seventeen* or, more specifically, the sophomoric inanities of "Mary Smith." The last section of the novel brings the premarital portrait of Claire to a close with her final acceptance of a suitor. There is an echo here of *Alice Adams,* for Claire, like Alice when she enters the business college, at last comes out of her world of self-dramatization and romantic dreams and accepts reality in marrying Walter Rackbridge. Always before, she was waiting for the perfect man.

Just as Tarkington had used his experiences and the exotic background of Algeria in *The Plutocrat,* he worked his memories of Taormina into *Claire Ambler.* The setting for most of the novel is his hotel (once a monastery), which overlooked the distant Straits of Messina from a rugged eminence near the foot of Mount Etna. The shifty-eyed Bastoni brothers and the pro-Fascist prince were suggested by Tarkington's observations of the political undercurrents in Sicily, and the most moving incident in the novel, the scene in the Greek theater, was transcribed from life almost as it occurred. Tarkington one evening went alone to a concert in the ancient amphitheater at Taormina and heard a woman, somewhere in the shadows high above him, sing an impromptu accompaniment to the string orchestra far below. It was a warm, clear night, the music from the stage enchantingly beautiful, and the unseen soprano's voice ethereal and inspired. Tarkington returned to the hotel in ecstasy and immediately scribbled his impressions of the music and the singer. When he wrote his novel of Taormina two years later, he described this experience (in the words of the dying Englishman) as the "final loveliness in the hour of greatest sheer beauty I've ever known in my life." Everything about Taormina was so different and engrossing that he wrote Woollcott: "I can no more work here than I could in Hell." The scenery was too beautiful, the music too abundant, the pretty women too numerous, the almond trees too fragrant.

After an interlude of writing about Americans abroad Tarkington returned to familiar scenes in Indianapolis for his next novel, *Young Mrs. Greeley*. This story, however, was a slight departure, because in it he turned his scrutiny to a previously unexamined phase of midland city life, apartment-house living. *Young Mrs. Greeley* concerns the jealousies, rivalries, and machinations that go on among the tightly packed residents of the Warwicke Armes. Its social drama is played against a background of business rivalry so that the work is an integrated socio-economic study. Tarkington planned it as another domestic comedy with serious consideration of marital and business relations, and it is noteworthy too for its recurrent use of the scheming, selfish wife. Yet this short tale barely scratches the surface of the problems it treats, and Tarkington gave the same subject a fuller and more penetrating analysis later in *The Lorenzo Bunch*.

There are four prominent characters in the novel: Will and Aurelia Hedge, Stella and Bill Greeley. These four become best friends when the Greeleys move to the city from a near-by small town. Bill gets a job at National Kitchen Utensils through Will, then in a short time demonstrates superior business talents which win him an executive position. When he passes up Will, Aurelia's jealousy is boundless; and in her schemes to capitalize on the rapid advancement of her husband's friend, she plays on the naïveté of Stella (a sort of sex-reversed Iago-Othello relationship) and nearly wrecks Stella

and Bill's happiness and security. In the end the president of
the company banishes the Hedges to a small-town, branch store,
a fate like death for the socially ambitious Aurelia.

The slightness of *Young Mrs. Greeley* is understandable in
light of biographical fact, and the real wonder is that the novel
was finished at all. During its composition Tarkington suffered
the physical blow that made him a semi-invalid for years and
seriously impaired his activities for the rest of his life: blindness. In the midst of the novel he had to alter radically his
entire procedure of literary composition, and while facing the
bleak prospect of blindness, he had to learn to write by dictating. By sheer force of will he made the abrupt transition,
accomplishing it so smoothly that *Young Mrs. Greeley* contains
neither rough joinery nor noticeable variations in style. He was
fortunate in securing at this critical juncture the services of a
talented young woman, Elizabeth Trotter, a Kennebunkport
summer resident from Philadelphia, who already was a close
friend. Miss Trotter served him with filial devotion as secretary for the rest of his life, wintering with him in Indianapolis
as well as summering in his employ in Maine.

Tarkington's sight did not fail without prior warning. His
eyes had troubled him for a decade, and recently the trouble
had been growing steadily more serious. For a time in 1922 he
had been ordered not to use his eyes while he underwent superficial treatment for the cataracts that were beginning to form,
but notwithstanding, three years later he had lost most of the
sight in his right eye. Press reports in 1927 that he was going
blind, however, were premature. Tarkington denied them vigorously, even going to the lengths of reading a newspaper clipping to a reporter to prove the groundlessness of the story. Yet
Mrs. Tarkington was seriously concerned by this time and
began urging her husband to consider an operation; but even
though he was suffering from impaired vision and headaches,
which were especially painful when he attended Commencement
at Princeton the next June, he held out adamantly against
surgery. His wife watched helplessly as his eyes grew dimmer.
When she suggested going to Baltimore to see William Wilmer,
the well-known opthalmologist, he excitedly made her promise
not to mention the subject again. He did not think he could
stand an operation and did not wish to talk about it; but by the

end of 1928, when the choice lay between blindness and surgery, he capitulated.

Once the decision had been made, Tarkington bore with cheerful stoicism five operations over a two-year period. He seemed to stand the repeated visits to the Wilmer Institute of Johns Hopkins better than the other members of his household, and once when a visit to the hospital produced only new glasses, he wrote cheerfully that he felt cheated. Going there and not being operated on, he reported, was "rather like going to Commencement at P[rinceton]. when it's not your reunion year." On other occasions he joked about his long time at Wilmer Institute, saying that he matriculated in 'twenty-nine and hoped to graduate in 'thirty-one, then become a member of the alumni association. The hardest trial of his hospital experience was getting used to the lack of privacy. "It was an advantage to be blind," he wrote George Ade, for "the first thing they remove is your modesty." He explained that pleasant ladylike voices constantly were ordering, "Mr. Tarkington, please take off your clothes"; and he quoted his wife as saying that "by the end of his first week he began to undress whenever he heard a strange woman's voice."

When Tarkington entered the hospital in November, 1928, preparatory to his first operation in February, his case did not seem especially difficult. Wilmer subsequently removed the cataract from his right eye (which he still had very slight use of) and optimistically wired Mrs. Jameson that "the operation was a remarkable success." It would only be a matter of weeks, he added, before his patient regained complete use of the eye; but the early report was too sanguine, and by the following summer Tarkington again was reading and writing with great difficulty. The next winter Wilmer operated once more on the right eye, and that time Tarkington went home seeing pretty well. During the summer of 1930, however, the eye began to misbehave, and in August a curtain seemed to be lowering, so that each day he had to throw his head back farther in order to see. Finally on August 25 the curtain came down completely, and he was totally blind.

The trouble was a detached retina, and after a hurried trip to see a Portland doctor Tarkington was rushed back to Baltimore. The Boston and Maine Railroad provided a special car for the journey, and Wilmer interrupted his vacation to operate on the right eye for the third time. When that operation failed, a fourth was attempted, also without success, in October. Then Wilmer decided to remove the cataract from the long-useless left eye, and after his patient had recuperated from the autumn ordeal, he operated again in the winter. After more than two years of discouraging failure the fifth and last effort was a success, and Tarkington subsequently was able to see better than he had for many years. By the time the bandages were removed at the end of January, he had been totally blind for more than five months and almost blind for nearly three years.

One might expect a novelist in the depths of physical affliction to interrupt creative activity for a period of emotional readjustment, but the writing habit was inveterate with Tarkington, and he took no pleasure in anything but literature. The bibliography of his works shows no break in published titles between 1929 and 1931. During this troubled time he collected, under the title *Penrod Jashber,* a volume of stories written much earlier; he also wrote the tales which made up *Mary's Neck;* a five-part serial, "High Summer," that he did not reprint in book form; and an excellent novel, *Mirthful Haven.*

During the anxious months of his eye operations Tarkington turned to literary material that was close at hand and, for him, relatively untapped—the Maine scene. Almost everything he wrote at this time was laid in the vicinity of Kennebunkport and drew its characters from the permanent residents of the place and the summer colony. Although he had used Maine as the locale for *The Wren* and *Tweedles,* he had not yet written a New England novel. But he was well prepared by this time to place his fiction in Maine, for he was thoroughly acclimated to Kennebunkport, well attuned to the local life, and accepted by the villagers more completely than any other non-resident. In fact, there is no good explanation why Tarkington had not written a Maine novel ten years earlier.

He had been a property-owner in Kennebunkport since 1916 when he had bought eighteen acres of land on a hill above the town, and he had been summering in Maine since 1903 when he went there to recuperate from typhoid fever. In 1917 he had added to his property and built a handsome colonial frame house that became one of the tourist attractions of Kennebunkport. Named Seawood, this pleasant house drew him back to Maine regularly each year, and if he ever had been forced to choose between his home in Indianapolis and Seawood, he probably would have forsworn Indiana. The place in Maine was a perfect setting for a man whose passion was to surround himself with beautiful things. His green-shuttered house over-looked flower-bordered terraces, groves of birch, oak, and juniper, meadows, and a strip of sea-bordering pine woods. From the west side of his hilltop he could catch glimpses of the Kennebunk River, beyond which lay Wells Harbor and Mount Agamenticus, and on the east he looked on a grassy field and thick woods. Nowhere was there a sign of habitation.

The interior of the house was decorated and furnished in harmony with the unspoiled natural surroundings, and one room in particular deserves special mention: the workroom which Tarkington planned to suit his personality and writing habits. Built at the end of the house, it was a two-storied room with a high arched ceiling and windows, simple decorations, and plenty of cupboards and books. It was originally furnished mostly in oak, large functional pieces which harmonized with the plain décor, and liberally ornamented with ship models. After his last eye operation, however, Tarkington wanted something more to look at and remodeled the workroom, replacing the rough plaster walls with carved wainscotting and panels in the eighteenth-century manner and filling the room with some of his most prized art objects, especially his eighteenth-century portraits. At the inside end of the room was a stairway leading to a balcony, on which Tarkington worked, facing the wall, secure from distractions. His bedroom, moreover, was reached from the gallery through a doorway that provided an escape route when visitors (of whom there were many) were shown through Seawood by feminine members of the household.

One visitor to Seawood, whose arrival never signaled Tarkington's retreat through the gallery door, was his neighbor Kenneth Roberts. The two men had met when Roberts returned in 1919 to his native Maine from service in the First World War, and a friendship had grown up during the succeeding years. Roberts at that time was chiefly occupied with writing articles for the *Saturday Evening Post,* but he hoped someday to do a novel, and Tarkington encouraged him in that ambition. For the first decade of their relationship, however, they met only socially, though they collaborated once, with Hugh Kahler, on a burlesque handbook for the antique collector, *The Collector's Whatnot* (1923), and five years later Tarkington illustrated a similar volume called *Antiquamania* that Roberts wrote alone.

The full story of Tarkington's part in Roberts' career as a novelist belongs in Roberts' biography; yet the relationship is so typical and revealing of Tarkington that it cannot be omitted altogether from this record. Without Tarkington's repeated encouragement and infinitely patient editorial assistance Roberts might never have written any novels. When his first novel, *Arundel,* was in the planning stage, Roberts talked over plot and characters with Tarkington at great length and was urged to drop everything to start on the story. Roberts took this advice and later, after he had written the first draft, read the entire manuscript to Tarkington, who gave him exhaustive criticism. Tarkington was enthusiastic, called for numerous stylistic revisions, wanted the love-making less explicit; but his most important service was in the matter of cutting. Roberts had a natural tendency to use twice as many words as necessary, and Tarkington wielded the editorial blue pencil vigorously. Yet "Booth was gentle, always, in his suggestions," says Roberts, "so gentle that I failed to grasp many of them. I think he was fearful of hurting my feelings or discouraging me."

Four novels later the same editorial process was going on during the writing of *Northwest Passage* (1937), and during the reading of the manuscript, after the two novelists had gone through only one hundred and seventy pages in fourteen nights, Roberts remarked that his writing must be deteriorating, judging from the amount of rewriting that was needed. When Tarkington replied, however, that *Northwest Passage* was the best Roberts had done thus far, the latter concluded: "If he had urged me to alter everything in *Arundel* that had been a little out of kilter, I'd have been discouraged, and we could never have got through it." Even though *Northwest Passage* was Roberts' fifth novel, Tarkington gave his time unstintingly during its revision, spending fifty-eight evenings between August 12 and November 19, 1936, listening to the manuscript and making suggestions. He dictated so many emendations that Roberts felt obliged to offer Tarkington joint authorship and half of the royalties, but Tarkington insisted modestly that he merely had played a Maxwell Perkins to Roberts' Tom Wolfe. Tarkington regarded Roberts as a gifted writer, though not an artist, one who could put memorable scenes into a reader's mind by "superhuman *labor*," and he was happy to have helped him become a distinguished novelist.

Tarkington's characteristic generosity never was shown more clearly than when Roberts began writing fiction, for his first two novels were produced during the exact period of Tarkington's most serious eye trouble. *Arundel* was planned and executed in 1928 and 1929 while Tarkington, apprehensively, was learning to dictate so that he could go on with his own literary career, and it was during the summer of 1930 when he was helping Roberts with *The Lively Lady* (1931) that he became totally blind. While Mrs. Tarkington made hurried arrangements for a special car to rush her husband to Baltimore, Tarkington put aside his own despair and concerned himself with Roberts' problems. The last thing he did before leaving Kennebunkport for Johns Hopkins, Roberts remembers, was to dictate suggestions for using material cut out of *The Lively Lady*.

Mirthful Haven (1930), written when Tarkington thought he was going to be permanently blind, reflects in its story something of the author's personal problems at the time of its composition. One of its reviewers, Robert E. Sherwood, called it Tarkington's bitterest and angriest book, "faithful to the unlovely truth," and inevitable in the resolution of its plot. Although the story is not a tragedy, Sherwood was correct in appraising it as "thoroughly and violently unneighborly," full of vigor and protest.

Not only was it written during his physical affliction, but it appeared soon after Tarkington had been disillusioned by the meanness of the summer residents in their treatment of an employee of the River Club. Captain Blynn Montgomery, who already was an old man, was fired summarily without any provision for other employment or pension. Tarkington tried hard to circumvent the firing, but a coup was brought off by a handful of the summer people who were determined to get rid of the captain. Tarkington proposed a compromise, got it accepted by the club's executive committee, then was defeated by a cabal within the committee. Despite a long career as a novelist he hardly could understand such pettiness and inhumanity: "I suppose I'll *never* get over it," he wrote Kahler, "that it's utterly *impossible* to reach either the imagination or the hearts of the —— in such a case."

The result of this incident, besides furnishing material for *Mirthful Haven,* was Tarkington's resignation from the club and permanent estrangement from some of the summer colony. He and his neighbor William Trotter then bought The Floats, a building on the river, which they turned into a rival clubhouse, and Tarkington never went back to the River Club. Tarkington and Trotter, moreover, hired the captain for life as caretaker of their new establishment, and Tarkington later put the old sailor into a series of stories about Captain Ambrose Valentine, a retired tugboat skipper.

Mirthful Haven is built around the mutual suspicion, distrust, and antagonism that Tarkington had observed between the natives of Kennebunkport and the summer people. Where he had used this antipathy humorously in *Tweedles,* he made it the vehicle for a poignant study of manners in his novel. The story concerns the love of Edna Pelter and Gordon Corning, two young people from opposite worlds, who are drawn together during a summer at Mirthful Haven. Ironically named, Mirthful Haven (Kennebunkport) belies its name in the course of the story, for the love which blossoms during the summer withers in the fall under extremely unmirthful circumstances. Edna has the misfortune to be the daughter of Harry Pelter, cantankerous native who stubbornly refuses to sell his land, which the summer people want for a yacht club site. He also feuds with the Cornings, the richest of the summer families, whose property adjoins his own, and through their malice is boycotted so that he cannot make a living as a fisherman. When he turns surreptitiously to rumrunning, he is found out by the Cornings, who tip off the Coast Guard, and is fatally shot during a running battle that takes place within sight of the beach. The Cornings then discover Gordon's affair with Edna and bring to bear more pressure on him to break off the romance than his weak character can stand. Edna is left heartbroken by the simultaneous loss of both father and lover.

Tarkington resists the impulse, however, to make the denouement melodramatic. As a practitioner of the Howells type of commonplace realism, he realized that life would go on for Edna, who was young and resilient; and just as Alice Adams had picked herself up after losing Arthur Russell, Edna would go on living and adapting herself to the situation. Tarkington, too, could not resist giving a highly original and humorous ending to his somber story. Although Edna has grown up in the Maine village, with the reputation of a wild, undisciplined girl, a frequent target for the scandalmongers, she has one good friend in Captain Embury, wealthy retired seaman who once captained a clipper ship, octogenarian of ancient lineage, and a personage looked on with awe both by the villagers and summer people. Some months after Harry Pelter's death and Gordon Corning's renunciation of her, the venerable captain marries Edna, thus giving her at one stroke the prospect of becoming soon the most respected widow in Mirthful Haven.

Mary's Neck, though written as a series of stories before the composition of *Mirthful Haven,* was not published until 1932. It also employs the Kennebunkport locale, but it is a slighter performance and draws its material almost entirely from the aimless amusements of the summer people. It is preoccupied mostly with the exhausting activities of the Massey family, an Illinois clan which is summering at Mary's Neck for the first time. The Masseys are tenderfeet when they deal with the local people; hence they are victimized by the sellers of goods and services. Their two eligible daughters, Enid and Clarissa, are continually besieged by fatuous males, much to the harassment of Mr. Massey, who would have preferred anyway to stay home in Logansville, Illinois.

Although Tarkington's humor was well subdued in *Mirthful Haven,* he infused *Mary's Neck* with a pleasing leaven of comedy. As humorous properties for the Massey doings, he created a group of "characters," both native and non-resident, including a visiting opera singer, a pedantic anthropologist, and a droll, taciturn Yankee caretaker, Zebias Flick, who looks after the Massey cottage. Even more amusing than these is the Masseys' gardener, Ananias P. Sweetmus, who provides several chapters of hilarity and was drawn from life. He is a garrulous, self-satisfied chucklehead, who does not have enough sense not to kick a skunk right in front of the fresh-air intake. His monologues bore everyone but the reader.

Tarkington also gets off some rather broad jokes at the expense of *avant-garde*-ism, making the hare-brained Enid Massey the champion of whatever is new in painting, sculpture, music, and letters. When Carlos Prang, fugitive from a near-by art colony, comes to call, Mr. Massey, an unashamed Philistine, suffers articulately from the jargon and ideas of modern art, but this reaction is mild compared to the assault on his sensibilities made later by an exhibit he sees on a visit to the art community. The picture gallery there makes him think that he has wandered into a paint factory which has been blown up by "an explosion that left the walls standing." The real climax to this good-natured satire, however, comes when Eddie Bullfinch, a clumsy admirer of Enid, accidentally breaks a group of Carlos Prang's art objects. He and Zebias Flick manufacture a substitute collection from odds and ends, and when they successfully pass it off on Enid as more of Prang's inimitable creations, the joke is complete.

Tarkington's use of Maine characters and settings in his fiction of this period leaves little to be desired. He handled this material with as much truth as he put into the Midwestern portraits of his earlier works. When he turned to Kennebunkport for literary capital, he captured the essence of heterogeneous society in a resort town. Although his gallery of Maine characters is less impressive quantitatively than his midland collection, the quality is high, and his work in this genre is authentic. Even a serial such as "High Summer," which Tarkington did not reprint as a book, contains a rich Maine flavor and genuine New England characters. This serial, in fact, suggests a key to Tarkington's ability to get inside his Kennebunkport neighbors far better than the average writing outlander: he was genuinely liked, respected, and admitted to the local society. As Ambrose Trainband, the gardener in "High Summer" says of Joe Nutter, an unpretentious summer resident: "Just as cawmun as the next man. Why I like Joe Nutter, it's because he's cawmun." This character might well have been

Francis Mulberry Chick, the 245-pound chauffeur who drove for Tarkington from 1913 on, speaking of his employer. His opinion of the Tarkingtons was well known around Kennebunkport and expressed the general sentiment: "We folks around here like the Tarkingtons. They're so common."

Letter to father of April 13, 1899. Judge Tarkington had written, after Booth had been in New York ten weeks: "Come home. 'The voice of the turtle is heard in the land.'"

FOURTEEN

THROUGH THE THIRTIES

During the tumultuous years of the depression when Tarkington was in his sixties, he lived quietly secluded and economically undisturbed in his Maine and Indiana homes. Although his sight had been partially restored, he never regained physical vigor and had to conserve his energy for the one indispensable activity of his life—writing. While many authors suffered from the economic disorders of the decade, Tarkington was able to go on writing as industriously as ever, and magazines that previously had been eager to buy his novels and stories still clamored for everything he could write. Hence he not only weathered the times with no financial discomfort but even benefited handsomely from the increased buying power of the depression dollar. The calm surface of his life frequently was ruffled by the political currents of the decade, and he watched the New Deal from his sheltered vantage point with bewilderment and dismay. However, he rarely made public pronouncements against it or concerned himself with politics in his writings. Often his fiction of the Thirties reflected the economic ordeal of individuals in the depression, but in the main his writing continued the major preoccupations of his life: he wrote of children, adolescents, domestic relations, and society in transition. His avocational interest in art, however, expanded spectacularly, and he bought many important paintings, wrote stories of art collecting, and produced a graceful volume of essays about his pictures.

Year after year Tarkington followed what one old friend called his exaggerated policeman's beat: from Indianapolis to Kennebunkport and from Kennebunkport to Indianapolis, east

282

in the spring and west in the winter. Yet despite the apparent regularity of his life Tarkington's domestic routine was never dull. In Indiana during the winter he was surrounded by relatives of all ages and relationships. The death of his sister in 1937 left him the sole survivor of his immediate family, but he still had his devoted nephews, John, Donald, and Booth Jameson, and by this time he also had six great-nephews and nieces, in whom he took a warm, avuncular interest. Weekday evenings often were given over to the nephews and nieces and sometimes a few cousins, while Sunday afternoons brought groups of friends to tea, usually a dozen well-assorted individuals at a time. The Tarkington household in this decade was predominantly feminine, including besides the novelist and his wife, Miss Keifer and Miss Trotter, but offsetting the female imbalance were Figaro, the French poodle; Rennie and Peter, both cocker spaniels.

Tarkington's circle of friends was large and varied: staid bankers, lawyers, and merchants, patrons and practitioners of art and peripatetic writers, old associates from the theater and musicians. Almost every year Woollcott's lecture tours brought him to Indianapolis, and Helen Hayes renewed her old friendship when she played in the Indiana capital. The Silberman brothers, New York art dealers, were occasional visitors; so were artist friends from eastern cities. Surviving from the literary circle of the Hoosier Golden Age were Meredith Nicholson, who remained in Indianapolis, and George Ade, who lived quietly on his farm in Newton County. Dr. McCulloch, who in the Thirties was an influential New Dealer, continued his old relationship, and late in the decade Fabien Sevitzky joined the group after becoming conductor of the Indianapolis Symphony.

Yet Tarkington's home was not a gathering place for all resident and visiting illuminati. When Sinclair Lewis came to town in 1939, Tarkington made no effort to see him, though Lewis told a reporter that he would like to meet the city's most famous native son. Tarkington wrote a friend at this time that he always had classed Lewis "among the people I don't want to sit down with" and went on to name several others. There was no malice in this statement, for he admitted that these people "may all be delightful in their ways," but he added candidly: "I'd feel a certain constraint in chatting with 'em." He had no taste for Lewis' barbed satires and simply felt there would be an inevitable clash of personalities.

Tarkington's daytime schedule did not change much as he grew old. He still spent the mornings writing, the afternoons resting and reading, and the evenings entertaining informally. He dictated the daily quota of fiction to Miss Trotter and listened while various members of the household read to him, and though he once had walked to the University Club for a convivial hour before dinner, he now was driven in the country in the late afternoons. Meanwhile, he carried on his large correspondence with friends, relatives, editors, and readers. To his friends he wrote personally in penciled longhand on heavy yellow legal covers that were easy on his eyes; but he dictated the bulk of his letters and delegated to his wife and his secretary an increasing amount of routine epistolary business. As a novelist with a large popular following, his fan mail by this time was huge and the demands on him extensive.

The daily regimen during the summer and autumn at Kennebunkport also was pleasantly interesting, though smoothly ordered. The seven bedrooms at Seawood often were filled with visiting friends and relatives, but Tarkington maintained a regular work schedule in the mornings, letting his guests take their breakfasts whenever they got up and spend the forenoons on the beach in Mrs. Tarkington's charge. In the afternoons he usually took visitors and neighbors to sea in his forty-five-foot motorboat, the *Zantre,* skippered by Harry Thirkell. During the mid-Thirties, when an unprecedented number of whales appeared off the Maine coast, Tarkington frequently amused himself and his passengers by giving chase. Late in the afternoons tea was served at The Floats, and after dinner, for which the Tarkingtons always dressed, the entertainment usually was music, cards, or, if the company was large, charades. Always a conscientious host, Tarkington put his guests instantly at ease, drew them out skillfully, and filled conversational gaps comfortably with his own wit and anecdotes.

The key person behind the scenes during the last decade and a half of Tarkington's life was his wife. As usual, she ran the domestic machinery with quiet efficiency, assisted by a loyal staff of servants. She long had taken partial charge of her husband's affairs, was a competent business manager; and after his

eye trouble began, she assumed an even greater responsibility
and more than ever made it possible for him to go on writing.
He was profoundly grateful to her for these ministrations, and
the debt he owed her, wrote a Maine neighbor after his death,
showed in his eyes when he looked at her.

Husband and wife grew increasingly close to each other as
time passed. Tarkington undoubtedly was thinking of Susanah
when he wrote an article in 1936 describing love at various
stages of life. Of the boy giving an apple to a little girl, the
adolescent carving initials on a tree, and young parents with
their first-born he wrote perceptively and characteristically, but
of aged love he wrote with more than usual feeling. Old lovers,
he said, "are released from a fiery master. The eyes are dim
but sight at last is in the heart. Love in old age is like quick-
sand that has become solid rock; the lovers stand upon it secure,
and there's no longer any possible danger . . . to their love . . .
they possess life's happiest prize, peace of mind." On other occasions Tarkington joked about his utter dependence upon his
wife, and once when he was asked by a correspondent if she had
in any way been a help or inspiration to him, he replied: "Mrs.
Tarkington does so many things to make my work possible that
I'm not able to list them. About all I do for myself is to shave
—but she changes the razor blades."

Tarkington further was relieved of many business problems
after about 1930 when he turned part of his affairs over to Carl
Brandt, who represented him from then on. Brandt acquired
this account at the beginning of the depression when Tarkington was having trouble with a theatrical agent over a motion
picture contract. During a visit to Maine Brandt heard of the
difficulty, offered to help, and was able to force a partial settlement of money due Tarkington. Subsequently Brandt was
asked to act as agent for the dramatic and serial rights to Tarkington's writings and in the next fifteen years sold his client's
serials, short stories, articles and marketed the appropriate
rights to Hollywood and the broadcasting industry. In all of
his negotiations and transactions Brandt handled Tarkington's
affairs expertly and profitably. Tarkington continued to deal
directly only with his old friend Lorimer, who remained editor
of the *Saturday Evening Post* until 1937, and the Doubledays,
who long had published his books.

Tarkington's prosperity (somewhat embarrassing) amid depression increased greatly the demands on his natural generosity. Throughout his life he experienced great difficulty in hanging on to the large amount of money he made. When old friends, relatives, and even strangers appealed to him for loans or gifts, he seldom could say no. Although his wife kept most of the demands from him and disbursed funds without bothering him, his own benefactions were extensive. The full scope of his giving cannot be disclosed, but he gave away tens of thousands of dollars to individuals and organizations. Among the institutions he supported were the Seeing Eye, Incorporated, John Herron Art Institute, the Indianapolis Symphony, Princeton University, Phillips Exeter Academy, and many regularly organized charities such as the Red Cross and the Community Chest. He also rationalized his affluence during the depression by remembering that he employed eleven persons, nine with families, all of whom were solely dependent on him; and when he bought expensive paintings, he reminded himself that he was a major source of revenue for an entire firm of art dealers. Early in the Thirties he even astonished the editors of the *Saturday Evening Post* by voluntarily asking that his rate of pay be cut. He then was one of the two highest paid writers among the magazine's contributors.

Paradoxically, Tarkington found himself at the peak of his grass-roots popularity during the depression but scorned by many critics. Certainly his most enduring books had been written at least ten years before, but he was still a conscientious craftsman and superb stylist, and the reason for the critical abuse he received lay outside his art. He was a conservative in an age of social revolution, felt uncomfortable in the new climate of opinion, and admitted publicly that the days of McKinley and Theodore Roosevelt had seemed pretty good; yet he did not engage in polemics, and his late novels are nearly all contemporary in action, albeit implicitly old-fashioned in their point of view. The critics of the Thirties, reflecting the liberalism of the New Deal, saw Tarkington as an enemy and dismissed and disparaged his books as no longer significant. He went on writing as he wished, however, though he complained privately: "I'm anathema—member of the Amer. Acad. . . . and recipient of Academy's medal for fiction . . . reactionary—[I've] written plays and satires agin socialism . . . I'm what they hate *every* way: if I'm right *they're* wrong."

Tarkington's approach to social and political problems was entirely consistent with his attitude towards the arts. In both respects he was a strong traditionalist and clung doggedly to the ideals of the pre-industrial Midwest of his boyhood. He disparaged non-representational art and esoteric literature as well as political experimentation and remained ideologically a passionate defender of individuality, a sort of Jeffersonian democrat, and a Republican (as he put it) "very much as Ignatius Loyola was a Catholic." That he did not become an embittered old man after twelve years of the New Deal may be explained by his optimistic faith in the ultimate triumph of conservative principles.

Although Tarkington pondered the problems of the depression, he believed steadfastly that the best government is that which governs least. "Pump-priming" with the taxpayers' dollars and creating innumerable government agencies to tinker with the economic machinery seemed to him entirely the wrong approach. When the Republican Convention of 1932 was about to convene, he wrote his Indianapolis Congressman to protest reckless governmental expenditures by the Hoover Administration and even then argued the necessity of a balanced budget. Later, as the Roosevelt Administration employed deficit financing, he was depressed by the large-scale federal spending. He believed that the depression resulted from a national loss of confidence in business and felt that the treatment indicated was public psychiatry rather than governmental specifics. To Tarkington, depressions were inevitable as long as nations could not conduct their affairs without periodic and cataclysmic wars.

There was a brief period in 1933, however, when Tarkington thought that Franklin D. Roosevelt might be able to lift the country out of the depression through inspired leadership. Although he had regarded Roosevelt as an impractical visionary during the campaign, he wrote a friend two weeks after the inauguration: "We have a great deal more faith in him than we formerly had." Roosevelt had just closed the banks and in a fireside chat argued for national confidence. But this honeymoon was short-lived, and by the following September Tarkington was writing privately: "It's almost always a disaster for this country when the Democratic Party comes into power." He then regarded the President as part Colonel Sellers in his "impractical, utopian economics," part politician, and part philanthropist.

After the national debt and taxes had soared to previously undreamed of heights, he wrote a friend that he had been reading Gibbon and had discovered that taxes had the most to do with the decline and fall of Rome. At that point philosophic anarchy seemed to him the most attractive ideology, but since anarchy was not practical, his reading of history convinced him that a republic was the best form of government "under which we make the most progress toward becoming civilized." The best republic, however, is one in which the government is by law, not officials, a highly decentralized state like the agrarian democracy Jefferson had envisioned. When Tarkington looked at history, he concluded, moreover, that the world by astronomical time is about fifteen minutes old on its way to ultimate perfection and, accordingly, "still in the tribal stage." Neither Coolidge nor Roosevelt, he argued, could do much to speed up the civilizing process.

It was a rare occasion when Tarkington broke a lance in public against the New Deal. He disliked the Roosevelt administration but had few economic remedies to offer and preferred to keep discreetly silent. He always was willing to endorse his candidates at election time, but beyond that he accepted with resignation the repeated votes of confidence that Franklin D. Roosevelt obtained. For the most part Tarkington spent the Thirties in the political storm cellars, but when a mass meeting was held in Indianapolis to protest the Supreme Court expansion bill in 1937, he wrote a message which was read at the rally. He then urged retention of the nine-man court as a bulwark to our liberties, for if the President's bill were passed, he urged, the Constitution would mean whatever any president said it meant. On another occasion he wrote against a bill before Congress to establish a federal bureau of the arts. He opposed mixing art and politics and noted that if the government had been subsidizing young artists in the Nineties, he undoubtedly would have spent his career as a mediocre illustrator and a public charge. If the government wanted to help artists, he suggested, it could grant tax exemption to all money spent buying American art.

Tarkington's solution to depression problems in his fiction of the Thirties is always personal, never collective. He focused his attention especially on the effect of hard times on the youngsters who had grown up during the prosperous Twenties. Between 1932 and 1934 he wrote two novelettes, a one-act play, and a full-length novel treating this topic from different angles and later returned to the same subject in *The Heritage of Hatcher Ide* (1941). In all these works he clung to a faith in individual solutions as the proper way to restore the more abundant life. Tarkington was artist enough to keep his political and economic convictions well in the background, and he never turned his fiction into soapbox orations. But to many of his critics he seemed hopelessly behind the times and completely out of touch with the realities of breadlines and Hoovervilles.

"Pretty Twenty," a four-part serial never reprinted, brought the depression seriously into his fiction for the first time. Written early in 1932, it has for a protagonist Henry Streamer, the son of a rich man who committed suicide after losing a fortune in the stock market crash. Henry flunks out of college about the time of the crash, then accepts the challenge of events, and takes the only job he can find, a highly unlikely and, for him, difficult position as a private tutor. In the course of the story he falls in love with Gabrielle Dart, who has been raised to adorn a wealthy man's establishment. She has character and nerve, however, and after Henry saves a little money, they elope and return to the soil on a rented farm. Gabrielle's mother is distraught, but her father takes the situation calmly and concludes (with the author's approval): "When the times get too bad, young people that are pushed pretty hard always have to go back to the soil, most likely. It seems to be our first resort and our last."

While many of the older generation struggled to keep their big houses and servants, Tarkington noted that the depression children rolled up their sleeves and went to work. This motif recurs in a better novelette, "Rennie Peddigoe," published serially in 1934-1935 and collected posthumously in *Three Selected Short Novels* (1947). Here Rennie Peddigoe, the shy, wistful child of divorced parents, grows up during the reckless Twenties and like the hero and heroine of "Pretty Twenty" reaches marriageable age just as the depression begins. She too reacts positively and unequivocally to the historical necessity of the Thirties.

The plot and theme of this story are revealed through the impressions, perceptions, opinions, and emotions of the girl as she passes from childhood to maturity. Raised without love or understanding in wealthy surroundings, Rennie grows up in a society as aimless, futile, and ruthlessly portrayed as Fitzgerald's world in *The Beautiful and Damned*. Her childhood memories are a procession of parental quarrels, adult philanderings, and drunken Prohibition revels. The emotional crisis of the story centers on the stock market crash, which destroys her parents' selfish way of life. As the depression begins, Rennie falls in love with Ward Macaulay, whose family's financial smash also carries the Peddigoes and others of the same set to ruin, and with Ward she leaves the rubble of her parents' world of selfish hedonism. They elope and start life together with little more than their love for each other and their determination to be their own agents. Ward gets a job as a high school basketball coach and begins his career humbly, just as his grandfather, the founder of the now-shattered family fortune, once had done.

Tarkington's most significant use of depression themes, however, is more somber, more searching, and virtually unknown among his works. Named "This Boy Joe," it is a problem novel of a middle-class youth who finds himself thrown unceremoniously into a hostile world. Joe is a naïve, likeable, good-natured boy reminiscent of Willie Baxter, but the stable social structure of *Seventeen* (before the First World War) vanished as Joe was born. He has to assume adult responsibilities at an age when Willie was concerned merely with getting ready for college. Nevertheless, Joe emerges from the crucible of his experience as steel rather than slag, and his story is a triumph of individual character over unpromising environment. During his ordeal he finds some pretty shoddy stuff in the moral fabric of his society and asks some disturbing questions about the ethics of his elders.

"This Boy Joe" grew from Tarkington's desire to help find a

way out of the economic wilderness. In 1933 when he was asked to write a radio play dramatizing the plight of unemployed youth, he responded with "The Help Each Other Club," produced over both NBC and CBS in October. This playlet is little more than a forum in which several young men discuss their future, but one character, a youth who has turned car thief, suggested interesting avenues of speculation. In the novel this boy became Yeastie Marshall, one of the tempters of the protagonist Joe Hadley. As ideas for "This Boy Joe" took shape, Tarkington examined various problems of adolescence in the context of the Thirties. He subjected Joe to two preliminary ordeals in his passage from youth to maturity—the painful rejection of his boyhood friend Yeastie and the disillusionment of a shabby love affair—then climaxed his story with a tough ethical problem.

The emotional core of the novel is Joe's decision to turn down a job that he needs badly. After his unfortunate romance, he rebounds to a girl he has known all through school, Anita Blythe, whose father is a respected lawyer. The future seems bright when Anita's father offers Joe work; but Joe finds he is not qualified for the position open, and the job, moreover, is on the padded payroll of a company that Blythe, as receiver, is conniving to wreck. The youth accidentally learns of the crooked scheme before accepting the job and must decide if he can afford the luxury of integrity. Joe's father, a member of the legislature, had been ruined for voting his principles against corporate interests that had elected him, and that experience, reflects Joe, brought about his early death. Society seems full of villains who go unpunished, and Gus Cooper, the rich man who destroyed the elder Hadley and "bought" Anita's father, probably will die honored. Yet Joe concludes, as he renounces the job and Anita, that he is compelled by something within him to follow his father's example. He recalls his father's oftenquoted lines from Wordsworth (*The Prelude,* xi, 394):

There is
One great society alone on earth:
The noble Living and the noble Dead

and he hopes that he always will be worthy to sit in the company of his father.

"This Boy Joe" is a strong, honest tale that deserved a better fate than it received. Of all Tarkington's novels, this story suffered the most from editorial vicissitudes. The *American Magazine,* which commissioned the story, turned it down after it was finished, and *This Week* magazine, eager to get the tale, could not use it unless cut to half its length. When the story finally was sold to the Chicago *Tribune* for serialization in the Sunday magazine, the paper professed to be delighted and promised to publish it without significant cuts. Yet the serial was slashed to ribbons and jammed into twelve short installments. All the reflective passages which give the story significance were deleted, and the remainder was a pale image of the original manuscript. Fortunately for Tarkington he never realized the extent of the mutilation, but he was by this time discouraged and decided not to publish "This Boy Joe" in book form. "It's a story that either gets you or doesn't," he wrote Brandt. "Some people are susceptible to it and some aren't."

Although Tarkington took little part in public debate during the Thirties, he expressed himself freely on political and economic questions to a large number of correspondents and guests. His friends ran the gamut of political and economic opinion from extreme left to far right, and he commiserated or argued with them as the situation required. When he wrote staunch Republican friends (who formed a big majority of his circle) like Harry Daniels, his Princeton classmate, Warrack Wallace , his lawyer, or Kenneth Roberts, he reiterated his conservative opinions, and they replied energetically in kind. On the other hand, he argued with a liberal Republican in Julian Street, a New Dealer in Dr. McCulloch, and a Socialist (Tarkington's designation) in Woollcott. Indicative of the variety found among his group is this report on a single week's activity: "Yesd'y at tea here I was gassing along with Mrs. —— . . . I mentioned that I'd begun the week with a Socialist . . . Tuesdayed with a New Dealer . . . Fridayed with a Communist. . . . 'And now me,' says she, 'a Fascist' "; to which Tarkington added: "What funny brains we all have!"

Carl McCulloch was the political adversary with whom he argued the most violently. The two had been friends for nearly a lifetime, and their assaults on each other inflicted no serious wounds. McCulloch always had been a Democrat, as Tarkington always had been a Republican, and during the Republican Twenties when McCulloch ran for Governor, Tarkington had gone so far as to concede that if the Democrats had to win he would feel the least uneasy with his friend in the State House. In the Democratic Thirties when McCulloch became director of the WPA for Indianapolis, the arguments increased in volume and frequency. Neither man ever moved the other an inch, though the debate was lively and barbed.

Not all the dealings between these two friends, however, erupted into serious political debate. There were frequent moments of byplay initiated by Tarkington's irrepressible comic sense. When McCulloch's ardent support of the New Deal could be joked about, Tarkington was quick to take advantage of the situation. Such an opening occurred in 1938 when McCulloch visited Kennebunkport. On the second day of his stay the phone rang after dinner: "Message for Dr. McCulloch— Washington calling." The doctor took the call, was gone for a long time, and finally returned greatly excited:

"It's Charlie Michelson," he told Tarkington. "He says the President wants you to say *something*—even if it's only a *little*— commending his Administration. I told him I was afraid you wouldn't."

"Certainly not," replied Tarkington.

When McCulloch went back to the phone, Tarkington followed and heard him saying:

"No, I'm afraid it can't be done . . . What? . . . No, he simply won't *do* it. . . . No, you don't *know* this bird as *I* do. I've known him since he was a BOY and *no*body could ever do anything WITH him. . . . He's the most rabid anti-New Dealer I ever saw. . . ."

Back in the drawing room a minute later, McCulloch implored Tarkington to humor the publicity director of the Democratic National Committee, and both men went to the phone. McCulloch picked up the receiver, then turned to his host: "The *President* wants to speak to you."

At this point Tarkington grabbed the phone and shouted into it that he was not going to say anything favorable about the administration for anybody. McCulloch, appalled at the turn of events, shuddered as he imagined dreadful consequences. At the other end of the line, however, was Kenneth Roberts,

who announced that he was coming right over to help heckle
McCulloch about politics.

Earlier in the decade Tarkington had needed no help in
heckling the doctor over a non-political matter. McCulloch
had ventured incautiously into the unfamiliar area of art, and
Tarkington had pounced on him gleefully. This byplay re-
volved around the selection of a sculptor to do a statue of Lincoln for University Park in Indianapolis. Henry C. Long, a
former resident of the city who died in 1901, had left ten
thousand dollars for the monument, but for years the money
had not been touched as successive park boards passed in and
out of office. In 1933 the money (then $25,000) was discovered
and plans finally made to spend some of it. McCulloch was a
member of the committee which carried out the project. Someone apparently suggested to the doctor that Daniel Chester
French, who had done the well-known Lincoln statue in Washington but who had died in 1931, would be an excellent choice
to execute the Indiana commission. When the probate court
released the bequest, McCulloch wrote Tarkington in Maine
to tell him of the plans. "I am sure that all would agree," concluded McCulloch, "that we would be very fortunate to have
Mr. French accept this commission." Tarkington saw his opening and wired a two-page answer, which concluded:

> I DO NOT MEAN TO DAMPEN ENTHUSIASM NATURAL UPON SE-
> CURING FRENCH BUT WHY STOP THERE SINCE COMMUNICATION
> IS OPEN. WHY NOT MICHELANGELO WHO WOULD BE DELIGHTED
> NEVER HAVING SEEN SIXTEEN THOUSAND DOLLARS.

McCulloch replied by telegram: "GO JOIN FRENCH."

The next day, after thanking his friend for the courteous
message, Tarkington wrote a long letter to follow up his lengthy
wire: "Now you've got Daniel Chester French," he observed,
"I'll admit at once that your Committee could hardly have done
better. My suggestion of Michelangelo is purely frivolous. . . .
[He] would probably take twenty years to do it and leave it in
an unfinished state, at that. Besides, he'd make Lincoln too
muscular, exaggerate the beard and wouldn't understand at all
what Indiana people want." At the same time Tarkington
noted that Hoosiers always seem reluctant to give Indiana sculp-
tors a "chance at a little Indiana money in hard times," and

although "we Hoosiers readily believe we've got plenty of favorite sons fit to be President . . . we can't imagine that anybody living amongst us could be an important artist." But maybe, he concluded, it was not Daniel Chester French after all who had been secured to do the statue but "Shorty French, the tombstone man who made the Fanny Lincoln Memorial in South Washington, Nebraska, showing Fanny with a kitten in her lap and a palm leaf fan in her hand."

A week later Tarkington continued his banter with another page-long telegram on the same topic. This time he wired Elmer Stout, Indianapolis banker and friend of McCulloch:

> I HAVE NEW ENGLAND CAST IRON STATUE GENERAL GRANT WHICH LOOKS AS MUCH LIKE LINCOLN AS IT DOES LIKE GRANT . . . HAS MORE ARTISTIC TREATMENT OF PLUG HAT . . . I WOULD LIKE TO TURN DEMOCRAT AND SELL THIS WORK OF ART AND OTHERS BESIDES, THROWING IN ONE OF WOODROW WILSON . . . [I WILL] PAY YOU COMMISSION IF YOU CAN WORK IT, THOUGH MY REAL MOTIVE IS TO SEE INDIANA GET BETTER ART . . . ALSO KNOW WHERE THERE IS SECOND HAND LONGFELLOW BY NEW ENGLAND WOOD CARVER . . . [WHICH COULD] BE PAINTED BRONZE AND MADE TO LOOK LIKE GOVERNOR HENDRICKS.

Some days later when Tarkington heard that the committee planned to have Henry Hering, who already had done the "Pro Patria" figure for the Indiana War Memorial, copy the French statue of Lincoln in Washington, he wired Stout again:

> NOW UNDERSTAND . . . PSYCHIC OPERATOR CALLED HERING . . . [WILL] COPY DANIEL CHESTER FRENCH LINCOLN HEROIC SIZE TO HARMONIZE WITH LITTLE FAT STATUETTE HARRISON, THE CHURCHES, AND ALL LAMP POSTS SO THAT WE SHALL HAVE CITY BEAUTIFUL AND MAKE INDIANA TRUE HOME OF ORIGINAL ART NOT PROTECTED BY COPYRIGHT AND HELP GIVE VISITING FOREIGNERS EVEN HEARTIER LAUGH THAN NOW.

Then he ended the month-long exchange of letters and telegrams by asking how the committee had discovered that the late sculptor French was a Democrat and therefore worthy of imitation.

Tarkington's amusement over the Lincoln statue occurred at a time when his interest in art was steadily consuming more and more of his time. He had been a modest collector since his youth, and by the early Thirties art had become both a major preoccupation and a source of literary material. He began his fictional use of art with a historical novel of Restoration England, *Wanton Mally* (1932), which was suggested by two seventeenth-century portraits in his collection—a French gentleman by Largillière and "The Ugly Lady" by an unknown artist. Tarkington wove a story about these pictures, much as he had done at the beginning of his career when he wrote *Monsieur Beaucaire*. He next made use of his experiences as a collector by creating the inimitable art dealer Mr. Rumbin, who sold paintings through sixteen stories. He also wrote a novel laid mostly in an art gallery, *Image of Josephine* (1945), a volume of essays about his own pictures, *Some Old Portraits* (1939), and served as a director of the John Herron Art Institute in Indianapolis.

Tarkington's plunge into large-scale collecting resulted from two factors: the final success of his eye operations and the bargain prices on paintings during the depression. When the bandages were removed from his eyes after the last operations in January, 1931, he was startled by the vivid colors he could see for the first time in years, and the canvases he already owned took on subtleties of texture and tone that he never had seen before. He subsequently could not resist surrounding himself with as many paintings as he could afford. When the bottom dropped out of the art market while his income dipped only slightly, he was able to buy an impressive number of works by Reynolds, Gainsborough, Lawrence, Lely, Stuart, Romney, Dobson, Raeburn, and even a Titian, a Velasquez, and a Goya. He wrote an English friend late in 1932 that he had been buying pictures heavily instead of stocks and argued that paintings were more depression-proof than securities.

Tarkington's taste in art was compatible with his attitude in other spheres of interest. As in politics and in literature, he was conservative and traditional. He actively disliked surrealism, thought Picasso an excellent draftsman though vastly overrated, and developed no enthusiasm for either the impressionists or post-impressionists. As a practitioner of literary realism, he demanded similar fidelity in painting—not photographic likeness but truth touched by insight and imagination. Competence in the artist's medium, of course, he required, for Tarkington

himself was thoroughly professional in his own field and intolerant of those with talent who would not learn their trade.
Rembrandt he regarded as the greatest of all painters, a wizard
in technique, candidly forthright, and a genius at revealing
character. This partiality for Rembrandt, the unexcelled portrait painter, suggests at once Tarkington's predilection for
portraiture, a taste in art that also parallels his literary career.
Tarkington agreed that the "proper study of mankind is man,"
and throughout his long procession of novel-portraits, from
The Gentleman from Indiana through the *Image of Josephine*,
he was absorbed in people. Proof of this interest lies in his
many novels which have for their titles the name or description
of the leading character: *The Flirt, Ramsay Milholland, Penrod, Alice Adams, Gentle Julia, The Plutocrat,* and eight or
ten others. It also is appropriate that Tarkington found his
greatest delight in the English portrait painters of the eighteenth century, the historical epoch that he had begun writing
about at the outset of his career.

His middle-of-the-road aesthetic principles applied equally
to art as to literature. Great novels and great paintings, he
wrote, must have in common a basic and indispensable ingredient—content. Before either the writer or the painter can
begin to create enduring art, he must have something to say,
something that exists independently of plot and character, form
and color. Tarkington took vigorous exception to an unidentified portrait painter who claimed that he would just as soon
paint his subjects upside down if they could be comfortable
that way. To such an artist, argued Tarkington, art is all form,
color, and paint, and the paintings of this particular man are
not arresting because they do not "in *themselves* hold a content that detains you." Titian, continued Tarkington by way
of example, was a greater painter than the upside-down artist,
because he began with the content of a picture in his mind,
then considered the form, color, and paint which could com-
municate his ideas. Yet the exact nature of the content is not
possible to express in words; it can only be experienced. When
Titian named a painting "Sacred and Profane Love," added
Tarkington, he did it for popularity with people "who can
only 'take' obvious allegory and wouldn't be able to reach the
real content of the painting."

Although Tarkington did not think the essence of a great picture could be put into words, he had no use for the completely subjective critic who defended his taste solely on the grounds of liking something. The person who knows what he likes, Tarkington declared, knows only something about himself. He is not a critic; he is merely autobiographical. "Bare naïveté is not more trustworthy in a gallery of paintings than in a chemist's laboratory. In either . . . ignorance can blow itself up." Yet Tarkington was patient with beginners and served with pleasure as a museum trustee. A start had to be made somewhere, for "art's what tells man about himself," he wrote Paul Manship. "History, in writing, is confused and confusing, partisan in spite of itself; geology, anthropology, etc. go dry as dust. . . . Get some benighted soul interested in art and you give him a world."

In 1935 after several years of large-scale collecting, Tarkington had accumulated a great deal of information about the mechanics of selling expensive pictures. More than once he had been talked into buying old paintings for more than he wanted to spend, or he had been persuaded to snap up bargains before other collectors saw them. He bought some of his pictures from the Robert C. Vose Galleries of Boston, others from the Newhouse Galleries of New York; but most of his transactions were made with Abris and David Silberman, New York dealers. Both of the Silbermans devoted a great deal of talent to selling him paintings, and when David died Tarkington wrote in tribute: "In his hands an object of art seemed to become both exquisite and sacred; and his reverent enticements were so vivid that the listener found life unbearable without a prospect of possessing the treasure." From the Silbermans he gathered anecdotes of the trade as well as first-hand experiences. Both brothers sat for the portrait of Mr. Rumbin, but David, who was fat and spoke a gorgeous broken-English, supplied the major part of the character. The Rumbin stories began in the *Post* in January, 1936, and continued sporadically for ten years, though half of them appeared within twelve months. Collected into a novel, *Rumbin Galleries* (1937), the first six stories made a highly entertaining book.

Although the Rumbin tales paid for a good many of his paintings, Tarkington lavished even more literary skill and knowledge of art on his essays. There was no magazine market for art essays, but Tarkington wrote them because he wanted to, and Doubleday brought them out in a handsome volume, excellently illustrated, under the title *Some Old Portraits* (1939). Tarkington described twenty-two of his own paintings in this volume, writing with affection amounting to inspiration, and the result is an exquisite book that tells the interested non-specialist more about its subject than an entire course in "art appreciation." Furthermore, the essays also contain insights for the specialist, for Tarkington had made himself an expert on his own collection, and concentrating on the English portrait painters of the eighteenth century, he mastered not only the art history of the period but also the political and social background. His knowledge of art was accurate, extensive, and perceptive.

What makes these essays valuable for layman and expert alike is their unusual approach to the subject. Tarkington writes about art like a novelist who "did gather humours of men dayly," as John Aubrey once said of Shakespeare and Jonson. Not only was he interested in the artist and the picture, but he was attracted equally to the subject. He considered the usual matters of form, space, mass, line, movement, color, and light, then added another dimension to his criticism—a complete knowledge of the sitter; and with this special competence he produced illuminating commentaries. Professor Erwin Panofsky, the art historian, who summered in Kennebunkport in the late Thirties, calls *Some Old Portraits* "a book the like of which no art historian could ever write—a book that compels the painter to tell us more about human nature than he revealed in the picture, and compels the sitter to tell us more about human nature than he revealed to the painter."

The catalogue of Tarkington's collection reveals that he bought paintings both for the artist and for the subject. A furrowed brow, a flashing eye, a bewitching smile, a resolute glance, all fired his imagination and dictated the choice of new accessions. He owned Dobson's portraits of Jonson and Milton, one of Lely's Nell Gwyns, Romney's Samuel Johnson, Gainsborough's Blackstone, and Titian's Ariosto. His gallery also contained many characters well known to history by relatively obscure painters, such as Paulus Van Somer's James I,

John Riley's Sir Isaac Newton, and Willem Wissing's Louise de Kérouallc, Duchess of Portsmouth, who was Nell Gwyn's chief rival for the affection of Charles II. There were, in addition, Gilbert Stuart's Augusta Montagu, Godfrey Kneller's Sarah Jennings, and John Singleton Copley's Mrs. Isaac Royall.

Always it was character as revealed by the artist that interested Tarkington. Gainsborough's "women too exquisite to have been of this earth" did not detain him, but he delighted in that master's moment of opposite extreme when he captured the pompous Blackstone almost with his dignity down. His essay on Reynolds' portrait of Mary Countess of Rothes, who married Bennet Langton, friend of Johnson, Burke, and Goldsmith, is especially revealing of his method and insight. This splendid woman is painted in full profile, a highly unusual position which most critics would note but not explain. Tarkington's knowledge of the sitter discloses what the art critic misses: the countess is painted in full profile because the position is completely in character. "The attitude," writes Tarkington, "is eloquent of a passivity entirely alive; the lady listens and waits—and is undisturbedly thinking, all the while." She was noted as a "listener, sympathetic but comprehending and never cajoled." She would not speak until her guest had finished, even when he was tiresomely prolix. All this is at once obvious to the viewer after it is pointed out, but it takes a novelist-turned-art-critic to explain the significance of Reynolds' remarkable portrait.

Before Tarkington began writing the Rumbin stories, he turned to a field that he long had specialized in, stories of children. During the early Thirties he found himself surrounded by great-nephews and nieces, all hovering about the age of seven. Their activities were as absorbing as those of the Jameson boys had been many years before when the Penrod stories were in embryo. Never having written about the age of seven, he tried the subject, found it congenial, and produced a volume of tales. First a popular serial in the *Saturday Evening Post,* the stories later were collected as *Little Orvie* (1934).

When Tarkington planned this series of tales, he noted in a prospectus that he already had scrutinized in *Penrod* and *Sev-*

enteen two of the key ages of youth. Penrod had been eleven, the age when a child is "no longer a little boy and feels somewhat emancipated," and Willie Baxter had been seventeen, the age when a "boy is thinking he ought to be [a] man but is still a boy." Now Tarkington wanted to "analyze . . . the age of seven and its adjacencies, reaching out, too, for some slight exhibition of the relationship between a child of that age and his parents, and also striving to know something of his viewpoint concerning his contemporaries, household pets, worldly distinctions and importances." This age, he thought, was another of the key years of childhood. The result was Orvie Stone, whose antics mirrored the activities of thousands of other little boys growing up in comfortably affluent urban families.

Tarkington's most serious fiction of the Thirties after "This Boy Joe" was *The Lorenzo Bunch* (1936), which carried on the problems of urban apartment life briefly considered earlier in *Young Mrs. Greeley.* But like the story of Joe Hadley, this novel raised too many problems to please the big-circulation magazines and encountered more than the usual editorial difficulties. The chief objection was the unhappy ending, which editors in the depression were reluctant to inflict on their readers. The *Pictorial Review* in 1921 had not objected to *Alice Adams'* denouement, nor had the *Ladies' Home Journal* refused to print the tragic conclusion of *The Midlander* in 1923; but *McCall's* flatly rejected the final chapter of *The Lorenzo Bunch.* The editors asked for numerous changes, and Tarkington, who always tried to oblige, made a few minor modifications, softening details of a female character's past and cutting objectionable passages from a scene laid in a philandering bachelor's bungalow; but none of his alterations was significant, and he refused, as he was requested, to eliminate the divorce which ended his story of domestic wrangling. Such a concession, he maintained, would emasculate the entire novel.

The Lorenzo Bunch, an unpleasant story, is likely to irritate all readers who enjoy vicariously the experiences of their heroines. Tarkington wrote it, he said, "for more rarefied minds, those capable of detachment." Its leading characters are Ernie and Irene Foote, a young couple who at the outset of the novel move to the city from the country. They become members of the "bunch" in the Lorenzo Apartment House and intimate friends of Roy and Arlene Parker. Although Irene is a dazzling beauty, the seeds of domestic tragedy are contained in her warped sense of values, foolish jealousy, and silly vanity. She fails to appreciate her husband's solid merit, prizes material possessions inordinately, and refuses to make sacrifices for her husband's career. During the course of the novel she succeeds in wrecking Ernie's life and nearly ruining the happiness of the Parkers.

In the final chapter, which was published only when the novel appeared as a book, Irene returns to the Lorenzo to see old friends after her second marriage. Tarkington makes it clear that she is unrepentant and unchanged, and already she has made an errand boy out of her new husband, whom she eventually will discard for still another, richer mate. Irene is the sort of woman who is forced to pay no visible price for the misery she causes others—"a lovely monster of egoism," Tarkington called the type. Some years before when he had placed a live specimen of this genus under his observation, he had written Kahler about it: "I love to see her look at him [her husband] and hear her voice when she speaks to him. *He* looks and sounds as if he'd beat hell out of her if he dared and could stop being amorous of her long enough—both of whiches she perfectly knows and despises." This is the kind of thing, he added, that "I get excited about, when there's any chance of 'getting *at* it!'" Such a character treated realistically obviously did not meet the standard specifications of popular magazine fiction for women.

FIFTEEN

LAST YEARS

From the days of his residence in Paris to his old age in Maine and Indiana, Tarkington kept firm emotional and cultural ties with Europe. During the Thirties, as the Nazi plague spread its contagion through Central Europe, he watched with fascinated horror. Having lived through the saber-rattling that preceded the First World War, he saw history repeating itself, and long before most Americans took alarm, he was talking and writing to friends about the danger. Within the meager budget of books that were read to him, he included *Mein Kampf*, one of Hermann Rauschning's exposés of Hitler, and other works of current history. As the Anschluss and the Munich Agreement passed and the war clouds gathered, Tarkington's letters reflected increasing concern. When the German juggernaut rolled over Europe for the second time in his adult life, his optimistic faith in man's destiny was shaken, and he conceded that "the future has never seemed more uncertain and dangerous." But even as events moved swiftly towards the attack on Pearl Harbor, he refused to admit defeat and wrote in the autumn of 1941 that "civilization cannot die."

The most striking effect of external danger was his emergence from behind the Republican barricades to join President Roosevelt in preparing the United States for war. For Tarkington the tradition to which many Americans give only lip-service, that politics ends at the water's edge, was a valid imperative. As war approached, he became increasingly able to live with the President, and by the time that Mr. Roosevelt died, he felt the same sense of loss that gripped the nation as a whole. Although he had disliked intensely nearly every New Deal domestic policy, he recognized that the President had been right about Hitler and Mussolini from the start and had acted greatly as a wartime leader.

For the second time in his career Tarkington found himself implementing his belief that in time of war an author's duty is to write propaganda. As in 1915 and 1916, he attacked all isolationists and others of myopic vision who thought the United States could stay out of a world conflict. He supported privately in 1940 the President's destroyers-for-bases swap with England and selective service legislation, then a few months later made his first public pronouncement of the pre-Pearl Harbor period. When the Lend-Lease Bill was before Congress, Tarkington urged Senator Van Nuys of Indiana to support the measure and ignore the flood of opposing mail from Midwestern constituents. Pointing out that American defenses were not yet very strong, he suggested that "our protection . . . and perhaps our existence as a free people . . . depend on the British wall against the barbarian." Van Nuys released the letter for publication in *Life* and then joined the successful backers of the bill. Tarkington continued his support of the President by arguing two months later that the United States must protect the supplies that were flowing to England under Lend-Lease. This was several months before Mr. Roosevelt ordered the navy and air force to shoot on sight at Axis submarines—"the rattlesnakes of the Atlantic."

After America entered the war, Tarkington placed his services at the disposal of war bond drives, ration regulation enforcement, and civilian defense measures. He never turned down requests for morale-building essays or specific home-front appeals but gave his services unsparingly in support of the war effort. Most of his propaganda was written gratis for government departments and war agencies, but magazine editors also besieged him for contributions, and he responded often with inspirational editorials. As he approached his seventy-fifth birthday in 1944, he was busier than he had been for years.

Though his propaganda output was ephemeral, one piece is noteworthy for his comments about it. In his wartime works he was willing to adopt the stereotypes of popular fiction, despite his normal abhorrence of formula writing. In 1943 he was commissioned by the *Saturday Evening Post* to write a brief article to accompany a Norman Rockwell illustration of the freedom of speech. Believing this freedom to be the most basic of all to democratic institutions, he gladly supplied text for the picture and wrote a parable describing the meeting of two youthful Europeans many years before at the Brenner Pass in northern Italy. As they spend an evening together at an inn, one character reveals himself to be a house painter, the other a journalist. They discuss their dreams of political power, ways of achieving their ambitions, and the necessity of muzzling free speech to obtain their goal. The strangers finally identify themselves as young Hitler and young Mussolini.

This is a highly contrived fable, a piece of slick fiction; and when a friend wrote that the story was reminiscent of O. Henry, Tarkington admitted the similarity. The device of the surprise ending was old, he replied. It had been used by Balzac, Maupassant, and Anatole France before O. Henry. "There are only a few patterns for stories . . . all of 'em ancient in origin. . . . For years I've been trying to discard pattern altogether; but now and then for a special job, like the Post bit, it's a convenience."

Meanwhile, Tarkington's health improved visibly under the strenuous regimen of writing both propaganda and fiction. During the year that war broke out in Europe he was able to attend symphony concerts for the first time in a decade, and later he was strong enough to revisit Princeton after a ten years' absence. In the months leading to Pearl Harbor he helped organize the Indiana Committee for National Defense, which later was absorbed by the National Committee to Defend America by Aiding the Allies. When the United States became a belligerent, he joined the Coast Guard Auxiliary and during the first summer and autumn of the war helped patrol the coast off Kennebunkport in his motorboat.

His domestic routine during the war underwent only minor changes, though the closeness of the conflict to the east coast and wartime rationing made life at Seawood seem strangely altered. When he returned to Maine in 1943, Kennebunkport looked almost like a ghost town. Hotels were shuttered and empty, cottages were blacked out after sunset, and private boats were all in dry-dock. Adding to the eeriness were the occasional earth-rocking reports of coastal defense guns and the presence of coast guardsmen patrolling the beach. For the first time since 1910 Tarkington found himself without a boat, but even if gasoline had been available, his skipper was working at a war plant in Portland. "We sit all afternoon on the 'Floats' veranda," wrote Tarkington to McCulloch, "and the only boat we see will be Francis Noble's old shingle floating him over for coffee," and the coffee, he added parenthetically, actually was "Karamalt." Tarkington's private club, however, still was open to all comers, whether they were aged beachcombers like Noble or bank presidents on vacation.

During the winters in Indiana his life went on much as it had for many years. He cut his morning work sessions down to three hours or less; yet even then he managed to dictate an average of eight hundred words a day to Miss Trotter when he was writing fiction. His industry between 1940 and 1945 did not flag, for he wrote, besides his war propaganda articles, four novels, seven stories, a novelette ("Walterson"), and the first part of his memoirs. He was cheerful throughout the war, accepting civilian restrictions without complaint, following the war news avidly, and writing long, newsy letters to friends and relatives in service. He hoped that the bureaucracy spawned by the needs of a war economy could be sloughed off after the conflict, but his letters of the period reflect no old-age petulance or impatience. Illness and age never made him self-centered, and during the war he was a steady source of spiritual strength to people far younger and physically more vigorous than he.

Consistent with his out-going personality was his keen interest in the war news, which he followed daily. With shrewd insight he sensed the ebbing of German power well before it was readily apparent and wrote as early as October, 1943, after the Allied invasion of Italy: "There's a 'feel' of the fatal hour coming out of Germany—almost a *sound* of it, like the strangled grunts of a ferocious wrestler who knows he's gone but still gouges and knees the inevitable conqueror." Later, after the Normandy landing and the unsuccessful attempt on Hitler's life, he observed of Germany: "The racket's gone rotten inside —apple's full of worms, so it splits at a push. Be same as if Mark Clark and Eisenhower tried to blow up F. D. R. with MacArthur and Bradley and Nimitz and Spruance helping. . . . If you were a soldier you'd certainly know there wouldn't be any use [of] *your* getting your legs shot off *now.* . . . Add to this that the Russians are . . . busting hell out of everything . . . and what have you! . . . Jeff Davis was running away in his wife's cloak and hood—still *sure* [in 1865] if he could get to Texas he could still win."

During the last years of his life Tarkington returned from the literary byways to the main thoroughfare of his ripest creative period—the Indiana scene. Late in 1939 he began writing *The Heritage of Hatcher Ide* (1941), which brought up to date the midland family sagas of the *Growth* trilogy. He followed this with *The Fighting Littles* (1941), a revival of Midwestern domestic comedy, then went on to write *Kate Fennigate* (1943) and *Image of Josephine* (1945), both of which are fictional portraits in an Indianapolis frame. Finally, an unfinished novel published posthumously, *The Show Piece* (1947), is a male character study of a young egoist reminiscent of George Minafer in *The Magnificent Ambersons*.

When *The Heritage of Hatcher Ide* (serialized as "The Man of the Family") appeared, Tarkington's old friends saw a quickening of the spark that had produced his most important novels. They were powerfully moved by his evocation of familiar things. For "Big" Murray, Tarkington's old Princeton roommate, the novel brought back the world he had known as a youth. Although the story is contemporary in its action, it recalls nostalgically at the opening the heyday of the Ambersons and the society that flourished prior to the First World War. "It awakened a melancholy streak in me," Murray wrote. "I wander around the streets of Flushing looking at the gaunt mansions, built in the '70s . . . and they stare back at me with lusterless windows, dirty and broken . . . The Turmoil, The Magnificent Ambersons and The Man of the Family, all dovetail together, singing of the days that have passed . . . when we ate from the garden and not out of tin cans, when if you came to visit there was no limit to the stay . . . AND WHEN EVERY GIRL WAS GOOD TO LOOK AT." Julian Street, who was similarly moved, saw the novel as a lone survivor of a once-graceful literary tradition. "You're the *only* one," he explained, "who writes about these times and people as we know them." To him the literature of Tobacco Road described an alien world.

The world of Hatcher Ide, however, is familiar to all old Tarkington readers: it has roots and tradition which underlie and buttress a story of 1939. In it the days of the Ambersons and Sheridans are evoked as a setting for Hatcher Ide, a youth who grew up between the wars. When Hatcher returns from college on the eve of the Second World War, the only job he can find in the lingering hours of the depression is collecting rents from the poor tenants of run-down real estate managed by his father's brokerage firm. Yet his subsequent industry and imagination make productive once more the dilapidated houses. In telling this tale Tarkington reaffirms his faith in the regeneration of America by her youth. Concurrently with the economic chronicle runs an integrated domestic plot in the author's most characteristic manner. As Hatcher begins his business career, the outbreak of war in Europe drives the rich, twice-divorced Sarah Florian back to her house next door to the Ides. Another of Tarkington's lovely "monsters of egoism," Sarah amuses herself both by fascinating Hatcher and by trying to rekindle an old spark in the breast of Victor Linley, Hatcher's gentlemanly but bankrupt architect-uncle. After causing a good bit of mischief, she ultimately passes on to Mexico, unrepentant and unscathed.

The Heritage of Hatcher Ide is perhaps Tarkington's best late novel, a well-constructed piece of fiction with depth and breadth. Hatcher is a vivid life-sized figure, and Sarah Florian, in the words of Kenneth Roberts, is "a terrible lady, beautifully done. I wish to God I could do it a quarter as well." The plot also is managed with real skill, especially in the interweaving of the business and social narratives. When Frederic Ide's business partner, Harry Aldrich, commits suicide and Sarah Florian's malice is fully revealed, Tarkington brings the novel to a powerful conclusion. The story is not tragedy, however, for the new generation is left afloat after their elders founder in the economic storm. Tarkington's prognosis that life would go on richly and more vigorously under young leadership was optimistic and, as subsequent events have shown, sound. Yet the story upset the editors of the *Saturday Evening Post,* who thought it too depressing for their readers. They were vastly relieved when Tarkington obligingly inserted, here and there, a few foreshadowings of the actual outcome.

His next novel, *The Fighting Littles,* which is loosely episodic and grew by accretion in the manner of *Women* or *Mary's Neck,* concerns the lively activities of the Little family, mostly in their comfortable midland city home. The inmates of this establishment include Filmer, fifteen, a youth to whom something always is happening; Goody, his eighteen-year-old sister, who is besieged by hare-brained males her own age; Ripley Little, the most irascible man in town; the fluttering and ineffectual Mrs. Little; and Cousin Olita Filmer, a middle-aged poor relation, who acts as housekeeper. This is not Tarkington at his best, though there are in the collection a good many amusing scenes. Filmer's first attempts at smoking, for example, are hilarious, and some of the adolescent capers of Goody and her boy friends are excellent Tarkington; but at its worst the novel descends to slapstick farce.

The chief importance of this book, which contains stories written as early as 1937, was to provide a safety valve for Tarkington. On the same day that the *Saturday Evening Post* rejected one of the stories because "it is anti-New Deal propaganda," he explained to Kahler: "Ripley Little is my own wax-image—by dropping hot lucifer-match ends on it I relieve my bone-aches. It's a most helpful device . . . If I 'make' the image screech, *my* voice need but murmur." In these stories Ripley Little attacks the New Deal, abuses the Democrats, resigns from his club when someone suggests a third term for the President, and takes it hard when Wendell Willkie is defeated in 1940. Little is, of course, a ridiculous figure—both a caricature of the rabid anti-New Dealer and an emotional outlet for the author.

Among the previously unpublished material that went into the book version of *The Fighting Littles* was a second story rejected by the *Post:* "Filmer's Fascinating Face," which the editors thought an incredible tale of adolescent inanity. The story describes Filmer's experiment with his sister's make-up and his later exposure to public ridicule when he forgets to wash his face. The *Post* thought that no boy could undergo such a mental lapse, but when the manuscript came back, Tarkington sent it to Woollcott, who promptly wrote that "it delights me all the way through." He could see nothing incredible about the tale and recounted in his letter the occasion when he had appeared at breakfast in a Philadelphia boardinghouse without his trousers. He had been a sophomore in high school at the time, had only a small mirror in his room, and simply had forgotten to finish dressing.

Tarkington's minor difficulties with the *Post* over *The Fighting Littles* and *The Heritage of Hatcher Ide* became a serious impasse when he wrote his next novel, *Kate Fennigate*. Wesley Winans Stout, the editor, asked Tarkington if he would care to write a story about a woman who is responsible for her husband's business success. He said the *Post* needed something to hold and to attract women readers. Tarkington was interested in the suggestion and wrote the novel, but when he submitted it to the magazine, the editors flatly turned it down. They complained that the husband got pushed around too much by his wife and that *Post* readers, who were mostly men, would not like the hero. Considering that the magazine received what it asked for, Tarkington was good-natured about the rejection and wrote Stout merely that he guessed the editors could not change their habits of a lifetime in selecting virile reading matter. To Adelaide Neall, a *Post* editor, he explained further that "your 'group mind'—inevitably develops the *Post* pattern of a reader and 'Mrs. Lanning' was, intentionally, of another pattern . . . and . . . *therefore* disturbing to the editors. . . . I'd got the idea you were *reaching* for this other reader-pattern . . . and would recognize a story that would interest it."

Tarkington had an inkling of trouble two months before finishing the serial. The *Post* editors then had asked to see the first part of the novel and had objected to the unattractiveness of the husband, Ames Lanning. At that time Tarkington had written: "I suppose—for a serial—that I should keep a reminder-slogan before me on the wall of my workroom: 'Reader's Got to LIKE Somebody!'—I'm too much interested in the human beings as such, in my stories, making 'em out of realities that swarm . . . together from mosaic memory cubes—too absorbed in that to remember that the reader, too, isn't (in numbers) of this persuasion." After the story was rejected, he added in his letter to Stout: "I *can* write regular patterns but don't get much interested that way, so I'd necessarily sometimes be a disappointment to editors." What was not sauce for the gander, however, was sauce for the goose, and Tarkington carved out of the novel a four-part serial that the *Ladies' Home Journal* was happy to publish.

There is no gainsaying that *Kate Fennigate* appeals more to women than to men, especially to the type of reader that Tarkington deprecated, the vicarious adventurer. Kate is a shrewd, brilliant woman who manages people without their being conscious of her doing it. Her assets are not all plus, for Tarkington made her "a dry little gal . . . generally lacking in what we used to call 'charm.'" But she married Ames Lanning at the nadir of his career and is in great measure responsible for the subsequent realization of his early promise. She is the fictional embodiment of what all women believe (and what often is the truth): that behind every successful man there is always a woman. Ames is, moreover, a somewhat contemptible figure, as he was intended to be; but he also is, indefensibly, slightly incredible. Although Tarkington recognized this weakness, his attention was fully engrossed by his heroine, whose portrait is undeniably interesting.

In developing his title character, Tarkington supplied background detail that also contributed to the novel's unsuitability as popular magazine fiction. Kate first is seen at the age of twelve bringing her drunken father home from his club, and the subsequent home life that Tarkington reveals is anything but reassuring. Kate's mother is a weak, self-indulged creature who has eaten herself into obesity and chronic ill-health, real and imaginary. Her father is a lawyer of brilliant parts, who unfortunately has a fatal weakness for liquor. The Fennigates, moreover, typify the shattered old families of their Midwestern city, a sorry remnant of the pre-industrial aristocracy. In addition to the unflattering picture of Kate's family, Tarkington creates an equally unlovely environment for Ames Lanning's early failure. About eight years older than Kate, he marries her cousin Mary, the frail daughter of an iron-willed shrew, while he still is in college, then has to live with his mother-in-law while he works his way through law school and begins to practice. It is not surprising that these early chapters were omitted from the version of the novel serialized by the *Journal*.

Tarkington's readers in Indianapolis found *Kate Fennigate* intriguing for reasons other than plot and character. The setting was again implicitly the capital of Indiana, as it had been

in *The Heritage of Hatcher Ide*. Those who had enjoyed iden-
tifying Butternut Lane in the former story found the old University Club and Tudor Hall (a girls' private school) in the new
novel. Once more Tarkington told his story against the social
and economic background of Indianapolis, beginning the tale
in 1920 and ending it with the year of its composition. The
growth of the city, the encroachment of industrial building on
old residential areas, the burgeoning of business enterprises are
the essential elements of the supporting data.

In a rather different fashion Tarkington went on with his
use of the Indianapolis milieu in his last completed long fiction,
Image of Josephine, written two years later. Economic and
social history, however, were employed only tangentially, for
in this novel he combined his interest in art collecting and his
experience as a museum trustee. The germ of the story had
been in his mind a dozen years, during which time he had
become more and more interested in art galleries. He thought
that a "house attached to a museum might engender a situation
in human lives that could be studied as the basis for a novel."
To implement this notion Tarkington created Josephine Oaklin, proud, spoiled granddaughter of a Midwestern millionaire,
Thomas Oaklin, who gives his city an art museum. The old
man builds the gallery in his own yard, endows it with most
of his wealth and his own extensive art collection, and stipu-
lates that Josephine is to be a permanent member of the board
of trustees.

From this provocative situation Tarkington evolved a story
that combined his dual interest in feminine portraiture and art
collecting. The story chronicles the troubles that the museum
director, his assistants, and other trustees have with Josephine,
who lives in her grandfather's old home attached to the museum. She has private access to the gallery, a nasty disposi-
tion, and a penchant for modern art. Characteristically up to
date, Tarkington makes his hero an army officer temporarily
invalided out of the service, who comes to work for the museum. The soldier, Bailey Fount, inevitably clashes with and
is attracted to Josephine, but the outcome is not conventional.
Bailey plays Petruchio, but Josephine is no ordinary Katharina,
as he realizes, and the novel ends with the couple engaged but

not destined for an easy life together, if indeed they ever are to get married. Josephine does not change.

Since the novel ends with an engagement, most readers probably discounted the author's explicit denial of Josephine's reformation. They bought well over half a million copies, making the novel one of Tarkington's most widely distributed works; but the fact remains that the heroine is purposely an elusive figure. "No man knows himself and even the shrewdest women have but a sketchy notion of themselves," wrote Tarkington at the time of the book's publication. "No two people have the same concept of a third person, and the person concerned has a third opinion of himself." Readers were not expected to like Josephine, and Tarkington was surprised at the popular success of the novel. He had written the story because it interested him, and once more, as with *Kate Fennigate*, he had published only an abridgment of the novel before book publication.

His townsmen again hunted for names and places that could be identified, though Tarkington denied that he had based his story either on the John Herron Art Institute in Indianapolis or on his activities as one of its trustees. However, the character John Constable Horne, an elderly trustee of the Oaklin Museum, frequently expresses Tarkington's own opinions about art, and, moreover, a controversy between Horne and Josephine over the nonrepresentational painting of one Harry Pilker seems freely adapted from fact. There actually had been a wide difference of opinion over modern art between most of the trustees, on one hand, and the director of John Herron and the museum's chief patroness, on the other. Nevertheless, Tarkington's experiences were only suggestive, and one particular tempest among the museum trustees over buying a Picasso painting actually occurred after he already had written the section on Harry Pilker. Tarkington's imagination had so transformed the factual basis of the novel that the director of John Herron read the story and wrote that he had found no similarities between characters and people he knew.

Tarkington's uncompleted last novel, *The Show Piece*, continued the fictional preoccupation of his final years. Like *Kate Fennigate* and *Image of Josephine*, it too is what he called an "investigatory novel," which is simply another name for realism that refuses to be bound by any set of rules. If the characters in a book are to come alive, he wrote, they "must be not easier to know . . . than actual people. They must be people about whom the reader could change his opinion, as he does, sometimes, of actual people . . . [They] must be as inconsistent, for instance, as human beings are, and must inspire in one another as diverse opinions of themselves as all human beings do." Irvie Pease, the protagonist in *The Show Piece,* is developed by this investigatory method and also like Kate and Josephine is a character not destined to be loved by the reader.

Although it was only two-thirds completed, the story of Irvie Pease is pretty well blocked out in the forty thousand words written. Moreover, the denouement had been dictated so that the plan for the story need not be conjectured. Irvie is a supreme egoist, raised by indulgent parents, adored by the author-narrator's niece, and patiently served by a self-effacing cousin. The elderly novelist who tells the story conveys his own prejudice against Irvie to the reader, but among the character's family and friends the verdict is widely varied. Before the story breaks off, Irvie passes obnoxiously through adolescence and college, trading all the while on his talent for self-dramatization and his cousin's brains, and then jilts his faithful fiancée for an heiress. But had the tale been finished, Irvie would have ended as a pricked balloon, for he was to marry a woman even more selfish than he. The jilted girl and the patient cousin, meanwhile, were to marry and settle down to a happy life together, unencumbered by their former delusions about Irvie.

The really interesting thing about *The Show Piece* is its final demonstration of a subject that held lifelong fascination for Tarkington. Studies of egoism, male and female, as we have seen, abound in his large output of novels, stories, and plays. While he was at work on this last book, he said that he might have named it *The Egoist* if Meredith had not already used the title. In fact, Meredith was one of the giants among novelists that Tarkington enjoyed reading in his old age. He was absorbed always by the secret workings of human beings, especially the type of individual whose world focuses inwardly. "Egoism," he wrote, "is the main and controlling force operative among human beings." Yet Tarkington himself focused outwardly on the world about him, a trait which is perhaps the essential requirement for a novelist who combines realism and social history.

Characteristic of Tarkington's outward focus was an intense concern over international problems that were to follow the Second World War. Even while he was helping the Treasury sell war bonds in 1943, he was assuming the role of elder statesman in matters of postwar policy. Soon after the Italian mainland had been invaded by Allied forces, he publicly supported the Roosevelt-Churchill decision made at Casablanca to accept only unconditional surrender, and before the Second Front was opened in France the next year, he was urging the creation of an international law enforcement organization. Just as he once had been an early advocate of the League of Nations, he later wrote passionately in favor of the United Nations. He felt a tremendous sense of urgency about these matters, even though he would be seventy-six when the war ended and not likely to live far into the postwar era.

He put his faith for world peace in an international organization that would have real power to enforce its decisions and resented the wartime "vaporings about 'what we're fighting for' from the politicians, debaters, propagandists, radioteers and newspaperettes" who thought we were struggling "to bring freedom from misery to every human being." Some people who stay miserable, he observed, "will be sore at us for failing. They'll say we were cheaters and failures, just as people say now we *flopped* in '17-'18 because we *didn't* 'end all wars' and 'make the world safe for democracy.' " He took comfort, however, that the men actually doing the fighting were not fooling themselves about why they were in uniform: their country was in danger, and they had to fight. "I 'get' a mighty wholesome spirit in Johnny's letter," he wrote after receiving a particularly sane communication from John Jameson, Jr., who was then in basic training.

Tarkington also hoped that the problems of peace could be placed in the hands of a revitalized Republican Party. He had hitched his faith in a renaissance of the G.O.P. to the political career of Wendell Willkie, whom he knew personally and admired greatly. He had been thrilled by the invigorating leadership of Willkie in 1940 and had concluded that an internationally minded Hoosier could shatter traditional Midwestern isolationism. Later Willkie's *One World* gave him an exciting glimpse of his friend's vision. Reviewing the book, Tarkington wrote of Willkie: "He is impelled by the strong necessity to make us comprehend at least a little of the dangers and of the noble possibilities that will be brought to all human lives by the modern annihilation of this earth's old distances." This also was Tarkington's vision. When Willkie's hopes for a second presidential nomination were wrecked by his failure in the Wisconsin primary election in April, 1944, Tarkington was tremendously disappointed.

A month afterwards, however, he struck out on his own in an effort to influence his party. Addressing an extraordinary letter to the Republicans in Indiana, he challenged his party to abandon all taint of isolationism and to come out strongly for a positive policy towards postwar problems. He specifically charged Indiana Congressmen who were up for re-election that year: "Our duty to our country . . . demands that we know clearly from you how you stand upon the question of a permanent peace and what you will do when the attempt is made, as it will be, to take such measures as will best serve to prevent future international wars." He was willing to throw overboard even the staunchest conservative who was unwilling to face up to the United States' future role in world affairs.

What made this letter even more arresting was his concluding admonition: " 'When the next war comes,' all of the military powers concerned will almost certainly be in possession of an implement able to wipe out such a city as New York within ten minutes so effectively that no living being could get anywhere near the place during the next three or four months." Tarkington, of course, was thinking of the atomic bomb, though the first nuclear explosion at White Sands, New Mexico, was still fourteen months in the future. The isolationist Congressmen to whom the message was directed may have thought that Tarkington was writing science fiction, but, in fact, he had known as early as 1942, when a visitor to Kennebunkport confirmed and amplified his own shrewd guesses, that scientists were trying to produce an atomic bomb. He immediately had grasped the implications of the bomb; hence the urgency in his writings about post-war problems.

After Hiroshima and Nagasaki were leveled by the bomb, Tarkington wrote: "But now . . . a hell's own flash . . . terrifies the world with a glimpse of Nature laughing murderously at the period-charting of politicians, economists and reformers." He warned then that the only hope of civilization lay in internationalizing the bomb under the United Nations. At the same time, he opposed vigorously any old-fashioned plan for national security, particularly the proposal for universal military training. "From now on," he added, "the nations are like a family living in a house with walls irretrievably built of dynamite," and they must walk softly and take care not to "be irritating to one another." Later he told an interviewer that "the principle of atomic energy is no more an American secret than 'raising tomatoes,' " and he repeated that the bomb must be controlled by an international authority. Fortunately he did not live to watch the present atomic arms race and to be disillusioned by Russian intransigeance but died confident that only "suicidal madmen" would care to take part in such a contest.

He did, however, live to see the organization of the United Nations at San Francisco in 1945 and the subsequent initial sessions of the General Assembly and Security Council in London the following January. He had high hopes for the success of the U. N. and never abandoned his faith that light and civilization would triumph over darkness and the jungle. He answered the objections of those who thought war could never be abolished by declaring that people once had believed human sacrifice was an essential part of religion and more recently had considered the burning of witches both legal and meritorious. Society no longer hangs pilferers of sixpence, he added, nor is it necessary for a secretary of the United States Treasury to let himself be shot simply because dueling is too ironclad a custom to be denied. Tarkington died believing that men would have the wisdom and intellect to control the awful products of their technical proficiency. In his last public statement, a New Year's Day message, he gazed ahead at a year that he was not destined to see end. "We can look 1946 in the face and make despair step behind us," he wrote with almost youthful confidence. "We have come through the dreadful night and tomorrow is here. Tomorrow is not our master; it is in our hands and will be what we make it."

Less than five months later Tarkington made his last appearance in public on March 7 when the Indianapolis Civic Theater produced Miss Trotter's dramatization of *Alice Adams*. Although he already was making plans for his annual return to Maine in May, towards the end of March he was stricken with vague arm and leg pains that foreshadowed a more serious internal disorder. In the midst of dictating *The Show Piece* he was forced to bed, and as the weeks of April passed, he slowly lost strength. Finally, surrounded by his beloved wife and nephews, he died after an illness of two months on the evening of May 19, nine weeks before his seventy-seventh birthday. Simple services were held at home, and he was buried in Crown Hill Cemetery with his parents and daughter and near the grave of his old friend Riley.

Tarkington died quietly and unostentatiously as he had lived. In his last years he had achieved the Olympian detachment he thought necessary for happiness. He had come to believe that "life is only an episode in our passage from infinity to infinity," and "there is no death, only change." His life had been rich with promise and fulfillment, industry and recognition, and he had lived generously, honestly, and modestly. Having kept faith in his life with the best traditions of American experience, he remained in death a member of Wordsworth's one great society—"the noble living and the noble dead."

A BIBLIOGRAPHICAL POSTSCRIPT

This book is based largely on the extensive collection of papers given to Princeton University by Mrs. Tarkington in 1951. This collection contains thousands of items: correspondence to and from Tarkington, manuscripts, periodicals, books, scrapbooks, photographs, and memorabilia. For a description of this material, see "The Tarkington Papers," *Princeton University Library Chronicle,* XVI (Winter, 1955). Other manuscript material at Princeton includes Tarkington's letters to Hugh Kahler, Erwin Panofsky, A. B. Maurice, Ruth Gordon, Gregory Kelly, George Tyler, Brandt & Brandt (literary agents), and Harper & Brothers. The last two groups of letters I consulted in New York before they were given to Princeton. I have used additional Tarkington letters among the George Ade Papers at Purdue University, the Alexander Woollcott Papers at Harvard University,[1] the Hamlin Garland Papers at the University of Southern California. Also I have been allowed to use Tarkington letters owned by Mrs. Julian Street, Barton Currie, John Jameson; and Doubleday and Company opened their Tarkington files to me.

Tarkington's printed work, including most of the ephemera and contributions to obscure publications, was not hard to find. The Princeton Papers are nearly complete, and what I could not find at Princeton I found in Indianapolis in the state and public libraries. Tarkington's life after 1899 was extensively reported by the newspapers, and the New York *Times Index* (1913-) is a useful guide for finding much of this coverage. Scrapbooks at Princeton contain many cuttings, but especially valuable are the clipping files of Tarkington material in the two Indiana libraries mentioned above. In addition, the New York Public Library has many pertinent newspaper cuttings in its theater collection. Finally, the Indiana State Library and the Butler University Library have supplied me with back volumes of Indianapolis newspapers.

Three specific works, which are indispensable for the biographer of Tarkington, I have cited frequently and referred to hereafter by symbol or abbreviation:

Bibliog.—Dorothy R. Russo and Thelma L. Sullivan, *A Bibliography of Booth Tarkington, 1869-1946* (1949). This volume contains a nearly complete listing of Tarkington's writings and gives abundant bibliographical data for his major works. In the following pages I have tried not to duplicate information found in this source.

AISTM—"As I Seem to Me," *Saturday Evening Post,* CCXIV (July 5-Aug. 23, 1941). This is Tarkington's autobiography down to 1899. I have used it frequently in chaps. 1-3, though in many instances I was able to verify its data from other sources. I have found that Tarkington's gift of almost total recall makes *AISTM* a valuable reference. My problem (except where he embroidered detail for dramatic effect) was to date events precisely and to supply real names for fictitious ones.

TWDM—*The World Does Move* (1928). This book is a collection of reminiscent essays strung on a loose thread of autobiography. The data here are accurate, but the problem of supplying referents is more difficult than in *AISTM*. This volume covers Tarkington's life, with gaps, from 1895 to the time it was published.

The specific chapter notes which follow are not a complete blueprint of this work, but they omit no important sources. In addition, I have included some interesting though peripheral data. Unless special note is made, all letters to or about Tarkington, cited or quoted, are at Princeton, while letters written by Tarkington are either at Princeton or owned as indicated in paragraph one. Indianapolis newspapers I have referred to by name only: *Star, News, Times,* etc. On occasion, when exact reproduction of manuscript sources might have caused confusion, I have silently supplied punctuation, corrected obvious slips of the pen, or spelled out abbreviations. To save space in the following pages, I have used T to represent Booth Tarkington.

Prologue

For Howells' visit to Indianapolis, see local newspapers of Nov. 19, 20, 1899; Mildred Howells, ed., *Life in Letters of William Dean Howells* (1928), II, 115-117; T's Preface to *The Rise of Silas Lapham* (1937). For Howells' remarks on Riley, see *North American Review,* CLXVIII, 588 (May, 1899) ; for his appreciation of T, see "Editor's Easy Chair," *Harper's,* CXXX, 798, 961 (April, May, 1915); and unpublished letters to T of Aug. 28, 1914, Jan. 9, 1915.

Two useful articles on Indiana literary history: Richard A. Cordell, "Limestone, Corn, and Literature," *Saturday Review of Liter-*

ature, XIX, 3-4, 14-15 (Dec. 17, 1938); Howard H. Peckham, "What Made Hoosiers Write," *American Heritage*, II, 24-27, 59-60 (Autumn, 1950). Cordell tells the lyceum-lecturer story, which he once heard Ade tell a Purdue audience. Peckham, a historian, suggests that the prodigious writing of Hoosiers resulted from several factors: rich natural resources that made life more abundant for the pioneers; diverse racial strains (French, German, Irish, and Anglo-Saxon) that mingled in Indiana and stimulated the development of an articulate population; the growth of a rich folklore resulting from the state's long delay in creating a public school system; and the intellectual stimulus of the New Harmony community.

Two other useful works: R. E. Banta, *Indiana Authors and Their Books, 1816-1916* (1949), which contains about one thousand bio-bibliographies of Indiana authors; Meredith Nicholson, *The Hoosiers* (1900).

Proof of Indiana book-writing lies in this article: John H. Moriarty, "Hoosiers Sell Best," *Indiana Quarterly for Bookmen*, III, 7-14 (Jan., 1947). Moriarty assigned from ten points down to one for each of the ten best sellers listed annually in Alice P. Hackett, *Fifty Years of Best Sellers, 1895-1945* (1945), and tabulated the points on the basis of the authors' native states. Results: Indiana, 216, New York, 215; Pennsylvania, 125.

A selected bibliography of Indiana and Indianapolis: Bowman, Heath, *Hoosier* (1941); Buley, Roscoe C., *The Old Northwest, Pioneer Period, 1815-1840*, 2 vols. (1951); Dunn, Jacob P., *Greater Indianapolis: The History, the Industries, the Institutions, and the People of a City of Homes*, 2 vols. (1910); Esarey, Logan, *History of Indiana from Its Exploration to 1922* (1922) ; Holloway, W. R., *Indianapolis* (1870); Hyman, Max R., *Handbook of Indianapolis* (1897); Martin, John B., *Indiana: An Interpretation* (1947); Nolan, Jeannette C., *Hoosier City* (1943) ; Roll, Charles, *Indiana, One Hundred and Fifty Years of American Development*, 5 vols. (1931); Rusk, Ralph L., *Literature of the Middle Western Frontier*, 2 vols. (1925).

Chapter One

For details of T's birth, see *Journal* of July 30, 1869, and letter to T from father on July 29, 1908. John Tarkington's career is documented in *AISTM*, *Who's Who*, obituary in the *News* on Jan. 31, 1923. Joseph Tarkington's life is fully covered in *Autobiography of Rev. Joseph Tarkington, One of the Pioneer Methodist Preachers of Indiana* (Cincinnati, 1899). Data on the Booth family are from

AISTM, a document at Princeton called "Crown Hill Cemetery—Tarkington," a letter from John E. Parker to T of Sept. 30, 1941.

Hauté Tarkington Jameson was christened Mary Booth Tarkington but always called Hauté for Terre Haute, which she was fond of visiting as a child.

The visit to California is reported in *AISTM* but dated from family letters. *Beasley's Christmas Party* was a book that Mark Twain liked. A. B. Paine reports in his *Mark Twain, A Biography* (1912), III, 1535: "He said [as Paine came in and found Twain propped up in bed reading]: 'I seldom read Christmas stories, but this is very beautiful. It has made me cry. I want you to read it . . . Tarkington has the true touch,' he said; 'his work always satisfies me.' "

Material on the house at 1100 N. Penn. St. appears in *AISTM; Star* of Nov. 12, 1929, Feb. 16, 1941; *Presenting Lily Mars,* chap. 1. The account of life in Indianapolis in the Seventies is from *The Magnificent Ambersons,* chap. 1. Data on the Panic of 1873, buying the needle, the children's party, and T's inability to get angry are from *AISTM.* The data on T's reading are from "Chronicle and Comment," *The Bookman,* XLII, 233 (Nov., 1915); "Children and Books," *Fashions of the Hour* (Autumn, 1932); *AISTM;* letter to mother of June 18, 1907 (MS owned by John Jameson).

T's juvenile writings, including the 1881 diary, are among the papers at Princeton. His sister's memory of his first story comes from an unidentified clipping in a scrapbook at Princeton. His fourth grade feud is told in *AISTM.* This also is the source for his memory of Marshall, Ill., plus chap. 7 of *The Gentleman from Indiana* and "The Better Man," *Nassau Literary Magazine,* XLVII, 233-234 (Nov., 1891).

Chapter Two

Material on "Jesse James" is from *AISTM;* data on the high school farce-comedy and the Hord-T theatrical plans are from copybooks and *AISTM.* T's first poem is reprinted in *AISTM;* but see also *Gentle Julia,* chaps. 15, 16. For data on spiritualism, see *AISTM;* letters to Garland of June 19, 1936, Aug. 17, 1939; posthumous tribute to Garland (*Bibliog.,* p. 189); Foreword to May Wright Sewall, *Neither Dead nor Sleeping* (1920); letter to John Jameson of Sept. 16, 1941. T's recollection of church and Sunday school is from letter to Gilson Willets of the *Christian Herald* on Dec. 26, 1904. His faith is outlined in a letter to Dan Calkins of Aug. 1, 1898.

Penrod's letter excusing himself from the dance appeared first in *Penrod,* chap. 14, was reprinted in *AISTM.* Also told in *AISTM* are the stories of the call on the Older Girl and the two shirts. Much material is available on T's relationship with Riley (see *Bibliog.,* Index); chief sources are *AISTM;* "Mr. Riley," *Collier's,* LVIII, 3-4, 22 (Dec. 30, 1916). T's high school truancy is told in *AISTM;* I have verified and added to this source from records of the Indianapolis public schools.

T's letters to his parents, and theirs to him, plus T's letters to Dan Calkins, provide the basis for recreating his Exeter experience. T's memory of Exeter in *AISTM* exaggerates his extravagance and unfilial willfulness in staying on after graduation. For other data on Exeter, I am indebted to W. G. Saltonstall, the present principal, and the *Exonian* for June 22, 1899. The spring visit to New York is recalled in T's Foreword to John Drew's memoir, *My Years on the Stage* (1922). The context of T's letter to his father of Nov. 28, 1888, indicates that Scott taught psychology, though academy records show only that he lectured on philosophy. The memory of Indianapolis at Christmas, 1888, is found in "Railroading a Christmas," *Collier's,* XXXIV, 8, 11 (Dec. 3, 1904).

T reported his autumn activities in a letter to Dan Calkins of Nov. 15, 1889. T's Purdue experiences come from *AISTM;* his weekly columns (Sept. 21, 1890-June 7, 1891) in the Lafayette *Sunday Times;* records in the registrar's office; three letters to his parents (MSS owned by John Jameson). T's memory of the dean is from John G. Coulter, *The Dean* (1940), pp. 166-167. For additional information about this period, I am indebted to Mrs. William V. Stuart (Geneve Reynolds) of Lafayette, Ind. The T-Ade relationship is well documented in letters (see the Ade Papers at Purdue) and printed sources (see *Bibliog.,* Index).

T's Princeton years are well documented in files of undergraduate publications, various reminiscences of friends, clippings, *AISTM,* four letters to his parents (MSS owned by John Jameson). The cousin in Princeton, to whom T's father wrote on July 25, 1891, was Charles A. Aiken, a professor at the theological seminary. For memoirs of T at Princeton, see A. P. Dennis, "Getting Booth Tarkington Educated," *Gods and Little Fishes* (1931), pp. 273-297; J. L. Williams, "Booth Tarkington '93: A Personal Impression," *Princeton Alumni Weekly,* XVI, 245-247 (Dec. 8, 1915). T's memories of Princeton are chiefly in "Personal Recollections of Princeton Undergraduate Life," *Princeton Alumni Weekly,* XVI, 819-822 (June 7, 1916) ; "Young Literary Princeton Fifty Years Ago," *Princeton University Library Chronicle,* VII, 1-5 (Nov., 1945); "Reminiscences of the Triangle Club," *Safety First* [a program] (1916); *AISTM.* The

Glee Club tour of Christmas, 1892-93, is recorded in a scrapbook of clippings. See also Mark Sullivan, *The Education of an American* (1938), pp. 98-100. T wrote about the Ivy Club to Kahler on Mar. 23, 1924. T's grades at Princeton, translated from the group grade system, consisted of four A's, seven B's, five C's, five D's. He apparently did not take the final exams in four of the seven courses he was enrolled in during his last semester.

Chapter Three

Hugh Kahler told me the story of the summer-colony mother. T reported his chance to work on the New York *Tribune* in a letter to his father on May 29, 1893 (MS owned by John Jameson). "I was for five years" is quoted from *Book News*, XVIII, 325-326 (Feb., 1900); the same source describes T's early draft of his first novel. About five columns of *AISTM* deal with his apprenticeship. The dialogue with the milkman comes from T's speech to the St. Andrew's Society of New York on Nov. 30, 1904. The T Papers contain several copies each, in various states, of "The Ruse" and "The Prodigals," one of the latter being a collaboration with James Barnes entitled "His Word of Honor." For data on Indianapolis performances of T's plays (and T's performances in various plays), see newspaper files and the annual booklets published by the Indianapolis Dramatic Club.

The genesis of *The Gentleman from Indiana* may be seen in several items extant in the T Collection: a sheaf of papers outlining the novel, a hand-drawn map of Marshall, Ill., several notebooks containing tentative starts. T contributed to the *Flower Mission Magazine* between 1891 and 1900 (see *Bibliog.*, pp. 155-158); the Indiana State Library has an almost complete file of this rare item. The interest of Mansfield and Barnes in "The Prodigals" is reported in the latter's memoir, *From Then Till Now* (1934), pp. 161-162; see also note from Mansfield's secretary of July 6, 1895. The drawing bought by *Life* is described in *Book News* (see above) and *AISTM*. The two-line joke sold to *Life*, probably in 1894, for $2.50 was illustrated, as T later remembered, by Charles Dana Gibson, but T could not identify it. Riley wrote W. M. Carey of the *Century* on Oct. 5, 15, 1895; see William Lyon Phelps, ed., *The Letters of James Whitcomb Riley* (1930), pp. 201-202.

T recalls his 1895-96 visit to New York in *TWDM*, chaps. 1-4. T's one work in the first person is "This Boy Joe" (see discussion in chap. 13 and T's letter to Susanah Jameson of May 5, 1939—copy at Princeton). His memory of Riley's criticism, recalled in *AISTM* with remarkable accuracy, may be checked against the extant, annotated manuscript. T's talk with Lew Wallace is in chap. 6, *TWDM.* For T's memory of Wallace, see *There Were Giants in the Land* (1942), pp. 75-82.

Indianapolis in June in the Nineties is described in *TWDM,* chap. 7. The Indiana State Library has a file of the rare *John-a-Dreams.* T's relationship with that periodical is recalled in Robert T. Sloss, "The Real Booth Tarkington," *Pearson's Magazine,* IX, 211-220 (March, 1903). For data on Helen Pitkin, see notes for chap. 4. T's unpublished poems, perhaps two dozen in all, are among the papers at Princeton. The publishing history of *Monsieur Beaucaire* is covered adequately in *Bibliog.,* pp. 6-9; the same is true of other works, on appropriate pages. Runyon's comment was in the *Star* on Aug. 7, 1937. The end of T's apprenticeship is recounted in *AISTM, Book News* (see above), letter to Garland of [Nov. ?, 1920], tribute to Garland *(Bibliog.,* p. 189). I am indebted to members of the Tarkington family for my knowledge of T's deep friendship with John Green.

Chapter Four

T's visit to New York (Feb.-May, 1899) is reconstructed from nineteen letters to his family, and their replies. A few are reproduced in the *Princeton University Library Chronicle,* XVI (Winter, 1955). The reception of *The Gentleman from Indiana* is recorded in several places: a letter apparently to McClure (though first page is missing) written in summer or early fall, 1899, about the Culver City banker (MS owned by John Jameson); "Temptations of a Young Author," *Cosmopolitan,* XXXIX, 665-666 (Oct., 1905); *TWDM,* chap. 8; *AISTM;* letter to Dan Calkins of Dec. 21, 1899; a scrapbook of newspaper reviews. For T's defense and interpretation of the Midwest, see "The Middle West," *Harper's,* CVI, 75-83 (Dec., 1902). Indiana papers, c. 1900, contain many reports of Whitecapping.

T's low opinion of fiction that gives reader vicarious adventure comes from the above cited letter to Susanah Jameson. For the publishing history of *The Gentleman,* see *Bibliog.,* pp. 3-6; best-seller lists in *The Bookman;* a letter from F. N. Doubleday of Aug. 1, 1919; various publisher's advertisements. T's book columns appeared in the *Press,* p. 2 of Sat. Supplement, from Jan. 27 to May 5, 1900. The history of *Cherry* is from various letters by Jaccaci, McClure, and Sears; an unpublished (?) reminiscence written c. 1916; a letter to Street on April 8, 1915.

326   BOOTH TARKINGTON

There are forty-five letters from Helen Pitkin in the T Collection. The other side of the correspondence, owned by her heirs in New Orleans, has not been available to me. This relationship is treated in *AISTM;* letters to Street on March 4, 1916, and George Tyler, March 17, 1916.

The dramatization of *Beaucaire* is documented by Mrs. Sutherland's letters; clippings; family letters to T; his article "The Actor and the Empress," *The Players' Book* (1938), pp. 73-81. "Incredibly prevalent . . . entertainment" is from the above-cited reminiscence of *Cherry.* For data on *The Two Vanrevels,* see T's tribute to St. Mary-of-the-Woods in the *Star* of Feb. 13, 1916, and *Fifty Years of Best Sellers.* About three weeks after the novel was issued the publisher advertised 63,000 copies sold. Two useful books on best sellers: James D. Hart, *The Popular Book* (1950), and Frank L. Mott, *Golden Multitudes* (1947).

T's publishing relations: See summarizing letters to F. A. Duneka of March 28 [1911] and to T. A. Lamont of Sept. 3, 1919. When McClure and F. N. Doubleday dissolved their partnership in 1900, T stayed with McClure. Later friendship with Colonel Harvey and Duneka took T to Harper, which published seven titles between 1903 and 1916. In 1907 T, reminded by McClure that he had been T's first publisher, gave McClure a contract for three books. Subsequently Doubleday, who had remained a friend, bought out McClure, including T's contract, after T had delivered only one book. From 1913 until 1916 Doubleday and Harper split his output, an arrangement T planned to continue; but after Duneka died in 1919, he went to Doubleday permanently.

There are about one hundred letters from girls other than Helen Pitkin among the T Papers. The comment on T's infinite tact appeared in the *Press* on Dec. 13, 1899. Mrs. Rombauer's memory of T I have had first-hand and from her letter to me of Nov. 15, 1953. The letter about T's frequent attendance at weddings was written to Dan Calkins on May 18, 1897. Data on T's courtship and marriage are mostly from newspaper reports. Fletcher family history is recorded in J. P. Dunn, *Memorial and Genealogical Record of Representative Citizens of Indiana* (1912).

Chapter Five

For data on *The Man on Horseback,* see *Star* on Feb. 19, 1905; *Sentinel* on Oct. 8, 1901; letter to Hauté on May 21, 1907 (MS owned by John Jameson) ; a review of Josephine Hart Phelps in the San Francisco *Argonaut* (Aug. 24, 1912), p. 123. The play ran from

Aug. 19 through Aug. 31 at the Columbia Theatre in San Francisco. The manuscript of this play, as well as the manuscripts of other unpublished plays, is among the papers at Princeton.

The record of T's term in the legislature is found in two main sources: Indianapolis newspapers of appropriate dates and the *Journal of the* [Indiana] *House of Representatives* . . . (1903). The Governor's opening address is on pp. 14-50 of this volume. T wrote of his public office in "My Political Career; or, When I Helped to Make the Laws," *Saturday Evening Post*, CCV, 10-11, 26-27, 29 (April 8, 1933). T made no effort to be accurate and was chiefly interested in making a sprightly narrative. Bryan's comments appeared in *The Commoner*, II, 5 (Nov. 7, 1902). T recalled Bryan's remarks in speeches before the Indiana Society of Chicago in 1908 and the Lotos Club in New York in 1916 (see *Bibliog.*, pp. 160, 172). T explained his feeling about making speeches in a letter to Garland of Nov. 29, 1920. In the T Collection there also is a letter from Carleton B. McCulloch to Will Hayes (Nov. 3, 1937) explaining Tarkington's inability to make public appearances.

T describes campaigning with Shank in " 'Lectioneering," *Collier's*, XXXIV, 12-13 (Oct. 22, 1904). His review of the legislative session is in the *News* for March 28, 1903. For the Governor's veto message, see the House *Journal* (1905), p. 152. The letter about Debs was written to Samuel Castleton on Jan. 10, 1945. When Debs was in prison after the First World War, T was one of the signers of a pardon petition. T wrote of Sam Arbaugh, the ward boss, in "The Priceless Ballot," *Collier's*, XXXIV, 13-14 (Oct. 29, 1904) .

T's luncheon at the White House was described to his father on Dec. 23, 1904. Theodore Roosevelt's views also are recalled in *TWDM*, chap. 9. For specific praise of *In the Arena*, see a letter of March 9, 1905, in J. B. Bishop, ed., *Theodore Roosevelt and His Times Shown in His Letters* (1920), I, 367. T recalled his siege with typhoid fever in "The Boastful Kennebunkporter" (see *Bibliog.*, p. 267).

Chapter Six

The letters T wrote his nephews from Europe, 1903-04, are collected in *Your Amiable Uncle* (1949). For other records of that year, see "Views of the Stage and Players," *Harper's Weekly*, XLVII, 1862 (Nov. 21, 1903); "The Next Time We See Paris," *American Legion Magazine*, XXXIV, 8-9, 44-45, 47 (March, 1943) ; "Knowing Paris," *American Legion Monthly*, III, 14-15, 90 (Aug., 1927). The visit to Waterloo and T's early automobiling experiences are given in *TWDM*, chaps. 10-12.

T's year in New York, 1904-05, is recorded in letters to and from his family. The data on the dramatization of *The Gentleman* come mostly from newspaper reports; but see also George Tyler's memoir, *Whatever Goes Up* (1934). For a good succinct treatment of periodicals, c. 1900, see Clarence Gohdes, "The Age of the Monthly Magazine," in *The Literature of the American People* (1951). T's memory of the Lakewood dinner is from a letter of June 27, 1944, to Burges Johnson, published in his *As Much as I Dare* (1944), pp. 227-233.

For details on the writing of *The Conquest of Canaan,* see letters to T's father of May 29, Aug. 18, 1905, and from John D. Thompson on July 28, 1905. T acknowledged Cherbuliez' "most persuasive" influence in an undated (c. 1923) interview in the Chicago *Tribune* with James Bennett, which is in the T Collection at Princeton. See also T's correspondence with Harper about the 1935 edition.

There are many letters to T's parents and sister written from Europe between 1905 and 1907. Most are at Princeton, but sixteen are owned by John Jameson. See also Julian Street, "When We Were Rather Young," *Saturday Evening Post,* CCV (Aug. 20, Nov. 19, Dec. 17, 1932); a letter to A. B. Maurice of Dec. 6, 1905. T's plans for playwriting while abroad were told to the *Sentinel* on Sept. 4, 1905. His relationship with Harry Leon Wilson is detailed in "H. L.: A Writing Man," *Saturday Review of Literature,* XX, 10-11 (Aug. 12, 1939); also in John Tebbel, *George Horace Lorimer and the Saturday Evening Post* (1948). Tebbel's version of Rose O'Neill and the "woses" seems garbled. I have had the tale orally from several sources, and my account is a mosaic of them all, buttressed by such contemporary records as I have found. Barnes' trip to Italy is reported in his memoirs (see above), also mentioned by Street (see above), and noted in T's letters.

The Wild-West-Show story exists in several forms: in "Indiana in Literature and Politics" (T's Lotos Club speech—see *Bibliog.,* p. 172); in "Some Americans Abroad," *Everybody's Magazine,* XVII, 168-174 (Aug., 1907); letter to Fred C. Kelly of July 18, 1945 (photostat at Princeton). Kelly tells it in his *George Ade, Warmhearted Satirist* (1947); so does Street in his reminiscent articles. Material about Antonio comes from his letters to T, T's letters home from Europe, and Street. The best account, however, is in an interview in the New York *Times* of May 7, 1905.

For T's troubles over *His Own People,* see letters to his family, also one to R. U. Johnson of Nov. 2, 1906 (copy at Princeton) and Johnson's reply of Nov. 17, 1906. The account of the orphans' picnic was printed in the *News* of Oct. 27, 1906, freely edited from a letter to T's mother of Sept. 28, 1906.

Chapter Seven

Rue de Tournon is described in a letter to A. B. Maurice published in his *Paris of the Novelists* (1919); also in letter to Hauté of April 28, 1908 (MS owned by John Jameson). Street's articles recall the American colony in Paris at that time. The sketch of people seen on the boulevards occurs at the opening of *The Guest of Quesnay*. The stories of Maxim's and the Minister of Agriculture, the tales of the derby hats, the fruit stand, and the cavalcade to Lafayette come from Street's articles. The episode at Fort Monroe was recalled to T by Colonel Frederic A. Price in a letter on Nov. 10, 1943, and its aftermath in a reply to Price of Nov. 14, 1943 (MS owned by Price).

Material about the writing of *The Guest* comes from T's letters to his parents; the letter to Maurice (see above), a letter to Street of May 5, 1921; an undated interview from a Cincinnati newspaper among the clippings at Princeton. For T's opinion of Cherbuliez, see his Foreword to an edition of *Samuel Brohl and Company* (1902). For quotations from the novel, see chaps. 18, 22.

The writing, casting, and production of *The Man from Home* are reconstructed from several general sources: Tyler's *Whatever Goes Up;* a letter from T to Burns Mantle partially printed in *The Best Plays of 1899-1909* (1944), the complete text of which is at Princeton; various newspaper reviews; T's article on Wilson (see above); Tyler's archives, which are in the Seymour Theatre Collection at Princeton. This last source is the repository of statistical data about many of T's plays produced by Tyler. Tyler's most profitable play, incidentally, was *Mrs. Wiggs of the Cabbage Patch,* which made $900,000. For T's memory of royalties from the play and for his later attitude towards it, see letters to Street of Jan. 14, 1915, and New York *Times* of Oct. 19, 1919. The play opened in Chicago on Sept. 29, 1907, in New York on Aug. 17, 1908.

Specific sources: "There is no spot" and "I can write plays" are from T's letters to his parents of Sept. 26, Nov. 10, 1906; T wrote of Stutesman's and Fletcher's response to Europe to his father on Feb. 15, 1906 (MS owned by John Jameson); the conversation between Stutesman and Lord Lascelles is reported by Street, *op. cit.;* the unexpected reaction to the play is quoted from T's article on Wilson.

The quotation from *Harlequin and Columbine* is from chap. 6. Other material on T's playwriting theories comes from "Sister Arts," *Collier's,* XLII, 15 (March 20, 1909). Not quoted but pertinent is "The Audience Makes the Play," *Theater,* XLVI, 12 (Sept.,

1927). The remark overheard at the box office is reported in "Indiana in Literature and Politics" (see above). Data on movie productions of *Cameo Kirby* are from *Bibliog.*, p. 150, and the files of Brandt & Brandt.

T's account of his mother's death occurs in a letter to F. A. Duneka of May 28, 1909; also see obituary in *Star* of April 18, 1909. The best account of *Your Humble Servant* is found in Otis Skinner's memoir, *Footlights and Spotlights* (1924). The New York *Tribune* review was published on Jan. 4, 1910. T wrote Dan Calkins of his weariness on Dec. 31, 1909. The limerick is quoted by T in a letter to Frank Crowninshield of May 20, 1942 (copy at Princeton).

Chapter Eight

The tour of Europe in the summer of 1911 is reconstructed from T's letters to his father and Dr. McCulloch; from an interview in the *Star* on Nov. 9, 1911. The account of troop movements on the German border is from *TWDM*, chap. 13.

Material pertaining to the divorce comes from Indianapolis newspapers of Oct. and Nov., 1911, family letters, and other documents among the papers at Princeton.

For material on Bennett's visit to the United States, see the *Journal of Arnold Bennett* (1933), Reginald Pound, *Arnold Bennett* (1952). T's entertainment of Bennett is specifically reported in the *Star* of Nov. 9, 21, 1911. His feeling about the old home is from a letter to Street, undated but written c. 1916. The interview recalling the moment T swore off liquor appeared in the *Times* of March 10, 1945. "Nipskillions" is collected in *Looking Forward and Others* (1926), pp. 31-47; the other article on this topic is "Holding More and Showing Less," *Nassau Literary Magazine*, LXXXI, 329-335 (Feb., 1916). Additional data on this subject I have had from T's family.

"Now I'm in condition" was written to F. A. Duneka on Sept. 19, 1912. The belief that a writer must "go into training" occurs in a letter to Street of June 29 [1914?]. T's plans to resume fiction-writing were reported in the *Star* of Nov. 9, 1911. Lorimer accepted "Mary Smith" in a letter of June 24, 1912. T quoted his nephew on the story in "Author's Explanation" to 1932 ed. of *Seventeen*. T wrote Street twice about *The Flirt*: March 26, April 21, 1913. His letter about plot as his "stumbling block," also to Street, is dated April 16, 1913. The quotations from the novel are from chap. 1.

Data pertaining to T's marriage to Susanah Robinson come from several sources: newspaper reports; letter to Hauté on Aug. 19, 1912 (MS owned by Susanah Tarkington), to Ade on Nov. 5, 1912, to Street on same date and Nov. 6, 1916; Susanah Tarkington, "Making a Home for my Husband," *McCall's,* LVI, 20-21, 97 (March, 1929); "The Hopeful Pessimist," *Looking Forward,* pp. 51-98; and Mrs. Tarkington's reminiscences.

Mrs. Tarkington also is the source for my account of Penrod's genesis. The dream en route to New York is reported in a letter to T's family of Feb. 1, 1899. That Booth Jameson was Penrod's prototype is stated in a *Times* interview c. 1933-35 (undated clipping at Indiana State Library). The origin of Georgie Bassett is recalled in a questionnaire T filled out for the Literary Guild in 1945 (copy at Princeton). T's remarks on *Tom Sawyer* are from his introduction to the book (see *Bibliog.,* p. 171). The sequence of realistic children is cited in a letter to Woollcott printed in *Woollcott's Second Reader* (1937), pp. 966-967. T's theory of child development comes from "What I Have Learned About Boys," *American Magazine,* XCIX, 5-7, 146-148 (Jan., 1925). T wrote several letters to Tyler about the dramatization of *Penrod* by E. E. Rose, beginning Feb. 28, 1918, some of which were printed in a corrupt text in the New York *Times* on Sept. 8, 1918. The story of Chase Walker is recalled in *AISTM,* Bob Philips in a letter to Carl Brandt of Sept. 8, 1940. T's letter to Street about rates is dated Sept. 9 [1914?]; Wilson's letter was written on June 26, 1913. "Teacher told us . . ." is recalled by T in the *Star* on Jan. 30, 1919 (reprinted from the New York *Sun). Penrod* sales to 1945 (see Hackett, *op. cit.)* totaled 586,000. There was also an Armed Forces Edition distributed in 1943. The combined sales of *Penrod, Penrod and Sam, Penrod Jashber,* and *Penrod: His Complete Story* have been over one million. For additional bibliographical data on *Penrod,* see Campbell R. Coxe, "The Pre-Publication Printings of Tarkington's *Penrod,*" *Studies in Bibliography,* V, 153-157 (1952).

Chapter Nine

T recalled his feelings on returning to Indiana in "I Live in Indiana and Like It," *Woman's Day,* II, 4-5, 46 (May, 1939). For his Maine preference, see a letter to Street of Nov. 10, 1945. The time of the Penrod stories is stated in the dedication to *Penrod Jashber* (1929).

The Turmoil: T's attitude towards smoke, commerce, bigness, corruption is found in chap. 1 and "The Second Name," *The Works of Booth Tarkington,* VIII (1918), pp. 317-359. "Commercialism is the savage" was written to Street on Nov. 21, 1914. T equated commercialism with greed in a letter to T. B. Wells of Dec. 22, 1914. Sheridan's view of smoke is in chap. 2; the quotation, "the kiln must be fired," and the description of Sheridan "struggling and inevitably conquering" both are from chap. 33.

One account of his writing *The Turmoil* in sixty days is in Kenneth Roberts, *I Wanted to Write* (1949), but T often referred to this fact. See, for example, his letter to Tyler of June 3, 1915. A good account of his writing habits at this time is in J. R. McMahon, "Booth Tarkington at Home," *Ladies' Home Journal*, XXXIX, 15-16 (Nov., 1922); also in a letter to Street of April 21, 1913.

T's letter to Howells is dated Sept. 7, 1914 (MS at Harvard). His letters to Ade were written on Sept. 14, Oct. 19, 22, 1916. His visit to York Harbor was described to Street on June 25, 1915. His feelings about Howells are best seen in his introduction to *The Rise of Silas Lapham* (1937), which was reprinted, with modifications, from an obituary article in *Harper's* of Aug., 1920.

It may seem surprising that T went back to Harper after they rejected *His Own People,* but T's loyalty to Duneka offset this single adverse incident. Just as T had stayed with McClure after the *Cherry* episode, which gave Harper its original entree, he let Duneka continue publishing his works: *The Man from Home* (1908), *Beasley's Christmas Party* (1909), *Beauty and the Jacobin* (1912). See also notes for chap. 4.

Seventeen: Data on the novel's history are from *Bibliog.,* pp. 36-40, and the files of Harper & Brothers. "Seventeen is Mr. Tarkington's high water mark" is quoted from Charles C. Baldwin, *The Men Who Make Our Novels* (1924), pp. 485-486. The letter to Broun was printed in his syndicated column for Jan. 12, 1924. The New York *Times* interview appeared in the *Book Review and Magazine* of Aug. 20, 1922. The letter to Garland was written on May 6, 1934.

Gentle Julia: Fenton Booth's newspaper is described in *AISTM.* T's letters are full of references to his dogs; but see specifically "Teach Me, My Dog," *American Magazine*, XCV, 5-7, 58, 60 (Jan., 1923), and "Fox Terrier or Something," *Country Life in America*, XXVII, 38-39 (Nov., 1914). T wrote Tyler on Feb. 17, 1922. "Are you a miserable sinner" is from Woollcott's letter to W. Graham Robertson of Aug. 1, 1935 (*The Letters of Alexander Woollcott*, 1944, p. 146). Chaps. 13, 14 deal particularly with Gamin. A footnote to T's interest in dogs is his letter to the Indianapolis City Council (*Star*, March 16, 1943), which resulted in the establishment of a municipal pet shop.

The Magnificent Ambersons: The rediscovery of Thackeray is described to Harrison Daniels in a letter of March 10, 1936. Lovett's review appeared in *The Dial*, LXVI, 86-87 (Jan. 25, 1919). For the identification of places in the novel, see *News* of Oct. 26, 1918, and T's letter to Tom Prideaux of *Life* on March 22, 1942 (copy at Princeton). Howells' letter of Aug. 20, 1919, is in *The Life in Letters of William Dean Howells*, II, 388-389; also T's reply of Aug. 28. T's wartime writings are listed in *Bibliog.*, p. 235 and *passim*. His letter to Barnes is in *From Then Till Now*, p. 459. The files of Indianapolis newspapers contain much data on his wartime activities. His statement about *Ramsay Milholland* appeared in "Gossip Shop," *Bookman*, L, 652 (Feb., 1920). Two letters quoted from this era were written to Dr. McCulloch on April 27, 1918; and to Ade, Aug. 14, 1917.

Chapter Ten

Among T's unpublished correspondence at Princeton there are about two hundred letters, telegrams, and miscellaneous documents written to and for Tyler. Much of my material for chaps. 10 and 11, though specific letters are not cited, is drawn from this source. I also have made extensive use of the various clipping files cited previously and, for about half of T's plays, the account books which survive among the Tyler Papers. A useful tabulation of production data for all of T's professionally performed plays except *The Man on Horseback* is found in the Appendix to A. D. Van Nostrand, "The Novels and Plays of Booth Tarkington" (Harvard, 1951), an unpublished dissertation.

Mr. Antonio: See Skinner's *Footlights and Spotlights*, pp. 344-346; T's letters to his father of May 20, 1915, Sept. 26, 1916, Oct. 19, 1916. "Poor Mrs. Tarkington" and a statement of the play's intent were written to Ade on Oct. 19, 1916. See also a review in the New York *Times* on Sept. 19, 1916. Data on the Buffalo criticism are from the undated and undirected draft of a letter to a Buffalo newspaper editor.

The Country Cousin: See Tyler's *Whatever Goes Up*, p. 273. The Tyler-T relationship is documented further in T's Foreword to Tyler's memoirs. For identification of Tyler as Hurley, see the *News* of Jan. 15, 1934. "Managing is really an art" is quoted from *Presenting Lily Mars,* chap. 7. See also a letter from Street of Feb. 12 [1916], and a review in the New York *Times* of Sept. 9, 1917. The same issue of the paper carried excerpts in a corrupt text of nine of T's letters to Tyler (several of which are here quoted) about the production and writing of the play.

Clarence: The T-Lunt relationship was described to me by Mrs. Tarkington and by Lunt in a letter of Feb. 27, 1954. See *Whatever Goes Up,* pp. 274, 294; Catherine Hayes Brown, *Letters to Mary* (1940), pp. 103-109, 135-137. Several letters to Tyler describe various aspects of T's relationship with Helen Hayes. Her letter of appreciation to T is undated. Stanhope's comment on the manuscript was reported in the New York *Times* of Sept. 28, 1919, which also printed T's congratulations to the cast. The same paper published Woollcott's review on Sept. 22, 1919. T summarized his playwriting career, attitude towards critics, and desire for a pen name in a letter to Tyler printed in the New York *Times* on Oct. 19, 1919.

Up from Nowhere: The early title was "George Washington Silver." Woollcott's review in the New York *Times* appeared on Sept. 9, 1919. Skinner rejected the play in a letter of Oct. 29? [1918?].

The Gibson Upright: See *News* of July 15, 1919; *Star* of Oct. 26, 1919; and *Bibliog.,* pp. 51-53. Also among the papers at Princeton are several letters from businessmen commending T for this play.

Poldekin: The New York *Times* for Sept. 12, 1920, contains details of the play's history. See also T's letter to his father of Oct. 4, 1920, and Broun's review in the New York *Tribune* for Sept. 10, 1920. T's letter to Broun is from an unidentified clipping at Princeton.

The Wren: See notes above on *Clarence.* Also see T's letters to his father on Sept. 18, 1921; from Helen Hayes on May 6, 1921; to Street on May 5, 1921. Woollcott's review appeared in the New York *Times* on Oct. 11, 1921; further remarks on Oct. 16. An interesting review is by H. T. Parker in the Boston *Transcript* of Sept. 20, 1921.

T recalled his meetings with Harding and Wilson in a letter to his father of Nov. 4, 1921.

Chapter Eleven

The Intimate Strangers: See Maude Adams' letter of Feb. 25, 1921, and T's letter to Street of July 25, 1921 (describing her visit). Hammond's review is reprinted in H. L. Cohen, *Longer Plays by Modern Authors (American)* (1922), pp. 251-253. Lunt's first letter, undated, probably was written in Aug.-Sept., 1921; the second [March 10?, 1922]. See also Billie Burke's memoir, *With a Feather on My Nose* (1949), pp. 197-200, and T's letter to his father of Nov. 4, 1921.

Rose Briar: Billie Burke, *op. cit.,* p. 209. T recalled the show's closing and the suggestion from James in letters to Brandt on Feb. 28, Nov. 3, 1936. The second letter also discussed plans for "Otherwise Kitty Swift." T characterized himself as a painter having "another go at the same landscape" to Woollcott in a letter of May 21, 1936. The summer of 1922 is well documented by the frequent letters T wrote home during the last few months of his father's life. See particularly letters of Aug. 11, 17, 1922; also Susanah Tarkington to Laurel on Nov. 22. Woollcott reviewed the play in the New York *Herald* on Dec. 27, 1922; Page, in a special dispatch to the *Star* on Jan. 7, 1923.

Tweedles: See letters to Gregory Kelly on Dec. 11, 1921; March 11, July 3, 1922; Jan. 11, April 12, May 7, Aug. 2, Oct. 23, 1923. For T on sex plays, see also *TWDM*, chap. 22. Woollcott's opinion is in his *Enchanted Aisles* (1924), pp. 121-123.

Magnolia: Its history is summarized in a manuscript dated June 26, 1931, in Susanah Tarkington's hand. T reported on the play's unfortunate New York run in a letter to Street of Sept. 21, 1923. His intent is explained in a letter to Ralph T. Jones of the Atlanta *Constitution* on Oct. 5, 1923. Lunt's view of the play was written to me on Feb. 27, 1954.

Colonel Satan: See undated letters from Arliss (Nov., 1928?) and to Winthrop Ames (Summer, 1929?—copy at Princeton). T and Tyler exchanged several letters about this play in 1930. The review quoted, by Robert Garland, appeared in the New York *Telegram* on Jan. 12, 1931. T was interviewed by the *News* on Jan. 31, 1931.

Details of the T Festival come from scrapbooks and program files at the Pasadena Playhouse. The forecast about television and comments on radio writing are from the New York *Times* of Feb. 19, 1933. The scripts for the radio serial "Maud and Cousin Bill" are among the papers at Princeton. After fourteen sustaining programs the series was sponsored for an additional eighty-six performances by the Atlantic & Pacific Tea Company, which paid $200 for each script.

There are at least six unproduced movie scenarios among the papers at Princeton, including sketches for Deanna Durbin, Will Rogers, and an Andy Hardy picture. T described the Maude Greenwood suit to Kahler in a letter of Jan. 1, 1925. See also the New York *Times* of Jan. 27, 1925. T's reaction to *Boy o' Mine* is from a letter to Kahler of Jan. 11, 1924. For his observations on the movies, see interviews in New York *Times* on July 18, 1920, and *Times* of March 10, 1945. T wrote Harrison Daniels on Nov. 24, 1935, about the dialogue for *The Millionaire.*

There is a great deal of correspondence about the Warner Brothers suit among the papers at Princeton, but see specifically T's letter to Brandt of July 24, 1938, and the correspondence between

T and his lawyer, Sidney R. Fleisher. Observations on the truth of Lily Mars come from a letter to Street of Nov. 20, 1932.

Chapter Twelve

T's views of twentieth-century change are found in *TWDM*, *passim*. The Carlyle retort, "misfortunes fall," and Twain's view of happiness come from "The Miracle," *Ladies' Home Journal*, XXXIX, 12 (Dec., 1922). The world as an "ascending spiral" is quoted from *TWDM*, chap. 25. The long passage summarizing the change, "That had been a great railroad making . . . period," is from *The Midlander*, chap. 24.

Alice Adams: For T's intentions in writing the novel (and the *Growth* trilogy), see a letter to A. B. Maurice of Jan. 23, 1924. Also see "How Could You," *Wings*, VII, 7-8 (Aug., 1933). Quotations from the novel are from chaps. 3, 25. See *Bibliog.*, pp. 53-55, for additional data on this work. The letters from Lewis and Glasgow were written on April 29 and May 26, 1921, respectively. Lewis also was the author of the citation read in New York on May 18, 1945, when T was awarded the Howells Medal by the American Academy of Arts and Letters. At that time he wrote: "Mr. Tarkington . . . has been one of the first, and he remains one of the chief, of all the discoverers of America in literature. . . . Perhaps as much as Hamlin Garland or Howells or Dreiser he was a pioneer in seeing that our wheatfields and apple trees and old brownstone-fronts are quite as romantic as European marble fauns and secret gardens. . . ."

T's letters to Garland are dated Feb. 26 and March 25, 1921; Garland's letter is of March 8 [1921]. Data about honorary degrees and popularity contests come from the clipping files and various letters from the institutions concerned. See also letters to Street of Aug. 4, 1922, March 14, 1924.

See *Bibliog.*, p. 263, for list of the eight *Redbook* stories published between May and Dec., 1921. "Jeannette" was reprinted, with alterations, in *TWDM*, chap. 20, and both "Jeannette" and "The One-Hundred-Dollar Bill" are in *The Fascinating Stranger and Other Stories* (1923).

"I don't doubt he worried" was written to John Jameson on May 22, 1937; the letter to Garland about John Tarkington's death is dated Feb. 10, 1923. Data on the death of Laurel come from unpublished family letters at Princeton. The letters quoted to Street and Tyler both were written on April 14, 1923. Also pertinent are letters to Maurice on April 7, 1923, and to Kahler on Jan. 15, April 12, 1923.

The Midlander: T's correspondence with Barton Currie contains important data on the writing of this novel. See specifically letters of Feb. 18, May 2, 31, June 8, July 14, 1923; also T's letters to Maurice of Jan. 23, 1924, and to Street of March 24, 1940. The clipping files in Indianapolis contain numerous articles about the house at 4270 N. Meridian St. T's memory of the first night spent there was written to John Jameson on Dec. 9, 1940. "The woodland was still there" and the following quotation are from *The Midlander,* chap. 31. Tyler's comment on the new house and the statement "We do enjoy" come from a letter to Kahler of Feb. 23, 1924. T wrote Street on Sept. 28, 1924, about his lazy summer.

Quotations from *Women* are found in the preamble and chaps. 1, 2, 4. The ten serials and story sequences not collected or reprinted are these: "Pretty Twenty," "High Summer," "Otherwise Kitty Swift," "This Boy Joe," "The Divine Evadne," stories of the Eliot-Mears families, the Belinda Dale series, additional Rumbin stories, the Susie Rollins stories, and the Captain Valentine stories. See *Bibliog.,* pp. 235-270, for publication data.

Chapter Thirteen

The trip to North Africa and Europe is well recorded in letters to friends and family. Some of the letters to Hauté are owned by John Jameson, but most of them are at Princeton. A sequence of these letters was published in the *Star* on April 5, 1925 (with some deletions). Specific letters I have used are these: to Linda Tarkington (Mrs. John S.) on Feb. 27, March 27, 1925; to Dr. McCulloch on April 22, May 15, 1925; from Susanah Tarkington to Dr. McCulloch on March 16, 1925. The memory of Hemingway comes from a letter to Street of March 7, 1932.

"If we have a type" T wrote to Currie on April 4, 1925; his description of Fisher as "an American Abroad" is from a letter to Linda Tarkington of Feb. 9, 1925. T pursued this topic in letters to Kahler on March 17, 1926, and Maurice on May 24, 1928. Dr. Medjila's remarks on Tinker and America as a modern Rome are in *The Plutocrat,* chap. 29. See also chaps. 14, 20, 21 for Tinker's exploits that reveal him as a modern Roman. The scene at St. Augustine's tomb is found in chap. 30. "Rotarian and Sophisticate" appeared in *The World's Work,* LVIII, 42-44, 146 (Jan., 1929). As a footnote to *The Plutocrat,* see Omar Bradley, *A Soldier's Story* (1951). In describing preparations for the invasion of Sicily General Bradley tells of cleaning up an entire Arab village before making it his headquarters. Also see Malcolm Cowley, *The Exile's Return* (1951), chap. 7, for a discussion of the controversy that raged in the Twenties between the aesthetes and their critics.

The unforgettable experience in the Greek Theater at Taormina was told to me by Mrs. Tarkington, but T refers to it in a letter to his sister on March 14, 1925 (MS owned by John Jameson). See *Claire Ambler*, chaps. 12, 13. The letter to Woollcott from Taormina was written on Feb. 27, 1925.

Printed sources relating to T's eye trouble are extensive. Among newspaper reports these are informative: *Star* of Dec. 6, 1927, March 12, 1929; Jan. 27, Feb. 4, March 1, 1931; Jan. 1, 1934; *News* of Oct. 27, 1927, and Jan. 31, 1931. See in addition Roberts, *I Wanted to Write*, p. 204, and the same author's "A Gentleman from Maine and Indiana," *Saturday Evening Post*, CCIV, 14-15, 50, 54, 57 (Aug. 8, 1931). T wrote of his affliction in "Out of the Dark," *American Magazine*, CXIII, 48-49, 111-114 (April, 1932); "The Seeing-Eye Dog," *Ladies' Home Journal*, LIV, 16-17, 58, 60-61 (Sept., 1937). I also have used these unpublished letters: T to his father on May 31, 1922; to Tyler on May 27, 1922, Aug. 12, 1929, April 14, 1930; to Ade on June 5, 1929; to Kahler on May 27, 1930; Susanah Tarkington to Dr. McCulloch on Sept. 12, 1928, Oct. 9, 1930; to Tyler on Dec. 12, 1928.

Seawood is described in several sources: "Making a Home for my Husband"; Ethel Davis Seal, "The Summer Home of Booth Tarkington," *Ladies' Home Journal*, XLII, 16-17 (April, 1925); "A Gentleman from Maine and Indiana." See also T's letter to his father of Oct. 19, 1916.

My chief source for the Roberts-T relationship is *I Wanted to Write*, p. 152 and *passim*. Roberts' letters to T are at Princeton, but T's letters, in Roberts' possession, have not been available. T's letters to Street contain many references to Roberts' work. For Sherwood's review, see "The Hidebound Coast," *Scribners*, LXXXVIII, 21 (Nov., 1920).

The controversy over Captain Montgomery I have had first-hand from Hugh Kahler. In addition, at Princeton are copies of the Tarkingtons' resignations from the Kennebunkport River Club. See also letters to Kahler of Jan. 29, March 30, May 28, 1928. The quotation from "High Summer" is from the *American Magazine*, CXI, 121 (June, 1931). Chick's comment was reported in the *News* on Dec. 11, 1941.

Chapter Fourteen

Domestic details of T's life in Indiana and Maine in the Thirties come from various sources: letters, newspaper interviews, first-hand reminiscences of family and friends. The letter about Lewis was written to Street on June 17, 1939. The papers at Princeton contain a large bloc of correspondence (both sides) written during this period by T and an old English friend, Aucher Warner. The Tarkingtons visited with the Warners when they went abroad in 1925 and entertained them at Seawood in 1931 and 1937. T's letters to Warner are filled with political comments and details of art collecting. Also during the Thirties and till he died in 1946 T was interviewed annually on his birthday and on his return to Indianapolis for the winter. The clipping files are full of data covering these years. See also Erwin Panofsky's reminiscence, "Humanitas Tarkingtoniana," in *An Exhibition of Booth Tarkington's Works* (Princeton, 1946). For T's view of old-age love, see "What Is the Age for Love?" *Pictorial Review,* XXXVII, 24-25 (Aug., 1936); his attitude towards his wife was reported by Alden Rogers to Julian Boyd in a letter of March 21, 1951. His answer to the query, "Has your wife been a help to you?" was written to Dora Albert on June 15, 1944 (copy at Princeton).

Details about T's relationship with Brandt & Brandt I have had first-hand from Carl Brandt. Additional data is summarized from an examination of the T correspondence in Brandt's files. T's generosity is well documented in letters scattered throughout the correspondence of a lifetime. The request that his *Post* pay rate be cut is reported by Tebbel, *op. cit.,* p. 71. "I'm anathema" is quoted from a letter to Harrison Daniels of Jan. 28[?], 1936. His comparison with Loyola was written to Woollcott on Jan. 15 [1933?].

For T's public attacks on the New Deal, see *Star* of June 5, 1932, April 17, 1938; *News* of Feb. 22, 1937; "Loss of Confidence in Business," *Saturday Evening Post,* CCVII, 79 (July 21, 1934); "Thought Contagions" [an editorial], *ibid.,* CCXI, 24 (March 25, 1939). T proposed tax relief to buyers of American art to Peyton Boswell, Jr., in a letter of May 18, 1938. His private comments on the New Deal are found in many letters, but see in particular those to Warner of March 17, Sept. 16, 1933; to Fred Kelly of May 7, 29, June 8, 9, 1939 (photostats at Princeton). T's letter about the political variety of his friends was written to Kahler on April 17, 1939. The quotation from "Pretty Twenty" is from *McCall's,* LIX, 76 (Oct., 1932).

The complete manuscript of "This Boy Joe," which never has been published, is at Princeton. Details of its publication history come from the T-Brandt correspondence. The extensive T-McCulloch correspondence at Princeton (extending from 1911 to 1946) contains the exchange over the Lincoln statue. The phone-call hoax is reported to John Jameson in a letter of Oct. 24, 1938. Other data on the Lincoln statue are from the *News* of Feb. 11, 1933; *Star* of Nov. 3, 1933, Dec. 27, 28, 1934, April 6, 1935.

For T's art criticism, see (besides *Some Old Portraits*) Preface to *Dutch Paintings* ... *of the Seventeenth Century* (Indianapolis, 1937); Foreword to Lionello Venturi, *Painting and Painters: How to Look at a Picture* (1946); letters to George W. Eggers of Feb. 17, 1936 (copy at Princeton), and Paul Manship of March 30, 1945 (copy in possession of Mrs. Tarkington). T's identification of the Silbermans as Mr. Rumbin was specifically stated in the Lewiston, Me., *Journal* of Aug. 6 [1936?]. The inspiration for the character, however, was widely commented on at the time, and there is much correspondence at Princeton from David and Abris Silberman. See T's "In Appreciation of the Late David Silberman," *Art Digest*, XVII, 13 (April 1, 1943). Professor Panofsky's view of *Some Old Portraits* is found in his "Humanitas Tarkingtoniana," and I am in his debt for calling my attention to T's discussion of Mrs. Bennet Langton *(Some Old Portraits,* pp. 129-133).

The prospectus for *Little Orvie* exists among the papers at Princeton as a one-page, undated carbon typescript. For data on *The Lorenzo Bunch,* see a letter to Harrison Daniels of Jan. 20, 1936, and an undated letter to Eleanor Jaschke. Also see various letters between T, Brandt, and Mabel Search in the Brandt & Brandt correspondence. "I love to see her look at him" is quoted from a letter to Kahler of March 30, 1928.

Chapter Fifteen

T's growing concern over events in Europe is best seen in the Warner correspondence. "Civilization cannot die" is quoted from "Thanksgiving—1941," *Cosmopolitan*, CXI, 15, 80 (Dec., 1941). T wrote a tribute to Roosevelt, which was read over WFBM, Indianapolis, on April 15, 1945. The Lend-Lease letter of Feb. 9, 1941, appeared in *Life*, X, 33 (March 10, 1941). His support for protecting lend-lease supplies was published in a broadside by the Indiana Committee for National Defense on April 18, 1941, and reprinted the next day in the *Star*. For details of his wartime propaganda, see *Bibliog.*, p. 235 and *passim*. His parable on freedom of speech appeared in the *Saturday Evening Post*, CCXV, 12 (Feb. 20, 1943).

His comments on the O. Henry ending were written to Howard Wetherell on March 4, 1943 (copy at Princeton).

T's account of life at Seawood during the war may be found in various letters of the period, but see specifically one to Dr. McCulloch of July 4, 1943. Also see *Star* of Dec. 20, 1942. A good account of his work habits in old age is contained in the *Times* for Jan. 12, 1940. Specific data on his following of the war news come from letters to John Jameson of Oct. 8, 1943, and July 24, 1944.

The novelette "Walterson" (not discussed in text) is a competent story of a magazine editor's career told from a minor-character point of view. T wrote the editor of *Good Housekeeping,* Max Wilkinson, on Feb. 11, 1945 (copy at Princeton), that he had Lorimer in mind for part of the characterization. He also refused to eliminate the marital break at the end of the story, as the editor wished.

The Heritage of Hatcher Ide: See letters from Harold Murray of Jan. 22, 1941; Street of March 24, 1941; Roberts of Feb. 24, 1941; Adelaide Neall of Feb. 12, 19, 26, March 18, April 22, 1940.

The Fighting Littles: See letters from Wesley Winans Stout of July 7, 1937, and April 17, 1939; from Woollcott on May 2, 1938; and to Kahler on April 17, 1939.

Kate Fennigate: A letter to Brandt of Feb. 25, 1942, summarizes the serial's history to that point. See also letters to Miss Neall of Dec. 30, 1941, Feb. 25, 1942 (copies at Princeton); to Stout on March 12, 1942 (copy at Princeton); to Malcolm Johnson of Jan. 11, 1943 (copy at Princeton); to Lucy Taggart of July 9, 1943.

Image of Josephine: The idea of the story is traced in the Literary Guild questionnaire previously cited. "No man knows himself" is quoted from *Wings*, XIX, 3-9 (March, 1945), part of which is reprinted in the introduction to *The Show Piece*. For data on the use of a museum as background and thoughts about the title character, see letters to LeBaron Barker on Sept. 30, 1944; to Warrack Wallace on Feb. 23, March 3, 27, 1945; to McCulloch on March 17, 1945 (copies at Princeton). See also a letter to Wilbur Peat (director of John Herron Art Institute) of Jan. 23, 1944, and one from Peat of March 16, 1945. Additional material is in letters to Caroline Fesler of Jan. 9, 1945; to Lucy Taggart on May 18, Dec. 7, 1944 (copies at Princeton).

The Show Piece: See pp. 208-210 for synopsis of planned ending; also see Introduction by Susanah Tarkington. In a letter to Woollcott of Feb. 2, 1935, T said that he had not read much nineteenth-century fiction in twenty-five years—only *Theron Ware, Salammbo,* James, Meredith, and a bit of Maurice Hewlett. The quotation about egoism is from a letter to Senator Edward Burke of Aug. 29, 1940 (copy at Princeton).

T's support of unconditional surrender is found in several places, but see in particular the *Star* on Nov. 27, 1943, and "An Unacceptable Peace," *American Legion Magazine*, XXXVI, 11 (Feb., 1944). T's attack on "vaporings" is from a letter to John Jameson of Oct. 8, 1943. For T's relationship with Willkie, see various entries in *Bibliog.*, Index. T's review of *One World* appeared in the *Star* on April 11, 1943. See also several letters to and from Willkie among the papers at Princeton. T's letter to Indiana Republicans was printed in part by the New York *Times* of May 7, 1944, and published on May 8 by the Indiana Committee for Victory. The same group issued his "Shall We Choose Insanity," a plea for an effective United Nations to forestall an atomic war, after it was read over WFBM on March 25, 1945.

T wrote extensively against universal military training during 1945-46 because he thought it represented false security—an antiquated reliance on traditional military power in an atomic age. There are many letters and documents at Princeton on this topic. See specifically "Booth Tarkington on Peacetime Conscription," *Congressional Record, Appendix*, XCI, part 12, p. A2909 (June 11-Oct. 11, 1945). His statements about the need for controlling atomic energy appeared in the *News* on Sept. 11, 1945, the *Star* on Dec. 4, 1945, Jan. 1, 1946.

For details of his final illness and death, see newspapers of May 20, 1946. Also see Street's obituary written for the Associated Press and published in the *News* on May 21, 1946. The funeral was held on May 21.

T speculated on death and immortality in a collection of stories, *Mr. White, Hell, The Red Barn, and Bridewater* (1935). See particularly the Preface to this volume and a newspaper interview about the book in the *Star* on Dec. 29, 1935.

INDEX

New York (1899), 76-80; reception of *The Gentleman*, 80-82; book columnist, 84-86; New Orleans and Helen Pitkin, 87-89; *Beaucaire* and Mansfield, 89-92; engagement and marriage, 94-96; candidate for legislature, 97-103; efforts and attitudes towards public speaking, 100-102, 105-107; legislative experiences, 103-110; fictional use of politics, 107, 108-109, 112-113; typhoid fever, 114; Europe (1903), 115-120; start of art collection, 119-120; year in New York (1904-1905), 120-126; popular magazine contributor and the Periodical Publishers Association, 122-124

Return to Europe (1905), 126; Capri, 124, 126-129; Rome, 129-132; birth of daughter, 130; automobile owner and motorist, 120, 133-135; Champigny-sur-Marne, 134-137; Rue de Tournon, 137-146; playwriting, 136-137, 146-157; views on theater, 149-150; Europe (1911), 159-162; divorce, 158, 162-163, 164; teetotalism, 165-166; marriage to Susanah Robinson, 171-174; return to fiction, 167-171; creation of Penrod, 174-180; Indianapolis family chronicles, 182-188, 245-250, 256-258; creation of Willie Baxter, 188-190; on sex in literature, 190-191; dogs, 193-194; Pulitzer Prizes and other honors, 194, 198, 250-251; propagandist in First World War, 198-203

Return to playwriting, 204-234; anti-Communist play, 215-218; one-act plays, 234-235; radio writing, 235; relationship with movies, 235-238; theater fiction, 238-241; philosophy at middle age, 242-245; deaths of father and daughter, 254-256; removal uptown, 258-259; North Africa and Europe (1925), 262-265; literary use of trip, 265-271; failing eyesight and operations, 272-274; house at Kennebunkport, 274-275; literary use of Maine, 218-220, 228-229, 277-281; life in the Thirties, 282-286; attacks on New Deal, 287-289; depression fiction, 289-292; Lincoln statue, 294-295; portrait collecting and writing on art, 295-300; propagandist in Second World War, 304-305; return to Indianapolis fiction, 307-315; postwar problems, 315-317; death, 318

NOVELS, NOVELETTES, SERIALS: *Alice Adams*, 63, 159, 169, 182, 226, 245-250, 270, 279, 297, 301, 318; *Beasley's Christmas Party*, 24, 157; *The Beau-*

tiful Lady, 121-122; *Cherry*, 86-87, 121; *Claire Ambler*, 262, 269-271; *The Conquest of Canaan*, 51, 63, 124-126, 127, 130, 146; "The Divine Evadne," 239; *The Fighting Littles*, 307, 309-310; *The Flirt*, 168-171, 182, 226, 261, 297; *Gentle Julia*, 39, 192-194, 235, 252, 297; *The Gentleman from Indiana*, 19, 35, 36, 61-62, 63, 65, 72-75, 77, 78, 79, 82-84, 86, 88, 92, 98, 115, 121, 122, 139, 158 175, 181, 261, 297; *Growth*, 244, 245, 256, 307; *The Guest of Quesnay*, 143-146, 154, 197; *Harlequin and Columbine*, 149, 188, 226, 239, 240; *The Heritage of Hatcher Ide* ("The Man of the Family"), 289, 307-308, 312; "High Summer," 274, 280; *His Own People,* 135-136, 146; *Image of Josephine*, 261, 296, 297, 307, 312-313; *Kate Fennigate*, 307, 310-312, 313; *Little Orvie*, 300-301; *The Lorenzo Bunch*, 226, 271, 301-302; *The Magnificent Ambersons*, 169, 182, 194-198, 203, 245, 307; *Mary's Neck*, 274, 279-280, 309; *The Midlander*, 182, 245, 256-258, 301; *Mirthful Haven*, 274, 277-279; *Monsieur Beaucaire*, 71-72, 73, 80, 86, 89, 115, 159, 237, 296; "Otherwise Kitty Swift," 226-227; *Penrod*, 174-180, 182, 188, 191, 202, 212, 231, 235, 238, 297, 300; *Penrod and Sam*, 180; *Penrod Jashber*, 180, 274; *The Plutocrat*, 262, 265-269, 270, 297; *Presenting Lily Mars*, 27, 209, 226, 239, 240-241; "Pretty Twenty," 289, 290; *Ramsay Milholland*, 201-202, 203, 297; "Rennie Peddigoe," 289-290; *Rumbin Galleries*, 298; *Seventeen*, 42, 129, 167, 188-190, 191, 192, 202, 228, 231, 234, 252, 270, 290, 300; *The Show Piece*, 307, 313-314, 318; "This Boy Joe," 290-292, 301; *Three Selected Short Novels*, 289; *The Turmoil*, 19, 182-188, 194, 198, 245, 307; *The Two Vanrevels*, 92-93, 95, 97, 115; "Walterson," 306; *Wanton Mally*, 296; *Women*, 259-261, 309; *Young Mrs. Greeley*, 226, 271-272, 301

STORIES AND STORY COLLECTIONS: "The Aliens," 112-113, 253; "The Better Man," 57; "Boss Gorgett," 112; "Captain Schlotterwerz," 201; *The Fascinating Stranger and Other Stories*, 252; "Filmer's Fascinating Face," 309; "Francine," 239; "Gay Fragments," 62-63; *In the Arena*, 112-114, 121, 253; "Jeannette," 252-

DATE DUE